BRITAIN'S HERITAGE

EDITED BY

JOHN JULIUS NORWICH
BRITAIN'S HERITAGE

CONTINUUM · New York

General Editor
JOHN JULIUS NORWICH
Assistant to General Editor
MOLLIE PHILIPPS

Managing Editor
JOHN GRISEWOOD
Production Editor
NICK HEARD
Design
JOHN STRANGE
Picture research
PENELOPE WARN
Diagrams
CHARLOTTE STYLES
Genealogical tables
T.A.S. LTD., LONDON
Cartography
Product Support Graphics, Derby
Manager: **Ralph Orme**
Map artwork: **Marion Dudley** (Control)
Kate Westcott

1983
The Continuum Publishing Company
575 Lexington Avenue
New York, New York 10022

Designed and produced by Grisewood & Dempsey Ltd.,
Elsley Court, 20-22 Great Titchfield Street,
London W1P 7AD

Copyright © Grisewood & Dempsey Limited 1983

Printed and bound by
Mohndruck Graphische Betriebe GmbH
Gütersloh, West Germany.

Library of Congress Catalog
Card Number: 82-074384

ISBN 0-8264-0234-8

Contributors

SIR WILLIAM ADDISON FSA
Landscape historian and English heritage conservator. Author of *Understanding English Place-Names*, *Understanding English Surnames*, and *The Old Roads of England*.

Dr J. H. BAKER MA, LL.B, Ph.D
Barrister at law, University of Cambridge. Author of *An Introduction to English Legal History*.

JOHN BARRETT MBE
Naturalist.

Dr DAVID BATES BA, Ph.D
University College, Cardiff. Author of *Normandy Before 1066*.

MICHAEL BERKELEY
Composer.

FELICITY BRYAN
Author of *The Town Gardener's Companion*.

MARGARET M. CASSON RIBA, FSIAD
Architect and designer.

ALEC CLIFTON-TAYLOR OBE, MA (Oxon), FSA, Hon. FRIBA
Author of *The Pattern of English Building*, *The Cathedrals of England*, *English Parish Churches as Works of Art*.

JOHN CORNFORTH
Architectural writer, *Country Life*.

PROFESSOR ROSEMARY CRAMP MA, B.Litt, FSA
University of Durham. Author of articles and books on Anglo-Saxon Monasticism and Sculpture.

PROFESSOR H. C. DARBY CBE, Litt.D, FBA
University of Cambridge. Editor and contributor to *A New Historical Geography of England*.

G. H. DOGGART MA Cantab.
Headmaster of King's School, Bruton. Editor of *The Heart of Cricket*.

STANLEY ELLIS MA, FIL
University of Leeds. Principal Fieldworker for *Survey of English Dialects*.

EDWARD FAWCETT
Director of Public Relations, The National Trust.

JANE FAWCETT MBE, Hon. FRIBA, ARcM AA Grad. Dip. Conservation.
Editor and co-author of *The Future of the Past: Attitudes to Conservation*.

Dr DAVID FISHLOCK D.Litt.
University of Salford. Science Editor, *The Financial Times*. Author of *The Business of Science*.

MARY GORDON WATSON MBE
Horse Trials World Champion 1970; Olympic Gold Medal 1972. Author of *Handbook on Riding*.

ST JOHN GORE
Adviser on Paintings, The National Trust Historic Buildings Secretary 1973–81.

PROFESSOR J. R. HALE FBA, FSA
University of London. Author of *Renaissance War Studies*.

CHRISTINA HOLE
Author of *British Folk Customs*, *English Folklore*, *English Traditional Customs*.

KENNETH HUDSON
Author of *The Good Museums Guide*, *World Industrial Archaeology*, and *Where We used to Work*.

GERVASE JACKSON-STOPS
Architectural adviser to the National Trust and a regular contributor to *Country Life*.

LT.-COMMANDER P. K. KEMP OBE, FRHistS.
Author of *The History of Ships*. Editor of *The Oxford Companion to Ships and the Sea*.

PROFESSOR (Emeritus) H. H. LAMB Sc.D (Cantab.)
University of East Anglia. Author of *Climate: Present, Past and Future* and *Climate, History and the Modern World*.

ROGER LONGRIGG
Author of *The English Squire and his Sport*.

HUGO MORLEY-FLETCHER MA, FSA
Director of Ceramics Department, Christie's.

Dr RICHARD MUIR MA, Ph.D.
Author of *The English Village*, *The Shell Guide to Reading the Landscape* and *The Lost Villages of Britain*.

MARY NORWAK
Author of *The Farmhouse Kitchen* and *Kitchen Antiques*.

LORD OAKSEY (John Oaksey)
Co-author of *The History of Steeplechasing*. Author of *The Story of Mill Reef*.

Dr DONALD PENNINGTON MA (Oxon)
Fellow and Tutor in Modern History, Balliol College, Oxford. Author of *Seventeenth-Century Europe*.

GERALD PRIESTLAND
Religious Affairs Correspondent BBC 1977–82. Author of *Yours Faithfully*.

Dr FRANCIS SHEPPARD PhD, FRHistS
General Editor of *The Survey of London*.

C. A. SINKER OBE MA (Cantab), FI Biol.
Botanist and Conservationist. Director of Field Studies Council.

N. H. H. SITWELL MA
Universities of Cambridge and London. Author of *Roman Roads of Europe*.

Dr DAVID SOUDEN MA, PhD
Research Fellow of Emmanuel College, Cambridge.

JOHN SPURLING
Playwright.

HILARY SPURLING
Literary critic, *The Observer*. Author of *Ivy When Young: the early life of I. Compton Burnett 1884–1919*.

Dr DAVID STARKEY MA, Ph.D
London School of Economics, University of London. Author of *Court and Kingdom*.

Dr R. N. SWANSON MA, Ph.D. FRHistS
University of Birmingham.

PHILIP VENNING
Educational journalist.

HUGO VICKERS
Author of *Debrett's Book of the Royal Wedding*.

JAMES WALVIN
University of York. Author of *Beside the Seaside: A Social History of the Popular Seaside Holiday*.

BRIGADIER P. YOUNG DSO, MC, MA (Oxon), FSA
Military historian. Author of *Civil War England*, *Edgehill 1642*, *World War 1939–45*.

Contents

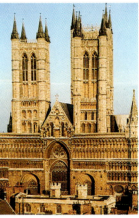

Introduction

'Heritage' is an overworked word. As a result, it has acquired in recent years a number of more or less emotive connotations which threaten to obscure its basic meaning. Sometimes it tends to suggest pomp and pageantry: Beef-eaters, the Crown Jewels, Westminster Abbey. Sometimes the images it conjures up are rather more homely: thatched cottages, village cricket, Victorian pubs. Nearly always, however, somewhere in the background, one seems to hear a distant flourish of trumpets. No three syllables are more loaded with national pride.

Nearly always, but not quite. In *Britain's Heritage*, the trumpets are silent, nor do we wish to beat any patriotic drum. We have adopted the title – after much soul-searching – only because there is no other word in the language that expresses so accurately what we have taken as our theme: all those various elements of the past that have shaped the present, and made us what we are today. Every country, to vary the metaphor, has a different hand to play – a hand dealt partly by nature, partly by fate and partly by the inscrutable workings of history. Britain, on the whole, has been lucky. Our climate is equable, our land fertile, our government stable, our culture rich and varied. But the purpose of this book is not to congratulate ourselves; it is, quite simply, to analyse some of the more important elements in our make-up, in the hope that Britain and the British people may emerge, at the end, just a little more comprehensible than they were before.

In choosing these elements we have tried, wherever possible, to follow a logical course. Thus we start off with the land itself, its climate, its fauna and flora and its natural wealth. Then, having set the scene, we are ready to introduce the characters: beginning with the earliest inhabitants of these islands and going on to the later, more sophisticated immigrants to our shores – Romans and Angles, Picts and Scots, Scandinavians, Normans and Jews, each group bringing its own linguistic and cultural traditions to enrich the new, national culture gradually taking shape. Now at last the action can begin; and we go on to describe how the British moulded their environment, over the past two thousand years or so, to their profit and advantage – how, in fact, they have played their hand.

The proper use of available resources is a valuable lesson, but only one of the many that have to be learned if people are to prosper. They must also cultivate the art of government, national and local; they must know how to establish and preserve law and order; last but not least, they must look to their defence. Our record in these fields is examined in Chapter Four. Since we are a monarchy, and since almost every monarch has left an indelible personal stamp on the Kingdom, we have devoted several sections to what we have called 'Royal Britain'. These sections are arranged chronologically; but our theme is heritage rather than history, and we have therefore tried to assess the principal legacies, political and material, that our Kings and Queens have left behind them rather than to give coherent historical accounts of their reigns.

In Chapter Five our field of vision narrows; the beam becomes more selective, the focus sharper. We look not at the country as a whole, but at the cities, towns and villages of which it is composed and the way its people express their personality: the houses they build, the gardens they so delight in, the food they eat, the games they play. Then, in Chapter Six, we turn our attention to their religion and their culture. In the religious section we have given particular attention to their ecclesiastical architecture – to the cathedrals and parish churches, the age, variety and profusion of which are unrivalled anywhere in the Christian world.

And so to our cultural heritage. Of all our sections this was the hardest to plan. It seemed sensible to begin with education: our universities and schools. After that, however, we consider people rather than places: the artists and scientists, architects and composers, the men of letters and of the theatre, whose work has enriched not only this country but the entire civilized world.

Up to this point we have considered our heritage in terms of the past and the present. In our final chapter we see it, for the first time, in a different light – that of the future. How is it to be protected against the inroads of a more and more competitive and grasping society, on an increasingly overcrowded island? The only solution is to combine constant vigilance with an ability to take swift and effective action when the need arises; and we are fortunate in possessing, up and down the country, an astonishing number of organizations admirably equipped to do exactly this. It is these organizations, varied in their individual objectives but united in their determination to preserve all that is best in Britain, that form the subject of our last chapter; and it is to them, with the National Trust at their head, that this book is dedicated.

John Julius Norwich.

Chapter One

Britain's Natural Heritage

Britain's countryside, from gentle farmland and rolling downs to granite peaks and the broad river-enriched Fens, is subtle and varied. No other country of comparable size possesses such a diversity of landscape. Much of what we see is of man's making – the hedgerows, the stone walls and pre-historic barrows. But the underlying shape of the land was forged in the fires of early geological upheavals, sculpted by ice and etched by erosion and weathering. Today Britain is a smiling land; its climate is kind, its wild life shy and its plant life – apart from a few berries and fungi – harmless. Its people are fortunate indeed.

Rocks – the Foundations of Landscape

Hardly any other part of the world can boast a geological map which is as gaudy and diverse as that of the British Isles. Almost every geological epoch is represented, with rocks ranging in age from youthful examples, like the glacial boulder clays of the Ice Ages, to those of Lewis and parts of the northern Scottish mainland, which may be more than 2500 million years old. Most of the main rock types are also well represented, including granites; basalts; schists, like those of the Scottish Highlands; gneisses, like the Lewisian gneiss of Lewis; slates; limestones, and a wide variety of sandstones. Each rock type tends to produce its own distinctive scenery; thus the contrasting landscapes of, say, the Carboniferous Limestone of the Pennine Dales, the chalk Downs of Sussex, and the granite scenery of Dartmoor are unmistakable.

Rocks can be classified according to their age or to their type. Geological time has been divided into a series of divisions so that, for example, the Cretaceous period was preceded by the Jurassic and the Jurassic by the Triassic (see map). In geological maps, the oldest rocks appear at the bottom of the scale and the youngest at the top. These age divisions, however, do not necessarily tell us much about the rock types concerned. Thus, the Cretaceous period includes most of the British chalk deposits, but also the green and brownish sandstones or 'Greensands' of the Weald and the sticky blue Gault Clay which often forms the vales between the chalk and Greensand scarps and ridges. Similarly, the Carboniferous division includes the Carboniferous Limestones, which produce bold scenery in the Mendips and parts of the Pennines and Derbyshire Peak, the Millstone Grit, so starkly displayed in the walls of Yorkshire mill towns, and most of the British coal deposits.

Each rock is of a particular type – chalk, slate, basalt and so on – while the types are parts of three broader groupings. 'Igneous' rocks result from the cooling of a molten rock mass or 'magma' originating from deep inside the Earth. When cooling at depth, the magma loses heat slowly and large crystals like the easily visible quartz, felspar and mica crystals of granite rocks are able to form. When cooling is rapid, as when the magma bursts to the surface through a fissure or in a volcanic eruption, then the resultant crystals are tiny, as in basalt. Granites, like

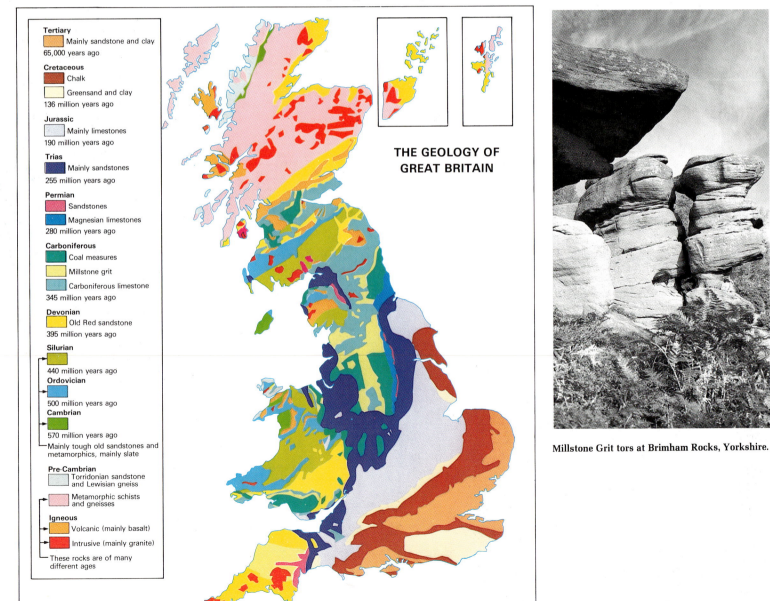

THE GEOLOGY OF GREAT BRITAIN

Tertiary
Mainly sandstone and clay
65,000 years ago

Cretaceous
Chalk
Greensand and clay
136 million years ago

Jurassic
Mainly limestones
190 million years ago

Trias
Mainly sandstones
255 million years ago

Permian
Sandstones
Magnesian limestones
280 million years ago

Carboniferous
Coal measures
Millstone grit
Carboniferous limestone
345 million years ago

Devonian
Old Red sandstone
395 million years ago

Silurian
440 million years ago

Ordovician
500 million years ago

Cambrian
570 million years ago
Mainly tough old sandstones and metamorphics, mainly slate

Pre-Cambrian
Torridonian sandstone and Lewisian gneiss
Metamorphic schists and gneisses

Igneous
Volcanic (mainly basalt)
Intrusive (mainly granite)
These rocks are of many different ages

Millstone Grit tors at Brimham Rocks, Yorkshire.

those of Dartmoor, Bodmin Moor, Land's End and the Cairngorms, and basalts, such as those seen in the Central Valley of Scotland or the Clee Hills of Shropshire, are the most common igneous rocks, but there are many less frequently seen types, like the volcanic ash or 'tuff' which forms the summit of Pike of Stickle in the Lake District.

Next come the 'sedimentary' rocks, which are formed after the deposition of debris eroded from older rocks; from the accumulated shells of marine organisms; or, in the case of coal, from thick deposits of swamp forest vegetation. Sandstones consist of eroded rock fragments and Britain has a wide range of them, including the coarse-grained Millstone Grit, the red desert sandstones of the West Midlands and Devon, and the 850 million-year-old Torridonian sandstones of north-west Scotland. Limestones, including chalk, mainly derive from the calcareous shells or skeletons of sea creatures and include the tough, silvery-grey Carboniferous Limestone; the oolitic limestones of Lincolnshire, Northamptonshire, the Cotswolds and parts of Dorset, which yield wonderful cream, buff and whitish building stones; and the soft white chalks of the North and South Downs, Chilterns, Dorset Downs and Norfolk.

Thirdly, there is the 'metamorphic' group of rocks, the members of which are igneous or sedimentary rocks which have been greatly altered by geological episodes of intense heat and pressure. Under pressure alone, a mud clay will become a mudstone and under greater pressure and baking a shale becomes a slate, while further increase in these processes may convert a slate into a tough, sparkling schist. Similarly, a sandstone may be changed into a form of quartzite, a limestone into marble, or a granite into a gneiss, a hard rock in which the different minerals have recrystallized in light and dark bands.

The enormous variety in the rocky foundations of Britain helps to produce the remarkably varied British landscapes. In general, the older and tougher rocks tend to lie to the north and west, often producing dramatic mountain scenery like the slate and volcanic rock landscapes of Snowdonia or the Lake District. The middle-aged Carboniferous Limestone and Millstone Grit produce the upland plateau scenery of the Pennines, while younger, softer rocks underlie the scarp and vale country of the English lowlands. With such a varied geological heritage, it is not surprising that Britain has produced so many illustrious geologists and geographers.

Left: A limestone gorge at Malham, Yorkshire.

Above: Granite forming rugged cliffs at Land's End, Cornwall.

Below: Basalt exposed as horizontal sheets in the Clee Hill quarries, Shropshire.

The Shape of the Landscape

What makes a landscape? A number of factors help to endow each area with its particular geographical and scenic personality. They include the geological character of the area, concerning the nature of the underlying rocks, their toughness, the ways in which they react to different kinds of weathering and the sorts of soils that form from their weathered particles. Equally important is the history of the erosion in the area concerned and the different processes involved. These include frost and ice, rivers and streams, the wind, the sea and the freeze and thaw effects which are experienced beyond the margins of active glaciers and ice sheets. Time is also an important factor, for landscapes tend to develop through different 'cycles of erosion' and so a newly uplifted landscape, with streams flowing swiftly through steep, narrow young valleys will (after

Left: Borrowdale, Cumbria – one of the most rugged and attractive areas of Lakeland scenery.

Above: The Eglwyseg Rocks in Clwyd mark a fault-line at the junction between the tough limestone rocks in the scarp and the less resistant shales near its foot.

Opposite, top: Lulworth Cove in Dorset. The sea has breached the relatively tough Purbeck Beds to carve out the Cove in the softer chalk rocks which lie behind.

Opposite, below: Scolt Head Island on the coast of Norfolk reveals a new coastline in the making.

many millions of years and the absence of new phases of uplift and mountain building) be reduced to a gently rolling plain with minimal slopes and slow, winding rivers. Finally, there are the landscape-making effects of human action such as the removal of the protective forest blanket and the over-use and destruction of soils by farming, which will accelerate erosion.

Distinctive landscapes

The air photographs show a selection of distinctive and contrasting British landscapes. That of Borrowdale shows an ancient mountain landscape composed of a complex mixture of slates and volcanic rocks which has, at several times, been uplifted and then reduced by the effects of erosion on the tough and vulnerable rocks, which now form one of the most rugged and attractive areas of Lakeland scenery. In relatively recent geological times, glaciation has acted upon the landscape. The air view shows how a glacier has ground its way along the main valley (which runs northwards towards Derwent Water), steepening and smoothing the sides of the valley which so gained a characteristic 'U'-shaped glaciated profile. The glaciers originated in upland basins which became deepened and bowl-shaped as ice and frosts shattered their floors and sides and are known as 'corries'. In the middle distance we can see a corrie and a frost-sharpened ridge or 'arrete', while a 'hanging valley' which held a less powerful tributary glacier joins the main valley in the foreground. Scenes such as this are typical of the hard rocks of the glaciated mountains of Britain.

The Eglwyseg Rocks in Clwyd mark a fault-line at the junction between the tough limestone rocks of the scarp and the less resistant shales near its foot. In the left foreground, the shale hill of Dinas Bran is prominent, though dwarfed by the towering limestone cliffs, and it is crowned by an Iron Age hillfort and Dark Age defences. The hard limestones of the scarp are interbedded with softer bends of shale, while erosion, particularly frost shattering during the Ice Ages, has attacked the softer beds to produce the stepped effect of the cliff-face. The indentations in the face of the scarp are the result of erosion by streams flowing in steep gullies which are gradually wearing back into the scarp.

Lulworth Cove in Dorset also reveals a juxtaposition of two different types of rock which vary in their toughness and ability to resist marine erosion. Here, the fossil-rich Jurassic rocks of the Purbeck Beds run parallel to the coastline and they are intensely folded by the Tertiary earth movements which created the Alps. At Lulworth, the sea has breached the relatively tough Purbeck Beds and so carved the Cove in the softer chalk rocks which lie behind.

Scolt Head Island on the coast of Norfolk reveals a new coastline in the making. Tides and current have cast up ridges of shingle to form a great island barrier beach which protects the low coastline behind. The shingle ridges are carpeted in sand dunes which are gradually colonized by vegetation such as marram grass which helps to bind and stabilize the shifting masses of sand, while behind the shingle and dunes salt marshes have developed where salt-tolerant plants trap tidal silts and assist the slow advance of the coastline. The accretion of new land is a slow and precarious process and the reclaimed farmlands which lie behind the salt marshes are protected by a number of man-made banks.

Climate

Britain's climate, at the eastern fringe of the Atlantic Ocean in the latitudes where westerly winds prevail, is warm for the latitude, thanks to the heat transported by those winds and to the warm water of Gulf Stream origin drifted by them towards our shores. Western districts, particularly those where mountain slopes confront the westerly winds, have a high rainfall; but parts of the country east of the hilly regions are much drier, except where local bodies of water act as a source of moisture or when winds from other directions enter without having passed over the mountains of the west. The weather, and in the longer run the climate also, varies as the winds vary. And in the Ice Ages, when the Gulf Stream water failed to extend north of latitudes 42° to 46°, the change of climate in these islands was greater than in most other parts of the world (*see* diagram opposite).

The rainfall map emphasizes the generally wet and very wet regions. The usually driest areas have climates where some irrigation is normally needed, particularly between March and June. Rain falls on about 250 days of the year in places near the Atlantic coasts, from Valentia in south-west Ireland to western parts of the Scottish Highlands and Islands and Shetland, while in more sheltered districts such as East Anglia averages may be as low as 140 to 150 days a year. Around London and the south and east coasts, as well as the higher-lying parts of the Midlands, totals are mostly around 170–180 days.

Thunderstorms are most frequent (averaging 15 to 22 days a year) in the broad lowland districts, especially the main river valleys where the local moisture source is important; but there are secondary maxima (10 to 17 days) over the hills and low plateaux adjacent to those lowlands, including the hills of Devon. And it is in the same areas that damaging tornadoes sometimes occur. Thunderstorms usually occur on 8 to 10 days a year at places in the Scottish lowlands. Winter thunderstorms are an occasional feature, especially near the Atlantic coasts, but usually pass over quickly.

The sunshine map may also be read as a cloudiness map, if the percentages are subtracted from 100. The bright areas along the coasts and inland in the east and south average less than 60 per cent cloud cover; the dullest areas have over 80 per cent cover. The distribution has an obvious relationship to rainfall, but day-time sea breezes in fine weather, absence of build-up of convection clouds in summer and of the fogs which form inland in winter account for high sunshine and low cloudiness figures along the coasts.

The temperature patterns are simpler: a general decrease from south to north in summer, when the coasts also tend to be cooler, and a decrease from west to east in winter, when the coasts are milder because of warmth lingering in the sea. Average temperatures decrease with height by 0.6° to 0.7°C per hundred metres or 7° to 9°C difference between sea level and the highest hilltops in Scotland. Nevertheless, on still, clear winter nights and days when the ground cools sharply, the variation with height may show an 'inversion' – the air aloft and on the hills being much less cold than nearby valleys and low ground.

Snowcover frequency shows a general gradient from south-west to north-east. The average frequency increases with height because of the lower temperatures generally prevailing. The figures range from one day in two years at Falmouth to 8 to 15 days a year in eastern and central England and near the coasts of Scotland. Inland in Scotland the figure increases to about 70 days at Braemar in upper Deeside and 215 days on the highest tops.

The variations in windiness are seen in the map of the average number of days with gale, defined as a day when wind speed averages more than 34 knots over any period of at least 10 minutes. The overall average wind speeds display a similar pattern. Average wind speeds and gale frequency increase strongly at and near the coasts. Great storms and high waves coming in from the Atlantic have caused many a shipwreck on our exposed coasts, particulary before the establishment of lighthouses. But the greatest historical weather-induced disasters in this part of the world have been produced by occasional northerly storms in the North Sea causing a surge of water up to 3 or 4 metres above the normal high tide level, with extensive flooding of the lowland near the coasts. London itself and other great cities around the North Sea are exposed to this risk.

Temperatures in Central England since the last Ice Age

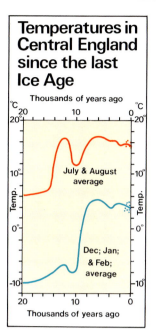

All the maps are based on data published by the Meteorological Office, generally for some 30-year period between about 1930–1970

AVERAGE RAINFALL, 1931-60

- Over 2400 mm / Over 95 ins
- 1000 to 2400 mm / 40 to 95 ins
- 600 to 1000 mm / 24 to 40 ins
- Under 600 mm / Under 24 ins

AVERAGE SUNSHINE/ CLOUDINESS, 1941-70

- Under 20% of possible sunshine
- 20 – 25%
- 25 – 30%
- 30 – 35%
- 35 – 40%
- Over 40% of possible sunshine

AVERAGE NUMBER OF DAYS A YEAR WITH SNOW LYING, 1931-60

- Less than 5
- 5 to 10

Lines on white portions of map mark frequencies of 20 and 50 days

TEMPERATURE JANUARY 1941-70

The temperatures shown on the map above are reduced to sea level averages.

TEMPERATURE JULY 1941-70

The temperatures shown on the map above are reduced to sea level averages.

GALES

The map shows the average number of days per year with gales (Beaufort Force 8 or over – over 34 knots). The map is generally for 1941–70.

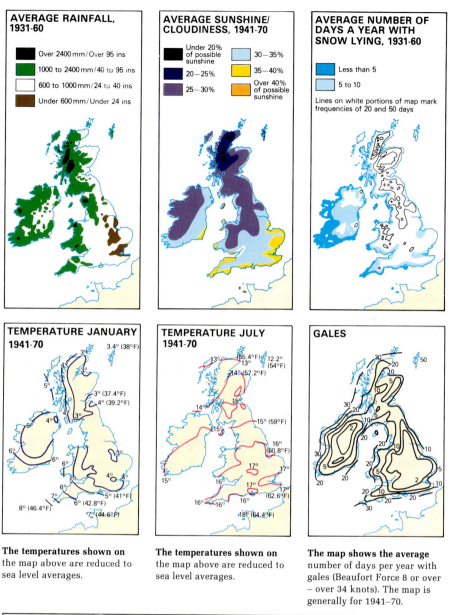

THE RECORDS SHOW OTHERWISE

Charles II's view of the English summer was that it consisted of three fine days and a thunderstorm. Byron, obviously being of much the same opinion, wrote 'the English winter – ending in July to recommence in August'. Such very British attitudes to our weather belie the statistical records. In a normal summer we can expect good spells of fine weather with temperatures soaring above the 80s (F) for about ten days and many more days with temperatures in the upper 70s. Years when our weather is unremittingly bad are very few and far between. The records also show that, contrary to popular belief, a cold winter does not promise a blazing summer. The 30 coldest winters during the past 300 years have been followed by cool summers on 20 occasions and by very warm summers on only three. (1947 was the last of such scorchers.) For summers with well below average temperatures we have to go back to 1903 and 1879. Outstandingly awful was 1816 – 'the year without summer' which is said to have inspired Mary Shelley to write *Frankenstein*. For consecutively dreadful summers we must go back even farther – to the 1690s and 1590s, a period sometimes known as the Little Ice Age.

During the winters of the Little Ice Age, which reached its nadir in the 1690s, the Thames frequently froze and in a number of years Frost Fairs were held. As Britain and Europe emerged from the Little Ice Age during the 1800s cold, snowy winters declined until, by the 1840s, mild winters became the norm. We owe our image of snowy Christmasses more to the childhood memories of Charles Dickens than to the climatic realities, for there were white Christmasses during two-fifths of the winters between 1782 and 1811 but only one in 12 during the first 60 years of this century.

Number of days with snow lying at Cambridge 1916-82

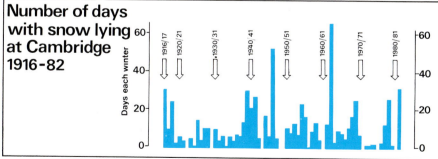

WEATHER RECORDS (annual mean)
Hottest place Penzance, Cornwall and Isles of Scilly both 11.5 °C (52.7 °F).
Coldest place Dalwhinnie, Scotland 6.1 °C (43 °F).
Wettest place Styhead Tarn, Cumbria 4391 mm (172.9 in).
Driest place Great Wakering, Essex 487 mm (19.2 in).

Plant Life: The Changing Habitat

The British are a nation of gardener-naturalists and in general value their heritage of trees and wildflowers as much as they treasure the works of people in the landscape. Plant communities or vegetation types, however, are not a set of fixed monuments like megalithic stone circles or the Suffolk wool-churches. They are as labile as language, shifting, flourishing and waning under the slow tides of environmental change.

The British flora is neither rich nor ancient. France has more than twice our total of about 2200 species. No major species is unique to Britain, and hardly any are more abundant here than on the continental mainland: bell-heather, bluebell and foxglove stand out among the favoured few.

The First Invaders

The Pleistocene Ice Ages repeatedly buried large parts of the British Isles under ice sheets and glacial deposits, while ice-free areas suffered an Arctic climate and frozen subsoil in which only stunted tundra vegetation could survive. A warmer climate finally melted the ice some 10,000 years ago, laying bare extensive tracts of fertile and well-watered ground. This was invaded by quick-spreading plants in great variety, including many opportunist species which we regard as weeds of cultivation today. Grasses and heath communities followed. These were succeeded by sallow and birch scrub, pine forest and hazel.

So far no major physical barrier hindered the spread of plants into Britain by seed or vegetative means, because Britain was not yet an island. By the time the replenished seas rose and joined to form the sundering Channel about 7000 years ago, all Britain's 'native' trees had returned. Most subsequent additions to the flora have been imported, wittingly or not, by people.

Britain makes up for its limited complement of species by an exceptional diversity of geology and local climate. There is a corresponding variety of soils and habitats, each with its own distinctive plant community whose members have been selected from the available stock by such factors as winter frost and summer heat; wind, rainfall and drainage; acid or lime-rich soil and the natural supply of phosphate and nitrogen.

In open ground (including flower-beds) mature plants can generally tolerate wide variations of weather and soil conditions. Not so in closed communities in the wild: here intense competition for living space, and above all for sunlight, favours those which can grow taller quicker. The less vigorous die, or else retreat to second-choice sanctuaries.

Foxglove (*Digitalis purpurea*) is more abundant in Britain than on the European mainland; dry acid soils and disturbed ground, especially in woodland clearings, are its typical habitat.

Purple Saxifrage (*Saxifraga oppositifolia*) is a small arctic-alpine plant found on damp rock ledges on mountains, mostly in Scotland.

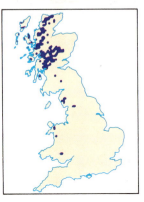

We think of bluebells as woodland flowers because they can tolerate shade. In fact they perform better in full sun, but are usually suppressed by the stronger grasses or by trampling and grazing. May sees bluebells at their elusive best in drifts on the hillsides of mid-Wales, where the fox-brown bracken is bloomed with grey like a child's breath on a morning window.

By the time of the Post-glacial Climatic Optimum 5500 years ago woodland had reached its greatest extent. Its canopy smothered the land in a tide of shade; sunloving plants of open habitats were confined to small fastness on mountain tops, crags and screes, unstable river banks, sea cliffs, sand dunes and marshes.

The oak and its broad-leaved companions were not destined to dominate the whole landscape for long. The climate became wetter as well as warmer; waterlogged peaty soils, unfavourable to tree growth, began to develop along the courses of sluggish lowland rivers and the gentler slopes of the hills in the North and West. At about the same time our ancestors made their first direct efforts to challenge the sovereignty of the plant kingdom: the agricultural revolution of the New Stone Age brought about the clearance of forest by felling and by fire, and led to the tilling of the soil for crops, the pasturage of dom-esticated livestock and the founding of more or less permanent settlements.

The ecological consequences were profound. There was a rapid diversification of open habitats, and the establish-ment of new, man-made vegetation types: pasture, arable crops with their attendant weeds, and the specialized communities of middens and trampled ground. Under human management the Grass Family became, and has remained, the most important group of plants economically and the most wide-spread, for it includes the cereals as well as the bulk of the herbage of grazing lands.

The gradual unfolding of the rural landscape, where farming expanded in slow step with the growing population, maintained and enhanced the diversity of vegetation until well into the 19th century. Somewhere in the quilted English landscape, seamed with hedges, or on the wilder downland, heaths or moors, the most exacting species could find a place in the sun.

Modern agriculture brings the latest tide of change. Fertilizers, mechanization and monoculture have made much of our flora fugitive again. Couch-grass, docks and nettles, the robust and greedy fellow-travellers of intensive farming, now line verges that were once bright-eyed with flowers.

Common Poppy (*Papaver rhoeas*), the most striking of Britain's cornfield weeds, is much reduced by modern farming methods.

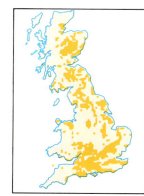

The maps are based on those published by the Botanical Society of the British Isles.

Western Gorse (*Ulex gallii*) is most common in the West and South-West; it is often associated with Bell Heather (*Erica cinerea*).

Paresly Fern (*Cryptogramma crispa*) grows on screes and rocky slopes in north-western Britain.

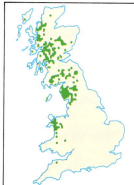

Common Rock-rose (*Helianthemum chamaecistus*) picks out the areas of chalk, limestone and other calcareous rocks on the map of Britain; dry, sunny grassland is its usual home.

Plant Life: Wetlands

Rivers, lakes and other wet habitats have a special place in Britain's natural heritage. Apart from their botanical importance, they provide some of the most valuable sites for bird life. They have in many cases escaped the changes due to forest cover and (until recently) those brought about by agricultural improvement.

In Upper Teesdale and parts of the Yorkshire Pennines there are calcareous springs and mires whose lime-rich but phosphate deficient waters sustain a remarkable community of arctic and alpine species. They represent a tiny surviving fragment of the flora of the Late Glacial period, frozen in time by the rigours of the habitat.

Such relict communities are rare, however. Aquatic and wetland plants are generally more notable for their talents as vegetable engineers: their capacity to modify, often on a large scale, the habitats in which they live. In doing this each dominant plant species may alter the conditions of the environment to its own ultimately fatal disadvantage, while favouring the growth of its successors.

Take, for example, a shallow lake in a lowland landscape recently vacated by an ice-sheet (lakes of this kind were formed in Cheshire and Shropshire, where they are known as *meres*). The shores slope gently, and underground waters feeding the lake are rich in mineral nutrients from the surrounding glacial drift. Seeds carried by wildfowl or the wind introduce larger plants into what is already a broth of micro-organisms. Water-lilies spread their pads on the surface, and the shores of sheltered bays are soon bearded with emergent reeds. Reed stems are fibrous and robust. When winter lays them low they accumulate on the bottom in a kind of waterlogged thatch, protected from bacterial decay. This is the beginning of the formation of peat.

When the rising reed-peat surface nears the normal lake level, conditions become suitable for colonization by sedges and other *fenland* plants. The reeds begin to die back. Sedges can build tussocks three feet or more in height, on whose crowns seedling willows and alders establish themselves. These succeed in their turn, shading out the sedges under fen woodland.

Woodland is not as a rule the climax of this succession. There comes a stage when the central area of the former lake basin ceases to be accessible to nutrient-rich groundwater, and is kept wet mainly by rain. This allows the peat to become very acid and leads to dramatic changes in the vegetation: trees die, and a specialized heath-like community takes over with the bog-moss *Sphagnum* playing a major part. Peat continues to build up, but it is now sterile, spongy, absorbent peat of a true *bog*.

Within the past few thousand years such plant successions have filled in many lowland meres, and made land out of flooded coastal flats from East Anglia to the Dyfi estuary. High rainfall and impermeable soil have also draped a blanket of peat over parts of our western upland from Dartmoor to Sutherland.

Fens and bogs may attract the ardent naturalist, but

Yellow water-lily, an early colonist of still lowland waters.

A red-fringed Shropshire mere in winter.

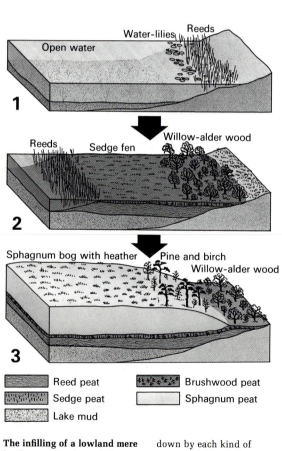

Reed peat
Sedge peat
Lake mud
Brushwood peat
Sphagnum peat

The infilling of a lowland mere by the growth of vegetation: three stages in a typical succession are shown in these diagrams with the peat laid down by each kind of vegetation. The full sequence may take a thousand years or more to complete.

what interest do they hold for anyone else? The most intriguing thing about them is that they have written their own history, and kept it in an ordered archive. Successive layers of peat are the actual (and recognizable) remains of plants that once grew there. Between these leaves of purely local history, moreover, is trapped a wind-borne sample of the seasonal pollen-clouds broadcast by trees, grasses and weeds growing in the surrounding region at any particular time. These grains of pollen, too, are preserved, and can be identified more or less precisely. It is from this *regional* vegetation record that we are able to speculate about past climates, and to visualize the changing landscapes in which our ancestors walked.

History in peat

In rare but important instances peat has preserved more direct evidence of human activity: log causeways and dugout canoes, leather and charcoal, weapons and bones of animals.

Peat has other uses. Our medieval forebears dug it for fuel, and left us the Norfolk Broads as a memorial to their labours. In areas such as the Fens and the Somerset Levels, agricultural land drainage and modern peat-cutting (for horticulture) have destroyed all but a few isolated remnants of the former habitats. Archaeologists stand to lose as much as biologists. Exceptional and co-ordinated efforts are needed to conserve what remains of the wetland archive.

Above: Peat digging near Scourie in Scotland.

Scanning electron micrograph of pine pollen grains, much magnified (right).

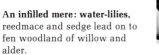

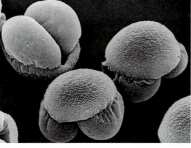

An infilled mere: water-lilies, reedmace and sedge lead on to fen woodland of willow and alder.

A dead sedge-tussock in the shade of dense alder woodland.

An acid peat bog: Sphagnum moss, heather and young pine trees in the foreground; a pool bordered with sedge, middle right; mature pine and birch in the background.

Plant Life: Trees

Oak tree in Somerset
parkland; Nettlecombe Court, in the background, is a Field Centre run by the Field Studies Council.

Thanks to pollen analysis we can now describe with some confidence, in terms of the species present, the *composition* of the wild woodland of Britain in pre-historic times. To picture its *character* is far less easy. Quantities are untrustworthy: hazel, with its copious pollen output, is over-represented, and pine grains may turn up a hundred miles or more from the nearest tree; lime and ash, by contrast, were probably more abundant than the records suggest. We are, moreover, unfamiliar with woods untouched by felling or thinning, in which saplings spring unhindered and stricken giants fall and rot where they lie.

The woods we know today are the product of a long history of use by human beings. They are a versatile resource, and have been managed and mismanaged with varying skill and foresight for a great variety of purposes. The hunting of wild prey for food and the gathering of wild fruits and firewood did not cease with the advent of settled agriculture. Norman overlords marked the chase as a privileged form of land use in introducing the term *forest*, not a synonym for woodland but a legal label denoting areas where potentially conflicting uses by the peasantry were proscribed. Hedges may have originated as carefully tended living barriers on the margins of hunting forest to keep domestic livestock out.

Woodland provided common pasturage for the animals of the local populace. Depending on their numbers and their kind (pigs are more destructive than sheep or cattle), such herds and flocks could shape a landscape varying from almost unaltered wildwood to open grassy parkland with a scatter of venerable, broad-crowned, lichen-encrusted trees.

When small wood was required for wood-pastures, for fuel or minor construction, the trees were often managed as pollards: cut well above head height, where they could sprout tufts of new growth out of reach of browsing animals. In most areas and periods, small wood was needed far more frequently than timber. A widespread custom was the management of woodland as *coppice*, by cutting the tree or bush close to the ground and harvesting at fairly regular intervals of a few years the many vigorous stems that spring from the cut stool.

In western Britain oak was commonly coppiced, and the product included bark for tanning leather as well as wood for charcoal and other uses. In the south-east, hazel was the most important coppice stock, as an understorey among well-spaced *standards* (or 'maidens') of oak allowed to grow to maturity on single trunks. These were the real timber-trees. Skilful selection and thinning could yield custom-grown timbers suitably shaped for anything from church roof to man-of-war.

Recurrent alarms over the nation's strategic stocks, from Tudor times to the present day, led to planned planting and modern forestry practice. Regular, even-aged, single species stands of certain exotic conifers are relatively cheap to establish, and yield a bigger volume of marketable timber and a quicker return on initial investment than native broad-leaved woodlands. They are not, however, so continuously productive, nor perpetually self-renewing, under rotational management.

The British oak (or rather two oaks, one more westerly than the other in its distribution) can tolerate a wide range of soil conditions. The dominance of oak in modern

Scots Pine in Rothiemurchus which is part of the Caledonian Forest in the Scottish Highlands.

Old beech pollards in Epping Forest near London.

woodlands may, however, be misleading. Until the dawn of agriculture, elm (of at least two kinds) was abundant too; and on richer soils the small-leaved lime. Beech often replace oak on dry sites, especially over chalk, and hornbeam is locally important in the south-east. Companions of the mixed oakwood, and indicators of its antiquity where several occur together, include hazel, holly, maple, the Midland hawthorn and the wild service tree.

Ash comes into its own in the North and West, especially on limestone. Chalk and limestone also favour a number of more or less restricted trees and shrubs, among them box, yew, buckthorn, whitebeam, dogwood, spindle and wild cherry.

Wet woodlands and river-banks are the home of bird cherry and the rare native black poplar, besides alder and at least a dozen kinds of willow.

Scots pine, as a native tree, has retreated to the fastnesses of the Caledonian forest, where another of the three British conifers, juniper, also flourishes. On lowland heaths, upland moors and poor soils anywhere the two birches are abundant, often in the form of secondary woodland; aspen and rowan may be found with them. Another secondary invader of great vigour is sycamore, thought to be a medieval introduction. The Romans probably brought the sweet chestnut.

Hawthorn and crab-apple are typically hedgerow plants, though both occur in other habitats. The well-laid hedge, low and trim, tree-punctuated, is still the peculiar glory of the English countryside; for how much longer? With its age often reflected in the diversity of woody species, it is green history in the landscape.

Wild Life: Fish

Nine Indigenous Freshwater Species with the Widest Distribution.

1 Roach 15–25 cm. Abundant in lakes and slow rivers. Eats plants, insects, snails. Spawns spring: eggs adhere to plants.

2 Perch Up to 40 cm. Ponds, lakes and lowland rivers. Eats invertebrates and small fish. Spawns spring.

3 Rudd 20–25 cm. Shallow, warm lakes and slow rivers. Eats surface insects and crustaceans. Spawns summer.

4 Tench Up to 40 cm. Slimy bottom fish in slow backwaters and lakes. Dormant in winter. Eats invertebrates. Spawns summer.

5 Pike 40–100 cm. Haunts quiet water, hidden among weeds. Eats invertebrates, frogs, fish. Spawns summer. May survive 20 years.

6 Common Bream 30–40 cm. Near stagnant large rivers and lakes. Active at night. Eats bottom-living invertebrates.

7 Stone Loach Up to 10 cm. Clear streams and lake shores. Active at night. Eats plants, insects, snails. Spawns summer.

8 Gudgeon Up to 15 cm. Gravelly fast streams. Feeds by sucking up invertebrates from bottom. Spawns summer.

9 Minnow 10 cm. Clean, gravelly streams and lakes. Eats insects and some plants. Spawns summer.

Living in the sea – which covers 70 per cent of the Earth's surface – are over 20,000 known species of fish, more than the number of amphibians, reptiles, birds and mammals (the other back-boned animals) put together. In diversity of shape and size they surpass in complexity the variety of insects, though not in the number of species. The 500-odd species of sharks, rays and dogfish have skeletons developed from elastic, flexible cartilage. All live in the sea. The rest, including all which live in fresh water, have fibrous, stiff, part-calcified skeletons of bone. Some 20 sharks and rays and 134 bony species live in the seas around Britain. None is peculiar to our waters. The fish of the sea are a multi-national heritage, much diminished in recent decades by ruthless commercial greed.

The freshwater fish, however, isolated from their relatives by the sea, are largely Britain's heritage and nobody else's.

The embryonic shape of what we call Europe began finally to emerge from the sea early in the Tertiary, 65 million years ago. However our present river systems and freshwater distribution patterns resulted from the uplift of land and the forming of new mountain chains which took place over the nine million years of the Pliocene which ended only three million years ago. Our freshwater populations stem from those nine million years: but it was not until 10,000 years ago that rising sea-levels, caused by melting ice, finally cut off Britain from the continental mainland and so isolated Britain's freshwater fish from all others.

If we remember that the severity of the ice had eliminated fish from Ireland, Scotland and all but southern England and Wales, it is not surprising that we have only some 23

indigenous wholly freshwater species in Britain. All of them occur in Yorkshire and nearly all in the Great Ouse and Trent drainages, and in Norfolk. The numbers fall away sharply northwards and westwards. Only three – the char, pike and minnow – live in the northern Highlands and only ten had time to re-occupy Ireland before rising sea-levels separated Ireland from Britain.

In Britain an additional eight species of fish come from salt water into fresh water to spawn – two lampreys, the sturgeon, two shads, salmon, sea-trout and smelt. Travellers in the opposite direction are the eel and the flounder which go down from fresh water to spawn in salt water. All these fish are found in Ireland and Scotland, and all except the sturgeon in the Isle of Man where perch and char are the only wholly freshwater species.

Another dozen species have been introduced to Britain, largely for food or fun. Both the carp and Crucian carp originated in Asia. (The Romans may have brought in the former.) Later, monasteries cultivated both. Their relation, the goldfish, a decorative curiosity from the Far East, reached us by 1630 via Portuguese sailors.

Attempts to improve the 'fishing', often on estate waters, led, around 1900, to the introduction from North America of the brook trout, the largemouth bass, pumpkinseed and rockbass; from Central Europe of the ide or orfe, the wels and the pikeperch. The rainbow trout has often and widely escaped from fish farms. In about 1920 the gaily coloured bitterling was liberated. Since 1960 isolated records have come from Scottish rivers of humpback salmon, strays from Arctic, Asian and American stock, which the Russians released in the Kola Peninsula.

Amphibians and Reptiles

Common Species Confined to England and Wales

Barbel Up to 50 cm (above). Middle reaches, clear, fast rivers. Eats bottom invertebrates at night. Spawns upstream, summer.

Silver Bream Up to 25 cm. Weedy lakes and slow rivers. Eats bottom invertebrates and plants. Spawns summer.

Chub Up to 30 cm. Clean rivers and lakes. Smaller eat invertebrates; larger, small fish. Spawns summer. Not edible.

Ruffe Up to 20 cm. Bottom of deep lakes and slow rivers. Eats invertebrates and some plants. Spawns spring.

Bleak 20 cm. Clean, slow streams and lakes. Eats insects, spawn and fry. Scales supply silvery crystals for artificial pearls. Spawns summer.

Bullhead 10 cm (below). Stony, clear streams and large lakes. Eats bottom invertebrates, mostly crustacea. Spawns spring.

The British inheritance of amphibians and reptiles is but a small reminder of the variety, numbers of individuals and range of size that occupied the land 100 million years ago. We are now left with only 12 species that are fully indigenous.

The fossil record shows that the first recognizable amphibians emerged in the humid swamp forests of some 300 million years ago, which constituted our Coal Measures. These amphibians were descended from a group of fishes which had fleshy lobes at the bases of their fins. With these primitive limbs they could heave themselves on to a muddy bank. As important, these 'fish' could breathe air, for the gills of some lobe-fin fishes developed into simple lungs.

The amphibians could now escape their marine predators – especially sharks – by seeking the safety of the land with its limitless supply of food, worms, snails, spiders and beetles, which were all impaled on their sharp teeth.

For 100 million years the amphibians diversified and flourished throughout the world. They were not, however, true conquerors of the land for, like nearly all modern amphibians – the frogs, toads and newts – they could not travel far from water and had to return to the water to breed. There – like their modern descendants – they laid soft, jelly-like eggs. These hatched out into free-swimming tadpoles which eventually changed into adults and left the water.

The first real conquerors of the land were the reptiles which evolved from amphibians. Their great advance was that they did not have to return to the water to breed. Instead, the young developed in hard, porous shells (to admit oxygen) that could be laid on land and hatch in the warmth of the sun. The still greater reptilian advance of retaining the egg within the body of the female until the young hatched (*ovoviviparity*) made it even easier for such reptiles to wander farther and farther afield. Reptiles also developed fully functioning lungs, allowing their skins to harden and thicken against the higher land temperatures which lasted during the Permian and Triassic periods for 100 million years. Amphibians died out while others retreated back to live wholly in water. The reptilian dinosaurs, in all their marvellous variety, dominated their long day which ended suddenly 65 million years ago. Why it ended is one of the unsolved puzzles of natural history. It did however, coincide with the start of the dominance of warm-blooded mammals.

Of the 12 remaining indigenous species of British amphibians and reptiles, the common frog, common lizard and the adder – three of the total of four species that still breed in Arctic Norway – may have survived in southern Britain during the last advance of the ice 120,000 years ago, which finally melted away by 8000 BC.

The European pond tortoise, *Emys orbicularis*, probably flourished here between 5000 and 3000 BC when Britain enjoyed a climate with an average temperature 2°C warmer than now. Then a series of cold, damp summers prevented tortoise eggs from hatching. The dead adults became fossils in East Anglian peat deposits. Today thousands of such tortoises are annually and ruthlessly imported to pet shops. Those which escape or are released may live years in the wild.

The rising sea-level from melting ice cut off all but the common frog, the natterjack toad, the smooth newt and the common lizard from Ireland. Only the common toad found its way to Orkney and, strangely, the slow worm to the Outer Hebrides.

The important biological advantage of hatching live young enabled the slow worm, common lizard and adder to spread all over mainland Scotland, whereas the wetter, colder summers of the far north of Britain restrict the egg-laying sand lizard and grass snake to England where the warmer climate allows the eggs to hatch.

No fossil has been found to confirm that the edible frog, *Rana esculenta*, lived in Britain during the 2000 years of warm climate between 5000 and 3000 BC. It may, however, claim residential status, having been brought into Britain on repeated occasions since the 1700s. As a result, colonies exist in Norfolk, Suffolk, Sussex and Kent.

The marsh frog, *Rana ridibunda*, also ranks as a British citizen. Largest of European frogs, its raucous laughing call prompted the Greek playwright Aristophanes to his choral refrain in *The Frogs*. The marsh frog was introduced in 1884 to Chilworth, Surrey. In 1934, 12 were released in Stone-in-Oxey, Kent; they started a fast colonization that now occupies over 150 sq km of Rother Levels and Romney Marsh up to the Isle of Sheppey.

More exotic creatures have been introduced to and then escaped from walled gardens, specialized collections and bored owners. Some survive a few years; some have even bred in hot summers. These displaced animals include the midwife toad, found in Worksop, York and Totnes; the Italian crested newt (Newdigate, Surrey); and the painted frog (Manchester and London fringes).

All these little creatures are so easily overlooked that isolated records may continue to turn up. Their chance of survival, notably for the few truly indigenous species, depends very much on human activities. The increasing disturbance of 'rough' ground, the drainage of meadows, the canalizing of streams and the use of agricultural/forestry chemicals all portend a decline more severe than was ever inflicted by ice.

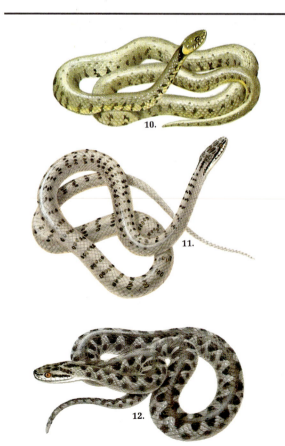

1. Common Frog 10 cm. Any damp habitat. Eats molluscs and insects. Spawns spring, quiet ditches and ponds.

2. Natterjack Toad 7 cm. Heathland and dunes. Largely nocturnal. Breeds in shallow ditches spring/summer. Rare.

3. Common Toad 12 cm. Various colours. Largely nocturnal. Voracious feeder insects, worms. Many breed simultaneously in favoured ponds.

4. Palmate Newt 7 cm. Smallest European newt. Breeds shallow, acid puddles, pools including uplands.

5. Warty Newt 11–17 cm. Largest European newt. Breeds in deeper lowland ponds. Courtship April: eggs summer. Crest of male absorbed after breeding season. Hibernates on land.

6. Smooth Newt 8–10 cm. Variously spotted; markings obscured after breeding. Courtship April. Nocturnal feeder.

7. Common (Viviparous) Lizard Up to 15 cm. Widely distributed: heaths, commons, banks, gardens to 915 m. Eats insects, spiders. Young born in July.

8. Sand Lizard Up to 17 cm. Variable colour. Sandy heaths and dunes: Surrey, Hants., Dorset and Lancs. Colonial. Eggs July; young August. Survival doubtful.

9. Slow-Worm 45 cm. Legless lizard. Found under cover; dryish heaths, commons, coasts, gardens. Serpentine movement. Mates spring; births August.

10. Grass Snake Up to 1.5 m. Preferably damp, open country. Eats mainly frogs. Diurnal. Mates spring. Hibernates in holes. Harmless.

11. Smooth Snake 60 cm. Only Surrey, Hampshire, Dorset in sandy heaths/woods. Eats insects and small mammals. Harmless.

12. Adder Up to 60 cm. Most common of the three British snakes. Dry, sunny open 'rough' country. Eats small mammals, frogs, carrion etc. Timid but bite can prove fatal.

Wild Life: Insects

Of the three quarters of a million or so of insects in the world that have been named at least 20,000 live in Britain. We have 300 species of wingless spring- and bristle-tails; 30 grasshoppers; 7 earwigs; 43 dragonflies; 540 sucking lice; 1650 aphids and scale insects; 200 caddis flies; 2380 moths and butterflies; 4000 beetles; 6200 ants, bees and wasps; 5200 flies; 50 fleas; and many others, all with three pairs of walking legs. Added to them are 550 species of spiders, 104 millipedes and centipedes, 180 slugs and snails, and many many more.

The river banks, heathland, hedgerows and meadow-lands of Britain teem with life. The 1000 million arthropods that live in the top nine inches (25 cm) of soil in an acre (0.40 ha) of English meadowland include 600 million mites, 250 million bristle-tails, 110 million bugs and beetles and 30 million centipedes and millipedes, as well as up to three million worms. A single nest may house a million ants or 20,000 wasps.

These wildlife habitats are now being severely threatened. Meadows, once a glorious mixture of natural grasses and wild flowers, are now more and more sprayed with herbicides and insecticides to maximize the weight of fodder grass. In summer the rasping song of the common green grasshopper is heard less and less and the sight of the gangly daddy-long-legs or crane-fly becomes ever more rare. The old meadow, bright with buttercup, ox-eye daisy, red clover and dandelion, was the home of ladybirds and dor beetles: now most of them are gone.

Despite ruthless grubbing out of our hedgerows in the 1950s and 1960s our hedgerows still provide a refuge for wildlife and for the wasp, the fly and peacock butterfly which feed on brambles. Along our river banks in summer can be found damsel flies, demoiselles and mayflies. In the precious relics of our wetlands the summer brings out numerous dragonflies: big hawker dragonflies with 4-inch (10-cm) wingspan and darter dragonflies (so named after their darting flight). On a floating leaf may be spied the Raft spider – biggest of Britain's spiders – watching for its insect prey. Oakwoods are the home of 500 or more species of insects. The leaf litter harbours a veritable zoo – spiders, mites, worms, springtails, centipedes, millipedes, ants, thrips and beetles and moths in all stages of their life cycles. Others in season, are behind the bark, on the open branches and trunks, in the buds, eating the leaves. Life quivers, night and day, at all levels on any oak. If we add to this the twilight world of moths, midges and dancing gnats and butterflies, those glorious creatures of the sun, then our heritage of insect life will be seen to be truly impressive.

Insects have bodies divided into three sections. The head is the sensory and feeding centre; the thorax carries three pairs of legs and usually two pairs of wings; the abdomen is the metabolic and re-productive centre. An insect's life cycle includes complicated stages between the egg and the adult.

Most insects can fly. Their adaptability enables species to live in every niche from the poles to the equator, from −50°C to +40°C. Their sizes range from 0·2 mm to 120 mm.

The number of named species of insects in the world exceeds three-quarters of a million, with perhaps another two million as yet unnamed – far more than the rest of the animal kingdom put together.

Stag Beetle, restricted to southern England. Mouth parts enlarged in male into antler-like structures. Flies in the evening.

Black Ant. Very common. Nests under stones. Eats other insects and is fond of honey-dew from aphids.

Wolf Spider. Makes no web; runs after prey to catch it.

Crane-fly, largest of many similar species also known as daddy-long-legs. Larvae are pests, eating roots of grass.

Seven-spot Ladybird – the most popular of Britain's beetles.

Centipede. Stone-dwelling with fifteen pairs of legs.

Meadow Grasshopper. Colour variable. The female is much larger than the male (shown).

Wild Life: Butterflies

The three upland, glacial survivors in Britain, which lay their eggs on moorland grasses on which the caterpillars feed.

The Scotch Argus. Widely found over mainland Scotland, some of the Inner Hebrides and, rarely, northern Pennines.

The Mountain Ringlet (above). Found in swampy hollows above 457 m near Perth and Inverness and on Langdale Pikes.

Large Heath (below). Common in Scotland; only indigenous butterfly on Western Isles and Orkney/Shetland.

Butterflies are perhaps the most emotive of all insects. Many have names as beautiful as their wings: purple emperor, orange tip, Adonis blue and clouded yellow. Of the 15,000 species which inhabit the Earth, fewer than 60 breed in Britain. There are another 20 species that visit Britain irregularly but do not breed.

Just why they are distributed as they are is much debated, but some of the outlines of the patterns are generally accepted.

No butterflies – and probably no insects – survived the long fierce third glaciation of 240,000 years ago. During the following interglacial a number of species made their way northwards only to be confronted by the fourth and last glaciation of 120,000 years ago. Some, like the hedge-brown, silver-washed fritillary and the brimstone, survived then only by retreating into the extreme south of Ireland and south-west Britain from where they edged northwards again when the climate improved; but they have not yet reached Scotland. Three upland species, the large heath, mountain ringlet and Scotch Argus, did manage to survive in sheltered nooks in the north. When the ice finally cleared away they found themselves for evermore separated from their relatives in the European mountains by the wide expanse of lowland plain. However the surviving pockets of the lowland brown Argus and speckled woods were eventually joined by new waves of their relatives from the south.

The return northwards of all those species which had been driven far to the south by ice was headed by a group which included the meadow brown, the common blue, orange tip, wall, grayling, ringlet, small blue and small copper. They are not strong fliers and there is no evidence that, since the final separation of these islands from the mainland of Europe 7000 years ago, our populations have ever been sustained by the arrival of immigrants from the south. The conclusion must be that this group, having reached Scotland, had time to curl down southwards into Ireland, where they all occur now, by crossing the last landbridge joining Argyll to the Inishaven Peninsula.

Those which delayed their move northwards until the climate had further improved never reached Ireland because the landbridge had been drowned before they reached it. The marbled white, purple emperor, chalk-hill blue, Adonis blue, black-veined white and small skipper are among those still slowly spreading from the south-east; some have hardly reached the northern English counties. Only the small pearl-bordered fritillary and the large skipper have extended their range to Scotland. Since 1940 the peacock has spread on north from the Lakes.

A few species reach us from the Mediterranean almost annually but in very varied numbers, occasionally in swarms outnumbering flakes of snow. Our indigenous green-veined, small and large whites and small tortoise-shells are almost regularly boosted in this way; our brimstones and peacocks may be too. Without the support of immigrants our native painted ladies and red admirals would not survive.

When clouded yellows and, less often, pale cloudeds arrive early enough they may lay eggs that hatch in August; but none survives the winter. The queen of Spain fritillary and Bath white from southern Europe and the Camberwell beauty from Scandinavia hardly ever lay an egg here, let alone survive. The swallow-tails and monarchs are probably no more than chance victims of the wind.

Some 1500 naturalists have not only mapped on the 10-km grid squares the numbers and distributions of our native butterflies, they have also repeated enough of their counts to show that the survival, let alone prosperity, of the group is now in doubt. Twenty-five per cent of the species are declining steeply; only eight are holding their own. What applies to the easily observed butterflies may well apply too to all the other groups of insects which are not so readily monitored.

The main cause of decline is without doubt the destruction of habitat that proceeds remorselessly all around us. New towns, motorways, and so-called 'greenfield' industrial building, the different kinds of aerial, water and soil poisoning, canalizing of streams and rivers, drainage of wetlands, and the large-scale changes that underlie the new agriculture all notably impoverish the natural world on which they are imposed.

The chalk downlands, grazed by sheep and full of flowers, used to support 25 species of butterflies. Those which are now ploughed up and sprayed with herbicides and insecticides to support the monoculture of barley are reduced to a biological desert. Human greed and need are often not distinguished.

The chequered skipper, extinct in England since 1976, may survive in Inverness. The silver-spotted skippers are

The story of the Large Copper (above) exemplifies the tenuous hold of butterflies in Britain. The butterfly lived long enough separated from its European relatives to have evolved into a unique subspecies. The drainage of wetlands had exterminated this brilliant flyer by 1850. Examples of the mid-European subspecies were introduced to Wicken Fen, Cambridgeshire, in 1909 but they died out because of the inadequacy of the supply of the great water-dock on which the caterpillars feed.

In 1915 a subspecies was found in Holland that was biologically closer to the original British version. That subspecies was itself becoming rare.

In 1927 another fen site in Cambridgeshire was carefully prepared. The great water-dock grows readily enough on stream banks, but large coppers require plants on flat, marshy areas among cover that must include purple loosestrife and common meadow rue. The new colony had to be large enough initially to survive heavy predation of the chrysalids by birds.

All these problems were overcome and that lovely colony survives now, but only because naturalists continue to support the unremitting cutting and 'gardening' of the fen without which the magnificent butterfly would again disappear.

The spring arrivals from the Mediterranean of the clouded yellows (above) and, in particular, of the pale cloudeds are erratic. In 'good' years early dates and warm sunshine may coincide to allow broods to hatch in Britain when the main August wave of migrants is arriving. Then we have one of those prodigious seasons that pass into folk memory. Britain's wet and cold winters eliminate all those summer stocks.

Red Admirals and Painted Ladies (right) migrate to Britain every year in varying numbers from as far south as the Mediterranean. Those that arrive as early as May have time to lay eggs on nettles and thistles which hatch in August just when the later waves of immigrants may be getting here. Neither species hibernates and only fragmentary evidence exists of an autumn migration southwards. If it were not for those April/May arrivals Britain's summers would then be without these two species.

The Swallowtail (right) is the largest British butterfly, with a wingspan of more than 7 cm. The subspecies particular to Britain has been almost eliminated by progressive drainage and pollution of wetlands. Now seen only over the Broads where the milk parsley still grows on which its caterpillars feed. Those swallowtails occasionally seen in Kent have been blown across from mainland Europe and belong to a distinct and smaller subspecies, whose caterpillars will survive on wild or cultivated carrots. They may even breed successfully but something prevents the establishment of even a semi-permanent colony in Britain.

Above: The Camberwell Beauty – a rare migrant to Britain.

critically few; they depend on downland turf but we do not know the links between cause and effect.

Another problem has been our ignorance of the precise biological requirements of each species. Only just in time was it discovered that the Adonis blue depended on well grazed downland, as its eggs are laid on the flowers of horse-shoe vetch on south-facing slopes. The Lulworth skipper will survive now that we understand its need for patches of chalk sward overgrown by tor-grass. The heath fritillary, reduced to only 31 small colonies, may now start to multiply in the sunny sheltered patches of open all-age woodland on which we know it depends. The black hair-streak was almost gone before the discovery that it needs blackthorn for its eggs in sunny woodland glades.

In each case, as soon as the biological requirements were understood, reserves that provided them were identified and bought by conservationists. If only we had known in time the relation between thyme, ants, rabbits and sheep on the downs we could easily have saved the large blue which disappeared in 1979 (unless rumours of survival in Gloucestershire are confirmed). Finding out is a slow process; the tempo of the natural world is timed by the lifespan of the creatures living in a particular habitat. People's impatience to impose their 'developments' will continue to do irreparable damage until they recognize their duty to the rest of Creation.

The Queen of Spain Fritillary (below) and the Bath White (below right), which were quite common in the 18th century, arrive nowadays at ever more irregular intervals and in numbers so small that several years may pass without a record of either.

The Long-Tailed Blue (right), first recorded in 1859, and seen less than 50 times since. The Short-Tailed Blue has been seen only four times since 1874. These four species breed all the year round in southern Europe and do not hibernate. Sightings in Britain are probably from the fringe of sudden bursts of breeding success far to the South. Why this happens nobody knows.

Wild Life: Birds

Some 20 subspecies, including wrens, hedge sparrow, twite, the Shetland starling, the bullfinch, goldfinch, long-tailed tit, nuthatch, dipper and Hebridean stonechat are recognizably different from their continental relatives. Nonetheless they are in contact with these relatives at some time of the year, usually during migrations, so their genetic structure does not qualify them for specific status.

The Red Grouse is the one species that lives and breeds only in Britain and is never in contact with its nearest relation on the Continent, the hazelhen.

Below: The Knot, a wading bird, is a winter visitor to Britain. This dumpy grey and white bird flies south from the Arctic in flocks of up to 10,000; in mid-winter there may be around a quarter of a million of them around the coasts of Britain.

Something like 480 species of birds have been recorded in Britain. This number has risen by 10 per cent in the last 20 years as ever more observers develop the skill needed to record new birds so accurately that their records have scientific validity.

About 135 species are resident here all the year round and breed with us. Another 55, including the warblers, flycatchers, wheatears, swallows, ring ouzels etc., come to us in spring from the south, nest here and leave us again for the winter. Another 30 species pass through northwards in the spring to breed in the Arctic regions and pass back again in the autumn as they fly down to their winter quarters in the south. A further 25 species, like the redwings, fieldfares, snow buntings, geese, some duck, swans and waders, are driven out by the cold from northern and central Europe to winter in Britain.

That still leaves some 200 species whose occurrences are so erratic that seeing any one of them in a particular year is unlikely. Probably 150 of them have been recorded less than 20 times in the whole history of birds in Britain.

Our commonest birds are the chaffinch and blackbird, each with a total of some 10 million; starlings, robins are at about seven million; house sparrows, hedge sparrows, song thrushes and meadow pipits are about three million each. Altogether about 14 species total more than one million each and another 15 species over 350,000 each. These 29 species between them constitute 75 per cent of Britain's total bird population. Four hundred species make up the other quarter.

In nearly every 10 square kilometres in England, Wales and Scotland 76 or more species will be found nesting.

The list of our breeding birds is always slowly changing. The great auk, great bustard and white-tailed eagle are wholly extinct. The ruff, black tern, spotted crake, avocet, black-tailed godwit, bittern, osprey and capercaillie were all once lost, largely through drainage, but have all re-established themselves, if marginally, encouraged by provisions made for them by the Royal Society for the Protection of Birds.

Modern agricultural methods have so reduced corn-crakes, stone curlew, nightjar, wryneck, red-backed shrike, cirl bunting and Dartford warbler that their survival is now doubtful. On the other hand, redwings, fieldfares, bluethroats, goldeneye and whimbrel are among those whose breeding range has recently spread from the north into

An untidy colony of rooks' nests, built high in the tree tops for safety. Rooks are gregarious; great flocks are often seen walking over fields, probing the ground for insect grubs.

Left: Large colonies of breeding guillemots are found on some of Britain's cliffs and offshore islands, crowded together, almost touching one another, as they incubate their eggs. The eggs, laid on bare rock, are sharply pear-shaped; If knocked, they roll round in a circle, and not over the cliff edge. Guillemots winter at sea; they are rarely driven into land by storms.

Above: Gannets are the largest European sea birds. About two-thirds of the world's breeding gannets nest in the British Isles, mainly on west coast and Scottish islands' cliffs. Sometimes these large white birds follow ships, making shallow dives for refuse; they also make spectacular dives for fish.

The direct ancestors of birds were a group of reptiles living 225 million years ago in the Lower Trias. The oldest known true bird is the Archaeopteryx whose fossil was found in 1861 in Bavaria in Jurassic rocks 135 million years old. The Archaeopteryx was the size of a crow, had a long feathered tail but still had reptilian teeth in both jaws. Moreover its bone structure indicates that it was a glider rather than a true flyer.

By the Eocene period of 50 million years ago adaptive radiation had progressed so far that the shape of a majority of our present groups of birds were already recognizable. In the late Miocene of 20 million years ago many modern genera were already flying.

The Red Kite is a great survivor. The commonest street scavenger in the 16th century and abundant across Britain, it was exterminated by intensive game preservation and by 1900 was extinct from Britain except for less than ten pairs in remote, wooded south-western central Wales. This remnant has been assiduously protected by devoted naturalists and the RSPB so that today there are known to be over 100 living. This illustration is from a poster produced by the National Museum of Wales.

Britain. Southern birds moving northwards include Savi's warbler, Cetti's warbler, serin, firecrest and little ringed plover. The extraordinary spread of the collared dove from Asia Minor reached Norfolk in 1955 and it now nests almost throughout Britain.

Many seabirds have increased during the last hundred years. The fulmar's spread from Iceland and St Kilda continues. Several gull species are now so numerous that (unwise) biologists think they should be 'controlled'. The gannet, shag, eider, and great skua are others that have increased. Unless even tighter control is exerted on the oil and chemical industries, their pollutions of the sea threaten to reverse these trends.

Nowhere else in the world is so much work and money provided by the public, in association with the statutory bodies, to look after its heritage of birds. The robin may yet supplant Britannia as our national symbol.

The Royal Society for the Protection of Birds
The Lodge, Sandy
Bedfordshire

Wild Life: Mammals

The last remaining descendants of Britain's original population of primitive mammal species were lost 450,000 years ago, during the second and harshest of our four glaciations. It lasted for 55,000 years. After that, during the 185,000 years of the second Inter-glacial Age, the weather improved and animals migrated slowly northward again. Some of those that arrived during this period have survived almost unchanged to the present day.

Our fox, wildcat and badger; our red and roe deer; our bank-, short-tailed and water voles and our mountain hare were among them. Later these old originals must have been pushed south again by the third onslaught of the ice which advanced as far as the Wash; but once again they all survived. So did bears, wolves and beavers. The musk ox and woolly rhinoceros were then hunted by Neanderthal people. As the climate became warmer again 180,000 years ago, surviving animals eased northward. Mammoths, aurochs, bison, lynx, hyena – even rhinoceros and hippopotamus – multiplied in Britain.

Then came the fourth Ice Age. Yet again cold eliminated all but the hardiest species. These included all those who had survived the third glaciation.

When the ice retreated northward for the last time 20,000 years ago (bringing in the Holocene modern times of *Homo sapiens*) these survivors occupied the land almost alone until new migrants joined them from the south. Today Britain's share of the world's species of mammals is only about 100. Most are descendants of those which existed in Holocene days.

As the ice melted and the sea-level rose, slowly the ark of Britain was set adrift. Those animals which moved northwards fast enough and early enough had time to occupy not only the central mass of Britain but also to reach the fringes of the land that the rising sea level would soon isolate as islands. By 5000 BC the English Channel barred further colonization from the south except by swimming and flying. The absence of 15 species of mammals in Ireland which flourish in mainland Britain is only because they did not move fast enough and so were cut off.

That the red squirrel, fox, and badger live in Ireland but not the Isle of Man is taken as evidence that Man was isolated by rising sea-level before Ireland was severed. The hedgehog had time enough to reach Man because it could sleep through the hard winters close to the ice edge. However the mole never reached Ireland, let alone Man, because it could not burrow in hard (frozen) ground. Strangely enough the pygmy shrew moved fast enough to occupy Ireland and all the islands except Shetland while the common and water shrews were cut off from all but some of the Inner Hebrides. The otter is the only carnivore on the off-shore islands: but he is the only one that can swim well.

Since then, some species have been deliberately exterminated (the wolf, the beaver and the bear). Many others have been introduced either deliberately or by accident. The rabbit, for example, is not a 'native' at all. Although the Romans may have brought in some from the western Mediterranean, there is no mention of rabbit warrens in Domesday Book (1086). The rabbit's main introduction is most likely to have been by returning crusaders before 1200. The return of farmland to wasteland after the Black Death in 1381 allowed rabbits to spread far and fast.

The black (ship) rat reached Britain from the East in the baggage of merchants, infested with fleas that spread the Black Death and Plague. Nowadays it is principally confined to larger ports and a few islands, although it retains a capacity for turning up in unlikely places. Its cousin, the common (brown) rat, arrived from Russia around 1682.

The Red deer (left) and Roe deer are the only deer native to Britain. The red deer, Britain's largest wild animal, lives on the open mountains and moorlands in Scotland, Cumbria and the West Country. During the autumn rutting season the stag rounds up as many hinds as he can find, and with his magnificent antlers drives off any intruders. The antlers are shed after rutting. All deer are shy animals.

1. The badger, relative of the stoat and weasel, lives throughout the British Isles. Being nocturnal, it is rarely seen.

2. The fox lives in dryish woodlands, copses, open moors and farmland. It is becoming increasingly common in suburbs and even in towns, scavenging from dustbins for food.

3. The Wild Cat, once found all over the British Isles, is now found only in the Scottish Highlands where, happily, its numbers are now increasing. It breeds with domestic cats which have 'gone wild'.

4. The Short-tailed or Field vole, found in long grass, hedges, marshes, river banks and woodlands, provides food for owls and kestrels.

TIME SCALE	
Beginning (years ago)	
1 million+	PLEISTOCENE
600,000	1st glaciation
540,000	1st interglacial
480,000	2nd glacial – harshest
425,000	2nd interglacial – warm
240,000	3rd glacial – severe
180,000	3rd interglacial – dry, cold
120,000	4th glacial – less harsh
35,000	*Homo sapiens* appears
20,000	HOLOCENE – still continues: ice retreats; sea level rises
7,000	Straits of Dover formed.

Within a hundred years it had spread right across the land and, by swimming from shipwrecks, on to almost all islands.

The 'native' brown hare was introduced as a game animal to Ireland and the larger Scottish islands.

Among deer, the red and the roe are the only true natives, having survived through the last glaciation. The fallow deer arrived later, having perhaps been introduced by Phoenician sailors or, more likely, by the Romans. Other more exotic species like the Sika, muntjacs and Chinese water deer were introduced from 1860 onwards to decorate gentlemen's parks – from which some of them inevitably escaped.

The North American grey squirrel was introduced still more recently – and more misguidedly – making its first appearance only in 1876. It spread fast just at the time when the numbers of the native red squirrel were falling steeply from a period of unusual abundance. Despite popular and persistent belief, the greys in no sense 'drove out' the reds, whose population may already have recently started upwards again on one of its long-term swings.

The recent escapes of various exotic animals, ranging from the coypu and the mink in 1919 to Mongolian gerbils in 1974, may have added interest to our native fauna; but they have certainly not improved it. The experience of rabbits in Australia should have been enough to teach us that the release of 'foreign' animals into the wild is not only a silly thing to do; it is biologically dangerous as well.

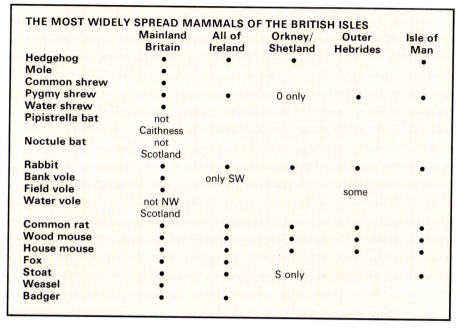

THE MOST WIDELY SPREAD MAMMALS OF THE BRITISH ISLES				
	Mainland Britain	All of Ireland	Orkney/ Shetland	Outer Hebrides	Isle of Man
Hedgehog	•	•	•		•
Mole	•				
Common shrew	•				
Pygmy shrew	•	•	0 only	•	•
Water shrew	•				
Pipistrella bat	not Caithness				
Noctule bat	not Scotland				
Rabbit	•	•	•	•	•
Bank vole	•	only SW			
Field vole	•			some	
Water vole	not NW Scotland				
Common rat	•	•	•	•	•
Wood mouse	•	•	•	•	•
House mouse	•	•	•	•	•
Fox	•	•			
Stoat	•	•	S only		•
Weasel	•	•			
Badger	•	•			

MAMMALS OF THE RIVER AND SEA

Pipistrelle, the smallest and commonest of the bats.

BATS

Bats are the only mammals that can fly, some like the noctule, powerfully and high while others, like the horseshoes, flutter rather feebly nearer the ground. Identification is sometimes difficult and even technical. The distribution and natural history of even the commonest of the 12 species in Britain are still shadowy.

Colonies of 100 or more breed in trees, buildings, crevices in masonry or caves. The males take no part in rearing the single young which is born blind. The first flight follows in three weeks. Bats are active at dusk and by night, finding their way about and detecting food by echolocation which may include little ticks or buzzes audible to the human ear. They hibernate, often in caves, sometimes away from the breeding site.

The long-eared bat, Natterers bat and pipistrelle – whose 12·5 cm wingspan makes it the smallest of all British bats – are common throughout England and Wales, though a good deal rarer in Scotland. Daubenton's bat may fly wherever woods surround open water. The noctule, our largest species (20–24 cm wingspan) is common as far as north Yorkshire: so is the whiskered, except for East Anglia. The greater and lesser horseshoe bats are confined to the south-west. The barbastelle flies in small numbers south of the Wash. The serotine is abudant only in the south-east and Devon. The distribution of Leisler's is uncertain and practically nothing is known of Bechstein's.

Otters

Nowadays otters flourish only in north-west Scotland, the Hebrides, Orkney and Shetland and northern Ireland. Until 1950 they were living almost throughout Britain. Then, within ten years of the sudden and widespread use of the organochlorine pesticide called dieldrin, the otter disappeared from nearly all the Midlands and South-East. The poison was concentrated through the food chains in which the otter was the last link. At the same time the wholesale destruction of habitats by canalizing rivers, draining wetlands and felling small woods all removed the secret undisturbed quiet these shy creatures require. Much is being done today to halt the otter's decline. Otter hunting is now illegal in England and Wales. Otter havens have been set up on some rivers. Since the otter's natural habitat is essential to its survival, conservationists have also worked tirelessly to slow down the rate at which these habitats are still being destroyed by Water Authorities (who are exempt from prosecution). In consequence the otter's future looks somewhat brighter; but until the radical measures required to save it become politically more acceptable, its long-term prospects remain grimly uncertain.

Seals

The Atlantic grey seal is a rare animal. In Britain we are responsible for looking after perhaps 75 per cent of the world's population. The best estimate is that around 70,000 live along the coasts of Scotland, the west of England and Ireland. Numbers are probably increasing.

In autumn the female comes ashore in caves, on to small islands or sheltered beaches, to drop a single white-coated pup weighing 13 kg. Each male protects a harem of five to ten females. After three weeks suckling, the females desert the pup. Copulation about a week after birth saves the adults from having to come ashore a second time. The females – 2 m long and weighing some 82 kg, are ready to breed when six years old and may live to be 30; the bulls are bigger but die younger.

Otters live by lakes and rivers. In Britain they flourish only in North-West Scotland, the Hebrides, Orkney and Shetland and northern Ireland. They eat fish and are mainly nocturnal. Otter hunting is now illegal in England and Wales.

A diving seal exhales air to reduce buoyancy. Its heart-beat falls from 150 to 10 per minute so conserving oxygen stored in blood and muscles. The fishing dive lasts about five minutes but can be 20. A few deep breaths after surfacing quickly eliminate carbon dioxide.

The grey seal eats crustaceans, octopus and squid as well as many fishes, including cod, salmon and sand-eels; but nobody knows the daily weight of its food. Thus there is no conclusive proof of the frequently made claim that seals damage commercial fishing and consequently no justification for the annual killing of seals in Scotland. In the Farne Islands, however, the situation is very different. Here, with serious overpopulation causing aggression and disease while abandoned pups die from wounds or starvation, humane culling is essential to the health of the community.

The pug-faced common seal is a creature of shallow, sheltered water, sand banks and sea lochs. Estimates of the total British population vary widely around 15,000, of which the largest colony, about 1500, live in the Wash. The rest are distributed along the east coast of England, around Scotland and Ireland. The diet of the common seal includes molluscs and crustaceans as well as a wide variety of fish.

MAMMALS ERADICATED IN HISTORICAL TIMES

As humans 'progressed' they tended to think of more and more carnivorous animals as 'vermin'. The larger the animal the worse it fared because of damage it did to flocks, herds, crops and, latterly, 'game'.

The **bear** still common (and protected) in eastern Europe, the Balkans and Pyrenees, was so common in Britain in Roman times that an export trade carried them to circuses. It was however extinct by the 10th century.

The **wild boar** still abounds in central European forests. It was widespread in deciduous woods in Britain but never in Ireland. The last were killed in England in the 17th century.

The **wolf**, that most gentle of animals, has always met with hostility in Britain. In the 10th century taxes were paid to King Edgar in wolves' heads. Bounties persisted into the 17th century; in 1652 Cromwell forbade the export of wolf-hounds from Ireland. Wolves were thus progressively driven into the remote mountains of Ireland and Scotland, where the last were killed in the mid-18th century.

The **beaver** was once common in East Anglia, where sub-fossil remnants are abundant in Fenland peat. It survived in Wales to the end of 12th century, and somewhat later in Scotland.

MAMMALS RECENTLY ESTABLISHED

The **coypu** was introduced in 1929 from 'wetland' South America to 50 farms in East Anglia where a number of them promptly escaped and spread fast along the drainage system. It burrows into drainage banks and ravages vegetation including farm crops and reed beds. Repeated campaigns of extermination have largely contained the incipient spread beyond the Broads but final elimination is almost certainly impossible.

The **mink** was widely introduced for fur in 1929 and immediately escaped to colonize 'wetlands' extensively but irregularly throughout Britain and north-eastern Ireland. It is a serious predator of poultry, game-birds and fisheries and may locally exterminate ducks and waders. Despite all counter-measures it is probably by now permanently established.

The **red-necked wallaby**, a native of Tasmania, escaped in 1939 from a private zoo in Staffordshire into the scrub and moorland of the Peak district. Despite harsh winters, the breeding colony is now around 50. A separate escape near Horsham produced 'wild' breeding in the Ashdown Forest area where a few continue to survive.

The **Mongolian gerbil** – in the East a known carrier of rabies and bubonic plague – was carelessly released by a film company in 1973 near Fishbourne, Isle of Wight. By 1976 its breeding colony was probably about 100.

The **golden hamster** has regularly escaped from pet shops; near Bath in 1957, Finchley in 1960, Barrow in 1961 and Manchester in 1964. Seventy were trapped near Bury St Edmunds in 1974. It can easily become a pest, particularly of fruit crops and in food stores.

The **reindeer** unaccountably failed to survive the ice in Britain. It was however introduced in 1952 to the Cairngorms by the Reindeer Council of the United Kingdom as a potential source of protein.

The **porcupine** is nocturnal and capable of doing much harm to our native flora and fauna. A number of Himalayan porcupines escaped in 1969 from a wildlife park near Okehampton in Devon, and although there are now probably less than 20 in the wild, they still seriously damage the local conifer plantations. In 1972 a pair of North African crested porcupines escaped from Alton Towers in Staffordshire. They may have bred, but apparently failed to establish a colony.

An Atlantic grey seal with its pup. Numbers around the coasts of Scotland, the West of England and Ireland are probably increasing and on some beaches overcrowding is causing serious problems. Grey seals come ashore in autumn to breed; at other times of year they can be seen basking on offshore rocks. The less gregarious common seal breeds on the sandbanks of the Wash (the largest single colony in Europe), off the coast of Norfolk and on the Scottish isles. The common seal pup, born in June and July, has the great advantage of being able to swim off on the rising tide after its birth, which helps to keep it safe from predatory humans.

The coypu, a rodent from South America, was brought to Britain to be farmed for its fur in 1929. Before long, enough had escaped to set up breeding colonies in East Anglia, and while it has been possible to stop these from spreading the coypu now seems to be a permanent British resident.

Wealth from the Land

Among the whole of Britain's natural resources, only the sea and the air are in as plentiful supply as they were 500 years ago. The native forests and woodland areas have been greatly reduced, despite extensive replanting by the Forestry Commission in more recent years; the acreage of agricultural land becomes less each year; and in Britain, as elsewhere, minerals are a rapidly wasting asset.

Britain's industrial development slackened in the second half of the 17th century, because the country was running out of wood. The first step towards a solution of the problem was to replace wood by coal as a domestic fuel, at least in the cities and larger towns. Coal production rose from 200,000 tons in 1560 to three million in 1690 and then remained stationary. The easily worked surface deposits were becoming exhausted and there was as yet no way of keeping deeper pits free of water. Consequently, the industrial use of coal did not begin to develop until first Newcomen's and then Watt's steam engine made mine pumping practicable. Even with the extra coal available, full use could not be made of it until the technique of using it for iron smelting had been perfected – two-thirds of Britain's iron was being imported as late as 1720 – and until a canal system made it possible to move coal relatively easily into the manufacturing areas.

The raw materials and fuels stored under the surface of the Earth and the sea are only useful if they can be extracted, processed and transported, and if customers can be found for them. Once the demand is proved to exist, means of production and marketing will eventually be found. It is easy to forget the small scale on which industry operated before the second half of the 18th century and how correspondingly limited its mineral requirements were. In the 14th century, for example, the peak year for Cornish tin production was 1332, yet the amount was less than 850 tons. Lead deposits were much more widely distributed than tin, and by Tudor times lead was extensively used for roofing and for waterpipes, for pewter, for bullets and shot, and for sheathing warships, yet even in 1600 it is doubtful if more than 5000 tons a year was being produced. There was, of course, considerable re-use of old lead.

Copper was being mined in the 16th century, but there was not a great demand for it, and the metal did not, indeed, really come into its own until the end of the last century, when the rise of the electrical and telephone industries created a totally new market. Much the same happened to china-clay, of which Britain has some of the largest deposits in the world. So long as the market was confined to the manufacture of porcelain, the output of the Cornish pits remained very small, but as soon as additional uses were discovered for the mineral, especially in paper-making and in the paint and pharmaceutical industries, the scale of the operations was transformed.

Britain has few of the rare metals, such as cadmium, platinum and thorium; it has to import all its bauxite or finished aluminium; and it is no longer able to meet its full requirements of copper, lead or tin from domestic sources. But it is well provided with coal, iron, brick and pottery clays, and building stone and, since the Second World War, with petroleum and natural gas.

In the case of coal and iron, however, there has been a considerable change in the relative importance of the different deposits. Some coalfields, such as those in the Birmingham, Bristol and Somerset areas, have ceased to operate altogether; others, in, for instance, South Yorkshire and Nottinghamshire, have been greatly developed. Many local links between coal-mining and iron-making have disappeared altogether.

Until 1820 most of the commercially worked iron in

Britain came from the carboniferous ores associated with the coal measures in South Wales, the West Midlands, Derbyshire, South Yorkshire and the lowlands of Scotland. When these had been worked out, the main centres of ore-extraction were located on the broad band of Jurassic ores extending from North Yorkshire through the East Midlands to the Cotswolds. These are not rich, but easy to extract. The small area of good quality ore in Kent and Sussex on which the medieval iron industry largely depended was worked out by the end of the 16th century. An excellent ore occurs as haematite in the Forest of Dean, South Wales, Cumbria and the Furness district of Lancashire.

One of today's most important minerals, sand and gravel for concrete aggregate, is becoming scarce in a number of previously well-provided areas, especially London and the South-East.

GAS

The first discovery of natural gas to be made in Britain was in 1919, near Dalkeith, in the course of an exploration programme started during the war, when oil supplies were threatened by German submarines. No oil was found and drilling did not continue. In 1936 BP began exploring for petroleum and, by accident, discovered gas in Eskdale.

Coalfields were developed on a large scale to provide fuel for industry, in particular iron smelting. Today more than half Britain's coal output is used to generate electricity. In the past, coal mining devastated the countryside with huge slag heaps and the scars of opencast workings; today every effort is made to minimize mining blight.

MINERALS PRODUCED IN GREAT BRITAIN		
Anhydrite	Fireclay	Sand in gravel
Ball clay	Fluorspar	Sandstone
Barytes	Fuller's earth	Silica stone and ganister
Brine salt	Granite	Silver
Calcspar	Grit and conglomerate	Slate
Celestite	Gypsum	Talc
Chalk	Honestone	Tin ore
Chert and flint	Igneous rock	Tungsten
China clay	Iron ore	Zinc ore
China stone	Limestone	
Coal	Lead ore	
Common clay and shale	Potash	
Copper-zinc ore	Potter's clay	
Crude petroleum	Rock salt	
Dolomite	Salt in brine	

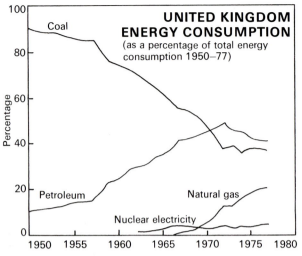

UNITED KINGDOM ENERGY CONSUMPTION
(as a percentage of total energy consumption 1950–77)

Drilling on a large scale started again in 1959, after huge gas reserves had been located in the Netherlands, near Groningen. The first gas discoveries of commercial importance in the British North Sea were made in 1965.

OIL

The first major discovery of oil in Britain was made near Nottingham in 1939. This has remained the principal on-shore region so far, although production on a smaller scale has been carried on at Gainsborough and Kimmeridge. Off-shore drilling in the North Sea went on throughout the 1960s and 1970s, with exploitable reserves at 8–10,000 feet (2400 m to 3000 m). The North Sea, with an average depth of 160 feet (48.75 m), is very shallow, compared with the 3 miles (5 kilometres) often encountered in the oceans.

The production of both oil and gas is expected to reach its peak in the late 1980s and after that to decline steadily until the end of the century.

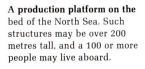

A production platform on the bed of the North Sea. Such structures may be over 200 metres tall, and a 100 or more people may live aboard.

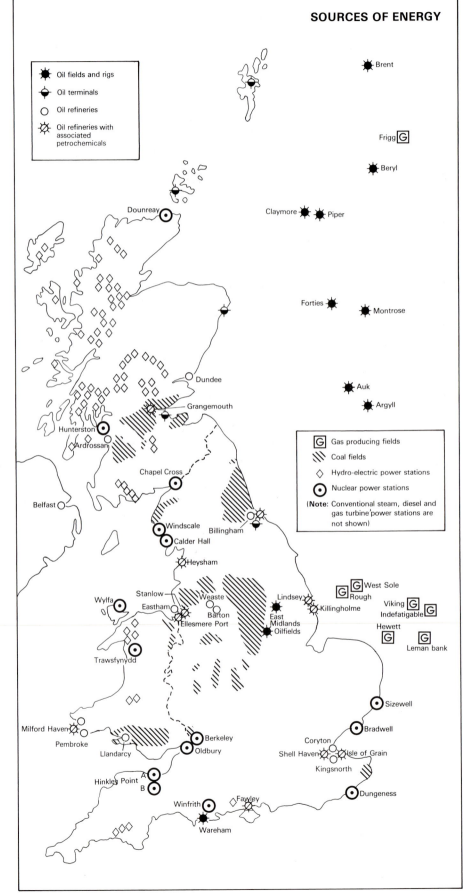

SOURCES OF ENERGY

- Oil fields and rigs
- Oil terminals
- Oil refineries
- Oil refineries with associated petrochemicals

G Gas producing fields
Coal fields
◇ Hydro-electric power stations
⊙ Nuclear power stations
(**Note:** Conventional steam, diesel and gas turbine power stations are not shown)

Chapter Two

The Origins of the British

The English language – subtle, rich, adaptable – is a living record of the various peoples who have contributed to the making of Britain's culture. The sinews of the language are to be found in the speech brought over by the Anglo-Saxon invaders. But their plain, practical tongue was enriched with a wealth of words from the indigenous Celtic languages (which still survive independently in Wales and parts of Scotland); from the Latin introduced by the Romans and preserved by monks and scholars; and from Viking raiders and settlers. The next influence – of immense importance – was that of the French-speaking Normans in the centuries after their conquest in 1066. Later immigrants – Dutch, Jews, Huguenots, Irish and most recently, settlers from the New Commonwealth, to say nothing of English-speaking peoples in America, Australia and elsewhere – have all contributed and continue to contribute, to the almost infinite richness of the language we still call 'English'.

The Archaeological Evidence 1

The study of the past was for centuries a matter of happy and usually unreliable conjecture, with theories often based on traditions and legends. The druids of ancient Britain, like the archdruid shown here, became the focus of much romantic speculation.

Below: Today archaeologists rely on meticulous examination of objects *in situ*, and of the site itself. Differences in soil colour and texture may show that the site has been disturbed; these diagrams show that three objects of widely different dates can be found at the same level owing to digging of pits, foundations and so on.

Although the 'antiquary', the person with a general interest in the past, has existed for some time, the 'archaeologist' is a different and more recent figure. Early antiquaries were interested mainly in the written records, or, where these failed, in traditions and legends – some of them totally unreliable. It was not until the 17th and 18th centuries that we first hear the fundamental question of archaeology being asked: 'Apart from records and traditions about it, what does this object – this building, this pot, this piece of metal – tell us about itself, simply by being what it is and not something else?'

Attempts to answer this question led to the classification of objects and hence to one method of dating them. If, for example, a certain kind of pottery is found associated with Roman coins at Casterbridge, it follows that the pottery is Roman and that Casterbridge was occupied in the Roman period; if the same type of pottery (but without coins) then turns up at Barchester, it follows that Barchester too was occupied in the Roman period. By comparing sites with one another, objects with one another, and sites with the objects that they produce, archaeologists can thus gradually build a framework for both dating and understanding the past.

Typology can be applied not only to the Roman period where we have at least some written records, but also to the pre-historic period where we have none. Whereas the 18th

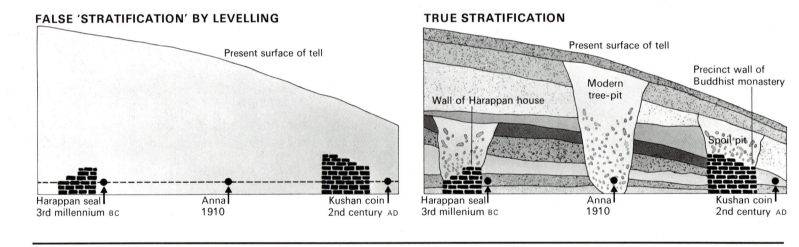

FALSE 'STRATIFICATION' BY LEVELLING

Present surface of tell

Harappan seal
3rd millennium BC

Anna
1910

Kushan coin
2nd century AD

TRUE STRATIFICATION

Present surface of tell

Wall of Harappan house

Modern tree-pit

Precinct wall of Buddhist monastery

Spoil pit

Harappan seal
3rd millenium BC

Anna
1910

Kushan coin
2nd century AD

century thought of all 'Ancient Britons' as being much the same from the earliest times to Julius Caesar's day, 19th-century work on ancient artifacts made clear that there had been a development – through the famous Three Ages of Stone, Bronze and Iron. Further subdivisions followed, such as that of the Stone Age into phases known as Palaeolithic, Mesolithic and Neolithic – Old, Middle and New. Even without actual dates one could thus build a relative chronology; some things were clearly older than others, even though one could not say just how much older. It could no longer be taken for granted, for instance, that Stonehenge and the Druids were connected, or even contemporary, just because both happened to be pre-Roman.

As well as typology, the study of *what* is found, archaeologists also need to deal with stratigraphy, the analysis of precisely *where* it is found. The basic principle of this is simple and well known: in any place of settlement rubbish tends to accumulate, and (other things being equal) the rubbish at the top will be the most recent and that at the bottom the most

ancient. The archaeologist's job, then, is to reverse the process by removing the piled-up layers of material in the opposite order to that of their deposition. In practice this can be complicated, largely because people not only dump new layers but dig into the ones already there. If someone digs a ditch and raises a rampart with the earth dug from it, then objects found in the rampart will mostly be those already in the ground before the digging started; objects found in the silt of the ditch, on the other hand will have been dropped into it after it was dug, so must be more recent than those in the rampart even though they are found at a lower level. And if someone else later slights the rampart and dumps its remains back into the ditch, one will be left with the seeming paradox of earlier material on top and later material underneath. But with care the sequence of events can still be worked out. Then if we can date the ditch (if, say, it surrounds a Roman camp in a part of Scotland which the Romans held only for a short and known period) we can gain an idea of the date of the objects in it; or conversely, if we can already date the objects we can gain an

THE THREE AGES
BC
Old Stone Age 350,000–8000
Middle Stone Age 8000–4500
New Stone Age 4500–2000
Early Bronze Age 2000–1400
Late Bronze Age 1400–700
Iron Age 700 to Roman Conquest

idea of when the ditch was dug and how long it remained in use. Therefore both stratigraphy and typology thus go hand in hand.

The Study of the Ordinary

From this arises the greatest principle of modern archaeology, the principle which distinguishes genuine archaeologists from tomb-robbers and treasure-hunters and which has become as important to them as the Hippocratic Oath to doctors: 'Objects Alone are Not Enough'. As General Pitt-Rivers, a pioneer of systematic excavation, remarked as long ago as 1892, 'The value of relics, viewed as evidence, may be said to be in an inverse ratio to their intrinsic value'. Valuable objects are rare, thus atypical, thus less helpful to our understanding of the past than everyday junk with no value at all; one reconstructs the past by the study of the ordinary, not the extraordinary. It is for this reason that archaeologists hold such a deep and passionate hatred of persons who go to an ancient site with metal-detectors, taking what they happen to value and destroying the rest.

The heritage of our past lies not only in museums and scheduled monuments, but in the earth itself, the patterns imposed upon that earth by people of former times and the story that these can tell us if we listen carefully and try not to interrupt.

Many Victorians were keen amateur archaeologists; outings to local excavations were popular and no doubt unintentionally destructive. Here a Bronze Age barrow is sliced through by the neighbourhood enthusiasts, treating archaeology as a happy day out.

Archaeology as a science: a modern site is marked out on a grid pattern so that the exact location of every find can be accurately recorded. The soil removed is sieved to make sure that even tiny fragments are not missed.

The Archaeological Evidence 2

The Power of Archaeology

The 20th century, and above all the past 40 years, have seen a revolution in archaeological thinking brought about largely by techniques derived from the physical sciences, above all the new methods of absolute dating of the past without using written records – something which until the 1940s was believed to be impossible.

The best known of these methods is radio-carbon dating. All living things contain carbon, and a small but measurable amount of it is of a type different from the rest, known as Carbon-14 and radio-active. Animals pick this up in their food (either other animals or plants); plants get it from the carbon dioxide in the air, where it is formed by the action of particles (cosmic rays) from the Sun. When an organism dies it can pick up no more Carbon-14 and the amount already in its body gradually decays and disappears at a known rate. By measuring the radio-activity of organic remains it is thus possible to estimate how old they are. Real, though not always very precise, dates in years BC can replace the older 'relative' chronology based on terms like 'Late Neolithic' or 'Middle Bronze Age'.

Other physical methods of dating followed. The fluorine test uses the fact that buried bones absorb fluorine from the ground, more and more of it the longer they stay buried. This was the test that finally proved the notorious 'Piltdown Man' to be a forgery; the skull and the jaw supposed to be from the same individual proved in testing to have entirely different fluorine contents and thus different dates. The thermo-luminescence test can be used in a similar way on pottery. A genuinely ancient pot absorbs energy from the ground in the form of radio-activity, and when heated will give this off again in the form of a special kind of light. The older the pot, other things being equal, the more of this light it will give off; but a modern forgery will produce none at all.

Yet another approach to dating comes from the study of tree-rings. The bristle-cone pine of California can live for 5000 years, and wood from such trees can be dated in two independent ways – by counting the rings, or by analysing them for radio-carbon. When this was done, the two sets of results did not agree, the counting dates being regularly older than the radio-carbon ones. 'Cosmic rays', it would seem, have not always reached the Earth at the same rate; the radio-carbon dates needed to be re-calibrated, and the results upset many earlier ideas about the order in which ancient societies developed.

In other fields besides dating, techniques from the physical sciences have proved valuable. Seeds and pollen grains can be recovered from sites and examined under the microscope, telling us what plants were growing in ancient times and hence something about ancient climates and farming methods. Stone objects can be analysed to find out how and where they were manufactured. X-rays provide a useful way of analysing valuable objects without cutting them up. Statistical methods and computers make it possible to handle large amounts of information more efficiently. Air photography can reveal sites totally invisible from ground level; many sites discovered in this way have still to be excavated, and will remain (one hopes) as a treat in store for archaeologists of the future.

The Limit Of Archaeology

The list of questions that archaeologists can answer is matched by a list that they cannot, which unfortunately includes many of the questions most often asked by the general public. Most people like to see the past in terms of individuals – 'Caesar's Camp', 'Arthur's Seat', 'Queen Elizabeth slept here'. At a pinch they will accept explanations based on groups of people – 'Celts' or 'Beaker Folk' or even 'Neanderthalers'. Archaeologists, however, now think in terms of what they call 'cultures', assemblages of material objects that signify certain ways of living. It is by no means guaranteed that a particular culture of this sort denotes a particular people, or even a particular period. Even a simple-sounding expression like 'Bronze Age' means one thing in Great Britain and something very different in Greece; and some regions (including most of Africa) seem never to have had a Bronze Age at all.

1066 and All That mentions 'that long succession of Waves of which History is chiefly composed'. Pre-history too has often been seen as a succession of waves, always flowing the same way, from south-east to north-west. 'Diffusionists' have maintained that all new ideas and techniques begin in the Near East, spreading thence to Greece and thence to the rest of Europe and reaching the British Isles last of all; 'invasionists' have gone on to claim that people as well as ideas move in the same one-way traffic system, and that every new 'culture' in Britain calls for a new 'people' to bring it. In real life human change and development are never as simple as this, and archaeologists are now realizing how very complex they can be and sometimes have been.

*'We think our fathers fools, so wise we grow;
Our wiser sons will no doubt think us so.'*

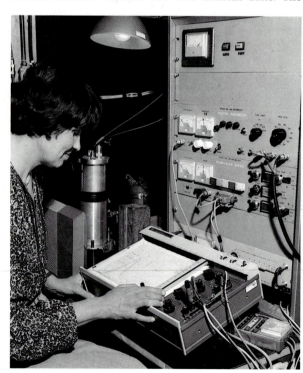

Scientific methods are increasingly used in dating objects. Here a sample of powder extracted from a pot is tested for thermoluminescence. Such methods are able to detect forgeries, and a number of once renowned museum showpieces have had to be banished to basements since modern tests have proved them fakes.

The Council for British Archaeology
112 Kennington Road, London SE11 6RE
Founded in 1944, the Council took over from the Society of Antiquaries the responsibility of recording and protecting ancient monuments and sites. It promotes, through its many regional groups, archaeological research and excavation and takes an active interest in archaeological education.

Aerial photography can reveal hitherto unsuspected remains. This picture shows the outlines of a Roman town at Wroxeter. When Osbert Crawford, archaeological officer for the Ordnance Survey just after the First World War, was shown strange markings in early air force photographs, he wrote: 'What I saw far surpassed my wildest dreams. . . . Here on these photographs was revealed the accurate plan of field systems . . . at least 2000 years old.' Aerial photographs can show up the pattern in a seeming jumble of mounds and banks, but they can also reveal a great deal that cannot be seen from the ground at all. Pictures taken at a low angle when the Sun is near the horizon show shadows thrown by very small bumps and dips, while difference in soil depth caused by hidden walls or filled up ditches leads to differences in vegetation and crop growth. Evidence of our past, lying concealed all around us, can now be studied and pieced together.

Prehistoric Migrations

Neolithic people were also in the habit of surrounding tracts of ground with banks and ditches, sometimes leaving many entrances to produce what is known as a 'causewayed camp' such as Windmill Hill in Wiltshire, and sometimes (at a rather later date) leaving only a few, to produce a 'henge' such as Maumbury Rings in Dorset or the earliest version of Stonehenge (with bank, ditch and numerous pits, but as yet without most of the stones visible today). The purpose of these enclosures is uncertain. They were not defended settlements at all; they may have been periodic tribal meeting-places – political, religious, commercial, or perhaps all of these together.

Beaker Culture

Round about 2500 BC a new culture, the Beaker Culture, makes its appearance in Britain; and (despite the dangers of linking 'culture' with a 'people') this does seem to have been introduced by new arrivals, the famous 'Beaker People' of the Rhineland, of noticeably different physical type from the earlier inhabitants. These newcomers, we think, brought to Britain the knowledge of metal – first gold and copper, then somewhat later the copper-tin alloy known as bronze, after which the next phase of pre-history is named.

The 'Early Bronze Age' (about 2000–1400 BC) is poor in settlement-sites, but rich in monumental ones. This is the age of the ubiquitous 'round barrow', the digging up of which was a favourite Victorian pastime; it is also the great age of the famous and enigmatic stone circles. More than 900 of these are known in the British Isles, Avebury being the largest but Stonehenge the most spectacular. They have been discussed at great length; all that can be said here is that their purpose was *probably* connected with astronomy, and *certainly* with religion.

Neolithic farmers in western and northern Europe buried their dead in elaborate 'family vaults'. Some, as in eastern Britain, were built of wood and turf, covered with a long mound or barrow. Where stone was available, as in western Britain, tombs might consist of a passage with small chambers opening off it, or of individual chambers, again covered with a long or round barrow. This picture, taken during excavations, shows a barrow at West Kennet in Wiltshire, an area particularly rich in Neolithic remains.

A Bronze Age necked beaker found at Sittingbourne in Kent. Objects of this culture seem to have been introduced by immigrants from the Rhineland, known as the 'Beaker People'.

The British Palaeolithic or Old Stone Age (about 350,000–8000 BC) and the succeeding Mesolithic or Middle Stone Age (about 8000–4500 BC) have produced numerous objects now in museums, but very little in the way of permanently visible monuments. In the Neolithic or New Stone Age, however (about 4500–2000 BC), people began to control their environment more effectively than before, and leave marks on it that are sometimes still easy to see. They grew crops, chiefly a type of wheat called emmer; they had domesticated cattle, sheep, goats and pigs; and they manufactured pottery. Though still ignorant of metalwork, they became highly skilled in stonework and in finding the most suitable types of stone for their implements. One late Neolithic industrial site, the flint mine at Grimes Graves in Norfolk, is still well preserved.

Neolithic houses were usually built of timber which has since perished, though often their plan can be reconstructed by study of the holes in which the timber uprights used to stand. Some parts of the country, however, were already short of timber, and here we sometimes find houses of stone. At Skara Brae in the Orkneys, an unusually well-preserved site, stone was used not only for the buildings but even for the furniture inside.

More widespread and conspicuous today than Neolithic settlements are Neolithic tombs. Among these are the well-known 'earthen long barrows' of southern England, also the more impressive 'chambered tombs' found mainly on the western side of Britain as well as in Ireland and along the Atlantic coast of the Continent. Some of these are built from very large stones indeed, and may be the oldest monumental stone structures in the world; Maes Howe, again in the Orkneys, is a particularly fine example.

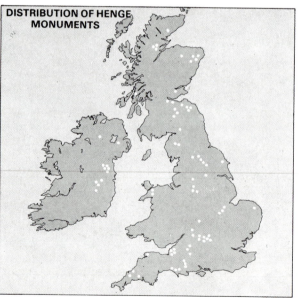

DISTRIBUTION OF HENGE MONUMENTS

The earliest visible monuments of the British Isles belong to the Neolithic period at a time when the early farming communities had mastered their environment, and developed the distinctive social organization celebrated by these monuments. In the early phase ancestral tombs and earthwork enclosures were the main forms of monument. The enclosures – whose functions ranged from settlements and defence to the disposal of the dead, were confined to southern Britain. Henge monuments, successors of these enclosures, are widely distributed, suggesting a general expansion of the settled area.

The 'Late Bronze Age' (about 1400–700 BC) has yielded no such impressive monuments. The climate at this time grew noticeably colder and wetter, perhaps causing much land to go out of cultivation. The political situation, too, changed for the worse. Sites on hilltops began to be fortified, and as time went on the fortifications grew more elaborate; the chief visible monuments of the succeeding 'Iron Age' (c 700 BC to the Roman Conquest) are its tremendous hilltop strongholds – Cissbury Ring in Sussex, Maiden Castle in Dorset, Old Oswestry in Shropshire and many others.

Just as the introduction of copper to the British Isles is associated with the Beaker People, so the introduction of iron is associated with the Celts. This raises problems: 'Celt' is not a racial or cultural term but a linguistic one, and without written records no archaeological technique can tell us what language a people spoke. We know that that in the Roman period (for which we *do* have written records) Celtic was the predominant language of Britain, and by combining archaeology with references in classical writing we are fairly sure that the Celtic-speakers reached Britain from France, and France from Central Europe; but the details of how this happened may be more complex than is generally supposed.

Pre-history is not an affair of one people replacing another, or of one idea replacing another; what happens far more often is that different peoples and ideas live side by side and mingle. (The Bronze Age is so called because some people sometimes used bronze, not because everyone always did; it did not simply replace the Stone Age, nor in turn was it simply replaced by the Iron Age). Race, religion, language and culture are formed, in Britain as in most other regions, by the combining of influences and traditions of diverse origins and equally diverse ages.

The standing stones at Callanish, on the island of Lewis in the Outer Hebrides. They date from about 2000 BC; the tallest stands some 5 metres high.

Silbury Hill in Wiltshire is the largest pre-historic mound in Europe. Despite a number of excavations, no one knows its original purpose. It was probably built about 1600 BC.

The Roman Legacy

Above: The first coin to show Britannia was minted by the Romans.

Below: The extensive Romano- British villa at Chedworth in Gloucestershire shows how the Mediterranean way of life was superimposed on the British landscape.

Though Julius Caesar's invasions of 55 and 54 BC mark the end of Britain's pre-history and the beginning of her history, they had no lasting effect on the tribes in the island. Not until AD 43 did Rome really make her presence felt; in that year the armies of the Emperor Claudius overran the south-east of Britain and established it as the Roman province of *Britannia*.

The first frontier of the province was the road called the Fosse Way, linking the military bases (later towns) of Exeter and Lincoln. This line gave Rome most of the rich 'Lowland Zone' of Britain; advance beyond it, into the poorer and more hostile 'Highland Zone' did later occur, but soon ran into the law of diminishing returns. The South-West was annexed with little difficulty, round about AD 60; Wales and northern England, however, were not conquered until the 70s, and never became wholly reliable. Throughout the Roman period both regions needed fairly large garrisons, and the remains visible in them today are for the most part military rather than civilian.

Scotland came under Roman rule only for short periods. Rome's 'Farthest North' was marked by the victory of Mons Graupius (perhaps Bannachie in Aberdeenshire) in AD 84. Soon afterwards the Roman army in Britain had to be reduced. Scotland was abandoned, and in AD 122 the Emperor Hadrian, making a personal visit, decided that it was not worth reconquering. The visible consequence of this was Hadrian's Wall, the most impressive military work to be found anywhere within the Roman Empire, and probably the second most spectacular 'Ancient Remain' (after Stonehenge) in the whole of Great Britain today. Hadrian's successor, the Emperor Antoninus Pius, organized a second northward advance – thereby producing another well-known monument, the Antonine Wall across central Scotland; but this seems to have been used for less than 40 years (built in about AD 142, abandoned in 180 or earlier). In their own way these two walls present a problem as tricky as that of Stonehenge: the 'where' of them is known, the 'when' fairly precise, the 'how' gradually yields to

study, but the 'why' – above all, why *two* walls in so short a space of time? – remains highly uncertain.

Behind the Roman soldiers, or sometimes even alongside them, came the Roman administrators, engineers and builders. 'Ancient Britons' of the Iron Age were by no means the half-naked savages they are sometimes made out to have been, and before the conquest had already built some very large permanent settlements; it is the Romans, however, who must receive the credit for the first true towns in Britain, as opposed to strongholds or overgrown villages. This town-planning made a shaky start, three of its most successful early specimens (Colchester, London and St Albans), being burned to the ground in AD 60 by the armies of Queen Boudica (Boadicea). Thereafter building went ahead more smoothly. At its height the province contained some 20 established centres of administration (*civitates* or 'cities') and nearly a hundred other settlements large enough to be called small towns. By modern standards all were small (London, the largest 'city' in the province and its capital, is believed to have had about 30,000 inhabitants), but they compare perfectly respectably with towns in Rome's other northern provinces, as with towns of medieval or even Elizabethan England – many of which, indeed, occupied Roman sites. These towns, and the network of roads which linked them, are probably Rome's most important contributions to Britain's heritage.

The Age of Villa-building

Roman rule brought rural as well as urban developments. As 'Britons' gradually evolved into 'Romano-British' they built their dwellings larger, more comfortable and more impressive than before. The great age of this villa-building came in the late 3rd and early 4th centuries, well after the greatest age of town-building; it was at this time that Lullingstone in Kent, Rockbourne in Hampshire and Chedworth in Gloucestershire reached their greatest splendour, as did many other villas whose sites happen to be less well-preserved today.

These developments in civilian life took place against a background of military problems still unsolved. The years round about AD 200 saw many towns of the province equipped with massive defensive walls; the 'Saxon Shore forts', whose walls are among the most prominent Roman remains in south-east England today, date mostly from the period round 270. In the 5th century we first hear of *Picti* from Scotland and *Scotti* from Ireland, menacing the northern coasts of Roman Britain with increasing boldness. And in 367 came what is known as the 'Barbarian Conspiracy', with Picts, Scots and Saxons attacking the province in collusion. They were beaten off, but life thereafter became noticeably less secure.

The final collapse of Roman rule came not from direct attack on Britain itself, but through invasion on the Continent combined with civil strife among the 'Romano-British'. The years 406 and 407 saw Gaul overrun by Germanic tribes and irrecoverably lost to Roman rule; they also saw mutiny in the army of Britain, which acclaimed three new leaders of its own in quick succession. The third of these withdrew troops from Britain to invade the Continent, met at first with some success, but was finally killed; this situation had occurred several times in the past, but now the 'legitimate' government in Italy had no force available to restore the *status quo*. In 410 the Emperor Honorius informed the cities of Britain that in future they would have to organize their own defence; the history of the province thus ends not with a bang but with a pause while people wait for the fireworks to ignite.

A map of Roman Britain showing the principal settlements, forts and roads.

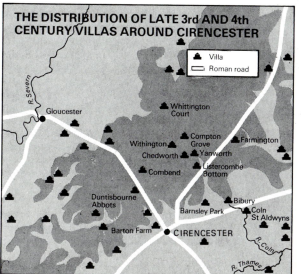

Roman roads and villas around Cirencester; the large number of villas indicates the prosperity of the area, and the importance of the local market town. After the withdrawal of the Romans, the breakdown of the Roman administrative structure and the arrival of invaders, prosperity decreased; soon soil covered the fine mosaic pavements of the Romans and many of their villas have now vanished.

The Coming of the English

The years that separated the end of Roman rule in Britain from the beginnings of the earliest English states are very obscure. The Roman legions were withdrawn in about AD 410, but long before this there had been plundering raids by the English from across the North Sea. At what date raiding passed into settlement is uncertain, but it would seem to have been about AD 450. The shadowy literary evidence tells how in 449, a British chieftain named Vortigern sought the help of the English under two brothers, Hengist and Horsa, to resist the raids of the Picts and the Scots from the North. But there were soon disputes, and the newcomers turned against their employers, and, says an early record, the fire of the Saxon burned across the island until 'it licked the western ocean with its red and savage tongue.' The result was a devastated countryside and the collapse of British resistance.

Bede, writing in about 730, divided the newcomers into Angles, Saxons and Jutes, but this is too simple a division, for the newcomers may also have included Frisians. The British called them all Saxons, a usage preserved in the Gaelic *Sassenach* and the Welsh *Seisnig*, but the descendants of the invaders came to call themselves English and their land England.

The English continued to arrive for another hundred years or more, but the details of their progress across Britain are lost to us. From these early years we hear of a Romano-British leader named Arthur who won great battles against the English; he was not called a king but a military commander. He has been described as the last of the Romano-Britons. Later ages were to add legend upon legend to his name. It may well be that at the core of the Arthurian cycle which so fascinated later generations lay something of the story of the defence of Britain against the English.

By 550 or so the Anglo-Saxon kingdoms were beginning to emerge. The earliest were those of the South-East – Sussex, Kent, and East Anglia bounded by wood or marsh. Then came the great powers of the later Anglo-Saxon period, each with possibilities of further advance towards the West – Wessex, Mercia and Northumbria. Decisive victories brought them to the western seas about 600 – to the estuaries of the Severn and the Dee, thus dividing the Britons into three groups. Soon they were being called Welsh from the English word *wealas* meaning slave or inferior person. They called, and still continue to call themselves Cymry, which means brethren.

The Advance of Wessex

In the South, the details of the advance are not many. Here was the Welsh kingdom of Dumnonia, the memory of which survives in the name Devon, and it passed into the hands of Wessex about AD 800. Beyond lay Cornwall (a name derived from the Celtic tribe of the Cornovii). It came under the overlordship of Wessex soon after AD 800 but it kept its native dynasty for some years. By this time the impetus of the advance of Wessex was dying down and Cornwall did not lose its Celtic character with its independence. Its place-names today are largely Welsh and incorporate a number of Celtic elements such as *pen*, *tre* and *pol*.

In the North, the kings of Northumbria conquered the Welsh kingdom of Elmet, north of what is now Leeds, and they extended their control into the lands around the Solway Firth. Amid much that is obscure, it is clear the Welsh survived in the Lakeland mountains and have left the name of Cumberland to remind us that this was once the land of the Cymry.

Between Wessex and Northumbria lay the kingdom of Mercia, with limits in the west set by the resistance of the Welsh and by the mountains of their country. It was in the reign of Offa (757–96) that it rose to a position of ascendancy among the English kingdoms. Offa corresponded with Charlemagne and brought his realm into the stream of European affairs. Among his problems was that of his Celtic neighbours. Little is known of the stages by which the frontiers between England and Wales evolved, but towards the end of his reign, Offa was able to mark the western limits of his kingdom by the greatest earthwork of the Anglo-Saxon age. Offa's Dyke seems to have been the result of a negotiated settlement, and after twelve centuries it stands as a reminder of ancient struggles.

Offa also negotiated over various matters with the Pope. By this time the heathen English had been converted to Christianity from two directions, from the Celtic monasteries of Ireland and Scotland and from the mission of St Augustine at Canterbury in 597. Differences between the two usages (especially over the date of Easter) were settled at the Synod of Whitby in 664. Certainly by the date of Offa Britain could be called a Christian country. Before Offa himself died in 796, his son Eigfrith was anointed king of the Mercians, the first recorded occasion that a religious element was made part of the inauguration of an English king.

A question that has often been debated is to what extent was there continuity between Roman Britain and the new England. The question is a difficult one. By continuity do we mean the survival of the native population, of language, of institutions or of social order? Or again, what of continuity as between one area and another? Whatever the answers may be, the balance of recent opinion is that there was a high degree of continuity to say nothing of survival. The process by which the two groups of people were fused was complicated by the arrival of yet another group. Under the year 787 the Anglo-Saxon Chronicle records the first coming of northern raiders to England. Not only Welsh and English but Scandinavians were to enter into the making of England.

Conjectural western limit of the English c.AD 570
Boundaries of English and Welsh kingdoms
B Brycheiniog
G Glywysing

LOTHIAN
STRATHCLYDE
NORTHUMBRIA
Hadrian's Wall
CUMBRIA
Chester 616
GWYNEDD
Offa's Dyke
POWIS
MERCIA
EAST ANGLIA
SEISYLLWG
DYFED
B
G
GWENT
Dyrham 577
ESSEX
WESSEX
KENT
SUSSEX
DUMNONIA

Based upon the work of H.C. Darby

THE ENGLISH IN BRITAIN TO AD c.800

OFFA'S DYKE c. AD 790

Chester
R. Dee
R. Severn
Knighton
Hereford
R. Avon
Gloucester
R. Wye

Land over 400 ft
Land over 800 ft

A section of Offa's Dyke at
Springhill, near Clun,
Shropshire. Offa's Dyke was
not the first attempt to delimit
a frontier between the English
and the Welsh. Wat's Dyke in
the North may date from about
AD 700 but it was superseded
by the greater achievement of
Offa. His frontier ran for nearly
240 km, and the length of the
earthwork itself is 130 km. It
crosses hill and valley alike,
often rising above the 240 m
contour, and even to over
425 m to the north of Knighton.
In the south, it becomes
intermittent and seems to have
been constructed in clearings
in woodland. From Bridge
Sollers (10 km north-west of
Hereford) the Wye replaces the
Dyke as a boundary until near
the Bristol Channel where it
reappears. The dimensions of
the Dyke vary today, but its
average height above the
ground is over 2 m and the
overall width of bank and
ditch is nearly 18 m.

A Mercian penny minted
during the reign of King Offa.
The issue of a royal coinage
bearing the name, even the
portrait of the King reflects the
growing power and prestige of
the Mercian monarchy.

The Vikings

The face of the aggressor: a helmeted head of a Viking warrior. It is carved from a piece of elkhorn and forms the handle of a stick. For nearly three centuries Britain was never entirely free from the Viking invader.

In 793 Vikings from Norway sacked the monastery at Lindisfarne. The English were filled with horror and surprise. The Vikings, in their recently improved design of swift ships, could sail across the North Sea and either land at any point along England's long coastline, or go up navigable river, ravage an area and sail away again with loot before the inhabitants could raise an effective force against them. Jarrow, Whitby, Dover and Folkestone were all monasteries with tempting treasure which were perilously exposed to such lightning attacks. From the time of the first raid on Lindisfarne until well into the reign of William the Conqueror Britain was never entirely free from the Viking menace.

Many of these Viking raiders overran huge territories in Britain and Ireland – the Danes in the lowlands of eastern England, the Norwegians in the islands of the north and west. During the course of the 10th century these Scandinavian conquerors and settlers assimilated with the people among whom they lived. They adopted their language while enriching it with hundreds of their own words. They accepted Christianity and many of their memorials survive in fascinating hybrids such as the stones of Middleton in Yorkshire which depict pagan Viking burials on the shaft panels of Christian crosses. (see page 163). Once they had integrated and settled, these Norsemen no longer presented a serious problem. On the move they continued to be formidable. During Alfred's reign (849–99) the English concern was with massive onslaughts from Danes 'on the move'.

The gradual build-up of Danish raids in the first half of the 9th century culminated in 865 with the invasion of the

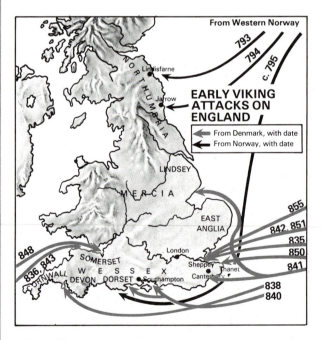

Viking raids on England in the 8th and 9th centuries. They culminated in 865 with the attack of the Danish Great Army, which destroyed all the former English kingdoms except Wessex.

Great Army. Under the impact of this enormous threat a land that had been several kingdoms – Northumbria, Mercia, East Anglia and Wessex – was quickly reduced to swordland ruled by Danish warriors, with Wessex, alone surviving as a focus for English resistance. This involved not only a permanent Danish settlement in Eastern England (the Danelaw) but the passing of the old order of Anglo-Saxon life and tribal kingship. The success of Alfred and his son and grandsons resulted in the conquest of the heathen Danes and in the unification of England – a unification achieved from within, unlike the earlier unification imposed from without by Imperial Rome.

Weak though it was in some areas, the administration of the newly united kingdom was strong enough to impose for the first time a uniform royal coinage and to keep the rewards of the country's growing prosperity. In the organization of the administrative areas of the kingdom the Danelaw boundary drawn between Alfred and Guthrum counted for far less than the older units of Mercia and East Anglia, ancient kingdoms which were preserved in the administrative geography of 10th-century England, and which continue to be used today as non-administrative regions. Mercia was divided up into neat shires. The centring of many of these shires on the English and Viking *burhs* or fortified towns underlines the military origins of the system which is largely intact to this day. Thus, for example, the Danish army forts of Northampton, Cambridge and Huntingdon (now defunct) gave their names to the new shires around them, as did such Saxon fortified towns as Oxford, Buckingham, Warwick and Hereford.

When the Vikings did come again, the prize at stake was nothing less than the Kingdom of England – a measure of the achievement of the House of Wessex.

Viking onslaughts resumed with renewed vigour during the reign of Aethelred (979–1016) which the *Anglo-Saxon Chronicle* presents as one of royal incompetence, internal treachery and cowardly collapse. Aethelred 'the Unready'

could be regarded as Aethelred 'the Unlucky'. However, he has gone down in history as the king who lost England to the Vikings. For after Aethelred's troubled reign the Viking conqueror Cnut was left to rule England.

Cnut's short-lived Empire

Cnut's conquest of England laid the foundation – a very unstable one – of a northern empire comprising England, Norway and Denmark. The kingdoms of Cnut's empire had little in common except allegiance to the King and no administrative structure existed to unite them. True, English traders and missionaries travelled to Scandinavia (as they had done before); many Danes settled in England and to some Cnut gave high administrative rank. But Cnut's empire was short-lived and collapsed after his death. This Danish conquest of England was a very different matter from the later Norman Conquest of 1066. The Normans forged close links across the Channel and England acquired a new dynasty as well as a new aristocracy, both secular and ecclesiastical. Cnut had few supporters he could trust and his rule of England depended on the English themselves. Cnut recognized the impossibility of unitary rule by partitioning his kingdoms among his sons. So within a few years of his death the component parts of his 'empire' all went their separate ways. England reverted to the old West Saxon line, although real power in the land was wielded by the family of the Earl Godwin.

Saxons, Norwegians, Danes and Celts integrated. Across the Channel a new military power had come of age – a Viking settlement founded in Normandy in the early 10th century.

In ships designed for speed and strength, like this 23-metre-long hafskip found buried at Gokstad in Norway, the Vikings struck terror into the hearts of the English. Coastal monasteries with their tempting treasure were perilously exposed to lightning raids.

Right: a page from the Anglo-Saxon Chronicle. Originally compiled during Alfred's reign, the Chronicle spans 200 years and was continued at several different places. The detail of the entries varies for different periods; it gives an excellent account of the incompetent reign of Aethelred, the king who lost England to the Vikings.

The Normans and After

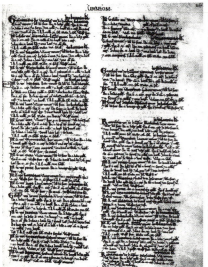

The Norman victory at Hastings was followed by a comprehensive colonization of the English kingdom. The effect of this conquest has for centuries been a controversial subject, principally because so much was left undisturbed and because the newcomers made great use of existing institutions.

No one can deny the sheer force of the Norman Conquest's impact; its physical legacy can still be seen today, not just in magnificent buildings such as the White Tower of London or Durham Cathedral, but in the numerous earthwork fortifications created after 1066, usually with wooden palisade and sometimes with the addition of a wooden tower on top of a mound, and in many fine churches, both large and small. Nor is it possible to overlook the intense administrative drive associated with the coming of the Normans, enshrined above all in that unprecedented record, *Domesday Book*. Finally, no one who reads the obituary of William the Conqueror in the *Anglo-Saxon Chronicle*, with its strictures against oppressive taxation and castle-building, can doubt the effectiveness and unaccustomed harshness of Norman rule.

After the rapid take-over of southern and western England between 1066 and 1068, the Norman settlement became a more gradual and piecemeal process. In the North and in Wales the Normans were still pushing forward in the early 12th century. Some of their campaigns were extremely brutal, most notably William I's devastation of northern England in 1070. Whatever the means, the final result was everywhere the same – the almost complete Normanization of England's ruling classes; the wholesale transfer to the newcomers of the lands of the Old English aristocracy; and the introduction of novel institutions of lordship and vassalage which focused more closely on the tenure of a fief than had the Old English relationship of commendation by which a freeman would voluntarily cede himself and his lands to the personal protection of a feudal Lord. Organization and respect for the law, nonetheless, were soon apparent in the more settled regions of England. Within weeks of the battle of Hastings, William was confirming to the city of London its liberties as in Edward the Confessor's time, while in 1072, at an enlarged meeting of the shire-court of Kent held at Penenden Heath near Maidstone, Archbishop Lanfranc of Canterbury embarked on the recovery of properties, most of which had been taken from his church before 1066. *Domesday Book*, the product of inquests conducted in the long-established courts of shire and hundred, and the records of land pleas such as Penenden show how, from an early date, the Normans utilized English institutions and through them sought a rational, legal basis for land tenure, usually conforming to the conditions of the Confessor's day. As befits a people emanating from what the recent work of French scholars has shown to have been a notably well-organized territorial principality, the Norman rulers soon began to control and to shape their conquest through the existing local and central institutions of the Old English monarchy.

Assimilation and Domination

The results of the Conquest must in many respects be seen in terms of the mutual assimilation of two races; several thousand Normans were after all at the cultural mercy of over a million English. The structure of rural society remained largely unaltered and England's long-standing economic prosperity was unaffected. It is likely that relatively few Norman women crossed the Channel, with inter-marriage between the two peoples therefore common from an early date. What needs emphasis is the political domination maintained by Normans over English well on into the 12th century. Even in the towns and the monasteries where the English survived as significant members of their communities, it was the Normans who were appointed as abbots and who had at Winchester taken over the best houses by the early 12th century. It was above all the related necessities of making a display of power and of organizing their conquest which ensured that England was significantly and conclusively changed by the

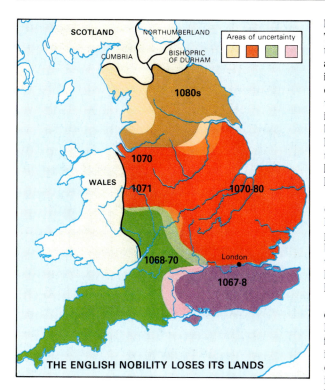

SCOTLAND | NORTHUMBERLAND
CUMBRIA | BISHOPRIC OF DURHAM
Areas of uncertainty

1080s

1070

WALES

1071

1070-80

1068-70

London

1067-8

THE ENGLISH NOBILITY LOSES ITS LANDS

The Domesday Book, completed in 1086, records how complete was the dispossession of the lands of the English lords by the Normans. The landowners of the South-East were the first to go, but it was not until the 1080s that the far northern areas were at risk.

coming of the Normans. The chief differences, well illustrated by the land pleas, *Domesday Book* and the Anglo-Saxon chronicler's complaints, were much stronger centralization, much more frequent intervention in the localities by royal officials and fiercer demands for money. The novel institutions of lordship, including the king's right to tax his vassals and conscript them for periods of military service, made for a more authoritarian monarchy. The English Church, with the Italian Lanfranc the presiding figure at Canterbury, became more open to continental influences, with its bishoprics better organized. In the fields of military and ecclesiastical architecture, the Conquest initiated a period of rapid development around forms which were mostly Norman. The Conqueror and his successors also began the development of a unified Common Law – which became a reality from Henry II's reign onwards – and initiated the political dialogue about the respective rights of kings and magnates, already evident in Henry I's Coronation Charter of 1100, which culminated in 1215 on the field of Runnymede. Historians rightly discern much continuity from Anglo-Saxon times in later medieval England. It is unlikely that they would have been able to describe anything like the same species of continuity if King Harold had been the victor on 14 October 1066.

IMMIGRANTS SINCE THE NORMAN CONQUEST

The common observation that Britain's population is one of the most ethnically composite in Europe demonstrates only a part of the contribution which incomers have made. For immigration has contributed substantially to the country's economic structure, its language, art and cuisine. In the wake of the Norman Conquest – the last of the great invasions from Europe – few groups of immigrants have been especially numerous. During the past four centuries at least it has been exceptional for the volume of immigration to exceed that of emigration. Nevertheless, while emigration has been broad-based, the variety of immigrant groups has helped further diversify the British population.

Over the long run, we may identify two distinct categories of immigrants. First, there have been those from Continental Europe driven out by religious persecution, many of whom possessed specialist economic skills; and second, there have been those moving from impoverished economies overseas whose main importance has been to provide low-skilled and low-paid labour force. Immigrants in the second category have been more numerous than in the first.

Within the first category, Jewish populations have been especially prominent – small populations in post-Conquest England until their proscription in 1290, Sephardic Jews from Spain and Portugal in the 17th century, and the mass influxes from Eastern Europe in the later years of the 19th century. Known for their involvement in finance, especially in the earlier years of immigration, they contrast with Protestant refugees – the Flemish in the 16th century, French Huguenots in the late 17th century – who were often involved in industry.

Large-scale Huguenot immigration, for example, may only have totalled some 100,000 of which many soon moved on elsewhere: the large number within our second category have often performed important work roles but usually had less significant economic impact. The Irish have historically been the most important, with a growing stream becoming a flood into early and mid-19th-century Britain. (In 1851 there were half a million Irish-born settled in England and Wales alone). While Irish immigration has never dried up, it has been surpassed by that from other less developed economies principally to fill unskilled positions in the labour force – streams of Chinese, Italians, East Europeans and, most recently and in the greatest numbers, New Commonwealth and Pakistani immigrants. Estimates in the mid-1970s put the population of New Commonwealth ethnic origin at 1.75 million.

Whatever their origins, immigrants have settled predominantly in towns, especially in London and the industrial centres of the Midlands and the North. Partly the result of urban demand for labour, this concentration has always permitted a cultural cohesiveness and community solidarity among initial generations providing support until those of immigrant descent have been – to a greater or lesser extent – assimilated into the population at large. This process has been most difficult where racial or religious prejudice has persisted.

British cultural diversity has always been due in considerable measure to the continued, if irregular, acceptance of immigrant groups.

Chronological table of British immigrants.

1100	1200	1300	1400	1500	1600	1700	1800	1900
Norman & Flemish conquerors				Flemish groups involved in textiles	Jews re-admitted		European political émigrés	
			Gypsies appear				Large-scale Irish immigration	
						French Huguenots		
French Jewish populations		Merchants and financiers from Italy & Germany		Aliens in mining, textiles, etc, principally from the Netherlands & Germany			Jews from Russia & Poland	
							Chinese, Italian & East European	

Language and Dialects

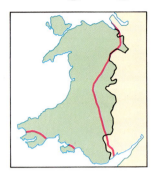

The Britons' Celtic language was displaced by the Germanic speech of the Angles and Saxons, which by the end of the 7th century had reached today's Welsh border. This map shows the boundary of Welsh-speaking in the 19th century. In this and the following maps Monmouthshire is shown as part of England.

The related languages, Welsh, Scots and Irish Gaelic, together with Manx and Cornish, represent the oldest spoken languages in Britain. Irish is now an 'official' language, taught compulsorily in schools. Regional feeling in Wales has acted to stem the decline in Welsh-speaking. Cornish and Manx disappeared, Cornish in the 18th century, Manx in the 20th, but enthusiasts have revived both and use them whenever possible. English, spoken throughout the world by millions, came to these islands as the Roman Empire crumbled. First as mercenaries to fight for the Romans and British against the Picts and Scots, then as conquerors and settlers, the Saxons and Angles came from the north of Germany. They had already dialectical differences when they first came.

Such literature as survives from the areas populated by the Angles – the Midlands and the North – makes it obvious that modern English descends from an Anglian Midland dialect. The West Saxon language of King Alfred survives more in manuscripts because it was less destroyed by the later raiders who came across the North Sea, the Scandinavian Vikings. These Danes and Norwegians who settled here from the late 9th century added much to the language of the English. In the north and east Midlands where everyday words in the dialects descend from the Norse tongue, such expressions as *lea* 'scythe', *lathe* 'barn', *beck* 'stream', to *addle* 'earn', to *laik* 'play' are all words which have entered local speech. Other terms such as *eggs*, *sky*, *outlaw* and *window* have replaced Anglo-Saxon words in the standard language.

After the Norman Conquest of 1066 French became the speech of gentlemen but English and its dialects remained the speech of the ordinary people. With the return of English as the language of the upper classes in 14th-century London English was well placed to become the desirable speech to be used by provincial visitors to the king's court. By the 16th century the dialect of the south-east Midland area had developed a form that became a class dialect and an acceptable (therefore 'correct') standard English emerged. Rustic and country speech was used by writers in the 16th century and after to indicate stupid and lowly characters. In 1674 John Ray produced his collection of *Words Not Generally Used* and began the fashion of taking the dialects more seriously that culminated in the founding of the English Dialect Society in 1873, a body wound up in 1895 when Joseph Wright's *English Dialect Dictionary* was in preparation.

Gaelic was spoken in the areas shaded blue, including Inverness, until the 18th century.

Variations in Middle English speech (in about 1400). In most of England *a* was written before *m* or *n* in such words as *kan* and *man*; only in the West was *o* used instead (above right). The map (right), shows present plural endings of verbs in Middle English. Written forms of such structures as *speketh* and *spekes* are found within the -en area marked, but the -en ending is found only in the Midland area. Below are shown the Scandinavian *th*- and English *h*- forms of pronouns in 1400. The Old English forms of the personal pronouns with *h*- have been replaced by the Scandinavian – except in 'em – today.

Our knowledge of varieties of speech in Middle English increases as more localized documents are studied. Before the introduction of printing people wrote phonetically, representing their own speech. Even in the few lines reproduced from Chaucer's *Wife of Bath's Tale* shown on the right we have evidence for composition in the South-East Midlands. The spelling of *kan*, *man*, and *many* excludes the West Midland area. *Speken* and *serchen* limit the speech to and area north of the Thames and roughly south of the Wash.

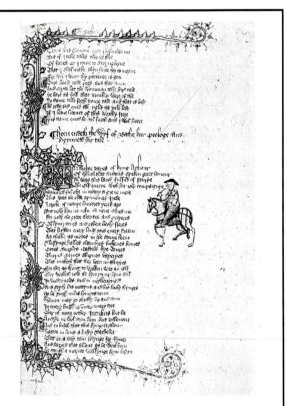

In tholde dayes of the Kyng Arthour
Of which that Britons speken greet honour
Al was this land fulfild of fayerie
The elf queene with hir joly compaignye
Daunced ful oft in many a grene mede
This was the olde opinion as I rede
I speke of manye hundred yeres ago
But now kan no man se none elves mo
For now the grete charitee and prayeres
Of Lymytours and oother hooly freres
That serchen every lond and every streem
As thikke as motes in the sonne beem
Blessynge halles chambres kichenes boures

The use of a pronounced *r* after a vowel in words like *turn, horse* died out in standard English by the 17th century. In Northumberland the use of a distinctive uvular r, often called the 'burr', continues. This is often claimed to be the speech defect described by Shakespeare as typical of Hotspur. Lancashire and the South-West have other types of *r*; that of the West Country may well be a survival of the Saxon *r*. Early emigrants from England may have taken this sound to North America.

The regional varieties for *grandfather* show interesting differences.

Below: An entry in Joseph Wright's *English Dialect Dictionary*, of 1895.

LOSS, *v.* Sc. Irel. Nhb. Cum. Yks. Also Som. Dev. Cor. Also in forms **lost** w.Som.[1] Dev.[1] Cor.[1]; *pp.* **lossen** n.Yks.[1] e.Yks.[1] [los.] **1.** To lose; a *vbl.* use of the *sb.* loss.
　Sc. Murray *Dial.* (1873) 206. Sh.I. Lossin' her grain o' 'oo', *Sh. News* (July 2, 1898). e.Sc. I'll loss my place, Setoun *Sunshine* (1895) 88. Abd. Lossin half a day seekin' ye, Alexander *Ain Flk.* (1882) 222. Per. Ye may loss it a', *Sandy Scott* (1897) 38; She did na loss heart, *Pitcoonans* (1899) 95. Dmb. Ye may loss your place as his secretary, Cross *Disruption* (1844) xxiv. Lnk. Dinna loss what ye've made, Roy *Generalship* (ed. 1895) 47. e.Lth. Ye never saw him loss his temper, Hunter *J. Inwick* (1895) 108. Edb. Women dinna understand what it wad be to loss bein' first cock o' the cless, Stevenson *Puddin* (1894) 87. N.I.[1] Ant. Patterson *Dial.* 24. Nhb. Tunbelly losses conceit iv his sel', Oliver *Sngs.* (1824) 12. Cum. It's a pity to loss them, Gwordie Greenup *Rhymes* (1876) 23. n.Yks.[2]; n.Yks.[4] Thoo'll loss thisel' (s.v. Lowse). ne.Yks.[1] Thoo'll a'e ti mahnd an' nut loss it. e.Yks.[1] w.Yks. A cross to loss, a ring to win, Binns *Vill. to Town* (1882) 82; Will thi moother flite the for lossin' it? (F.P.T.) Som. Ay, 'tis better to lost a little 'an what 'tis to breed ill-will, Raymond *Men o' Mendip* (1898) ii; (F.A.A.) w.Som.[1] Muy·n ùd·n nuudh·ur oa·l een dhu bai·g, uls dhee·t lau·st aa·f oa ut [See that there is no hole in the bag, otherwise you will lose half of it]. I count that there'll be a lostin job, they can't never do it vor the money. Dev. I hadd'n no mind vur ta loss zich a trait, Nathan Hogg *Poet. Lett.* (ed. 1865) 18; I can't afford to lost it, *Reports Provinc.* (1884) 23; Dev.[1] How did I lost tha? 8. Cor. For fear I should be tooken faint like, with losten' so much blood, Forfar *Pentowan* (1859) i; Cor.[1] Our horse is losting his coat.
　2. To go to the bad.
　N.I.[1] Them childre's lossin' for the want o' somebuddy t'see afther them.

'Neat' was another word for cow, used widely up to the 19th century. The place where cows are kept for milking is called a *neat-house* today only in the border areas of Norfolk and Suffolk. The name of this street almost opposite Victoria Station in London commemorates neat-houses shown near the site on an 18th-century map. In the north of England and in Scotland the word used is *byre*, in West Yorkshire *mistal*, and in north Lincolnshire and the Isle of Wight *cowstable*.

Modern regional dialects have been considerably modified under the influence of the standard language. Fine differences that made it possible to identify speakers from within very small areas before the 20th century are less usual today, though it is still possible in many parts of England to find speakers of very strong dialect: they are usually bi-lingual in that they use one form of speech with their friends and workmates and change to a form modified by the standard pronunciation, grammar and vocabulary when with strangers. Because many people regard a strongly regional speech as funny or indicative of lower-class origins socially ambitious people often abandon the dialect of their early years. Women are usually most conscious of social pressure and feel the need to speak a standard form.

Ever since the emergence of a standard language there has been serious writing in dialect varieties of English and Scots. Poets who feel they need to express themselves in a regional speech can expect only a limited audience. The barrier between the written and the spoken forms of the dialect is such that many people familiar with the spoken dialect cannot come to terms with the written form.

Wi' glowrin een, and lifted han's,
Poor Hughoc like a statue stan's;
He saw her days were near hand ended,
But waes my heart! he could na mend it!
He gaped wide, but naething spak,
At length poor Mailie silence brak.
Robert Burns 1786

Are you, bricht sandbird, o'the earth or sun?
Or baith? and tell me, gin the last, O! can
A like sublime duality – in life,
No' daith – no whiles be won to by a man?
Hugh MacDiarmid 1962

T'maister nobbut just buried, and Sabbath nut
oer'd, und t'sahnd uh t'gospel still i' yer lugs,
and yah darr be laiking! shame on ye! sit ye
dahn, ill childer! they's good books eneugh if
ye'll read 'em; sit ye dahn, and think uh yer sowls.
Emily Brontë 1847

Emily Brontë's dialect passages do not seem to have limited the appeal of *Wuthering Heights* – a quarter of a million copies have been sold in Japanese translation. But few readers from outside the West Riding of Yorkshire can be very aware of what Joseph means.

Then they took en in hwome to his bed,
An he rose vrom his pillow no mwore.
Vor the curls on his sleek little head
To be blown by the wind out o' door.
Vor he died while the hay russled grey
On the staddle so leately begun:
Lik' the mown grass a-dried by the day –
Aye! the zwath-flow'r's a-kill'd by the zun.
William Barnes

Barnes would be identified as a Southern poet by some of the same criteria as would have identified Middle English from the South: *v* for *f*, *z* for *s* and the verbal prefix, now *a-*, are all significant.

PLACE NAMES AND SURNAMES

More than 50 per cent of Britain's surnames come from place names with origins that can be classified broadly as Celtic, Anglo-Saxon and Scandinavian. The oldest British stocks are in Cornwall, Wales, and the Scottish Highlands. But their hereditary isolation is more apparent than real. There is no significant difference between the blood-groups of the inhabitants of Devon or Cornwall and those of Somerset or Dorset, while blood-groups in Kent are almost identical with those in Cornwall.

　The chief continuing factor in local types, from the pre-Norman period in which places got names to the post-

COMMON TOPOGRAPHICAL ELEMENTS

A, Ay River, stream, in Brathay, Greta *Old Norse, Old English*

Acre Cultivated piece of land *O.E. aecer, O.N. akr*

Barton Barley farm, demesne farm, monastic grange, in 24 counties

Bent Coarse grass, as in Bentham, Bentley *O.E.*

Burn Stream, associated with Scotland but pure Anglo-Saxon

Clough Narrow valley, ravine *O.E.*

Frith Covert for game, earlier simply woodland *O.E.*

Gill Ravine, as in Scargill, N. of E. *O.N.*

Hale Nook, corner, common in W. Mid.

Hay, Hayes Enclosure in De. and Do.

Holt Wood, often combined with tree name *O.E.*

Lound, Lund Grove, a La. surname *O.N. lundr*

Rain Boundary strip in places of Dutch settlement

Scough Wood, in N. of E. names, Myerscough 'miry wood' *O.N.*

Shaw Wood or copse, common N. of the Wash into Scotland *O.E.*

Syke Stream, trench *O.E.*

DISTINCTIVELY SCOTTISH SURNAMES

GAELIC

Buchanan *Both chanain*, canon's bothy

Campbell *Cam beul*, crooked mouth

Douglas *Dubh glais*, black water

Drummond *Druim*, spine or ridge

Duncan *Donn cath*, brown warrior

Farquhar *Fear char*, dear one

McAlister Son of Alastair

MacIntosh *Toiseach*, tribal chief

MacRae Son of grace

Malcolm *Maol Colm*, follower of St Columba, the dove

LOCALITY

Barclay 'Birch lea'

Crawford 'Ford of the crows'

Cunningham In Ayrshire

Forbes In Aberdeenshire

Murray Seabord settlement, Moray

COMMONEST PATRONYMICS:

Thomson; MacDonald; Robertson; Wilson; Anderson; Johnston.

Norman in which families got surnames, is geographical. Where the land was fertile both surnames and place names tell the story of how the native British settled down with Saxon and Viking invaders. Early Saxon names abound in Sussex (the kingdom of the South Saxons) and Essex (the kingdom of the East Saxons) both of which have high concentrations of names with tribal *-ing* endings, derived from *-ingas*, 'people of'. Names ending in *-ham* (homestead, village) have wider distribution; but *Domesday* recorded concentrations of between 21 and 26 per cent in eastern counties south of the Wash, whereas none of the West Midland counties had more than five per cent. In those *-ton*, with the same meaning as *-ham* but indicating later Saxon settlement, was common. In Herefordshire, for example, where Celtic names are frequent, there were only three percent ending in *-ham*, 66 percent in *-ton*. The extremely common *-ley* ending may denote either a wood or a clearing that became pasture or meadow.

Under the Treaty of Wedmore (878), Danish and Saxon spheres of influence were designated, with the region north and east of Watling Street being ceded to the Danes (the *Danelaw*). During the bitter struggle between contending armies the native British retreated into Wales in the west, the Cumbrian mountains and the Pennine foothills in the north-west, where Celtic place names, such as those beginning with *Pen* (top, hill) and *Blen* (hill farm), are common, and such ethnic characteristics as small bones and dark hair survive in the indigenous population. These were the last parts of England in which surnames became hereditary. In Wales they were not generally adopted until the 16th century.

Welsh patronymics have a final 's' for 'son' – for example Williams, Jones. This un-Gaelic brevity may be explained by surnames being given in this simplified form in Shropshire to immigrants from Wales in the 13th century. The characteristic Welsh patronymic has a prefixed 'Ap', abbreviated to 'P' for 'son of', as in Powell or Pritchard. Welsh place names, by contrast, are eloquent. They are the elements we call British in the names of all our principal rivers and hills, extending from the Avons, from *afon* 'river', to the many *Blens* (hills) in the Pennine and Lakeland fells.

Ireland, often by way of the Isle of Man, was the immediate source of northern infiltration from the west. The original Scots infiltrated the south-west Highlands from Ireland. Most of the ancient Scottish clans claim descent from a Gaelic-speaking people who landed *c.*500 under the leadership of Fergus Mor, whose name means 'super choice'. 'Clan' is Gaelic for children, 'Mac' means 'son of'. So to be a member of a Scottish clan there must be blood relationship between the chief and his followers. When Dr Johnson visited the Isle of Mull in 1773 he remarked that every man's name was MacLean. The clan still flourishes. Most Scottish names other than Gaelic are either French, like Mitchell (from Michel), or Norse, like MacKay, the second commonest Mac name in Scotland, or MacLeod. MacKay means 'son of Aodh', which has no English counterpart; MacLeod is from the Old Norse *Liotr*, the name of a Norse king of Man.

The northern counties of England now united in Cumbria (Welsh *Cymry*, 'the brethren'), like their neighbours, Durham and Northumberland, have curious local differences in both surnames and place names. Although both Cumberland and Westmorland were settled by Scandinavians there are 56 Danish *-by* (farmstead, village) endings in Cumberland, only 16 in Westmorland. The explanation is both historical and geographical. The region around Carlisle was Celtic and Northumbrian influences dominated the line of Hadrian's Wall. The kingdom of Northumbria

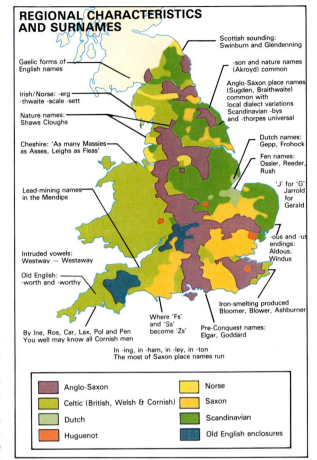

REGIONAL CHARACTERISTICS AND SURNAMES

Scottish sounding: Swinburn and Glendenning

Gaelic forms of English names

-son and nature names (Akroyd) common

Anglo-Saxon place names (Sugden, Braithwaite) common with local dialect variations Scandinavian -bys and -thorpes universal

Irish/Norse: -erg -thwaite -scale -sett

Nature names: Shaws Cloughs

Dutch names: Gepp, Frohock

Fen names: Ossler, Reeder, Rush

Cheshire: 'As many Massies as Asses, Leighs as Fleas'

'J' for 'G' Jarrold for Gerald

Lead-mining names in the Mendips

-ous and -us endings: Aldous, Windus

Intruded vowels: Westway — Westaway

Old English: -worth and -worthy

Iron-smelting produced Bloomer, Blower, Ashburner

By Ine, Ros, Car, Lax, Pol and Pen You well may know all Cornish men

Where 'Fs' and 'Ss' become 'Zs'

Pre-Conquest names: Elgar, Goddard

In -ing, in -ham, in -ley, in -ton The most of Saxon place names run

Anglo-Saxon	Norse
Celtic (British, Welsh & Cornish)	Saxon
Dutch	Scandinavian
Huguenot	Old English enclosures

---

extended from the Humber to the Forth, and under weak government was exposed to Danish raids and infiltration resulting in the region being peppered with Danish *-bys*.

There was little for the Danes as a pastoral people to go for in Westmorland. So the fells were left to the Norse shepherds to settle in the 10th century, when they began to come in from Ireland and found the mountains reminiscent of their native Norway. Their sheep created the Lakeland landscape. So we find Danish and Anglo-Saxon names petering out west of Barnard Castle, and small mountain pastures giving rise to settlements called *-thwaites* (O. Norse, 'meadow'), summer pastures called *-ergs* and *-setts*, on which temporary huts and shielings were built. Old Norse is similarly the origin of gill for ravine, rigg for ridge, and holm for the islands in lakes and rivers.

Danish names run through all the Danelaw shires with the exception of Essex, which has only a small group of them near the coast. *Domesday* records 700 *-bys*, of which 217 are in Lincolnshire, with secondary settlements called *-thorp*, making Lincolnshire as Viking as Cornwall is Celtic and Westmorland is Norse. Along with Danish names there are names with Anglo-Saxon endings all down eastern England, and pockets of Dutch, Flemish and Huguenot surnames introduced by peaceful settlers from Europe, some of which have been Anglicized. Jeeps and Frohocks are descendants of Dutchmen who came to work on the dykes; Flemish weavers were given the name Fleming to identify them. Among Huguenot refugees from religious persecution on the Continent who have enriched English life have been the Bosanquets, Courtaulds, and Houblons. These settlers introduced an astonishing variety of occupation names, most of which end in *-er* from the Latin *-arius*. They are a separate subject.

Chapter Three
The Imprint of Man

Very little of Britain's landscape has entirely escaped the efforts of human beings to 'improve' nature. The quilted hedgerow pattern of the 'typically' English landscape is man-made, the result of 18th-century enclosures. And everywhere we can see traces of human activity – in winding lanes, in woodlands, in the outlines of ancient field systems, in the remains of pre-historic flint mines and in surviving earthworks such as hill-forts and Offa's Dyke. Canal-building, the railways and the exploitation of iron and coal fields have all left their marks on the landscape. Today it is airfields and motorways which are moulding (or marring) Britain's scenic heritage.

The Changing Landscape: Woodlands

Autumn in the lovely 18th-century beech woods at Wandlebury in Cambridgeshire.

The Council for the Protection of Rural England
4 Hobart Place, London SW1W OHY
Campaigns to save unspoilt countryside from pollution and from destructive development.
CPRE–Wales
14 Broad Street Welshpool, Powys
Association for the Protection of Rural Scotland
20 Falkland Avenue, Newton Mearns, Renfrewshire

Healthy deciduous woodland is one of the loveliest features of the British countryside, but in the face of modern farming practices it is now in rapid retreat. Around 8000 years ago, most of Britain was covered in an almost continuous forest blanket but, with the possible exception of tiny pockets of woodland in the Lake District, Devon and near Loch Maree in Scotland, the natural forest cover has entirely disappeared. The greater part of the primeval forest was removed or subjected by 'unnatural' human management well before the end of the pre-historic period. Those woods which still survive are not the fragments of the ancient wildwood, but the remnants of medieval or more recent woods which were well-managed and highly valued.

The best evidence of the composition of the ancient wildwood has come from the analysis of pollen grains which have been preserved in damp and acid soils. The grains tell us that in the Scottish Highlands, birch and pine were the commonest species while a pocket of birch and pine existed in the northern Lake District. Elsewhere, there was mixed broad-leafed forest containing elm, hazel, oak, ash and lime.

The lime seems to have been very common on the better Lowland soils while alder thrived in the poorly drained areas.

Human interference with the natural woodland seems to have begun in the later stages of the Middle Stone Age (8000–4500 BC) with the local removal of patches of woodland, perhaps to create open hunting ranges or to improve the browse for prey animals such as the red deer. The rate of clearance accelerated during the New Stone Age (about 4500–2000 BC) when arable farming was introduced. Elm branches and ivy may have been gathered at an early stage as fodder for domestic animals, while in the course of the New Stone Age, the expanding agricultural clearings began to merge. A reasonable amount of natural woodland survived into the Bronze Age (about 2000–700 BC), but by the start of the Iron Age (700 BC to the Roman Conquest) relatively little remained.

The deliberate management of woodlands probably began in the New Stone Age with the 'coppicing' of trees, which were cut at ground level so that numerous new shoots would spring from the 'stool' and which could be harvested after five or more years to produce quantities of poles necessary for home-, tool- and enclosure-making, or be pegged down to provide roadways through marshy country. For the remainder of the pre-historic period, the demands for coppiced poles and for larger timber was enormous. Each hut of timber, mud, wattle and thatch consumed enormous quantities of poles. Wood was also necessary for domestic fuel, (in the form of charcoal) for smelting, for fencing, for reinforcing ramparts of hill-forts or for building protective palisades. Such immense demands could never have been met without organized skills of woodmanship.

The exploitation of woodland resources probably increased during the Roman period, when pockets of mature, natural or semi-natural woodland may still have existed. Recent excavations of Roman London have revealed the use of gigantic oaks, probably floated down the Thames from ancient woods surviving in the upper reaches of the river. After the collapse of Roman power, however, there seem to have been crises and retreats of farming which allowed the forest to advance over areas of abandoned farmland. The woods so created had later to be cleared on a piecemeal basis by grubbing up the trees and the bushes by hand – a practice which was known in medieval times as 'assarting'.

Throughout the Middle Ages, woodland was a precious resource, valued by the lord for its hunting assets, but more important still as a source of indispensible timber. Different systems of woodmanship were practised and most forests and woods were divided into sections which were cleared and allowed to regenerate according to different rotations. Some areas provided light, coppiced timber; in others there was a two-tier system, with some trees growing tall as 'standards' to provide heavy constructional timber while underwood beneath was coppiced. Other areas existed as more open 'woodland pasture' with livestock grazing in the spaces between the trees. Many areas of wood pasture were associated with 'pollards', trees cut off above the reach of browsing animals, which produced a regular crop of coppice-like poles from their crowns. A value was assessed for each tree and there were severe penalties for un-licensed felling or assarting. Many peasants, however, enjoyed the right to gather timber from the commons for essential uses.

In the post-medieval centuries, some new plantations were made for landscaping purposes, to provide shelter belts for crops and as cover for game and foxes. Popular choices of trees for these purposes included the Scots pine, the beech which does not seem to have been common in Britain before the Iron Age, and more recent introductions like the sycamore and the Lombardy poplar.

The degeneration of the British woodlands seems to have been apparent in the 19th-century, when cheap imported timber became increasingly available and new materials began to replace timber in the manufacture of many products. Gradually, the old woodland skills were forgotten so that today most woods are poorly managed while coppices and pollards grow unchecked and mis-shapen. The grand old deciduous woods, so essential a part of the lowland scene, are increasingly being grubbed-out to create featureless modern fields, while upland areas which supported marginally profitable livestock pastures submit to the dark embrace of monotonous commercial plantations of alien species like the Sitka spruce and lodgepole pine. It would be very hard to argue that any of these changes are in the national interest; the woodland story is one of the most depressing chapters in the story of the destruction of our scenic heritage.

Coniferous woodland extends across many attractive upland landscapes, creating monotonous scenery as here, on the flanks of the North Yorkshire Moors.

Below left: Coppiced timber produced long poles used for a host of purposes in the pre-industrial age.

Long-neglected pollards such as these are common features of the lowland landscape.

The Changing Landscape: Fields

Massive boulders were used in the walls to divide the fields around the Bronze Age village of Kestor on Dartmoor.

Most local patterns of fields contain a wealth of fascinating historical information. Their long story begins with the pioneering farming activities of the New Stone Age (about 4500–2000 BC). Much remains to be learned about ancient farming practices: did, for example, the Stone Age farmers tend to clear patches of woodland, burn the timber and grow crops until the lands were exhausted? Or, instead of moving on, did they renew the fertility of farmlands under pastures grazed by their livestock? The activities of later farmers seem almost invariably to have obliterated the traces of fields dating from the New Stone Age, although an area of walled fields of this period has recently been identified in the peat moors of Co. Mayo in Ireland.

The Bronze Age landscape included extensive networks of fields. Although the traces of most Bronze Age fields have long since been destroyed, on parts of Dartmoor one can still detect the ancient field patterns, consisting of small fields divided sometimes by streams, and sometimes by low stone walls or 'reaves'.

Although it is often difficult to date a field pattern without excavation, the evidence from the Iron Age (from c. 700 BC) and Romano-British period is much more extensive. Networks of smallish, roughly rectangular fields have often survived in areas which have not been ploughed since Roman times. Extensive areas of 'Celtic' fields, their boundaries defined by step-like banks or 'lynchets' are very obvious on the Pennine plateau above Grassington in Yorkshire, where the outlines of fields which may date from the Roman period loom through the later pattern of stone-walled pastures. In parts of Cornwall fields set out in Roman times appear to be still in use.

The Saxons, on their arrival in Britain adopted the traditional field pattern; however, the growth of population seems to have placed stresses on the agricultural resources of the countryside and more productive forms of farming were needed. An answer was found in 'open-field' farming. The arable land was divided into two, three or more vast open-fields, the fields into blocks of strips or 'furlongs'. Each peasant family held a number of strips (often around 30 strips each of around an acre in area) which were dispersed throughout the different furlongs. By using the open-field ploughland more intensively, other areas of land may have been freed to provide the essential livestock pastures and hay meadows, while each English *vill* (estate) normally included a tract of common pasture as well as some woodland.

In the uplands of northern and western Britain, where good ploughland was in short supply, the emphasis lay on livestock farming. Little villages and hamlets often lay beside small areas of ploughland which were generously manured and kept in production as 'infields', while areas of the surrounding 'outfield' pasture were periodically ploughed, cropped to exhaustion and then rested under long periods of fallow. As in the open fields, the infields were divided into strips, each consisting of around a half a dozen parallel 'plough ridges'. Ridges of this kind are often seen in old ploughland which has been preserved through conversion to pasture.

Early enclosures

Open-field farming could be efficient and productive, but it demanded high levels of peasant co-operation and organization. In the course of the Middle Ages numbers of peasants and landowners agreed to enclose sections of open-field land. These 'early enclosure' fields, generally small in size with curving hedged or walled boundaries, often survive to provide some of the most delicious passages in the English and Welsh borderland countrysides. Similar fields which can be seen in parts of the West Country and some upland areas in southern England may have existed as hedged pastures since the Dark Ages, or even earlier, and were never incorporated in open-field farming. The principle of hedgerow dating states – very loosely – that a hedge will naturally acquire one new species of tree or shrub every century, and the hedgerows of old enclosures may contain ten or more species in each 100-feet (30-metre) length.

Virtually all the open-field and common lands which had not already been enclosed by private agreements were the object of Parliamentary Enclosure in the period about 1750–1850. The ribbon-like patterns of attenuated 'S'-or 'C'-shaped strips were overlain by geometrical networks of hedgerows while the old common land was normally partitioned among the leading landowners of each parish. The hedgerows marked out by the enclosure surveyors tended to be straight and less visually attractive than the rich, winding hedgerows of the older enclosures; but like the copse and spinney plantations which often followed enclosure, they may still provide welcome detail and patterning in the countryside – to say nothing of invaluable refuges for wildlife and nesting birds.

Less common facets of the rural scene include 'strip lynchets' and water meadows. Strip lynchets are terrace-like features which roughly follow hillside contours and were created by ploughing. They are thought to date from the Middle Ages – probably from the period of over-population before the arrival of the Black Death in 1348, when peasants were forced to plough the most marginal lands. There are fine examples on the hillsides above Linton in Wharfedale and on the valley sides to the west of Worth Matravers in Dorset. Water meadows, often dating from the 18th century, can occasionally be traced in valley-bottom pastures. These were criss-crossed by patterns of artificial water channels which were used to flood the grazing in the spring and so stimulate early growths of grass. Good examples survive in the valley below Castle Acre in Norfolk and beside a long stretch of the Cambridge–Liverpool Street railway.

The Last Sad Chapter

The latest chapter in the field story is concerned entirely with destruction. Mechanized arable farming – generously financed by a labyrinth of public subsidies – is creating featureless prairie fields at the expense of the beautiful hedgerow patterning of the countryside which has so long delighted the traveller and has harboured a myriad of wild plants and creatures. Much of East Anglia, the East Midlands and even the lovely Dorset Downs have thus been rendered biologically sterile and visually boring. Old hedgerows enjoy no legal protection and there are no signs of the purposeful controls which are needed to preserve or salvage the glories of the British countrysides. A comparison between southern Cambridgeshire or northern Suffolk, where most of the beauty and interest have been destroyed and Shropshire, where much of the wonder remains, will show what is at stake.

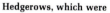

Hedgerows, which were established during the period of Parliamentary Enclosure in 1795, overlie the ridge and furrow patterns of medieval farming at Padbury in Buckinghamshire.

Britain at Work: Before the Industrial Revolution

Below right: The English cloth industry in the late 14th century. At this time the export of wool was more important than that of woollen cloth, which increased from 315 bales between 1350 and 1380 to 2,575,000 bales in 1501–1530. The important cloth-making areas were all largely pastoral. Today the wealth of the wool-merchants is recalled by the magnificent churches they built, particularly those of the Cotswolds and East Anglia, some ornamented with carvings of the sheep and the shears on which their riches were founded: 'Thank God, and ever shall, it is the sheepe, hath paid for all.'

greater financial return. Even where important and wealthy entrepreneurs existed, as they did in the textile industry, the domestic system of manufacturing was the norm. The capitalist distributed the raw material to men and women working in their own homes and bought the finished goods from them. Under this system, the county with the highest industrial production and the greatest population density at the beginning of the 15th century was Somerset, closely followed by Wiltshire. In the third league were Devon, Hampshire, Kent, Essex, Suffolk and Yorkshire.

Although the manufacture of woollen textiles was, apart from agriculture and milling, by far the most important industry right up to the last quarter of the 18th century, others were steadily gaining ground from the Tudor times onwards. Tin was increasingly important, as an ingredient of pewter and bronze. It was supplied from small, individually run mines in Cornwall and on Dartmoor. Lead

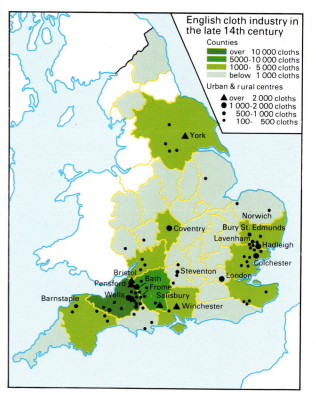

English cloth industry in the late 14th century
Counties
over 10 000 cloths
5000-10 000 cloths
1000- 5 000 cloths
below 1 000 cloths
Urban & rural centres
▲ over 2 000 cloths
● 1 000-2 000 cloths
● 500-1 000 cloths
• 100- 500 cloths

The English countryside is dotted with mills driven by wind or water – the main sources of power before the Industrial Revolution. This windmill is at Pitstone Green, Buckinghamshire. It is one of Britain's oldest post mills, bearing the date 1627. It is still in working order.

In 1700 two-thirds of the working population of Britain earned their livings directly from agriculture, and most industrial occupations were connected in some way with agriculture. Tanning, waggon-building and tallow-making are typical examples. With few exceptions, goods were made within a few miles of the place where they were to be used, and they were made with a particular customer in mind. One of the most significant features of the Industrial Revolution was that it changed the relationship between the manufacturer and his customer. The mills and workshops of the pre-industrial age produced, for the most part, commodities for people who were personally known to the craftsmen concerned and whose requirements were individually met, while a large part of the production of the factories, forges and mines which the Industrial Revolution brought into being was aimed at a speculative market.

Until the 18th century, such units of industrial production as did exist were, with few exceptions, small. Size was governed primarily by technical factors, the possibility of investing in capital equipment, not by the expectation of a

production, too, was carried on in Yorkshire, Derbyshire and Cumberland, and on Mendip, by undertakings which rarely employed more than ten men. By the late 17th century nearly all the main coalfields had manufacturing industries scattered around them, especially in the North-East and Midlands, but the most notable industrial concentration, outside textile manufacturing, was in Kent, which in the 16th century had most of the nation's blast furnaces and forges. During the following century iron-making established itself in Wales, the Forest of Dean and Yorkshire, as the forests of the Weald ceased to provide enough timber for charcoal-making. By the late 17th century, too, Kent had acquired a much wider range of industries – lime-burning and copperas along the Thames estuary, gunpowder at Faversham, paper-making at Dover and Dartford, shipbuilding and repairing at Chatham Dockyard. All these required considerable capital and, with the possible exception of lime-burning, were outside the range of domestic producers.

An essential feature of the capitalist industries, such as

the manufacture of paper, cloth and gunpowder, was that their products were sold over the whole country and in some cases exported. Except for London, however, most of the nation's requirements in the matter of food and drink, clothing, building materials, domestic equipment, furniture and tools were met locally. Even a small town was likely to contain the full range of craftsmen, who earned their living by supplying customers within a range of 20 miles or so, often much less. Only luxuries could absorb the high transport costs involved over long distances unless, as with Portland stone and Newcastle coal on their way to London, the journey was almost entirely by water. The only pre-industrial workshops to have survived in any numbers are windmills and watermills, although, as with the rapidly dwindling supply of blacksmiths' shops of the traditional type, one can still discover clues of other types of local craftsmanship of the old rural society.

For the rest, one has to depend largely on what has been preserved or reconstructed in museums, some of which, most fortunately, occupy the premises in which the industry or craft was originally carried on.

Museums are now almost the only places where some traditional trades and skills are practised. This cobbler is working in the Colne Valley Museum, Huddersfield.

Before the Industrial Revolution the making of woollen textiles, one of Britain's most important industries, was carried out almost entirely as a cottage industry. The whole family could join in, the children carding the wool, the women spinning it and the men weaving and finishing the cloth. It was particularly suitable for farms too small to provide a regular income.

There were two main types of loom in use; the horizontal loom, the warp threads of which passed horizontally from rollers to the weaver, and the high-warp loom in which the threads passed vertically in front of him. This type of loom was found in East Anglia, and the weavers' cottages there all had a high enough room to accommodate it. The weaver here is using a hand-operated horizontal loom.

Another cottage industry was the making of furniture. In the area around High Wycombe in Buckinghamshire, 'bodgers' used beech wood from the beech hangers to fashion parts of chairs which they took down to the town. Today beech chairs are still made there to the traditional designs.

SOME MUSEUM DISPLAYS WORTH VISITING
Curtis Museum, Alton, Hampshire Wide range of crafts, but especially shoemaking, millstone dressing
Wye College Agricultural Museum, Kent Especially waggons, implements
Weald & Downland Open Air Museum, Singleton, Chichester Building materials and techniques
Bridport Museum, Dorset Ropemaking
Somerset Rural Life Museum, Glastonbury, Somerset Cheese and butter-making
Tiverton Museum, Devon Waggons, smithy
Wookey Hole Museum, Somerset Papermaking
Norfolk Rural Life Museum, Gressenhall Wheelwright's shop, saddler's, smithy, basketmaker's
Buckinghamshire County Museum, Aylesbury Gallery of Rural Life
Manor Farm, Cogges, Oxfordshire Hurdlemaking
Wycombe Chair Museum, High Wycombe, Buckinghamshire Chairmaking
Avoncroft Museum of Buildings, Bromsgrove, Herefs. and Worcs. Building and techniques
Welsh Folk Museum, St Fagans, Cardiff Rural workshops
Ryedale Folk Museum, Hutton-le-Hole, Yorkshire Smithy, Elizabethan glass-furnace
Cregneash Folk Museum, Isle of Man Turner's shop, weaving shed
Abbot Hall Museum, Kendal, Cumbria Bobbin-making
Bishop Hooper's Lodging, Gloucester Pinmaker's workshop

Britain at Work: The Industrial Revolution

The traveller in 18th-century Britain moved through one largely self-sufficient area to another, each with its own pattern of industry and agriculture closely interwoven. Halfway through the century, London was still the only really large urban community. Most of the principal industries, especially iron and cloth, were well distributed throughout the country, although specialization existed in a few districts. The fast-running streams and local supplies of millstone grit gave the Sheffield and Rotherham areas, for instance, natural advantages for making cutlery.

In 1700, outside the London area, the density of population had been determined largely by the location of the woollen industry, which was carried out mainly in three areas – the South-West, parts of East Anglia and the West Riding. By 1750 this was no longer true. Even before turnpikes and canals improved communications, the distribution of the population was changing rapidly, with textiles moving north and the areas where coal and iron were readily available beginning to be more thickly settled. Between about 1750 and 1850, a series of inter-related developments gradually changed the economy of Great Britain from one which was based on agriculture and handicrafts to one characterized by concentrated urban communities and large-scale manufacturing units.

That the Industrial Revolution did happen is indisputable, but why it happened has been a matter of much argument. War, always a prodigious consumer of iron and iron products, certainly had something to do with it, but the major reason is probably that from about 1750 onwards the population of Britain began to grow at an unprecedented rate. In order to meet the basic needs of the extra millions, industrial and agricultural production had to be greatly increased. It is remarkable that the people who ultimately financed the Industrial Revolution were humble and impoverished people. Goods sold to them had to be cheap to sell at all, and that involved a revolution in production techniques.

The use of coal developed much earlier and faster in Britain than on the Continent, partly because outcropping seams were well spread over the whole country, so that the distances between the pit and the consumer were not impossibly great, partly because the fact that Britain is an island made it easier to ship coal over long distances, but even more because of a serious timber crisis. The demand for

With the coming of the railways, goods and people could for the first time be transported quickly, easily, and relatively cheaply. This print shows part of the Liverpool–Manchester Railway, opened in 1830, which was the first on which all trains were drawn by steam engines.

MONUMENTS OF THE INDUSTRIAL REVOLUTION

South-West
Avoncliff canal aqueduct, Avon
Bath Green Park station, Avon
Box railway tunnel, Wilts.
Bristol Temple Meads station, Avon
Claverton canal pumping station, Avon
Clifton suspension bridge, Bristol, Avon
Devizes Locks, Kennet and Avon Canal.
Dundas canal aqueduct, Monkton Combet, Avon
Dunkirk Mill, Nailsworth, Gloucs.
Great Western Dock, Bristol, Avon (and SS *Great Britain*)
Morwellham Quay and tramway, Devon.
Mythe road bridge, Tewkesbury, Gloucs.
Over road bridge, Gloucs.
Portland stone quarries, Dorset
Royal Albert Bridge, Saltash, Cornwall.
Sapperton canal tunnel, Gloucs.
Stanley Mill, Stroud, Gloucs.
Tolgus tin works, Cornwall.
Wheal Martyn china clay works, Cornwall.
Wookey Hole paper mill, Somerset.

West Midlands
Bage's Cotton Mill, Shrops.
Bedlam Furnaces and Iron Bridge (road), Ironbridge, Shrops.
Carby Furnace, Coalbrookdale, Shrops.
Coalport pottery and canal inclined plane, Shrops.
Curzon Street station, Birmingham
Forge Needle Mill, Redditch, Herefs. and Worcs.
Gladstone Pottery, Longton, Staffs.
Longdon-upon-Tern canal aqueduct, Shrops.

East Midlands
Abbey Lane pumping station, Leicester
Blisworth canal and railway tunnels, Northants.
Kilsby railway tunnel, Northants.
North Mill, Belper, Derbys.
Old Mill, Cromford, Derbys.
Papplewick pumping station, Notts.

South-East
Bembridge windmill, Isle of Wight
Chatham boat store, Kent
Cranbrook windmill, Kent
Cross-in-Hand windmill, Sussex
Eastney pumping station, Portsmouth, Hants.
Fakenham Gasworks, Norfolk
Faversham gunpowder mills, Kent
Great Bardfield windmill, Essex
Horsey windmill, Norfolk
Kew Bridge pumping station, London
King's Cross station, London
Maidenhead railway viaduct, Berks.
Polegate windmill, Sussex
Portsmouth dockyard storehouses, Hants.
St Katharine's Dock, London
St Pancras station, London
Saxted Green windmill, Suffolk
Sheerness boat shed, Kent
Tring railway cutting, Herts.
West Wratting windmill, Cambs.
Woodbridge tide mill, Suffolk

North-East
Abbeydale Industrial Hamlet, Sheffield, Yorks.
Bingley canal locks, Yorks.
Catcliffe glass cone, Yorks.
Monkwearmouth station, Tyne and Wear
Newcastle Central station, Tyne and Wear
Ryhope pumping station, Tyne and Wear
Saltaire textile village, Yorks.

North-West
Albert Dock, Liverpool
Barton canal aqueduct, Lancs.
Ellesmere Port warehouses, Ches.
Laxey waterwheel, Isle of Man
Liverpool Road station, Manchester
Lune canal aqueduct, Cumbria
Manchester Central station
Marple canal aqueduct, Ches.
Runcorn Viaduct, Ches.
Styal cotton mill and workers' housing, Ches.
Thornton Cleveleys windmill, Lancs.

SCOTLAND
Carron Ironworks, Falkirk, Central
Forth Railway Bridge Lothian/Fife
New Lanark, Borders
Tay Railway Bridge, Fife/Tayside

WALES
Blaenau Ffestiniog slate quarries, Gwynedd
Blaenavon ironworks, Gwent
Conway road suspension bridge and railway bridge, Gwynedd
Llanberis slate quarries, Gwynedd
Menai road suspension bridge, Gwynedd
Parys Mountain copper mine, Gwynedd
Penrhyn slate quarries, Gwynedd

wood as fuel, especially from the iron and glass industries, forced up the price to a point where coal was more economic, despite the high transport cost.

In its earlier stages, the Industrial Revolution was centred on villages and small towns, rather than on large urban communities. In the Midlands especially, people lived and worked in an industrialized countryside. Even during the 19th century, much of the land was not built over because it was covered by waste heaps and stagnant lakes; The Black Country was a pleasant green landscape until the middle of the 18th century. The mountains of rubbish which changed its appearance were the result of primitive iron-smelting methods. Of every 24 tons of material which was loaded into the furnaces, 11 went away into the atmosphere as gas and soot and 5 were dumped on the meadows of rural Staffordshire. Chemical works destroyed the countryside and polluted the rivers and streams in areas like Tipton, Widnes and Wigan, as ruthlessly as iron and coal did.

Cornwall has nearly as high a proportion of murdered acres as Lancashire, but its industrial tips – the waste sand from the china-clay pits – are 20th century and white,

rather than 19th century and black. These enormous and imprudently sited heaps have sterilized millions of tons of valuable china-clay, which lie untouched and untouchable beneath them and millions of tons more in pits cannot be worked any deeper, because there is nowhere to dump the waste and sand washed out of the clay.

The Wounds are Healing

The industrial deserts are gradually vanishing now, as land becomes scarcer and more valuable and as heavy equipment is available to carry out the levelling more quickly and cheaply. Large areas between Birmingham and Wolverhampton, for instance, and around Swansea, have completely lost their old dreadfulness, and the same is true of much of South Lancashire and parts of Fife. The wounds caused by the Industrial Revolution are slowly healing.

The architectural monuments of the age of coal, iron and steam are also being steadily swept back. Dynamite and the bulldozers are making short work of the great multi-storey cotton and woollen mills, the forests of factory chimneys, the acres of back-to-back terrace houses which characterized the industrial areas for so long.

A pit head in about 1820, showing the steam winding gear. At first the Industrial Revolution was powered by water, and water still predominated at the beginning of the 19th century. Steam power was developed for use in coal mining, and itself was a formidable consumer of coal. As steam engines became increasingly efficient their use spread throughout industry, which now concentrated in the towns.

Britain at Work: The Second Industrial Revolution

Mini Metro bodies travelling down the robot line for finishing welding. Robot welders can spot-weld car bodies with a precision far greater than their human counterparts could consistently achieve, and they can continue doing so indefinitely without ever tiring, needing refreshment or getting bored. Such devices are increasingly being used in factories where materials handled are too heavy, hot or dangerous for workers to handle directly. Unlike the first industrial revolution, the second one is being established without bloodshed or human misery.

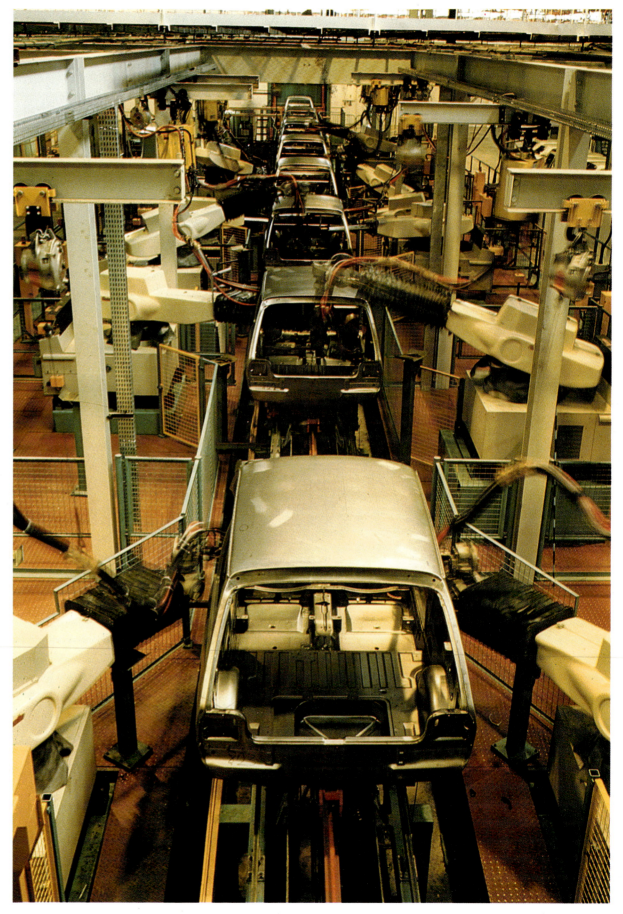

British coal was the basis of the First Industrial Revolution. It was required to raise steam to power the machinery that British engineers were inventing so prolifically.

Nuclear energy will be the basis of the Second Industrial revolution, generating electricity to underpin advances in electronic computing, information technology, control engineering and electro-refining and working of semi-conductors and superalloys for the new Revolution. No less important, it is having a seminal influence on the standards of health and safety at work.

Briefly, between the two Industrial Revolutions, Britain is enjoying a period in which it has an abundance of oil and natural gas to use as fuels and as feedstocks for its chemical industries. But peak production of indigenous oil is likely to be reached by the mid-1980s and of natural gas before the end of the century.

Today, Britain produces about one-fifth of its electricity from nuclear energy and over three-fifths from coal. As more nuclear stations are built the nuclear proportion will rise steadily. Already it is much higher in Belgium, Finland, France, Sweden and Switzerland. Meanwhile, plans are already well advanced to produce natural gas, oil and chemicals from coal, by techniques far more efficient than similar attempts made earlier this century.

No industry before or since – not excepting the aero-space industry – has depended so heavily on untried materials, some of which had never been produced commercially before, much less to the quality and purity demanded by nuclear technology. Nevertheless, Britain's first experimental nuclear reactor (GLEEP) operated as early as 1947, and the second (BEPO) in 1948, paving the way for the plutonium production 'piles' at Windscale in 1950. These piles made explosive for Britain's first nuclear weapon test in 1952.

The piles produced no power. But Christopher Hinton and John Çockroft were pursuing schemes for more advanced technology which would simultaneously make plutonium and capture the heat of fissioning atoms to make steam. The outcome was Calder Hall, where the piles were put into pressure vessels and cooled with carbon dioxide under high pressure. The gas, thus heated, was used to raise steam for turbo-generators. Thus the plutonium pile became a nuclear boiler – the first in the world which is of commercial size.

In addition to Calder Hall, Britain has other nuclear power stations generating electricity today. The original nuclear factories have been extensively adapted for a new role predominantly in support of the nuclear electricity programme. New factories have been designed exclusively to make parts and assemblies for nuclear reactors, using advanced manufacturing methods, in conditions as clean as medical suppliers must use. Others are making radio-chemicals, byproducts of the reactors, mainly for use in medicine and medical research.

This revolution in power production has not been achieved without great political and technical agonizing, as the opportunities unfolded. The discovery of plentiful hydrocarbon resources offshore proved a major national distraction for both financial and industrial resources in the 1960s and 1970s, just when the industrial problems of nuclear energy loomed largest. But unlike the energy of the first industrial revolution, this one is being established without bloodshed and human misery. From its inception the nuclear industry established standards of health and safety to which other industries – new as well as old – are just beginning to aspire. The Health and Safety at Work Act 1975, itself inspired by a major accident in the British coal industry, is helping to spread the nuclear industry's experience more widely.

Electronics

Electronics, the twin strand of the new industrial revolution, contrasts with it in some important ways. Electronics lies at the heart of the machinery of the new revolution. But where nuclear plant has grown rapidly bigger, to spread the heavy cost of safety, electronics over the same three decades has shrunk to microscopic proportions. Its great strength lies in the speed with which information can be gathered and sorted, separating precisely that which is needed to perform a given task. Moreover, this strength can be imparted for a price which has been and is still falling steadily.

In 1952, soon after the invention of the transistor, a British scientist publicized in the USA ideas which were being discussed by defence scientists in Britain. Geoffrey Dummer of the (then) Royal Radar Establishment told a Washington audience of electronic engineers: 'At this stage, I would like to take a peep into the future. With the advent of the transistor and the work in semi-conductors generally, it now seems possible to envisage electronic equipment in a solid block with no connecting wires'.

The first 'solid circuit' was patented in the USA in 1959. Since then the number of electronic components put into such circuits – 'silicon chips' as they are called nowadays – has roughly doubled each year. By 1982 they totalled about one million, within an area about the size of a small fingernail. Silicon chips are being sold having the data storage capacity (memory) and data processing capacity of machines which once filled a large room.

Silicon, to the second industrial revolution, is what steel was to the first one. The power of the chip in the form of micro-processors is pervading every commercial and industrial activity.

On a modern machine tool the electronics, not the craftsman, decide when a part has been cut to the desired shape and accuracy. Other robots with 'arms' and 'finger-nails', programmed to know when to remove and replace the part, also perform factory activities which may be particularly tiring and risky for people.

In the design office another kind of robot called computer-aided design (CAD) can transform an engineer's sketches and doodles into TV-like images on a screen. He can change these images, twist them round, view them from any angle, slice sections away to peer within. Then, when the engineer is satisfied with his creation, he can tell the computer to translate it into engineering instructions for the robots on the factory floor.

In the home

Neither is the home immune from the impact of the second industrial revolution. The TV screen, round which domestic life has centred increasingly in the past three decades, is also evolving into a far more powerful apparatus. Television viewing is essentially a passive occupation. But the computing power and low cost of the silicon chip can transform TV technology into an apparatus with which the viewer can interact, or question until he is satisfied with its answers. The telephone system, itself increasingly controlled by computers, is putting the viewer in touch with libraries of electronic data every bit as powerful as those available to the designer. Whether the questioner is in search of a purchase or engaged in some more esoteric investigation, a worldwide network of electronic libraries is beginning to open at his command.

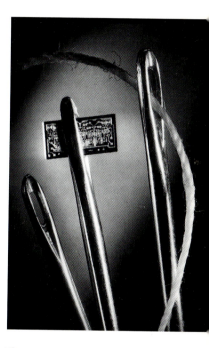

The compactness and cheapness of the silicon chip is likely to bring about what may be the greatest industrial and social revolution in human history. Silicon is to the second industrial revolution what steel was to the first.

Opening up Britain: Roads

The hub of Britain's pre-historic roadway system was Salisbury Plain, a plateau from which ridgeways had been provided by nature for transport east and west with shorter tracks to the coast for trade with Europe, and inland to the Cotswolds for links with other long-distance trackways. In the North-West through-routes were restricted to mountain passes reached from such centres as Keswick and Kendal, and northward via Carlisle into Scotland, where ridgeways continued to determine the lines of roads in the Lowlands and mountain passes in the Highlands.

The first made-up roads in the South were the North Downs Ridgeway from Stonehenge to Canterbury (*Durovernum*), the South Downs from Old Winchester to Beachy Head, the Icknield Way from Wessex to the Wash, and the Fosse Way from Axminster to the Humber.

The Romans shifted the hub from Salisbury Plain to London, from which main roads radiated to the Channel ports via Canterbury, to the Fosse via Silchester, and to Colchester, the tribal *Camulodunum*, with access to the prehistoric Peddars Way across East Anglia. They made a new road to Chichester, and because their prime object was to bring the whole of Britain into subjection they constructed the two main highways to the North: Watling Street and Ermine Street, the forerunners respectively of the Holyhead Road and the Great North Road. Before their withdrawal the Romans had given the country its first transport framework.

From the point of view of daily needs, the first important long-distance trackways were flintways and saltways. Salt is so basic a human need that the word salary is derived from *salarium*, the money allowed to the legionaries for salt. *Domesday* records 294 saltings producing salt by evaporation of sea water in Sussex alone, and saltings along the Solent continued to flourish throughout the 18th century. Flintways came even earlier. Among those that can still be traced are those leading to chalk pits in the South Downs and to the crystalline rocks deposits of the Langdale Pikes in Cumbria, which came into use for axe-heads in Neolithic times. Quarries like those of Grimes Graves in East Anglia, where antler picks have been found, were England's first factories.

Few long-distance roads were made in the 12th and 13th centuries. Throughout the Middle Ages road-making was in general confined to market- and farm-ways maintained by parish labour, which explains why their increasing use by waggons and coaches for long-distance transport was so stoutly resisted towards the end of that period. The exceptions were roads made by religious orders or wealthy landowners for convenience in visiting outlying estates, or for travelling either to London or to one of the provincial

Below: The remains of a Roman road at Wheeldale in Yorkshire. The Romans were excellent road-builders, digging deep foundations, and their roads remained in use long after all visible traces of their villas had been swept away. These roads were laid on almost straight paths from one town or fort to another; along them travelled merchants and above all the Roman army, which could march for a steady 30 miles a day with full equipment. A comparison of the main Roman roads from London, shown below right, with the 18th-century coaching roads on the opposite page shows how many Roman roads were still in use.

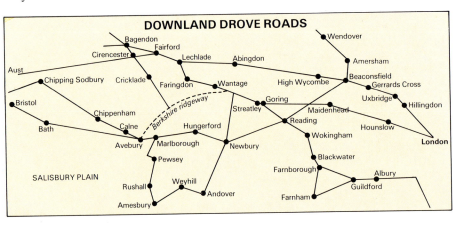

DOWNLAND DROVE ROADS

Left: Drove roads across the downs in South-West England. Before the days of cattle trucks animals had to be herded to market on foot, often travelling very long distances to get the best prices. Cattle from Scotland were driven to Norfolk where they were fattened on the marshes; some were then sold near Norwich, but some were taken on to London. Pigs, sheep, and even geese also travelled these roads, and farmers along the way let out grazing to the travelling flocks and herds.

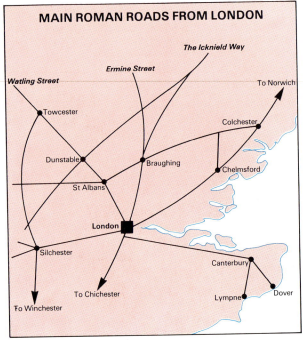

MAIN ROMAN ROADS FROM LONDON

capitals in which they had town residences. These roads can often be identified by such names as Abbot's Way in mid-Devon or Earlsway (Yelsway) in the North Midlands. To encourage such work the Church was generous in granting 'indulgencies' for what were described as 'pious and meritorious works before God'.

The parishes could be relied upon to keep bridges on packhorse routes in repair. The entire life of rural communities in hill country depended on them – so much so that by tracing the long-distance routes that converge on these narrow, humped bridges, with parapets low enough to be cleared by the panniers strapped to the backs of the ponies that trotted across them in single file, the whole pattern of life in the Age when every stream had its mill for local employment can be reconstructed. Parish records abound with reference to these 'pack and prime ways'.

Packhorse trails were narrow, and by that feature can be distinguished from the old 'green roads', along which herds of up to 200 head of cattle, with one drover and two dogs to every 40 beasts, were kept open along routes extending to Scotland in the North and Wales in the West. The Cotswolds and the Pennines are criss-crossed by what came to be known as 'Drover Roads'. 'The Feathers' at Ledbury and the ancestor of the 'Lygon Arms' at Broadway were drovers' inns. The most renowned of the drovers, John Birtwhistle of Skipton, who fattened cattle on Malham Moor before his men drove them on to the South, claimed to have up to 10,000 beasts on the road at any time.

The condition of metalled highways continued to be scandalous until, towards the middle of the 18th century, the principle of Turnpike Trusts, which since 1663 had been empowered to construct roads and recoup the cost by levying tolls, was reluctantly accepted. Three hundred and eighty-nine Trusts were established between 1750 and 1772. Then in 1784 John Palmer of Bath inaugurated a transport revolution with his plans for carrying mail by coach. By 1800 mail coaches drawn by four horses, each with an armed guard carrying a blunderbuss, had become the major form of public transport. Between 20 and 30 coaches a day would be changing horses in the inn yards of market towns with not more than two to three hundred inhabitants.

The challenge of constructing highways on this unprecedented scale was met by three men of immense drive: 'Blind Jack of Knaresborough', John Metcalf (1717–1810), who had been soldier, pedlar and horse-dealer before taking to road-making, and the two professional surveyors, Thomas Telford (1757–1834), and John Loudon McAdam (1756–1836), the favourite of the Turnpike Trusts, who at the peak of his prosperity had 300 sub-surveyors to assist him and who gave the language a new word. But their prosperity was not inherited by their successors: the Turnpikes were killed in stages by the extension of main line railways. Their number declined from 854 in the 1870s to 2 in the 90s. The last went into liquidation in 1895.

The Age of 'Pickwick' and 'Tony Weller' lasted for little more than a single generation. Nothing, it was thought, could bring life back to the roads on this exuberant Dickensian scale. But then came the motor car, and by the 1930s road transport had returned in such volume that it was being argued that many roads had become too dangerous for casual use, and that the pressure on these should be reduced by providing a national system of specially designed roads, restricted to cars only. The Second World War intervened. So it was not until the 1950s that a start could be made on this motorway scheme, and in 1982 London still awaits the completion of its orbital road.

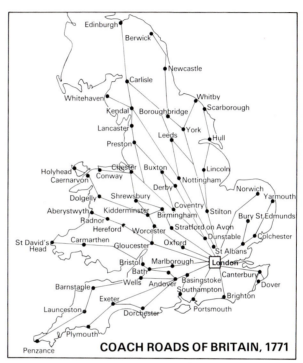

COACH ROADS OF BRITAIN, 1771

Above: Hyde Park Corner in 1797, showing the turnpike on the left. The tolls collected by the turnpikes were used to meet the cost of road building. By this time more and more coaches were trundling along Britain's inadequate road system.

'Spaghetti Junction', the complicated motorway interchange system at Birmingham. Today's motorways consume vast tracts of land; but their construction helps to save old towns and villages from the menace of unceasing streams of traffic, which disrupt everyday life and damage centuries-old buildings by their vibration.

Opening up Britain: Canals

Life on the narrow boats – as the long barges that nosed their way through the network of Britain's canals were called – was often gruellingly hard for the men and their families. Nevertheless they found time to develop a distinctive form of art: the colourful painting with which they decorated both their boats and many of their everyday utensils.

Below: Built by Telford between 1795 and 1805, the Pont-Cysyllte aqueduct at Acrefair near Llangollen carries the Shropshire Union Canal 120 feet above the Dee Valley.

Until the mid-18th century, the rivers were the main arteries of communication in Britain. The roads were almost uniformly bad – the excellent Roman road system had not been maintained – and in winter often barely passable, especially where they crossed clay areas. During the 16th century eight Acts of Parliament were passed to allow river navigation to be improved. As a result of one such Act, in 1571, the River Lea was brought to the north of London by means of an artificial cut. The process of improvement continued throughout the 17th century and by 1750, when the great period of canal building began, Britain had about 1000 miles (1600 km) of navigable rivers. During the next hundred years, approximately 3000 miles (4825 km) of canals were added to our waterways system. Most of this construction took place between 1765 and 1805. After 1850, mainly as a result of competition from the railways, little was done to extend the network, although the largest canal, the Manchester Ship Canal, was opened in 1894. It is the only canal in Britain to have been constructed by machinery. All the others were dug by hand.

Canals in Britain are of four types. A few were designed and built in the first place to take sea-going ships. The earliest of these was the Exeter Canal, linking Exeter with Topsham, which was begun in 1594. This has another claim to distinction, as the first British canal to use the modern pound-lock, which allows the level of the water to rise and fall between two pairs of gates. Those in the second group, the more important main line canals, are about 14 feet (4.25 m) wide. These are to be found mainly in the East Midlands and in Lancashire and Cheshire, although there are some examples in the South, especially where there was a connection with a tidal river. The narrow canals, with locks only 7 feet (2 m) wide, were built in hilly districts, where large numbers of locks and tunnels were needed and where the water supply was poor, especially in summer. There are a number of canals of this type in the Birmingham area and in South Wales. The fourth type were the tub-boat canals. These are found chiefly in the hilly parts of the South-West and Shropshire. They took small boats or barges, about 20 feet (6 m) long and 5 feet (1.5 m) wide, which could be hauled out of the water and carried up and down inclined planes, which was cheaper than building tunnels or flights of locks.

Britain, unlike the Netherlands, north-west Germany and much of France, presented canal engineers with great problems. In many regions, the geography meant a great deal of locking and sometimes tunnels, which were even more expensive, and some areas, such as the South-West, the far north and much of Scotland, were quite unsuitable for the construction of artificial waterways.

The main lines of canal and their more important branches were usually built by public companies formed for the purpose, but individual entrepreneurs sometimes undertook the venture. Many of the smaller branch canals, however, – especially to coalmines or factories – were financed privately by the people who stood to benefit most by them. In general, the canals in the largely agricultural South were a poor commercial bargain, since they did not have the traffic potential to make adequate profits. The Loughborough Navigation in Leicestershire, on the other hand, which carried large quantities of raw materials and manufactured goods, paid a dividend of 197 per cent in 1824.

The early canals were built as cheaply as possible, following the contours to avoid constructing tunnels or cuttings. Later, when competition from the railways made it necessary to shorten the time taken by canal journeys, the routes for new canals were made more direct, despite the greatly increased engineering costs. In other instances, the line of an old canal was straightened. The length of the Oxford Canal, for example, was reduced by nearly 14 miles (22.50 km) between 1829 and 1834.

Thirty-seven British canals are still navigable, at least for part of their length. Some, such as the Aire and Calder Navigation, are still commercially active, but most carry only pleasure boats nowadays and extensive restoration work has been done to allow them to be used for this purpose. Tunnels, however, present a major maintenance and repair problem. Tunnel repairs are expensive and, for this reason, some stretches of our canals are likely to be closed for a long time, perhaps for ever.

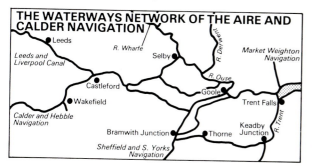

THE WATERWAYS NETWORK OF THE AIRE AND CALDER NAVIGATION

The network of the Aire and Calder Navigation, showing how rivers were linked by man-made waterways.

THE GREAT CANAL BUILDERS

James Brindley (1716–1772) has been called the father of canals in Britain. His ambition was to unite by means of canals the four great rivers – Mersey, Trent, Severn and Thames. He surveyed the whole network and, at the time of his death, the task of linking the first three rivers by means of the Trent and Mersey and the Stafford and Worcestershire Canals had been all but completed. The remaining link, the great Harecastle Tunnel at Kidgrove, was finished in 1777. The canal between the Thames and the Midlands was not opened until 1790. Brindley's canals followed a winding route, partly to avoid building locks, tunnels and embankments wherever possible and partly to bring as many villages as possible within the system.

Thomas Telford (1757–1834) worked for some years as an architect and bridge specialist before he became engineer to the Ellesmere Canal Company in 1793. This had been formed to connect the Mersey and the Dee to the Severn at Shrewsbury.

The canal had to run through very difficult country and at Pont-Cysyllte it crosses the Vale of Llangollen by means of a 1007-foot cast-iron aqueduct. After a great programme of road building in Scotland, he constructed first the Caledonian Canal, completed in 1822, and then the Gotha Canal in Sweden (1832).

John Rennie (1761–1821) built canals distinguished particularly by adventurous aqueducts and locks. These include the Lune Aqueduct, Lancaster, which carries the Lancaster Canal 51 feet above the river; the Dundas and Avoncliff Aqueducts, taking the Kennet and Avon Canal over the river Avon near Bath; and the series of 29 locks (1810) on the Kennet and Avon Canal near Devizes. Rennie was also responsible for Claverton Pumping Station, where the pumps that lift water to the 9-mile length of the Kennet and Avon between Bath and Bradford-on-Avon are driven by two waterwheels, and for Crofton Pumping Station, farther east on the Kennet and Avon, near Marlborough. The two beam engines at Crofton still work.

Further information can be obtained from: The Inland Waterways Association Ltd, 114 Regent's Park Road, London N.W.1, which campaigns for the restoration and retention of inland waterways in Britain, and encourages the fullest commercial and recreational use of them.

James Brindley came from a poor background and was a millwright by trade before he embarked on his great programme of canal building.

BRITAIN'S NETWORK OF CANALS

By the 1830s, Britain had constructed, entirely with pick and shovel labour, a network of canals and navigable rivers far more complex and comprehensive than the one achieved by the railways during the remainder of the century. Cheap to run and to use and causing no noise or atmospheric pollution, waterways lacked only the advantage of speed, which became increasingly important as Victorian industrialization gathered momentum and as the middle and upper classes came to appreciate quick journeys between one city and another.

This list shows the pattern of canal arteries in the heyday of the system. Many lock gates have rotted away and tunnels have fallen in. But most of the canals are still passable, at least for a substantial part of their length.

Aire and Calder Navigation Goole Docks to Leeds, with branches to Wakefield and Selby.

Avon Navigation From the Severn at Tewkesbury to Alverston, connecting with the Stratford-upon-Avon Canal at Stratford.

Basingstoke Canal From Basingstoke to the Wey, at Byfleet.

Birmingham Canal Navigations A complicated narrow canal system within the area Birmingham-Stourbridge-Wolverhampton-Cannock-Walsall.

Bridgewater Canal Manchester to Runcorn, with connections to the Leeds and Liverpool, Trent and Mersey and Manchester Ship Canal.

Calder and Hebble Navigation Wakefield, junction with Aire and Calder Navigation, to Sowerby Bridge, junction with Rochdale Canal.

Caledonian Canal Near Inverness to near Fort William.

Coventry Canal Coventry to Hawkesbury (junction with Northern Oxford Canal) and Fradley (junction with Trent and Mersey Canal).

Crinan Canal Ardrishaig to Crinan.

River Derwent Barmby-on-the-March to Malton.

Forth and Clyde Navigation Coast to coast navigation between the two estuaries.

Grand Union Canal Thames at Brentford to Birmingham.

Grand Union Canal, (Leicester section) From the Grand Union main line at Norton Junction to the Trent near Sawley.

Great Ouse Navigation Bedford to the Wash, near King's Lynn.

Kennet and Avon Canal From the Thames at Reading to Hanham Lock on the Bristol Avon.

Lancaster Canal Preston to Kendal.

Lee and Stort Navigation From the Thames at Limehouse to Bishop's Stortford.

Leeds and Liverpool Canal From Aire and Calder Navigation at Leeds to Liverpool.

Llangollen Canal From the Shropshire Union Canal at Hurleston to Llantysilio.

Macclesfield Canal From the Trent and Mersey Canal at Hall Green to the Peak Forest Canal at Marple.

Ouse Navigation From the Ure to the Humber.

Oxford Canal From the Thames at Oxford to the Coventry Canal at Hawkesbury, with connection with the Grand Union Canal at Napton and Braunston.

Peak Forest Canal Manchester to Whaley Bridge and Bucksworth.

Severn Navigation From the Staffordshire and Worcestershire Canal at Stourport to Gloucester Docks.

Sheffield and South Yorkshire Navigation A combination of rivers and canals, from Keadby on the Trent to Sheffield.

Shropshire Union Canal From the Staffordshire and Worcestershire Canal at Autherley, near Wolverhampton, to the Manchester Ship Canal at Ellesmere Port. Connections at Nantwich with the Trent and Mersey and Llangollen Canals.

Staffordshire and Worcestershire Canal From the Severn at Stourport to the Trent and Mersey Canal near Stafford. Connections at Wolverhampton with the Birmingham Canal Navigation and the Shropshire Union Canal, and at Stourton with the Stourbridge Canal.

Stourbridge Canal From the Stafford and Worcestershire Canal at Stourton to Stourbridge, with a branch to the Dudley Canal.

Stratford-upon-Avon Canal From the Worcester and Birmingham Canal at King's Norton to the Upper Avon Navigation at Stratford-upon-Avon, with a link with the Grand Union Canal at Lapworth.

Thames Navigation From Lechlade to Teddington, where it joins the tidal river to the sea.

Trent Navigation From the Trent and Mersey Navigation at Shardlow to the junction of the Yorkshire Ouse and the Humber.

Trent and Mersey Canal From the Bridgewater Canal to the Trent Navigation at Shardlow. Branches to Stoke-on-Trent and Leek, and links with the Macclesfield, Shropshire Union, Staffordshire and Worcestershire, and Coventry Canals, and with the Weaver Navigation.

Union Canal Falkirk to Port Hopetown, Edinburgh.

Weaver Navigation Winsford to the Manchester Ship Canal, with a connection with the Trent and Mersey Canal at Northwich.

Wey Navigation From the Thames at Weybridge to Godalming, with a connection to the Basingstoke Canal at West Byfleet.

Worcester and Birmingham Canal Birmingham to the Severn at Worcester. Connection with the Stratford-upon-Avon Canal at King's Norton.

Opening up Britain: Railways

This painting of Paddington Station, by William Frith, R.A. was painted between 1860 and 1862. By this time most of the main trunk routes had been built. People and goods could be carried quickly and cheaply over long distances; soon even small villages would have their own stations. Now it was becoming possible for excursion trains to take parties of people to the coast, while at the other end of the scale private parties – families going on holiday, for instance – could hire carriages for themselves, their servants, and their extensive luggage.

The earliest railway in Britain, at Wollaton near Northampton, is known to have been in use in 1604. It had wooden rails. From then on there was a continuous growth of horse-worked waggon-ways operated in connection with the mining and smelting industries. These were particularly common in Shropshire, Durham and Northumberland. Railways used as feeders to canals date from the 1770s. The first public railway, the Surrey Iron Railway, opened in 1803 and from then until 1830, most railways of this type resembled the turnpike roads, in that anyone who paid a toll could used them. Hauliers provided their own waggons and horses, and in one or two instances, their own locomotives.

The first steam railway locomotives were built by Richard Trevithick in 1802 and for the next 25 years there were many experiments both with steam locomotives and with cable-hauled trains drawn by stationary steam engines. The Rainhill Trials of 1829, won by George Stephenson's locomotive, *Rocket*, finally tipped the scales in favour of the locomotive. The Liverpool and Manchester Railway, built by Stephenson and opened in 1830, was the first railway to carry passengers on a regular basis and the first to be worked completely by steam from the beginning.

The railway network in Britain was built with great speed. The main line system, with more than 13,000 miles (21,000 km) open to traffic, was virtually complete in 1870 and most subsequent developments consisted of branch and feeder lines. The building of these secondary railway links went on at the same time as the development of an extensive system of electric tramways and, in the London area, of an underground railway system. By the outbreak of war in 1914, Britain had about 2700 miles (4800 km) of electric tramways.

From their earliest days, each of the passenger-carrying railways developed individual characteristics of its own. The engineers and architects had freedom to work out their own ideas, in the design of the stations, bridges, signal boxes, tunnels, station masters' houses and railway hotels. Architectural historians have devoted an understandable but disproportionate amount of attention to the grand urban terminals, such as King's Cross, Paddington and St

Pancras; the large number of small provincial stations, especially those in rural areas, were much more typical. Many of them have survived as private houses, long after their railway usefulness has ended.

The railways changed the landscape of Britain to a far greater extent than the canals. Their huge cuttings and embankments, their innumerable bridges and viaducts, and, in cities, the pollution caused by the soot-laden smoke they poured into the atmosphere, were an unmistakable mark of the Industrial Revolution. But they contributed to the industrialization of our society in other and possibly more fundamental ways. The development of the modern postal system and of national newspapers would not have been possible without railways. Nor, too, would the commuting habit, the large-scale movement of perishable foodstuffs, holidays by the sea, the transport of racing pigeons, and the availability of cheap domestic coal in practically every town and village.

The great Victorian railway-building boom stimulated the economy much as the automobile industry has done in our own times. In the mid-1840s railway investment absorbed between 5 and 7 percent of the national income each year and accounted for half the total capital investment. The demand for iron rails was almost entirely responsible for the unprecedented growth in rolling mills during the 1850s and 1860s and the railways' demand for bricks transformed the scale of the brick industry, creating new manufacturing capacity, which was put to good use in the building boom of the late Victorian period. On the debit side, the railways bankrupted many of the canals, made the turnpike trusts unprofitable, and brought about a serious deterioration in the condition of the roads.

Since the end of the Second World War, and especially since the Beeching Report of 1963, the railways have been in decline. Many lines and stations have been closed, bridges demolished, cuttings filled in and embankments levelled. The total railway mileage now is less than half what it was 40 years ago and within the next ten years it may well be halved again. The physical remains of our great railway heritage are year by year becoming steadily fewer and fewer.

In 1850 the Great Northern Railway built this viaduct at Welwyn, to carry part of its line from Peterborough to King's Cross. The different railway lines soon developed their own styles of engineering and architecture, and their own devotees. Their trains had their distinctive liveries – the cream and chocolate brown of the Great Western, for instance. For some time there was a large number of different companies, but after the First World War most amalgamated to form four main line railways: the Great Western, the London and North Eastern, London Midland and Scottish, and the Southern. In 1948 the railways were taken into state ownership.

THE GREAT RAILWAY BUILDERS

George Stephenson (1781–1848). The son of a colliery engine man, George Stephenson himself worked with pit winding and pumping engines. He was barely literate until the end of his life. With the construction of the Stockton and Darlington Railway, which opened in 1825, he became a railway engineer in his own right. Essentially a practical man, he made many mistakes, but his deserved reputation as a pioneer gave him the contract for the Darlington–Newcastle and Birmingham–Manchester railway. Like his son Robert, he refused a knighthood. He was not admitted as a member of the Institution of Civil Engineers, but was elected the first president of the Institution of Mechanical Engineers.

Robert Stephenson (1803–59). The Newcastle firm of Robert Stephenson and Co. was established in 1823 to build locomotives when Robert Stephenson was only 20. He was responsible for building many of the early locomotives including *Locomotion* and *Rocket*. After gaining experience as contractor for the Canterbury and Whitstable Railway and three other lines, he became engineer to the London to Birmingham Railway. Assisted by his father George, he advised the Belgian, Spanish and Norwegian governments on railway construction. As part of the Stephensons' line from Newcastle to Scotland, Robert was responsible for the great cast-iron bridge over the Tyne and for the Royal Border Bridge over the Tweed at Berwick. As Engineer-in-Chief to the Chester and Holyhead Railway, he also designed the Conway Bridge and the Britannia Bridge over the Menai Straits, to be followed by other tubular bridges in Egypt and Canada. He succeeded his father as president of the Institution of Mechanical Engineers.

Isambard Kingdom Brunel (1806–59). The son of the engineer Sir Marc Brunel, I. K. Brunel was educated in France and later apprenticed there to a celebrated maker of scientific instruments. In 1833 he was appointed engineer for the London to Bristol Railway. The construction involved cutting two miles through solid rock at Box Hill, the longest tunnel so far planned. By 1844 the line was through to Exeter, with a branch to Oxford, and in the following year the Swindon–Gloucester line was opened. The Devon and Corn- wall section of the Great Western necessitated major bridging works across deep valleys and the Tamar. He was the protagonist of the broad 6 foot gauge, which he believed gave safer and more comfortable travel; but in the end the 4 foot 8½-inch gauge, favoured by the Stephensons, won the day. Brunel was also a naval architect of distinction. His *Great Britain*, *Great Western* and *Great Eastern* all made important contributions to the progress of ship design.

Thomas Brassey (1805–70). Born into a farming and land-owning family, Brassey became a surveyor and began his career as a railway contractor through an association with the Stephensons. He achieved his reputation as Britain's leading railway builder as a result of exceptional honesty and remarkable powers of organization. He carried out a great deal of work abroad. By 1870 he had built one out of every 20 miles of the railways then existing in the world, and something like one in three of those in Britain. He enjoyed exceptionally good relationships with the thousands of men who worked for him and frequently took large numbers of them abroad on foreign contracts.

Thomas Brassey was considered the father of the British railway system.

Opening up Britain: Ports, Harbours and Airports

Britain's first wave of port-building took place while she was a colony of Rome and her second, a much more important process, while she was developing a commercial and political empire of her own. Of the main Roman coastal ports – Dover, Lympne, Richborough, Portchester, Southampton – little evidence remains. Their quays and jetties were built of wood, because there was little money to spend on them, and with the collapse of Roman power they soon rotted away. Even in London, the Roman quays contained little stonework.

The Saxons and Normans mostly made do with beaching their small ships, although some rudimentary jetties were constructed. By the 12th century, however, commerce was flourishing again and more solid and ambitious installations were developed at the more important ports serving the coastal, cross-Channel and Mediterranean trade – London, Bristol, Newcastle, Shoreham, Exeter and King's Lynn.

In the 17th century, the growth of the navy and of long-distance voyages for trading and exploration necessitated more elaborate docks where ships could be fitted out and repaired and loaded and unloaded. The first wet docks in Britain, at Blackwall and Rotherhithe on the Thames, date from this period. From the first half of the 18th century and throughout the 19th, a great programme of dock and harbour construction was carried through, in order to accommodate the huge increase in the volume of shipping which made Britain the world's leading maritime power.

The first docks in Liverpool were built in 1720 and the West India Docks, London, in 1799–1802. John Rennie's breakwater at Plymouth, which formed part of the Admiralty dock project at the port, took from 1811 to 1848 to construct. In London, St Katherine's Dock, designed by Telford, was built between 1825 and 1828, and in Liverpool the Royal Albert Dock was begun in 1874 and completed in 1880. The first stone of the modern docks in Southampton was laid in 1838 and the development of the Welsh ports, to cater for the expansion of coal and steel exports, began at about the same time. Swansea's first dock was opened in 1855, in the same year as the West Bute Dock in Cardiff.

Since 1945, British ports as a whole have been in a state of steady and in some instances spectacular decline. Most of the great engineering achievements at Liverpool and Southampton are now of purely archaeological interest, with the liner trade entirely gone – the aeroplane has taken it over – and much of the freight business transferred to more enterprising ports, such as Felixstowe, Yarmouth and Shoreham, where trade union problems have been less serious and where the facilities for container

Above left: Southampton is Britain's leading passenger port and also has a considerable cargo traffic. Its sheltered waters, which (probably because of the Isle of Wight nearby) have a double high tide, have made it a port since Roman times. Military and commercial traffic to France added to its prosperity.

Left: Brixham in Devon was the leading 19th-century fishing port in South-West Britain. A reason for this was the development here, in the 18th century, of the technique of trawling. Today the decline of the fishing industry has left Brixham largely to the tourists, though it still has a fishing fleet.

GROWING PORTS 1660–1851					
	1660	1700	1750	1801	1851
Bristol	18,000	20,000	50,000	61,000	137,000
Glasgow	11,000	12,600	23,000	77,000	345,000
Liverpool	5,100	6,000	22,000	82,000	376,000
London	486,000	550,000	657,000	1,088,000	2,481,000

The Second World War saw an enormous expansion in the building of airfields for fighter and bomber stations, and the remains of many of these can still be seen. Today's major airfields have grown up since the War. This picture shows Glasgow airport sprawling across the countryside. Modern aircraft need long runways and are very noisy; the siting of new airports is a cause of great controversy.

Croydon aerodrome in 1935. This departure hall was then considered 'magnificent'. The departure board, together with the times shown on clock faces, gives some idea of the tiny number of flights.

ships have been better. The withering away of Britain's once prosperous deep-sea fishing industry has also turned places like Hull into ghost ports, a sad process which the once great naval dockyards – Chatham, Portsmouth and Devonport – are also experiencing and which is producing a further great addition to our stock of maritime archaeology.

But there is development elsewhere. Specialist ports, like Par and Fowey for china-clay, and Aberdeen, serving the North Sea oil-rigs, are booming, and Dover, Ramsgate, Fishguard, Folkestone and the other car-ferry and hovercraft terminals have acquired a business success which would have seemed impossible 50 years ago. Marinas and yacht harbours have shown an equally impressive growth. In many small harbours along the coasts of south and south-west England, pleasure boats have taken the place of fishing boats, and in some places, such as Brighton, new harbours have been created especially for them. Where the coastal waters are unsuitable for pleasure sailing, that is, in the West and the North, the smaller ports and harbours have tended to fall into decay.

As sea ports have gone down, airports have come up. The present big airports are a post-war creation, but some of the airfields in use before 1939 are still operating. Outstanding among them is Shoreham, which opened for flying during the First World War, and still runs scheduled passenger services today, from grass runways. It is the oldest passenger airport in the world. Another all-grass veteran is at Locking, near Weston-super-Mare. Hendon and Croydon, the pre-war termini of British international flights, have long since been built over, although parts of the original buildings remain.

Even the largest airfields of the 1920s and 1930s caused few changes in the local environment. Aircraft were small and flights were few, and hard runways, where they existed, were short. But the airports and airfields demanded by today's big jets have revolutionized the landscape and affected the peace and quiet of many thousand people living in the district to an extent which is comparable to the results of railway building a century and more ago.

Britain's Inventive Genius

An invention, like a Nobel Prize, is not always what it seems. Sometimes it really is the product of a single brain — Fox Talbot's collotype negative and Harrison's chronometer were probably inventions of this kind — but more often it is the result of the combined efforts of a number of people or of the cumulative improvements brought about by a succession of scientists and technicians. There have been many occasions on which a successful patent has given X the credit for an invention, although the achievement of X would have been impossible without the previous work carried out by Y and Z. To say that a particular person 'invented' this or that is often a convenient and dramatic way of interpreting and presenting a more prosaic state of affairs, that the 'inventor' in question was the latest link in a chain of researchers and improvers.

It is also necessary to distinguish between 'inventions', which are creations of human brains and hands, and 'discoveries', which amount to the revelation of something which has been there all the time. The British 'invented' the pneumatic bicycle tyre, the steam turbine and the gas meter, but 'discovered' benzene, the electron, and the use of carbolic as an antiseptic.

Within the British Isles, both the inventors and discoverers have tended overwhelmingly to be either English or Scottish. The contribution of the Irish and Welsh has, for some unexplained reason, been in quite different fields, so that it might be more accurate to speak of the English and Scottish, rather than the British inventive genius.

A superficial look at the long list of our inventions might well suggest that the great period of what could be termed British inventions began in the 1720s and lasted for about 150 years. This would suggest that it coincided with the First Industrial Revolution, which was based on coal, steam and iron, and that it did not continue into the Second, which has depended on electricity, petroleum, aviation, a wide range of synthetic materials, and electronics. Such an interpretation of the facts is only partly true. It is not so much that British inventions became fewer as that those made in other countries became more numerous, as industrialization and scientific and technical education and research spread across the world.

At the same time, many British people of exceptional abilities found it more rewarding to emigrate. An 'American' inventor of, say, 1900 or 1930, might well have found himself classified as British, if he or his parents had not decided to settle on the other side of the Atlantic. The impressive flowering of American engineering and scientific innovation during the past hundred years or so has been due not to the talents of native American Indians, but to those of transplanted Europeans, among whom the British, of course, figured prominently. In the 18th and early 19th centuries, the British genius for invention was to be found almost exclusively in Britain; nowadays it is concealed by a variety of new national labels.

There has, even so, been a certain worsening of conditions under which the inventor or potential inventor in Britain has had to work. Technical education has been considerably better on the Continent and in Japan than in Britain. British industry and British governments have devoted inadequate resources to research and development. The prestige of the engineer and the industrialist has been lower here than elsewhere, and for too long our best brains tended to be applied to the study of the humanities, rather than to engineering, science and industrial management.

One can group the most important inventions in several different ways. It is interesting, for example, to consider them according to the industry which they particularly benefitted — textile manufacturing, food processing, electric power, and so on. Or one can plot them decade by decade, to show how the volume of inventions has varied with the years. Yet another approach is to observe the decline in importance of the individual inventor, working on his own, and the gradual domination of what one might call the institutional inventor, the leader and the front man of an industrial or academic team, paid a salary in order to develop new products and new processes and with large resources of money and equipment to draw on. In Britain, as elsewhere, an invention is something to which it is increasingly more difficult to attach one person's name.

IMPORTANT BRITISH INVENTIONS AND DISCOVERIES

Metals
1709	Abraham Darby smelts iron with coke
1740	Benjamin Huntsman produces crucible steel
1856	Henry Bessemer's converter for steel making
1868	R. F. Mushet makes tungsten steel
1875	Sidney Thomas and Percy Gilchrist's process for smelting phosphoric iron ore
1913	H. Brearley produces stainless steel

Instruments and machine tools
1622	Slide-rule invented by William Oughtred
1755	Thomas Mudge's lever escapement for watches
1772	James Watt's micrometer
1778	Jesse Ramsden's precision screw-cutting lathe
1796	Joseph Bramah's hydraulic press
c.1821	Richard Roberts' gear-cutting machine
1827	Joseph Clement's facing lathe
1839	James Nasmyth's steam hammer
1841	Joseph Whitworth's standard threads
1856	Whitworth's machine for measuring millionths of an inch

Steam power
1698	Thomas Savery patents the first steam engine put to industrial use
1705	Thomas Newcomen's pumping engine
1769	James Watt's patent for a separate condenser
1789	Watt's patent for a double-acting engine
1884	Charles Parson's steam turbine

Ships and Navigation
c.1590	Captain John Davis's quadrant or backstaff
1731	John Hadley's navigational sextant
1787	John Wilkinson builds the first iron boat
1838	The Sirius, the first ship to cross the Atlantic under continuous steam. The Archimedes, the first successful screw-steamer
1843	The Great Britain, the first screw-propelled, iron-hulled merchant ship
1959	Hovercraft invented by Christopher Cockerell

Land transport
1706	Carriage springs invented by Henry Mill
1801	Richard Trevithick's steam engine
1804	Trevithick's railway locomotive
1814	George Stephenson builds the fist efficient steam locomotive
1845	R. W. Thompson's patent for a pneumatic tyre
1885	H. J. Lawson's safety bicycle with a chain-driven back wheel
1962	Alex Moulton's small-wheeled bicycle

Air transport
1930	Frank Whittle starts jet propulsion experiments
1937	First successful jet engine tested

Building and civil engineering
1779	The first iron bridge built by Abraham Darby III
1825	Joseph Aspdin makes Patent Portland Cement
1851	Joseph Paxton's Crystal Palace, the first great iron and glass building
1854	W. B. Wilkinson's patent for reinforced concrete

Textiles and textile machinery
1589	Rev. William Lee's stocking frame
1733	John Kay's flying shuttle
1764	Thomas Hughes' spinning jenny
1767	James Hargreaves' improved spinning jenny
1769	Richard Arkwright's water-frame brings spinning into the factory system
1779	Samuel Crompton's spinning mule
1785	Edmund Cartwright's power loom
1809	John Heathcoat's lace-making machine
1883	Sir Joseph Swan makes Rayon
1941	J. R. Whinfield and J. T. Dickson invent Terylene

Agriculture and food
1787	Andrew Meikle's threshing machine
1789	Robert Ransome's cast-iron ploughshare
1877	H. and J. Bell and J. J. Cameron patent air-refrigeration plant for ships

Chemicals
1825	Michael Faraday discovers benzene
1855	Alexander Parkes makes celluloid
1856	W. H. Perkins makes the first commercially useful synthetic dyestuff
1888	J. Dewar and F. Abel produce cordite

Public utilities
1778	Joseph Bramah's valve water closet
1792	William Murdock demonstrates lighting by coal gas
1815	Samuel Clegg's gas meter
c.1845	Doulton's produce glazed stoneware drainpipes

Electricity, radio, television
1831	Michael Faraday's electric generator
1904	John Fleming's thermionic valve
1926	J. L. Baird demonstrates his television system, using mechanical scanning
1935	Robert Watson-Watt's plan for radio pulse echo aircraft detection
1956	Calder Hall, the first commercial nuclear power station in the world

The useful fringe
1824	Charles Macintosh opens his raincoat factory
1835	Charles Chubb's burglar-proof safe
1840	W. H. Fox-Talbot's collotype negative
1852	Samuel Foxes steel frames for umbrellas
1860	Frederick Walton produces cork lino
1928	Dunlop Co. develops latex foam rubber

Chapter Four

Government and the Law

The British are eccentrically unique. In a world of republics they have a monarchy stripped of any real power, but whose popularity and prestige has never been greater; they are governed by Parliament – 'the Mother of Parliaments' – which conducts its business by ancient ritual; and they possess, in English Common Law, an insular achievement which owes very little to other legal systems of the world. These institutions, and many others which, like them, have developed slowly over the centuries, may often seem illogical; in practice, however, they work with remarkable efficiency, and in so doing continue to preserve the freedoms on which the British have long set so much store.

Royal Britain: Normans and Plantagenets

The English Succession

The rival claimants to the throne are underlined: where no specific dates are given, it can be assumed that the person was a claimant through to his death. This table does not include those who may have raised a claim to the throne, and were treated on occasion as rivals; for example Theobald, the elder brother of King Stephen, who was considered but rejected as Duke of Normandy following the death of Henry I, and might therefore be considered as a claimant to the English throne; Henry, the eldest son of Henry II, often in rebellion against his father (as were his brothers), and actually crowned as joint-king in his father's lifetime; or Eleanor, the sister of Arthur of Brittany, who was kept in captivity by John and Henry III until her death in 1241.

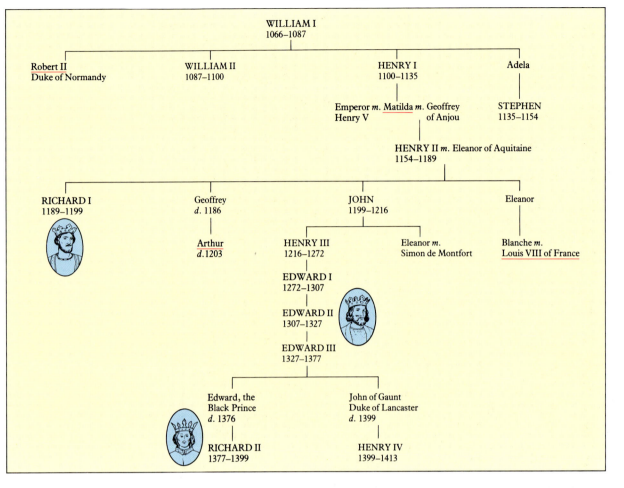

The death of Harold II at Hastings in October 1066 opened the way for the coronation of the Duke of Normandy as William at Westminster on Christmas Day 1066. His dynasty was thereby established, and his heirs retained the throne thereafter. But their tenure was by no means peaceful, and succession disputes continued until the 13th century. Most dramatic of these was the civil war between Stephen (1135–54) and his cousin, the empress Matilda, during which the King himself was captured following the battle of Lincoln (1141). The longest reign of this period, that of Henry III (1216–72), was troubled initially (1215–17) by the rival claims of France, and later by major baronial revolts, in which the King's own brother-in-law, Simon de Montfort, was a principal participant (1258–65). This period witnessed perhaps the most important battles in England in which a king participated: Lewes (1264), where the King and his son (later Edward I) were captured; Evesham (1265) and Kenilworth (1265). After the authority of Edward I (1272–1307) had waned, the incompetence of Edward II (1307–27) again produced instability, culminating in the King's forcible removal from office and eventual murder at Berkeley Castle. These events overshadowed the reigns of his successors, and may have provided the precedent for the forced abdication of Richard II in 1399.

Despite these political problems and rivalries, the status of the monarchy was nevertheless being raised, by developments within the coronation ceremony (essentially that still used) and the strengthening of the concept of hereditary right. The ceremonial itself became more elaborate and impressive; the previously strong elective element in king-making was diminished as the rite became the confirmation of a succession rather than an inauguration; and the act of anointing was interpreted as endowing the king with a semi-priestly character. The uniqueness of coronation, with the symbolic interpretation of investiture with the regalia (some fragments of which may survive from this period) as a divine grant of authority, led to the development of a formalized concept of kingship apparent in the first surviving royal portrait, of Richard II. The claims made for the Crown are also evident in the acceptance of the power to heal King's Evil (scrofula) by touch, and from the reign of Henry III in a claim to share in the saintly aura of Edward the Confessor (Richard II even using his coat of arms alongside his own). But these developments were not all one way: the coronation oath also imposed obligation on the monarchs to their subjects.

The Crown could not be divorced from politics. Kings needed to rule, and to live. England's royal heritage from this period is primarily architectural. To rule, kings need to control castles, and from the reign of the Conqueror castles were dotted throughout the land, from Dover in the south to Newcastle-upon-Tyne in the north (and, later, Berwick-upon-Tweed); from Leeds Castle in the east to Totnes in the west. But, at some stage, almost every castle in England fell, if only for a few years, into royal hands. Conversely, as the centuries passed, a number of castles were alienated from royal control. The largest such alienation occurred with the creation of the earldom (later duchy) of Lancaster for the younger son of Henry III in 1267, although most of the castles concerned reverted to the Crown with the accession of the Lancaster heir as Henry IV in 1399.

Many of the castles, such as Scarborough and Dover, were

ELEANOR CROSSES

Eleanor Crosses were built at the order of Edward I to mark the funeral route of his first wife, Eleanor of Castile, to her tomb in Westminster Abbey. Of the original twelve, only three still stand, that at Geddington being the best preserved. The most familiar cross, outside London's Charing Cross station, is a modern reconstruction. The elaborate marking of the route reflects the strong sense of monarchy with which Edward I was imbued, and which is apparent in several of his other activities, particularly his castle-building in Wales. The use of crosses to mark the route seems to be part of an attempt by the king to emulate the development of a cult of monarchy which was occurring in France at this time, following the death of Louis IX (St Louis).

for defence against external threats; others, such as those at York and other county towns, were for garrison duties and local government; yet others, such as Leeds Castle in Kent, seem to have been used more as palaces. Most of them have now decayed, either through neglect or, as at Corfe, slighted by the Parliamentarians in the Civil War and left in ruins. Others, of which the Tower of London, Windsor Castle and Bamburgh Castle are prime examples, remain largely intact, though overlaid with later accretions.

The fate of the royal castles is more than matched by the losses among the non-military royal buildings of the period 1066–1399. The medieval kings were prolific builders, but very little of their work now survives; it has either been rebuilt, or else allowed to collapse altogether. The only really major survival is Westminster Hall, begun under William II (1087–1100), but with its magnificent roof added in the reign of Richard II. Other parts of the old Palace of Westminster survived into the 19th century to be then demolished or destroyed by fire, so that only drawings remain of its former state. Often no more than the site of a royal residence is known, as at Radmore; elsewhere, for example at Cheddar and Clarendon archaeological investigation has proved more revealing.

The medieval kings, despite the demands made of them, were not expected to demand much of their subjects. The Crown was expected to 'live off its own', and to this end was endowed with extensive lands. Place-names sometimes testify to this association. But the greatest mark made on the land was in the creation of royal forests, vast hunting preserves which were not always as wooded as their title suggests. Fragments of several of them survive.

If the lives of royalty have left their mark on England, so have their deaths. For the first 150 years after the Conquest, the close association between England and the dynastic continental possessions resulted in few royal burials within England; but from the reign of John (the first king whose tomb survives, at Worcester Cathedral) all English kings were buried within the kingdom. Henry III rebuilt Westminster Abbey as a royal mausoleum, and royal burials were usually there. At times this posed problems: the body of Edward I had to be transported back from Scotland at his death (1307); while the journey of his queen, Eleanor of Castile, from her deathbed at Harby, Nottinghamshire, in 1290 was marked by the erection of Eleanor Crosses. But not all royal tombs were at Westminster: that of Edward II is in Canterbury, while his younger brother, William of Hatfield lies in York Minster.

What survives to illustrate the impact of the monarchs and the monarchy on England between the Conquest and the death of Richard II is clearly only a fragment of what there was; but it provides more than sufficient testimony to the wealth, power, authority and piety of the rulers of England during those turbulent 350 years.

The interior of Westminster Hall, with the undercroft of St Stephen's chapel, is virtually all that remains of the old Palace of Westminster. The dimensions of the Hall are essentially the same as those of the original building begun by William II, and which was in its time the largest royal hall in Europe. The original walls hide behind the reconstruction in the reign of Richard II (1377–99), who was also responsible for adding the magnificent hammerbeam roof, one of the masterpieces of medieval woodwork.

Below left: Edward III's tomb (d.1377) in Westminster Abbey.

Left: Richard II. The idealization and formalized status of the monarch is obvious in this, the first surviving contemporary portrait of an English king (ignoring manuscript illustrations, which have a doubtful resemblance to their supposed models). The status of the crown, and its elevation, was a major concern of Richard II, who also sought to proclaim his special role by adopting, along with the traditional royal arms, those popularly linked with Edward the Confessor, and thereby emphasizing a claim to some sort of Divine Right to rule.

Royal Britain: Scotland and Wales

Right: The Scottish crown jewels are the oldest surviving examples of regalia in the British Isles. The crown was made, or at least remodelled, for James V in 1540. The sceptre and sword are even older, both being gifts from popes to King James IV. The regalia was last used at a coronation when Charles II was crowned at Scone in 1651. They are now displayed in Edinburgh Castle.

The union between England and Wales in 1536, and that between England and Scotland in 1707, marked the end of a lengthy process towards linking the Celtic states with their English neighbour. From Anglo-Saxon times, the English had sought to dominate the whole of Great Britain, and this desire for domination increased from the mid-13th century. But whereas in the Welsh case conquest in the reign of Edward I (1272–1307) led to subjection, the attempts to dominate Scotland were thwarted, and the union when it eventually came was initially personal by succession, James VI of Scotland becoming James I of England in 1603, and only institutionalized by the Act of Union of 1707.

SCOTLAND

The origins of the Scottish monarchy are lost in an unfathomable past. The realm itself represents a slow accumulation of territories: the dynastic union of the Picts and Scots under Kenneth MacAlpin in the 9th century, the slow winning of the Western Isles in the 13th and 14th centuries and the acquisition of the Orkney and Shetlands in 1468–69 as the unredeemed pledge for the dowry of Margaret of Denmark, queen to James III were all important stages in the process. The complex Celtic system for succession to the Crown developed in the 12th century into the normal hereditary scheme, possibly under Norman influence. The extinction of the native line of rulers in 1290 led to a major succession crisis in which Edward I of England intervened, first to adjudge the Crown to John Baliol (1292–96), and later to try to take over the govern-

ment himself. But Robert the Bruce emerged as national champion and secured the throne, his line being succeeded in 1371 by the first of the Stewarts (the spelling was changed to Stuart by Mary Queen of Scots). That dynasty maintained a tenuous hold on the Crown thereafter, suffering civil wars, violent deaths and frequently lengthy minorities. When Charles I acceded in 1625 he was the second king in over two centuries – the first being James IV – not to require a regent in the first years of his reign.

Throughout the centuries, Scotland and England were frequently at odds. The frontier often shifted, and the conflicts were usually border skirmishes. Sometimes greater efforts were involved: David I's intervention in the English

Below: The opening stanzas of *The Kingis Quair*, written in England by King James I of Scotland during the later years of his captivity, probably in 1422–3. Only one manuscript survives – in the Bodleian Library at Oxford. It dates from about 1488. The style of the piece is similar to English poetry of the same period, and bears witness to the king's highly cultivated personality.

The origins of the Scottish monarchy are not clear but the realm itself seems to have evolved with the acquisition of lands. This began with the joining together of the Picts and Scots under Kenneth MacAlpin in the 9th century.

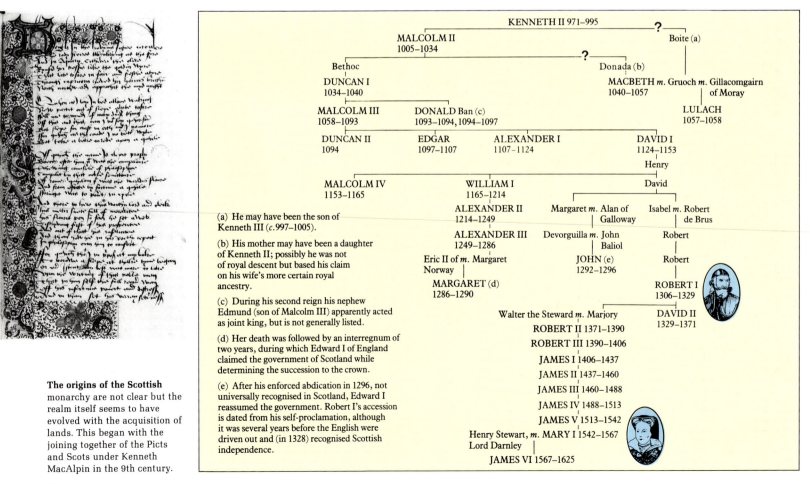

(a) He may have been the son of Kenneth III (c.997–1005).

(b) His mother may have been a daughter of Kenneth II; possibly he was not of royal descent but based his claim on his wife's more certain royal ancestry.

(c) During his second reign his nephew Edmund (son of Malcolm III) apparently acted as joint king, but is not generally listed.

(d) Her death was followed by an interregnum of two years, during which Edward I of England claimed the government of Scotland while determining the succession to the crown.

(e) After his enforced abdication in 1296, not universally recognised in Scotland, Edward I reassumed the government. Robert I's accession is dated from his self-proclamation, although it was several years before the English were driven out and (in 1328) recognised Scottish independence.

Genealogical chart:

KENNETH II 971–995

MALCOLM II 1005–1034 — Boite (a)

Bethoc — ? — Donada (b)

DUNCAN I 1034–1040 — MACBETH m. Gruoch m. Gillacomgairn of Moray 1040–1057

MALCOLM III 1058–1093 — DONALD Ban (c) 1093–1094, 1094–1097 — LULACH 1057–1058

DUNCAN II 1094 — EDGAR 1097–1107 — ALEXANDER I 1107–1124 — DAVID I 1124–1153 — Henry

MALCOLM IV 1153–1165 — WILLIAM I 1165–1214 — David

ALEXANDER II 1214–1249 — Margaret m. Alan of Galloway — Isabel m. Robert de Brus

ALEXANDER III 1249–1286 — Devorguilla m. John Baliol — Robert

Eric II of Norway m. Margaret — JOHN (e) 1292–1296 — Robert

MARGARET (d) 1286–1290 — ROBERT I 1306–1329

Walter the Steward m. Marjory — DAVID II 1329–1371

ROBERT II 1371–1390

ROBERT III 1390–1406

JAMES I 1406–1437

JAMES II 1437–1460

JAMES III 1460–1488

JAMES IV 1488–1513

JAMES V 1513–1542

Henry Stewart, m. MARY I 1542–1567 Lord Darnley

JAMES VI 1567–1625

civil wars under Stephen; the struggles for the Scottish throne in 1296–1328; the war which brought the death of James IV at Flodden in 1513; and in the 17th century the Bishops' Wars of 1639–41 and the later Cromwellian conquest.

The lengthy minorities and early deaths meant that the monarchs could rarely exert themselves, but they nevertheless left their mark. The old Celtic inauguration rituals at Scone were interrupted with the removal of the Stone of Destiny by Edward I, and thereafter the Scottish kings were instituted by coronation. But there was no specific coronation church, the inauguration being held in various locations, such as Kelso Abbey (James III) and Stirling (Mary I, James VI). Scone itself was the site of the last Scottish coronation, of Charles II in 1651. Unlike their English counterparts, the Scottish crown jewels were successfully kept out of the hands of the Cromwellians, and contain some of the oldest royal regalia in Britain.

Like their English cousins, the Scots monarchs were prolific builders, both of castles and palaces. Several survive either intact (as at Holyrood) or in ruins (as at Linlithgow). Edinburgh Castle, Stirling Castle, and Falkland Palace were also favoured residences, often reflecting the continental influences brought to the Scottish court by successive marriage alliances.

WALES

Only when the threat of an English conquest overshadowed them in the 13th century did the Welsh show signs of uniting into one state. Earlier there had been a patchwork of petty princedoms, occasionally united under one especially strong individual, such as Rhodri Mawr (844–78) or his grandson Hywel Dda (c. 918–c. 950). The three main principalities – Gwynedd in the north, centred on Aberffraw; Deheubarth in the south, based on Dynevar; and Powys in the centre, with Mathrafal as its capital – were troubled by frequent divisions of the inheritance and rivalry both within and between the dynasties. From the mid-11th century increasing Anglo-Norman penetration also posed a threat.

In the early 13th century Llewelyn I secured the supremacy of Gwynedd, but two generations later the death of Llewelyn II at Irfon Bridge in December 1282 opened the way for completion of the English conquest. This, however, was not secured for some time, as the large-scale revolt of Owain Glyndŵr – better known in England as Owen Glendower (1400–15) – made obvious.

The intended permanence of the English conquest was exemplified in the series of castles constructed by Edward I to encircle the Welsh heartland. Some of these incorporated buildings erected by the native princes. Royal influence had been felt earlier in the south, with control of some of the castles there; but only with Edward I's great enterprises (too great actually to be accomplished) did the English hand rest heavily on the Welsh. Ironically, the Act of Union of 1536 was passed under a king himself of Welsh descent: the tomb of Henry VIII's grandfather, Edmund Tudor, can still be seen in St David's cathedral.

THE EDWARDIAN CASTLES IN WALES

Rhuddlan
Beaumaris · Conway · Flint · Chester
Caernarfon · Hope
Criccieth · Dolwyddelan
Harlech · Shrewsbury
Castell-y-Bere · Montgomery
Aberystwyth
Builth
Cardigan
Carmarthen · Dynevar
Dryslwyn

▣ Castles built or wholly rebuilt by Edward I
▪ Other royal Castles
Ⓜ Castles repaired by Edward I

Above: Following his Welsh wars and the eventual conquest of Gwynedd, Edward I embarked on an ambitious building programme, establishing new royal castles and repairing a number of stone-built Welsh fortresses. In the North, his aim was clearly to encircle the Snowdonian heartland, principally by the construction of a string of fortresses along the coast but including also alterations to the ancient castle of Dolwyddelan – the birthplace of Llewellyn the Great.

Left: Stirling Castle. The original structure dates back to the 14th century, and it was a favoured royal residence during the 15th. The extensive additions made by James V reflect the French influence brought to bear on the Scottish court by his second wife, Mary of Guise. This is evident also in the remains of other contemporary palaces, making them reminiscent of French châteaux.

Above: The most ambitious of the castles planned by Edward I in Wales, Caernarfon was clearly from the first intended to be an enduring symbol of the English conquest and a fitting administrative centre for the new principality in North Wales. At the same time, its unique style reveals a more romantic side to Edward's plans. Welsh legends, influenced by the location nearby of the ruined fortress of Segontium, associated the area with the Roman emperors, especially Magnus Maximus (383–8).

Royal Britain: Lancaster and York

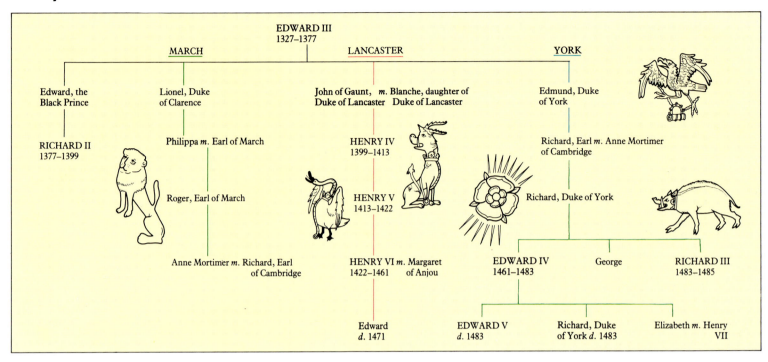

EDWARD III
1327–1377

MARCH — **LANCASTER** — **YORK**

Edward, the Black Prince

Lionel, Duke of Clarence

John of Gaunt, *m.* Blanche, daughter of Duke of Lancaster — Duke of Lancaster

Edmund, Duke of York

RICHARD II 1377–1399

Philippa *m.* Earl of March

HENRY IV 1399–1413

Richard, Earl *m.* Anne Mortimer of Cambridge

Roger, Earl of March

HENRY V 1413–1422

Richard, Duke of York

Anne Mortimer *m.* Richard, Earl of Cambridge

HENRY VI 1422–1461 *m.* Margaret of Anjou

EDWARD IV 1461–1483 — George — RICHARD III 1483–1485

Edward *d.* 1471

EDWARD V *d.* 1483

Richard, Duke of York *d.* 1483

Elizabeth *m.* Henry VII

Dynasticism was not the key element in the Wars of the Roses (itself something of a misnomer, as the badges show). Ignored in 1399, the March claim (now invested in the Duke of York) was only revived after Henry VI's humiliating loss of Normandy in 1450. Badges were crucial. Each branch of the royal house (and the King himself) had badges which were worn by household servants and retainers in peace and war and were also used to decorate buildings.

The great lands of the Duchy of Lancaster formed the power-base of the Lancastrians. Annexed to the Crown in 1399 (but preserving a separate existence to the present day), the Duchy provided both money and the key royal servants who (as the inset shows) wore gold or silver livery collars of 'SS' design.

Between 1399 and 1485 England was ruled successively by the three kings of the House of Lancaster and the three kings of the House of York. Each dynasty began with usurpation and each ended with the disaster of civil war. These events were given shape and meaning in Shakespeare's great cycle of Histories, and they received their name, the 'Wars of the Roses,' from Sir Walter Scott. Shakespeare and Scott overplayed the element of dynastic struggle but they grasped the essentials: that the chief political fact was the king's character and the chief political symbol the household badges (like the red and white roses) of the king and his lords.

Henry Bolingbroke, the exiled son of John of Gaunt, Duke of Lancaster, seized the throne in 1399 from the vainglorious and vindictive Richard II. Henry doctored genealogy to make himself 'true heir' of Henry III; he was anointed at his coronation with a specially sacred oil from the gold eagle-

shaped *ampulla* or flask which (much remade) is still in use; but his main strength came from the great Duchy of Lancaster. Nevertheless he had to face major rebellions: with his son Henry, Prince of Wales, he broke the power of the Percies at Shrewsbury in 1403; the young Prince continued his apprenticeship in war by waging a successful campaign of attrition against Glyndŵr (Owen Glendower), the Welsh patriot. Latterly, the King had bouts of prostrating illness, and he finally died in 1413. He was buried at Canterbury, under a fine alabaster effigy.

Henry V began by laying the ghost of the past. Richard II, probably murdered at Pontefract in 1400 and obscurely buried at King's Langley, was reinterred in a splendid tomb in Westminster Abbey; the dispossessed heirs of the rebels against Henry IV were restored to their former titles and estates. Then he revived the English claim to France. In 1415 Harfleur was taken and Agincourt won. In the battle – in which the flower of the French nobility was killed or captured – Henry wore in his helmet-crown the Black Prince's great irregular ruby, which is now the centrepiece of the Crown of State. Thereafter, thanks to French weakness and division, Henry carried all before him; and in 1420, by the Treaty of Troyes, he married Charles VI's daughter Catherine, thus becoming heir to the French kingdom. Two years later he was dead. His whirlwind career left little time for building, but his will made elaborate provisions for his great two-storied tomb-chapel directly behind the Confessor's shrine in Westminster Abbey.

Henry V's heir was his son Henry VI, child-King of England and France. Following in the steps of his uncle Humphrey, Duke of Gloucester, Protector during his minority, who founded Oxford University library, Henry and his Queen, Margaret of Anjou, set up major educational foundations at Eton and Cambridge. Politically, however, he was a disaster. Silly rather than saintly, he lost France and factionalized the nobility. Chief of the aggrieved was Richard, Duke of York, the heir presumptive. Helped by the powerful Earl of Warwick, York took over the government after the battle of St Albans (1455); Queen Margaret fought back; then York went further still and claimed the throne after his victory at Northampton (1460). Finally he

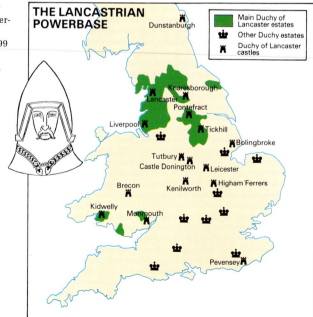

THE LANCASTRIAN POWERBASE

Dunstanburgh

	Main Duchy of Lancaster estates
	Other Duchy estates
	Duchy of Lancaster castles

Knaresborough
Lancaster
Pontefract
Liverpool
Tickhill
Bolingbroke
Tutbury
Castle Donington
Leicester
Brecon
Kenilworth
Higham Ferrers
Kidwelly
Monmouth
Pevensey

TITLES AND HONOURS

All officially recognized titles in the United Kingdom derive directly or indirectly from the sole 'Fount of Honour', the Sovereign. Only the Queen herself, and Queen Elizabeth the Queen Mother, have the right to the honorific title Her (or Your) Majesty (H.M.). The Prince of Wales, the Duke of Edinburgh and other members of the Royal Family bear the title of His (or Her) Royal Highness (H.R.H.).

The Peerage consists of five ranks – in diminishing order of seniority these are Dukes, Marquesses, Earls, Viscounts and Barons. The last four of these can all be referred to as 'Lord'; thus the Marquess of Salisbury is often known as 'Lord Salisbury'. All are members of the House of Lords, and until 1958 all were hereditary; since that year there has been an additional category of non-hereditary 'Life Peers', with the rank of Baron.

Below the Peerage and with no automatic seat in Parliament are two more ranks which carry the title 'Sir', always used with the Christian name. These are Baronets, where the title is hereditary, and Knights, where it is not. Their wives are known as 'Lady' – used, however, with the surname only.

When 'Lord' and 'Lady' are used with the Christian name as well as the surname (e.g. Lord David Cecil, Lady Antonia Fraser) these are known as 'courtesy titles' and merely signify that the bearer is the son or daughter of a duke or marquess – or, in the case of daughters only, an earl.

There are several orders of Chivalry, of which the senior is the Order of the Garter (K.G.). This has no other grades. The other orders have up to five grades. The Order of the British Empire will serve as a good example: within it are the Knights Grand Cross (G.B.E.), the Knights Commander (K.B.E.), the Commanders (C.B.E.), the Officers (O.B.E.) and the Members (M.B.E.). The two senior grades carry the title 'Sir'. Female holders of the second grade are known as 'Dames', and the 'K' is changed to 'D', i.e. D.B.E. The other principal Orders of Chivalry are those of the Bath (G.C.B., etc.), St Michael and St George (G.C.M.G., etc.) and the Royal Victorian Order (G.C.V.O., etc.).

There are in addition two orders normally awarded to outstanding figures in the Arts and Sciences; the Order of Merit (O.M.) and the Order of the Companions of Honour (C.H.).

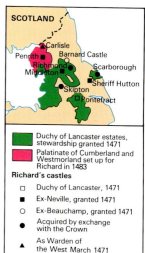

Duchy of Lancaster estates, stewardship granted 1471
Palatinate of Cumberland and Westmorland set up for Richard in 1483
Richard's castles
□ Duchy of Lancaster, 1471
■ Ex-Neville, granted 1471
○ Ex-Beauchamp, granted 1471
● Acquired by exchange with the Crown
▲ As Warden of the West March 1471

was defeated at Wakefield in 1460 and executed. Desperate, Warwick's faction gave their allegiance to Richard's son Edward, Earl of March, proclaimed him King as Edward IV, and then won the crushing victory at Towton. Henry VI himself was captured and imprisoned in the Tower in 1464.

Edward IV, however, held the throne only by courtesy of Warwick, and in 1469–70 he was driven into exile by an unholy alliance of Warwick, Clarence (his own brother) and Queen Margaret. But Clarence soon betrayed his allies; in 1471 Edward returned to defeat Warwick at Barnet and Margaret at Tewkesbury. It was the end of the Lancastrians. Henry VI, nominally restored during Edward's exile, was murdered and buried at Chertsey. Secure and increasingly rich, Edward now began to build at St George's, Windsor (where he is buried), Fotheringhay, Canterbury and Eltham.

But despite his successes, Edward's Queen, Elizabeth Woodville, and her upstart family sowed dangerous dissent.

After the King's premature death in 1483, his brother Richard of Gloucester exploited these divisions to make himself first Protector to the young Edward V and then King. On his way to the throne he eliminated his opponents; subsequently he murdered both Edward and his brother Richard, whose presumed remains were reburied at Westminster in 1674.

Richard III's strength was in the north; in the south he was a hated interloper, whose only real support came from a handful of die-hard Lancastrians. These he conciliated by giving Henry VI honourable burial at Windsor. In contrast, the leading southern gentry, the Yorkist backbone, rose in 1483. They failed but had their revenge two years later when Richard was defeated and killed at Bosworth. He was buried obscurely at Leicester; after the Reformation his bones were thrown out and the coffin used as a horse-trough. Even that has gone.

Richard's lands, castles and privileges in the North made him the mightiest of subjects. Even after he became Richard III, Northerners made up the bulk of his servants and, following the rebellions of 1483, he planted them in the South like colonists.
King's College Chapel, Cambridge is the most magnificent example of Perpendicular architecture in England. Begun by Henry VI in 1446, it was not completed until 1515. Every Christmas Eve the famous Festival of Nine Lessons and Carols is held there.

The plans for Henry VI's linked foundations of Eton and King's College, Cambridge emerged only slowly. Even then they were bedevilled by frequent and ever more grandiose changes of plan: at Eton (below) all the work carried out under stages 1 and 2 (to 1448) was demolished to make way for plan 3 (1449). Only the chancel was finished at Henry VI's death and the remainder was abandoned; at King's, even less was completed in Henry's lifetime.

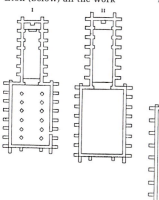

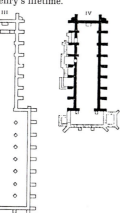

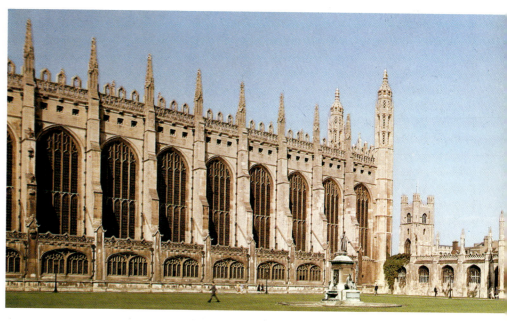

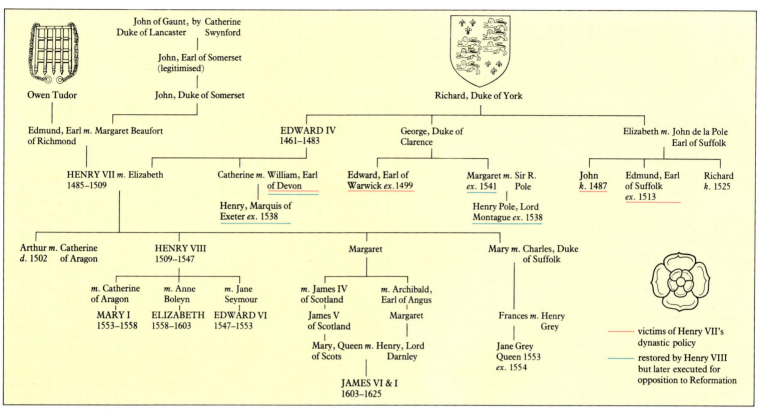

Family tree:

John of Gaunt, by Catherine
Duke of Lancaster Swynford
|
John, Earl of Somerset
(legitimised)
|
Owen Tudor   John, Duke of Somerset   Richard, Duke of York

Edmund, Earl *m.* Margaret Beaufort
of Richmond

EDWARD IV
1461–1483

George, Duke of
Clarence

Elizabeth *m.* John de la Pole
Earl of Suffolk

HENRY VII *m.* Elizabeth
1485–1509

Catherine *m.* William, Earl
of Devon

Edward, Earl of
Warwick *ex.* 1499

Margaret *m.* Sir R.
ex. 1541   Pole

John
k. 1487

Edmund, Earl
of Suffolk
ex. 1513

Richard
k. 1525

Henry, Marquis of
Exeter *ex.* 1538

Henry Pole, Lord
Montague *ex.* 1538

Arthur *m.* Catherine
d. 1502   of Aragon

HENRY VIII
1509–1547

Margaret

Mary *m.* Charles, Duke
of Suffolk

m. Catherine
of Aragon
MARY I
1553–1558

m. Anne
Boleyn
ELIZABETH
1558–1603

m. Jane
Seymour
EDWARD VI
1547–1553

m. James IV
of Scotland
James V
of Scotland

m. Archibald,
Earl of Angus
Margaret

Frances *m.* Henry
Grey
Jane Grey
Queen 1553
ex. 1554

Mary, Queen *m.* Henry, Lord
of Scots   Darnley

JAMES VI & I
1603–1625

— victims of Henry VII's
dynastic policy

— restored by Henry VIII
but later executed for
opposition to Reformation

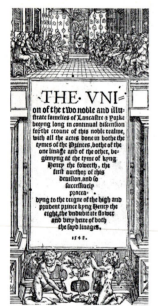

The title-page of Hall's
Chronicle, whose intertwining
roses celebrate the 'Union of
the two noble and illustrate
families of Lancaster and
York', and its culmination in
the 'Triumphal Reign of
Henry VIII'!

The Tudor Succession

With a weak claim to the throne, Henry VII's dynastic policy was harsh; more secure, as the title-page to Hall's *Chronicle* suggests, Henry VIII at first reversed it (save for the vendetta against the de la Poles), but many of the beneficiaries later opposed the Reformation and were executed. Henry VIII's own marriages created a second crisis, which was made worse by the failure of his children to produce heirs. In this eventuality, the King's will had excluded the descendants of his elder sister, Margaret, in favour of the issue of his younger sister Mary. But the former were to succeed in the person of James I (VI of Scotland).

The Tudors, perhaps the most remarkable English dynasty, came to the throne against all the odds. In 1483 the Yorkists were solidly established and it was only Richard III's murderous ambition – not Lancastrian sentiment that was virtually non-existent – that opened the way to the obscure young Henry Tudor's victory at Bosworth in August 1485. Moreover, though Tudor propaganda constantly emphasized the theme of dynastic unity, Henry VII in practice followed in the footsteps of Edward IV. Thus he completed Edward's rebuilding of St George's Chapel, Windsor, and continued the main lines of his policy – peace and money-making. But Henry VII went further; the reorganization of his court, its magnificence and his ruthless dynastic policy distanced him from the nobility; while his hold over the localities and the South-East in particular was strengthened through his huge number of gentlemen servants. The most hard-working as well as the most isolated of kings, he died in 1509 and was buried in the great Henry VII Chapel at Westminster that is both the symbol and the summary of his regime.

Henry VIII, who began his reign as a handsome athlete and ended it as a bloated monster, broke with some aspects of his father's policy. His thirst for pleasure led to favouritism and faction, while his vainglory demanded ruinously expensive wars against France (in 1513 and 1544) and scarcely less costly summit conferences like the Field of Cloth of Gold in 1520. Nevertheless, for all his idleness and changeability, the Tudor achievement was preserved and even extended: brilliantly projected by Holbein, his superficially overwhelming personality dominated the public political stage (whatever went on in private) while his acquisition and building of palaces – unprecedented in both numbers and magnificence – provided the setting for the English monarchy until the catastrophe of the Civil War.

But it was his dynasticism that was decisive. For – despite the early orthodoxy that had earned him the title 'Defender of the Faith' from the Pope – his search for a male heir drove him to repudiate his Queen, Catherine of Aragon (who had produced only a daughter) and to marry Anne Boleyn. In so doing he opened the corridors of power to the small group of intellectuals and aristocrats who engineered the break with Rome and shaped the main course of the English Reformation. Their leaders, Anne Boleyn herself and the minister Thomas Cromwell, were executed but the 'Reforming' clique survived and with Henry's death in 1547 seized control of the government of his son and successor, the young Edward VI.

The Reformation (despite the advanced Renaissance taste of some of the first generation of Reformers) emphasized the verbal rather than the visual: words not things. The result (especially when combined with the financial crisis arising from Henry VIII's last wars) was a collapse of royal artistic patronage; the buildings of Henry VIII's death-bed foundation of Trinity College, Cambridge were not completed until the end of the century and even his vast tomb at Windsor was left unfinished. The King was buried instead under a plain slab – as Edward VI was to be at Westminster. Even the accession in 1553 of Edward's half-sister Mary, the resolutely Papist daughter of Catherine of Aragon, changed little. Edward the Confessor's shrine at Westminster – dismantled rather than smashed in the 1530s –

Elizabeth's portraits, which were carefully regulated to approved models, are her principal monument. The legend 'Queen Elizabeth slept here', can only begin to be true within the points marked on the map below, as her progresses never ventured farther.

was partially restored, but Mary's Catholicism, legalistic not evangelical, inspired none of the fervent artistic glories of the Continental Counter-Reformation. And in any case it was soon over. Mary, who had married Philip of Spain, died childless in 1558 (her tomb is in the Henry VII Chapel) and was succeeded by Elizabeth I, daughter of Anne Boleyn. (Elizabeth received news of her accession in the Old Palace at Hatfield which still stands.) Rome was repudiated again and a Church set up that was reformed in doctrine, though conservative in government and ceremonial. The latter reflected Elizabeth's own taste which – as her portraits show – was ornate and traditional. But this taste received little direct expression since Elizabeth carefully husbanded her resources and instead of building new palaces relied on being invited to the 'prodigy houses' of her favourites and councillors.

All that she saved and more, however, was spent in coping with wars and rebellions, most of which involved her silly and scheming cousin Mary, Queen of Scots, who had to flee from her outraged subjects to refuge in England in 1586. And even Mary's embarrassing execution in 1587 played a part in precipitating the Spanish Armada.

But the Armada, the greatest challenge to her regime, showed the Queen at her best. At Tilbury, mounted and with a marshal's baton in her hand, she reviewed her troops and flung defiance at Spain. For Elizabeth – humanistically educated and always interested in learning, as her progress at Oxford and Cambridge shows – her supreme artistic achievement was herself: that creation of an image of monarchy which dazzled her own subjects almost to the last and presented her successors with a model that could only expose their own insufficiencies. She died in 1603 and was buried in Henry VII's chapel. Her successor James I (VI), who had been anxious to ensure his own succession to England to help his mother, Mary, Queen of Scots, while she lived, reinterred her, in an equally splendid tomb, immediately opposite.

The dynastic shrine
Henry VII's Chapel, Westminster, built between 1503 and 1519, was conceived as a shrine for Henry VI, whose (never-achieved) canonization as king-and-martyr was intended to put the ultimate accolade of respectability on the usurping Tudor dynasty.

But even without its centrepiece, the Chapel gives the lie to the two usual assumptions about its builder: its ornate magnificence shows that Henry VII was no miser; while the riot of royal badges in metal and stone demonstrates that Henry, far from destroying bastard feudalism (as the

system of badge-wearing is known) in fact enthusiastically supported it.

Henry VIII's 50-odd palaces, densely concentrated round London, were all organized on the same basic plan (below). Henry's successors disposed of most of this great heritage.

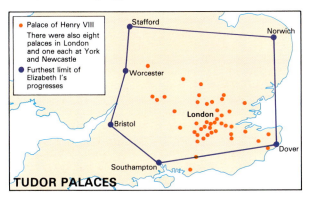

TUDOR PALACES

- • Palace of Henry VIII
  There were also eight palaces in London and one each at York and Newcastle
- • Furthest limit of Elizabeth I's progresses

Stafford
Norwich
Worcester
Bristol
London
Dover
Southampton

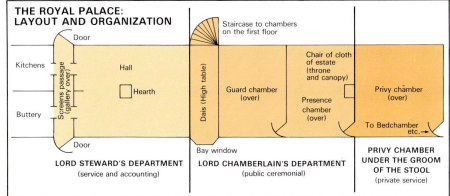

THE ROYAL PALACE: LAYOUT AND ORGANIZATION

Staircase to chambers on the first floor
Door
Kitchens
Screens passage (gallery over)
Hall
Hearth
Buttery
Dais (High table)
Chair of cloth of estate (throne and canopy)
Guard chamber (over)
Presence chamber (over)
Privy chamber (over)
To Bedchamber etc.→
Door
Bay window

LORD STEWARD'S DEPARTMENT (service and accounting)

LORD CHAMBERLAIN'S DEPARTMENT (public ceremonial)

PRIVY CHAMBER UNDER THE GROOM OF THE STOOL (private service)

Royal Britain: The Stuarts

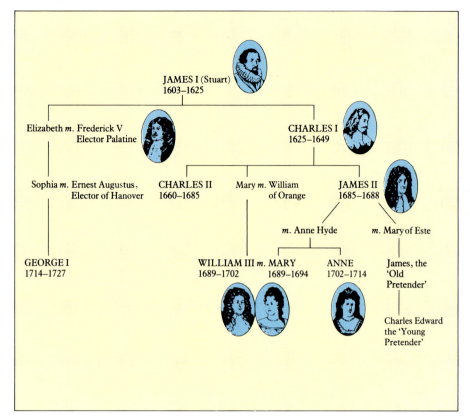

JAMES I (Stuart)
1603–1625

Elizabeth *m.* Frederick V
Elector Palatine

CHARLES I
1625–1649

Sophia *m.* Ernest Augustus,
Elector of Hanover

CHARLES II
1660–1685

Mary *m.* William
of Orange

JAMES II
1685–1688

m. Anne Hyde

m. Mary of Este

GEORGE I
1714–1727

WILLIAM III *m.* MARY
1689–1702   1689–1694

ANNE
1702–1714

James, the
'Old
Pretender'

Charles Edward
the 'Young
Pretender'

increased the power of the navy. James I held a conference out of which grew the Authorized Version of the Bible. Charles II gave a character to the Royal Society, of which in due course Isaac Newton was elected Fellow, (see page 175).

It is to the more extravagant monarchs that we owe our greatest heritage. Foremost in this respect was Charles I, who formed one of the greatest of all royal collections. This was dispersed after his execution but much has survived and been retrieved. The Banqueting Hall in Whitehall is the finest survival of his reign. Built by Inigo Jones in 1622, it possesses a magnificent ceiling by Rubens, the only major such decoration to remain in its original setting. Inigo Jones also built the Queen's House at Greenwich and Queen's Chapel in St James's Palace. Charles I was the patron of Rubens and Van Dyck, 26 of whose works are in the royal collection today. He founded the Mortlake tapestry factory, an example of whose work can be seen on the rear of the altar at St George's Chapel, Windsor. His library of one thousand manuscripts and books from the very earliest days of printing is now kept in the British Museum.

Charles II also loved pictures and at his Restoration set about the recovery of Charles I's collections. He appointed Peter Lely to be the King's Painter. He acquired new Coronation regalia, much of which is still used and can be seen in the Tower of London. He was a patron of the theatre and of racing. He instituted the Royal Gold Plate races at Newmarket, while Queen Anne later created Royal Ascot, with the Sovereign's procession up the course, still a feature of the June meeting. Charles II began to make Windsor Castle more comfortable, commissioning Hugh May to build new apartments for himself and the Queen. Of these, the Queen's Presence Chamber is the best lasting example with its painted ceiling by Verrio and carvings by Grinling Gibbons. Also during this reign, 779 drawings by Leonardo da Vinci, spanning his artistic life, were added to the Royal Library.

Yachtsmen brothers

Navigation interested both Charles II and his brother, James II. They were keen yachtsmen at a time when the designing of yachts was improving rapidly. Yacht racing dates from this period. Charles II founded the Royal Observatory at Greenwich for the study of navigation. He established a permanent British Army and founded the Royal Hospital at Chelsea, commissioning Sir Christopher Wren to design it. Wren went on to build the Fountain Court at Hampton Court and to redesign the fronts of the Palace. In Mary II's reign, Wren's pupil, Nicholas Hawksmoor, completed the Greenwich Hospital, now deemed one of Britain's finest buildings.

Mary II was also responsible for the decoration of Hampton Court. She added important Dutch furniture and fine Delft china. After her death, William III lost interest in Hampton Court, though he and later Queen Anne created the gardens there to designs by Henry Wise. It was William III who bought Nottingham House and converted it into Kensington Palace. Once again Wren did the remodelling. Kensington Palace is now the London home of the Prince and Princess of Wales and other members of the Royal family.

Queen Anne's reign, in which occurred the great victories of Blenheim and Ramillies, found her mainly at St James's Palace. Here she built a ballroom and a suite of state rooms. At last the Crown was stable and parliamentary monarchy established. Queen Anne was succeeded by her Hanoverian second cousin, George I.

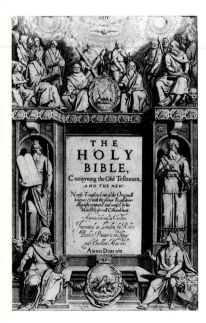

The frontispiece of the Authorized or King James' Version of the Bible. The result of a religious conference called by King James I at Hampton Court in 1611 the A.V. has probably had a deeper influence on the thought and literature of the English-speaking world than any other book ever published and is an abiding part of Britain's literary heritage.

The Stuarts, founded by James VI of Scotland, were an unlucky house, whose kings resisted as best they could the growth of English parliamentary democracy. With the exception of Charles II and William III they lacked statesmanship. There were no great military glories until Queen Anne's reign and the only great naval victory was the defeat of the Dutch in 1665. Meanwhile Parliament grew in stature and power. The increasing wealth of the country gentry and merchant classes brought the House of Commons into the front line. The Stuarts were forever in conflict with Parliament over religion and money and during the century of their dynasty there was civil war, the execution of Charles I and the permanent exile of James II. After the Glorious Revolution the doctrine of the Divine Right of Kings was laid aside for ever, the Crown was no longer permitted to raise a standing army in peace time, and Parliaments had to be summoned at least every three years, lasting no longer than that period.

Meanwhile there was tremendous economic growth in Britain. Science, literature and the arts flourished. Charles I and Charles II encouraged colonization and Charles II

ROYAL MONUMENTS

Charles I is in Whitehall; Charles II is in the centre court of the Royal Hospital, Chelsea; James II (by Grinling Gibbons) is in front of the National Gallery; William III is in St James's Square and Kensington Palace Gardens, and Queen Anne outside St Paul's Cathedral and in Queen Anne's Gate.

ROYAL TOMBS

James I and his Queen, Charles I, Anne (wife of James II), William III, Mary II, Queen Anne and George of Denmark are buried in Westminster Abbey. Charles II is buried in a vault in St George's Chapel, Windsor. Queens Henrietta Maria and Catherine of Breganza are buried abroad, and James II lies at St Germain in France.

The Banqueting Hall, Whitehall, was built by Inigo Jones in 1619–22 and is the finest survival of James I's reign. The magnificent ceiling panels by Rubens represent the 'Apotheosis of James I' and the 'Union of England and Scotland'.

Royal Britain: The Hanoverians

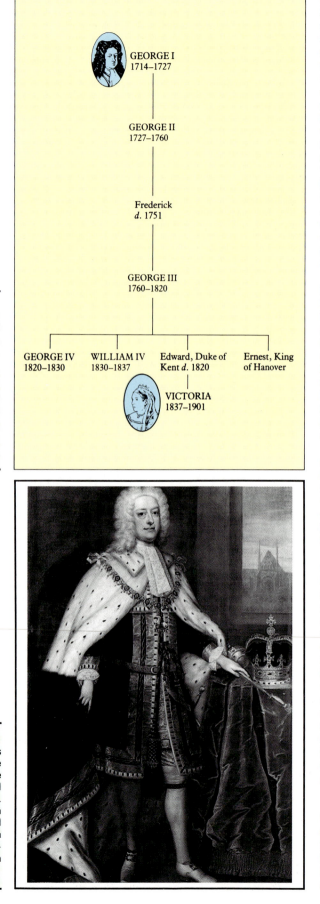

GEORGE I
1714–1727

GEORGE II
1727–1760

Frederick
d. 1751

GEORGE III
1760–1820

GEORGE IV
1820–1830

WILLIAM IV
1830–1837

Edward, Duke of
Kent *d.* 1820

Ernest, King
of Hanover

VICTORIA
1837–1901

George I (1714–27), the grandson of Charles I's sister Elizabeth, succeeded to the throne at the age of 54. He spoke no English and had deserted his wife 20 years earlier in favour of two German mistresses nicknamed the Maypole and the Elephant. He arrived from Hanover surrounded by German advisers and with the reputation of being a brave soldier. He was not a man of taste, though Handel composed the Water Music for him. During his reign the royal prerogative was further curtailed owing to the King's frequent absence from cabinet meetings, partly because he was often in Hanover and partly because he was uninterested in English politics. Thus, by 1721, with the Whigs reigning supreme, the way was paved for the rise of Walpole, the first Prime Minister. During his reign the King lived modestly, although he did commission William Kent to remodel the state rooms at Kensington Palace, London, and to redecorate Wren's staircase there. Kensington Gardens were completed in 1731 and the Serpentine created in its present form. Sir James Thornhill was meanwhile completing the ceiling of the Painted Hall at Greenwich Hospital.

George II (1727–60) was the last British monarch to lead his troops to war – at Dettingen in 1743. He did speak English but still with a strong German accent. He gave way frequently to Parliament, whose power continued to grow steadily. Meanwhile British influence was rapidly growing in Canada, and also in India – the King had a great admiration for Clive. George II loved the army, remodelled Horse Guards Parade where Trooping the Colour takes place today, and was a patron of musicians, especially of Handel. His Queen, Caroline, was very intelligent. She enhanced the Royal Collection by buying a set of royal portraits from Lord Cornwallis and she discovered a collection of Holbein drawings at Kensington Palace.

George's ill-fated son, Frederick, Prince of Wales, formed an outstanding collection of Spanish, Italian, French and Flemish paintings. He got William Kent to build his house at Kew and the Royal Botanical Gardens began there. His widow built the Orangery and Sir William Chambers designed the octagonal Pagoda. William Kent also made the Prince's state barge, which is now in the National Martitime Museum.

George III (1760–1820) who succeeded his grandfather, was wholly English, a popular man with simple tastes. Known as Farmer George, he was an enthusiastic cattle and sheep farmer; but he was also the first monarch to study physics, chemistry and astronomy. He set an example of happy domesticity and assumed the role of country squire, travelling informally among his people. This is one of the roles of the sovereign today. He is also remembered as the king who resisted Catholic emancipation and who lost the American colonies. Among his lasting achievements were the founding of the Royal Academy and the endowing of the British Library with 67,000 books. He purchased the collection of Consul Smith at Venice in 1762 and commissioned works by Gainsborough, Zoffany and Allan Ramsay. Towards the end of his life he suffered increasingly from fits of insanity and his son – later to become king as George IV – assumed, with the title of Prince Regent, the duties of kingship for the last ten years of his father's life.

Unparalleled magnificance
George IV (1820–30) was too dedicated to pleasure to keep control of what survived of the royal prerogative, and he was unpopular because of his unseemly private life and his extravagance. Nevertheless he was a great lover and connoisseur of the arts. He was the leader of fashion and

The Waterloo Chamber, Windsor was built by George IV as a memorial to the great battle.

Brighton Pavilion – one of George IV's many lasting architectural achievements With its onion-shaped domes and small minarets it creates an exotic skyline.

established an informal relationship between the monarch and society. He was the first king since the 17th century to visit Scotland, where he re-opened Holyroodhouse, and Ireland.

Among George IV's many lasting achievements are the improvements at Windsor Castle and the creation of the Brighton Pavilion. At Windsor, with the architect Sir Jeffry Wyatville, he set about a massive medievalization (doubling the height of the Round Tower) and roofed in an open courtyard to form the Waterloo Chamber as a memorial to the great battle. In London he commissioned John Nash to turn Buckingham House into a Palace, at a cost which became a national scandal and gave rise in 1828 to a parliamentary enquiry. The King patronized the Royal Institution, founded the Royal Society of Literature and brought the National Gallery into being. Forever in debt, he spent huge sums on tapestries, rugs, jewels, theatrical prints, Dutch and Flemish paintings and military accoutrements. (These last are now in the Queen's Guard Chamber at Windsor Castle.) He commissioned works from painters such as George Stubbs. He created for the monarchy an unparalleled magnificence and bequeathed to us much of our finest heritage today.

William IV (1830–37), the Sailor King, was a great support to his ministers and consequently a relief after George IV. He was the last sovereign ever to dismiss his Government. He and Queen Adelaide were much more accessible to their subjects than previous sovereigns. He added two rings to the coronation regalia and bought porcelain. During his reign much of the architectural work begun by George IV was completed. In 1837 he was succeeded by his niece, Queen Victoria.

Royal Britain: From Queen Victoria to Today

ROYAL TOMBS
Queen Victoria and Prince Albert are buried in the Royal Mausoleum at Frogmore. Edward VII and Queen Alexandra, and George V and Queen Mary have tombs within St George's Chapel, Windsor. Edward VIII is buried in the private burial ground at Frogmore and George VI is buried in the King George VI Memorial Chapel in St George's Chapel.

Queen Victoria (1837–1901) inherited the throne at the age of 18. In her long reign she rescued the monarchy from a period of unpopularity and brought it to a position of public respect and affection not known since the days of Elizabeth I. In the later years of her reign she wielded considerable political influence, with a first-hand knowledge of politics acquired at a time when her ministers were still at school. And in Prince Albert she had a husband who understood the British thoroughly and helped the development of a constitutional monarchy. Believing that art had an uplifting influence on society, he patronized sculptors and painters. He bought German, Italian and French art, favoured Winterhalter, and was a leading figure in the creation of the complex of museums at South Kensington. Prince Albert also designed the Royal Dairy at Windsor, created jewellery for his wife and was a patron of the

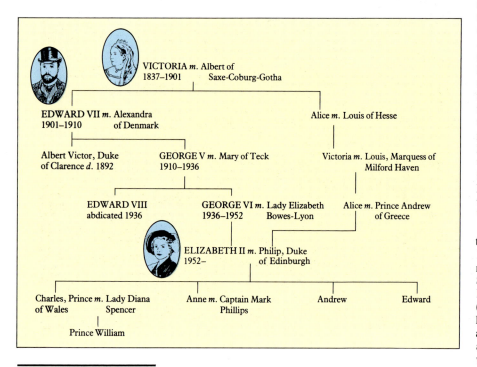

VICTORIA *m.* Albert of
1837–1901   Saxe-Coburg-Gotha

EDWARD VII *m.* Alexandra
1901–1910   of Denmark

Alice *m.* Louis of Hesse

Albert Victor, Duke
of Clarence *d.* 1892

GEORGE V *m.* Mary of Teck
1910–1936

Victoria *m.* Louis, Marquess of
Milford Haven

EDWARD VIII
abdicated 1936

GEORGE VI *m.* Lady Elizabeth
1936–1952   Bowes-Lyon

Alice *m.* Prince Andrew
of Greece

ELIZABETH II *m.* Philip, Duke
1952–   of Edinburgh

Charles, Prince *m.* Lady Diana
of Wales   Spencer

Anne *m.* Captain Mark
Phillips

Andrew

Edward

Prince William

ROYAL MONUMENTS
Queen Victoria's most famous memorial is the one by Sir Aston Webb outside Buckingham Palace. She can also be seen at Blackfriars' Bridge, London, in Kensington Gardens, and with the Prince of Wales at Temple Bar. The Albert Memorial by Sir Gilbert Scott is opposite the Albert Hall. Edward VII has an equestrian statue at Waterloo Place, George V faces the House of Lords and George VI is in Carlton Gardens.

composer Mendelssohn. The Queen and the Prince Consort undertook many royal tours throughout the land, being seen by as many subjects as possible. They bought Osborne and Balmoral, and extensive work was carried out in both properties. They catalogued the drawings at Windsor and established the very comprehensive photographic collection there. In London, Marble Arch was moved to its present site from outside Buckingham Palace, where a new ballroom was built for grand entertaining and the balcony added, now so much a focal point of great royal events. The Palace of Westminster was also rebuilt, following the fire of 1834. After Prince Albert's death in 1861 Queen Victoria constructed the Royal Mausoleum at Frogmore and erected the Albert Memorial in Kensington, on the site of the Great Exhibition of 1851 for which he had provided much of the inspiration and driving force. She became Empress of India, and at Osborne the Durbar Room represents her interest in her new empire. In the eyes of her subjects the Queen was a great matriarch and her two Jubilees (1887 and 1891) were times of national rejoicing.

Edward VII (1901–10) succeeded when he was 59. In his long years as Prince of Wales he had established the royal practice of visiting hospitals and laying foundation stones. An accomplished public speaker, he travelled abroad,

developing the talent for diplomacy which bore fruit in the *Entente Cordiale* with France. He was a most sociable monarch with an aptitude for mixing pleasure and business. He loved shooting, racing (his horse, Persimmon, won the Derby in 1896), regattas, early motoring and the theatre. He and the unfailingly elegant Queen Alexandra – she was the daughter of King Christian IX of Denmark – led their lives fully in the public eye, giving magnificent dinners and balls. He was particularly popular with the working class, though the middle class was censorious of his gambling and promiscuity. As Prince of Wales he acquired Sandringham in Norfolk, furnishing it and laying out the gardens. Here he and Queen Alexandra lived in an atmosphere of friendly domesticity, which later generations of royalty have continued to enjoy.

George V (1910–36) was more reserved. He had a difficult reign which encompassed the Great War, the General Strike of 1926 and other crises, yet he dealt sensibly and carefully with all the political problems that arose. His dominions extended farther than those of any monarch before or since. Significantly he was the only British king to wear the Indian Crown – at the Delhi Durbar of 1911. In 1932 he became the first king to broadcast to the nation. George V's great passion was his stamp collection to which he devoted three afternoons a week. Queen Mary was an avid collector of furniture, antiques, porcelain and notably of Chinese snuff boxes. She restored to the Brighton Pavilion much of its original furniture. In Edinburgh work was also undertaken at Holyroodhouse. In the 1920s the Queen was presented with a Doll's House, designed by Sir Edwin Lutyens, in which all the contents are perfect working reproductions in miniature. It can now be seen at Windsor Castle.

Edward VIII who had been a popular and widely travelled Prince of Wales reigned for only a few months in 1936. In December of that year he abdicated in order to marry a twice-divorced American lady, Mrs Wallis Simpson. He was made Duke of Windsor and lived mostly in France until his death. The reign of his brother George VI (1936–52) was overshadowed by the Second World War. His health was never good, he suffered from a bad stammer and was very shy. But in his wife, Queen Elizabeth, he had an admirable support. The war and the way they coped with it made heroes of them both. The King oversaw the creation of the Valley Gardens and Savill Gardens and took a keen interest in the garden at Royal Lodge, Windsor. The Queen Mother has continued to collect since the King's death, buying Chelsea porcelain for Clarence House and restoring the Castle of Mey in Scotland.

The present Queen, Elizabeth II, succeeded her father in 1952. She continues to work extremely hard and has a deep interest in the Commonwealth, visiting its member countries as often as possible and presiding over its conferences. She is yet more informal with her people, and the royal walkabout is now a popular part of a royal visit. To the royal collection, she and Prince Philip have added many contemporary paintings including works by L. S. Lowry and Graham Sutherland. In 1962 she opened the Queen's Gallery at Buckingham Palace where royal exhibitions are held. The Royal Yacht *Britannia* was commissioned in 1959 for use, among other duties, on overseas tours. The monarchy today has adapted to the demands of television, allowing the cameras behind the scenes on many occasions in the last decade. Besides showing the Queen at work, television has also enabled millions of viewers to appreciate the artistic heritage of Britain's sovereigns from the mists of ancient times to the present day.

Above: The Durbar Room at Osborne represents Queen Victoria's interest in her new Empire after she became Empress of India.

Below: Edward VII as Prince of Wales boards a motor car for the first time on 4th July 1900. He was to add motoring to his other interests – racing, shooting and the theatre.

George V delivering his Christmas broadcast – the first king to do so – and starting a tradition which has continued to this day.

Adapting to informal times. Her Majesty the Queen on a walkabout in Birmingham. Her tireless dedication has enhanced British pride in constitutional monarchy.

The Government of Britain: Parliament

Britain, it is often supposed, is governed by Parliament; and Parliament represents the people. To a Prime Minister with a secure majority, or a Permanent Secretary in Whitehall, this must seem a convenient myth. Realistically Parliament's functions are to formulate and express opinions, to protest against misdeeds of government, to give publicity to some of the governing process, and to ensure that a ministry that loses support will eventually be thrown out. It does so without making government unstable or ineffective. This may not be the ideal form of democratic government; but no modern nation has found one manifestly better.

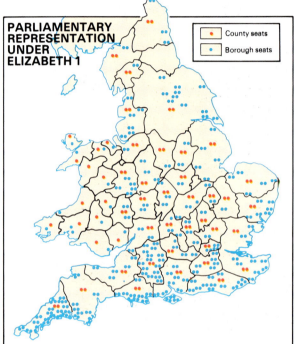

PARLIAMENTARY REPRESENTATION UNDER ELIZABETH 1

County seats
Borough seats

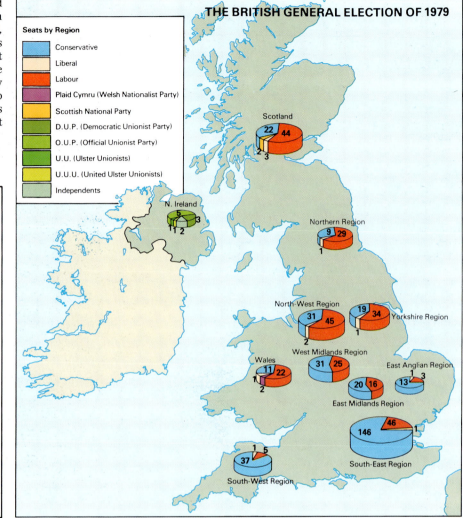

THE BRITISH GENERAL ELECTION OF 1979

Seats by Region

- Conservative
- Liberal
- Labour
- Plaid Cymru (Welsh Nationalist Party)
- Scottish National Party
- D.U.P. (Democratic Unionist Party)
- O.U.P. (Official Unionist Party)
- U.U. (Ulster Unionists)
- U.U.U. (United Ulster Unionists)
- Independents

Parliamentary representation during the reign of Queen Elizabeth I. A few more boroughs were created in the early 17th century; otherwise the system changed little before the Reform Act of 1832. Notice that the number of seats varied irrationally from 44 in Cornwall to none in County Durham.

Above right: The results in the 1979 general election, showing the proportion of seats held by the different parties in each region.

The earliest assemblies recognizable as parliaments, in the 13th century, originated mainly in conflicts between kings and noblemen. But from the beginning an 'estate' of the commons was there too, formed of the 'knights' of each shire and an assortment of 'burgesses' from boroughs. They were summoned partly to hear, and convey to their communities, the wishes of the king, partly to bring to him the grievances of his subjects. Petitions became their main business. Very slowly there evolved the procedure by which redress of grievances and acceptance of royal policies could be embodied in Statutes – a form of making or declaring law that became more binding than the pronouncements of kings, counsellors or judges. But Parliament's survival depended on its other main function – to provide the king with money. MPs recognized their duty to supply the Crown's exceptional needs – usually for war; but they did so

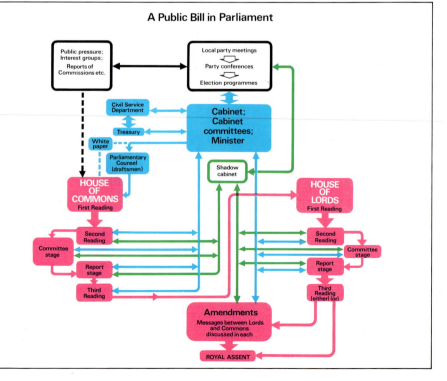

A Public Bill in Parliament

only after bargaining and persuasion. The theory that the king had resources of his own adequate for peace-time needs became less and less plausible.

As Parliament's activities expanded, men became more eager to be, or to choose, MPs. New boroughs were created, often returning county gentry or nominees of the Crown or of local magnates rather than true townsmen. In the Commons distinctions developed between the councillors and courtiers gathered round the Speaker's chair, the few regular opponents of ministerial policies, and the mass of uncommitted members ready to be influenced by what they heard at Westminster. Enthusiasm for the traditions and privileges of Parliament increased. Elizabeth exploited her popularity to limit the demands for parliamentary discussion of ministers and policies. Under James I and Charles I parliaments still essentially loyal to the monarchy felt their powers and their very existence repeatedly threatened. The Civil Wars in the 1640s were much more than a dispute about Parliament's power; but they showed how far it could develop. For a few years MPs undertook themselves all the main tasks of government. Their victory was not a democratic triumph: behind the successive regimes that dispensed with monarchy and peers lay the power of the army and the failure to reunite the nation. In 1660 the old constitution was restored and acclaimed. But Parliament had emerged from the conflicts as a permanent and essential centre of power. Without its consent no ministry and – as was tellingly shown in 1688 – no king could survive for long.

Reform and change

In the turmoil of the 1640s there emerged the astonishing idea that all, or nearly all, men should share equally in choosing their rulers. From the Levellers to the Suffragettes campaigns for democracy assumed that their first aim must be to extend the parliamentary franchise. In 1832, amid fears of popular revolution, the first major changes were introduced. It took another century of piecemeal reform before virtually every adult had a vote, in secret ballots guarded from illicit pressures. In that sense parliamentary democracy was achieved. But the power of the ordinary MP has declined.

In the later part of the 19th century the two huge political parties established rigid control over parliamentary proceedings. The replacement of the Liberals by Labour as the main rival to the Conservatives did nothing to reduce the grip of parties and ministers. Newspapers, and then radio, helped to turn elections into national campaigns, with voters choosing a Prime Minister rather than a local MP. There are always occasional 'revolts' in the House; loyalty in voting can conceal effective pressure in the lobbies and committee-rooms. The demand for more information, greater accountability of Whitehall departments, and genuine policy-making debates could become a new movement for parliamentary reform. The Cabinet is already seen to be less totally united and secret than was once pretended. Major decisions of policy can still be taken in secret, but at the risk of provoking eventually some healthy parliamentary anger. The century-old Public Accounts Committee, and the new Expenditure Committee with its sub-committees, can probe into a wide range of departmental activities. Critics can still describe British government as the least open among western democracies; supporters can claim it as the least susceptible to corruption and back-stairs pressures. But whatever the merits and defects they are less permanent than Parliament itself, able when it will to combine tradition with change and tolerant of almost every opinion.

Queen Elizabeth I in Parliament – in the House of Lords with members of the Commons at the bar of the house (in the foreground). Today, at State Openings of Parliament, the Queen delivers her speech outlining her government's programme from the throne. As in the days of Elizabeth I, members of the Commons stand at the bar of the House.

British Elections 1832–1980 (seats gained by each party)								
	C	**L**						
1832 Dec	185	473						
1835 Jan	279	379						
1837 Aug	314	344						
1841 July	367	291						
			P					
1847 July	243	324	89					
1852 July	290	319	45					
1857 March	256	372	26					
1859 May	306	348						
1865 July	300	358						
1868 Nov	279	379						
			IN					
1874 Feb	352	243	57					
1880 April	238	352	62					
1885 Nov	250	334	86					
			IN	**LU**				
1886 July	316	191	85	78				
1892 July	268	274	81	47				
1895 July	341	177	82	70				
1900 Oct	334	186	82	68				
	C&LU		**IN**	**Lab**				
1906 Jan	156	379	83	52				
1910 Jan	273	275	82	40				
1910 Dec	272	272	84	42				

	Coal.	**Opp.**		
1918 Dec	478	229		
	C	**Lab**	**L**	**Others**
1922 Nov	345	142	116	12
1923 Dec	258	191	159	7
1924 Oct	419	151	40	5
1929 May	260	288	59	8
	Coal.	**Lab**		
1931 Oct	554	52		11
1935 Nov	429	154	21	11
	C	**Lab**	**L**	**Others**
1945 July	213	393	12	22
1950 Feb	298	315	9	3
1951 Oct	321	295	6	3
1955 May	344	277	6	3
1959 Oct	365	258	6	1
1964 Oct	304	317	9	0
1966 March	253	363	12	2
1970 June	330	288	6	6
1974 Feb	297	301	14	23
1974 Oct	277	319	13	26
1979 May	339	269	11	16

C	Conservative	IN	Irish Nationalist
L	Liberal	LU	Liberal Unionist
P	Peelite	Lab	Labour

Note: 'Liberal' pre-1865 denotes a loose group of Whigs, Liberals, Radicals and Peelites, and Irish, often held together only by being anti-Conservative.

The Government of Britain: Freedom of Speech

The poet John Milton. His *Areopagitica* was an eloquent demand for the 'liberty of unlicensed printing' but did little to change the assumption that the written and spoken word must be firmly controlled.

John Wilkes – among the many reformers who owed their success to an alliance between moderate constitutionalism and popular radicalism.

Political institutions matter less in the long run than a truly free and well-informed public opinion. Such freedom is always a nuisance to governments. It is a heritage that has been won in centuries of struggle; and it can be preserved and improved only with active and constant determination.

In medieval England the notion of free speech was at most a matter for scholarly theory. The occasional rebel or outlaw might protest against oppression; but the essentials of Society, State and Church were hardly questioned. The Reformation, the new humanist confidence in the individual, printing, wider literacy, and economic change all contributed to a conflict between the spreading of ideas and the fear that the social and political order might be shaken. The crisis of the 17th century produced a sudden outpouring of pamphlets and newspapers; public gathering, from the village sermon to the violence of the London mob, became an ordinary part of life; and successive rulers resisted, exploited, or guided it all as best they could. The most eloquent of demands for the 'liberty of unlicensed printing', Milton's *Areopagitica* (1644) did little to change the assumption that the written and spoken word must be firmly controlled. With a few exceptions – William Walwyn was one and Oliver Cromwell, within limits, another – puritans and radicals were reluctant to give their enemies the freedom they demanded for themselves. The Restoration of the Stuarts brought a new intolerance. John Bunyan and George Fox were two of the many whose imprisonment failed to silence them. As religious passions and the fear of revolutions receded, the printed word seemed less danger-ous. In 1695 the licensing of the press was quietly dropped. But stamp duties soon made newspapers as expensive as government chose. The laws of sedition, blasphemy and libel enabled judges to condemn almost any attack on the powerful.

Against the arbitrary use of legal judgments to supress political opinions John Wilkes, in the 1760s, fought his spectacular campaigns, important mainly for the public enthusiasm in the cause of 'liberty' he was able to sustain. Wilkes was among the many reformers who owed their success to an alliance between moderate constitutionalism and popular radicalism. A generation later the French Revolution made compromise less easy. The decisive period began when repressive governments confronted the ideals of liberty and equality. Legislation culminating in the 'Six Acts' of 1819, and heavier stamp duties on news-papers, meant that political and social propaganda risked fierce punishment. The response was a campaign for freedom of the press which after years of defiant struggle ended in the gradual abandonment of prosecutions. Publishers like Richard Carlile of *The Republican* and Henry Hetherington of *The Poor Man's Guardian*, who were repeatedly imprisoned, were supported by a mass of news-vendors and local pamphleteers in the creation of the 'great unstamped' press. By the middle of the century printing in Britain had a freedom that has never again been openly threatened.

'Outrageous Demands'

Another of the Six Acts made virtually all public meetings illegal. The Acts followed the 'massacre' at St Peter's Fields, Manchester, in 1819, when a large meeting addressed by the radical orator Henry Hunt was dispersed by soldiers. Eleven people died. The Prince Regent and the Home Secretary thanked the soldiers for their prompt and efficient action. But Peterloo was only one episode in the heyday of the radical political meeting and the mass campaign. It had begun in the 1790s with the popular reform organizations for which Tom Paine's *Rights of Man* was the great source of inspiration; it included the great demonstration for the reform Bill of 1832; and it culminated in the Chartist movement of 1839, nearly all of whose seemingly outrageous demands have now become uncontroversial parts of the constitution. More restrained middle-class campaigns used the public meeting too – for Catholic Emancipation, the abolition of the slave-trade, the repeal of the Corn Laws. Their success established an era in which the citizen's welfare was a necessary part of every political programme and pressure for specific reforms an accepted part of the national scene. But more significant in the end than temporary campaigns was the beginning of permanent organizations of workers, against which the Combination Laws of 1800 had been directed. The six labourers of Tolpuddle sentenced to transportation in 1834 and pardoned two years later, became symbols of the demand for freedom of association. The Trade Union movement from its earliest days experienced the divisions between right and left, small-scale and large-scale, that still remain. These divisions did not however prevent its growth into one of the main moulders of policital and social opinion.

The absence of censorship and persecution is only one step towards the effective expression of public opinion. The history of British newspapers since their liberation has not been one of unmitigated triumph. With ten national dailies struggling to survive, evening papers nearly all having a local monopoly, and two ponderously impartial television news services selecting much the same material, access to information and ideas is in some ways more restricted than it was a century ago. But it is a different world from that of state-controlled information and repression of protest.

Above: The 'Peterloo Massacre' in St Peter's Fields, Manchester, in 1819. In this incident a large open-air meeting petitioning for parliamentary reform was brutally dispersed by yeomanry and hussars; 11 people were killed. Subsequent indignation accelerated the reform movement.

Right: Some 150 years later: a peaceful march by the Campaign for Nuclear Disarmament.

Left: The banner of the Operative Bricklayers Society, one of the many new mass organizations of the late 19th century. The six labourers of Tolpuddle sentenced to transportation in 1834 became symbols for the demand for freedom of association. Today the Trades Union Movement is one of the main moulders of political and social opinion.

The Government of Britain: Local Government

A **council in session. The** diagram on the opposite page shows the main functions of local government as divided between the new administrative units.

A **delivery of books and music** cassettes to a household by a local council's domiciliary librarian – one of the many services provided by local social services departments.

Britons seldom regard local government as one of the brightest jewels in their heritage: it is more readily seen as an incomprehensible tangle of bureaucracies and inefficient councils than as a benificent system responsive to the wishes of the people. But it has in many ways proved more adaptable to changing needs than the central legislature and executive. Here and there the apathy and hostility towards it may be diminishing, and the councillors and officials coming closer to the community.

The British Isles have never been a wholly unified country; and it is outside England that, for better or worse, awareness of loyalty to an area is strongest. Wales, despite its emotional and cultural identity, has remained firmly within the English legal and administrative system. Scotland's relations with English government are however full of anomalies. When James VI acquired the English throne in 1603, English statesmen refused to support his plans for a union of the kingdoms. The Act of Union of 1707 was a hasty political expedient, which nevertheless began the transformation of the Scotland of hostile clans and despotic magnates into a firmly administered unit. English institutions were not imposed outright: the very different system of law remained, and English legislation did not automatically apply to Scotland. It was a compromise that brought benefits to many Scots and aroused the bitter nationalist fervour of others. In 1978 proposals for elected assemblies in Wales and Scotland were rejected in referenda, decisively in Wales, less so in Scotland.

Within England communal tensions and thoughts of regional autonomy hardly exist. Local government has always been based on a single distinction – between rural and urban areas. Except in the North the counties were well defined well before the Norman Conquest and survived, with occasional boundary changes, until 1972. Boroughs within them rose, and sometimes fell; a few great cities, like Bristol or Peterborough, detached themselves from the county system completely; smaller units within the county developed – the medieval hundreds, the 17th-century divisions, and the 19th-century districts. But the shire remained the area with its own character, within which men of property built their influence, patronage and alliances. As sheriffs, Justices of the Peace, Deputy-

Lieutenants of the militia, and members of a variety of commissions, the gentry ran the affairs of the county with little opposition. Below them the hierarchy of lesser officials extended down to the parish constables and overseers of the poor — mainly unpaid and seldom devoted to their office. Only at parish level was there widespread participation in local affairs. The Parish Meeting was almost the only instance of direct democracy in British government.

The first general reform of the old system, the Municipal Corporations Act of 1835, established in most boroughs elected corporations meeting openly. In 1888 a unit better suited to industrialized Britain was created — the County Borough. In 1894 some of the powers of counties were distributed to urban and rural district councils. It was never a well-planned arrangement and it often had difficulty in taking on new functions.

In 1974 a drastic reform of local government accepted that the old Britain of the counties and scattered towns had been half-submerged by a new Britain of huge urban areas. Six 'metropolitan counties', together with Greater London, now have a third of the population. Of the remaining 'shire' counties some, in Wales especially, have been merged and others greatly changed. In Scotland nine 'regions' have replaced the counties. It is a striking victory for convenience over tradition, and its critics can point out that it still leaves many local services outside its scope. The National Health Service has its own 14 regions and 90 areas, with local authorities represented on its committees; for water supplies there is a different division into ten regions; for gas there are twelve. Police areas coincide sometimes but not always with local authority units. It works, on the whole, better than the complexities would suggest. Opportunities for citizens to seek redress exist everywhere. They are sometimes denounced as window-dressing by one side and as obstacles to efficiency by the other; but they are among the many institutions whose survival may depend on the use made of them.

Right: In 1974 the local government structure was drastically reformed to take account of a new Britain of huge urban areas. In Scotland nine regions have replaced the counties. Among the English counties to disappear altogether are Cumberland and Westmorland (now Cumbria), Huntingdonshire and Rutland (absorbed into neighbouring counties), while Herefordshire and Worcestershire combined, retaining their names after strongly protesting against the proposed new name Malvernshire. In Wales most of the old county names went and the reorganized units adopted historic regional names.

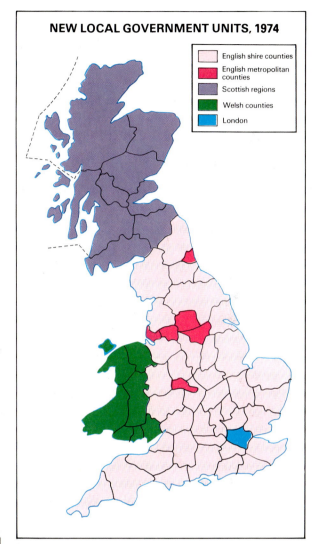

NEW LOCAL GOVERNMENT UNITS, 1974

English shire counties
English metropolitan counties
Scottish regions
Welsh counties
London

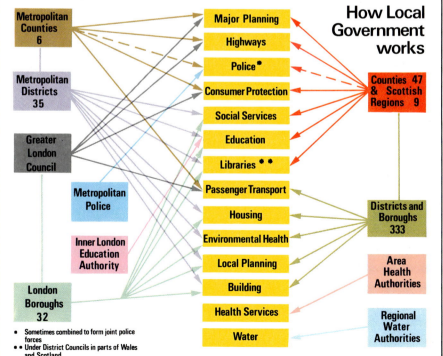

How Local Government works

Metropolitan Counties 6

Metropolitan Districts 35

Greater London Council

Metropolitan Police

Inner London Education Authority

London Boroughs 32

Major Planning
Highways
Police *
Consumer Protection
Social Services
Education
Libraries * *
Passenger Transport
Housing
Environmental Health
Local Planning
Building
Health Services
Water

Counties 47 & Scottish Regions 9

Districts and Boroughs 333

Area Health Authorities

Regional Water Authorities

* Sometimes combined to form joint police forces
* * Under District Councils in parts of Wales and Scotland

IRELAND

The problems of Scotland and Wales seem trivial in comparison with those of Ireland. For centuries successive waves of English and Scottish settlers or absentee proprietors seized Irish land at the expense of the native Irish. Cromwell, regarding Irish Catholic rebels as beyond mercy, imposed the most extensive confiscations of all, which were confirmed by king Charles II.

Stronger and more tolerant administration in the 19th century did nothing to mitigate the horrors of famine, depopulation and economic injustice. The bitter struggle for Home Rule shook the English political system and brought repeated threats of Civil War. The unhappy solution that separated six Ulster counties, where Protestantism and comparative prosperity gave a basis for attachment to Britain, from an independent Irish state arose from intricate manoeuvres in all the parties involved. It left British governments with by far their hardest administrative task. The 'direct rule' imposed in 1972 has avoided the total collapse of order, but a stable settlement still seems far away.

The Law of the Land: The Common Law

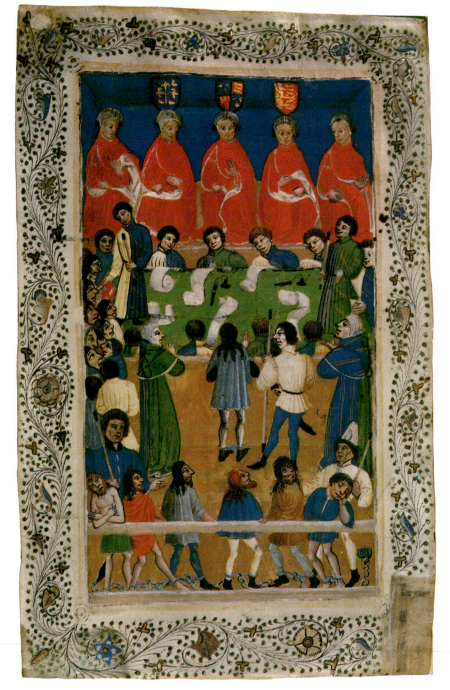

The Court of King's Bench
This miniature, painted in the 1450s, shows a prisoner being tried at the bar of the King's Bench in Westminster Hall. In this court the justices 'assigned to hold pleas before the king himself' dealt chiefly with criminal cases and actions for wrongs against the King's Peace. They are shown in their scarlet robes, sitting beneath a blue cloth of estate with embroidered arms. In the centre is the Chief Justice of England, Sir John Fortescue, who wrote an important book *In Praise of the Laws of England* while exiled in France in the 1460s. Beneath him are the clerks with their pens and records. At the left a crier is swearing in the jury. The prisoner, brought to the bar in the custody of the marshal of the Marshalsea (with sword and staff), raises his hand as his name is called. On either side of him stand serjeants at law, in their parti-coloured robes and hoods. The serjeants and judges alike wear on their heads the white coifs of their order. In the foreground six more prisoners are chained, waiting for their cases to be heard.

In all the history of the western world there have been only two complete and coherent systems of legal ideas, each with its own method and terminology. The 'civil' law of Rome, and its younger sister the Canon law of western Christendom, were taught in medieval universities and provided the framework of legal thought in most European countries. The common law of England, created by a comparatively tiny body of judges and advocates working in the Great Hall of Westminster Palace, was an insular achievement which owed little to Romanist influence. Even in medieval times it had its own literature and law schools. It survived the renaissance of classical wisdom, the Civil War, and the codification movement which transformed continental jurisprudence after the Code Napoléon of 1804. Within Europe, England became a legal island, cut off from the juristic learning of the mainland. Yet the expansion of

English trade and empire in the 18th and 19th centuries introduced one-third of the peoples of the Earth to the common law, so that the jurisprudence of Westminster Hall took root and flourished on every continent. In many parts of the world the common law, adapted to suit local requirement, lives on in countries which have become independent from the political rule of the mother country.

Medieval English lawyers were wont to regard their law as being of immemorial antiquity. Many of its institutions can indeed be traced back to Anglo-Saxon times: for instance, the king's council, or *witan*, the royal chancery and its writs and charters, the shires and their sheriffs. There were decision-making bodies at all levels from the witan, through the counties and hundreds, down to the village meeting, and they dealt with private disputes alongside public affairs. But these were hardly courts of law in any modern sense. Their decisions were doubtless guided by custom and experience, but did not themselves make law and were not constrained by the reasoning behind earlier decisions: there was no clear distinction between adjudication, administration and legislation.

The Circuits

Several interrelated factors combined in the 12th and 13th centuries to generate in England a distinct body of jurisprudence worthy to rival that of ancient Rome. The first was the regularization and centralization of royal justice under the Angevin and early Plantagenet kings. The appointment of justices enabled the king to delegate his regal powers to skilled advisers, who might serve in the royal palace or wander abroad the realm on circuit. Only by delegation was the king's justice capable of becoming the ordinary law of the land, available to all. By 1250 there were two major royal courts, the King's Bench and the Common Bench (or Common Pleas), and a third (the Court of the Exchequer) which was to gain in importance later. Twice a year the judges of the two benches went on circuit to try both criminal and civil cases with juries drawn from the vicinities where the facts occurred. These bi-annual visitations came to be called assizes. By such means the kings came to provide a uniform system of legal administration for the whole nation. Two further factors enabled that system to produce the common law. One was the use of parchment rolls to record the business of the royal courts. These durable records preserved decisions not merely for the benefit of the parties, itself a valuable boon, but also for the benefit of posterity. The plea rolls were a vast store of procedural and legal information, for those skilled to interpret them, and they gave consistency to the practice of the king's justices. The second factor was the appearance of a legal profession. Legal professionalism began with the bench, with the 12th-century royal councillors who devoted their lives to judicial work and settled the outlines of common-law procedure. By 1250 both bench and bar at Westminster were composed of men trained in the practice of the royal courts. The leaders of the Common Pleas bar were men of the highest intellectual distinction, who in the 14th century became a closed order called the serjeants at law. Yet these were not university men. Their language was not the Latin of the academical law schools, but the homely French dialect of the medieval court. They learned their law not by reading textbooks but through experience, by observation of proceedings in court and by discussion with their fellows. In their own language and by their own spontaneous processes of reasoning these men made the common law.

The Court of Common Pleas was the busiest royal court and until Tudor times was the hub of the common law. Here were heard cases concerning property and debt, mostly between subject and subject. In the miniature seven judges are shown sitting 'in banc' at some time in the 1450s. At the table, covered in green baize, the protonotaries, exigenters, filazers and other clerks keep their rolls. There would have been many more officers attending the court than are shown. The criers are calling on a case, and the defendant is being brought to the bar by the warden of the Fleet Prison. Five serjeants at law are present at the bar, and the two at the left appear to be taking last-minute instructions from an attorney.

Plea rolls. By the 15th century the central courts were generating about a mile of closely written Latin rolls every year. These mountains of parchment, which have survived virtually intact, are crammed with historical information and legal precedents.

THE LAW OF SCOTLAND

Scotland in the Middle Ages shared many legal and administrative notions with England, and if Edward I had not been defeated at Bannockburn its law might well have developed (like that of Dublin) along the same lines as that of Westminster. But conditions there made centralization more difficult, and continuous war prevented regular intellectual contact with English lawyers. Scots law therefore developed in its own way, chiefly through the work of the Court of Session, a royal court rather like the English King's Council. In Scotland, textbooks or 'institutions' had more influence than in England, and since the advocates were learned in Roman law the law of Scotland had some affinity with that of pre-Napoleonic continental systems. The merger of the Crown of Scotland with that of England in 1603 and the political union of 1707 did not affect the independent character of Scottish law. Appeals now lie from the Court of Session to the House of Lords at Westminster, but the terminology, principles and procedures of Scots law continue to be quite different (except in a few areas) from those of England and Wales.

The Law of the Land: The Common Lawyers

The Inner Temple, London.
The buildings in this view from the Embankment were erected in the 1950s to replace those badly damaged by bombing during the war. Yet the tranquillity of Temple Gardens is as timeless as that of the gardens of Lincoln's Inn and Gray's Inn walks. The Hall of the Inner Temple (centre) occupies the site of the medieval refectory of the Knights Templar, whose round church (also restored after bombing) serves as a place of worship for the lawyer Templars. Lawyers succeeded the Knights Hospitaller, as tenants of the Temple, and by 1388 had formed the two societies of the Inner Temple and Middle Temple.

Gray's Inn Hall (right) was
rebuilt in the mid-16th century and, despite severe damage in the blitz, still retains its Tudor appearance. This drawing was made by John Crowther about a century ago. At the far end is the screen supposed to have been carved from the timbers of a Spanish Armada galleon in 1588. The windows carry the arms of distinguished former members. The bay window (above right) contains those of noblemen, judges and serjeants at law, including Sir Francis Bacon, who lectured in the hall in 1600.

Two of the most distinctive features of the common law were the making of law in open court and the emergence of law schools, within reach of the courts, where that law could be learned and discussed. The process whereby nascent principles of law were tested by the serjeants in the Common Pleas, and either rejected or distinguished or refined for further use, can be glimpsed in the 'year books'. These remarkable volumes report the arguments and interchanges of opinion in the Common Pleas from the 1280s until the 1530s. They are not easy reading today, but few other kinds of literature bring us closer to our forbears and their ways of thinking about human relationships. Unlike carefully worded treatises they have the immediacy of oral debate, not omitting even the odd expletive! The skill of the serjeants in wriggling out of adverse propositions, by drawing distinctions and shifting ground, is breathtaking, even if the atmosphere more closely resembles that of a chess-match than that of a modern court. When a distinction or new proposition found general acceptance it became the law of England, though there might be years of doubt before acceptance or rejection was definite. The year books were the lawyers' guide to the doubts as well as the certainties. Although the last reports called year books relate to the year 1535, the tradition of reporting cases continued without break in various overlapping series known mostly by the names of the reporters, and continues to this day. Together with Acts of Parliament, these seven centuries of law reports

form the core of every English law library.

The serjeants at law were the leaders of the bar in the days of the year books, losing their supremacy in later times to king's counsel (a rank introduced in the 17th century). But even in the 13th century there was a sizeable body of lesser lawyers attending the royal courts, comprising not only the court officials and attorneys but also the 'apprentices of the law'. In a learned profession all are students, and the word 'apprentice' came by 1500 to denote senior advocates who were not serjeants. The serjeants were sometimes likened to doctors in a university, and although they did not teach directly it was from their performances in court that the younger apprentices learned. During the 14th and 15th centuries the apprentices and attorneys of the courts began to live together as learned communities in inns (or _hospicia_, town-houses) located in the western suburbs of London. The origins of these fellowships remain obscure, since they were never incorporated and had unwritten constitutions. By the 15th century they provided not only commons (food and drink taken in hall) but also learning exercises: lectures (called 'readings') and disputations (called 'moots'). The four greater inns (the Inner Temple and Middle Temple, Gray's Inn and Lincoln's Inn) were known by the 1420s as inns of the men

of court: it was their senior members who acted as counsel in the King's Bench when serjeants were absent, and from whom serjeants were chosen. There were in addition at least nine lesser inns, which came to be called the inns 'of chancery' because some of them had been associated with chancery clerks and provided students with an elementary grounding in the chancery writs upon which the law depended. The inns of chancery accommodated mainly younger students, together with attorneys and officials. In all the inns there were ranks or degrees connected with the exercises, as in the universities. When qualified to take a full part at moots the student became an 'utter barrister', so called because he stood outside the bar of the inn to argue (like a serjeant at Westminster). When he lectured he became a reader, and could take the part of a judge on the bench at moots, as a 'bencher'. In the 16th century the degree of barrister at law became an essential qualification for practice as an advocate, and so it has remained ever since. The degree of barrister is still conferred by the benchers, who are the governing body of each inn.

The Third University

Until the Civil War the inns of court and chancery received a considerable part of the gentry of England besides intending lawyers, and together they formed a body not much smaller than the University of Cambridge. It was no accident that so many chose to spend time there, since the spirit of the common law was in their blood. English

landowners loved to chase in the courts as much as they loved to chase in the fields, and their very lives were mapped out in parchment and wax. Moreover, by bringing these young men together in the metropolis, introducing them to each other and to the culture of the 'court' in its non-legal sense, the inns contributed in a broader way to the character of English society. The halls of the inns resounded not only to learned arguments of law but also to masques and interludes, plays and music. Among their members were many of the nation's finest thinkers and writers. Sir Thomas More was a bencher of Lincoln's Inn, Sir Francis Bacon a bencher of Gray's. Truly did Elizabethan writers call this law school The Third University of England.

INNS OF COURT
Inner Temple
Middle Temple
Gray's Inn
Lincoln's Inn

INNS OF CHANCERY
Barnard's Inn
Clement's Inn
Clifford's Inn
Furnival's Inn
Lyon's Inn
New Inn
Staple Inn
Strand Inn
Thavie's Inn

OTHER LEGAL SOCIETIES
Serjeants' Inn, Chancery Lane
Serjeants' Inn, Fleet Street
Doctors' Commons (for advocates in the ecclesiastical and admiralty courts)
Harflew Inn or Kidermister's Inn (for the six clerks of the Chancery)
Cursitors' Inn (for the cursitors of the Chancery)

Far left: A year book. This early manuscript shows on the right-hand page the beginning of some reports taken in the Common Pleas in Michaelmas term 1293. On the preceding page are some circuit cases from Shropshire.

Furnival's Inn from High Holborn in about 1720. This view shows how closely an inn of chancery resembled an Oxford or Cambridge college. The inn is divided into two courts by the dining hall, which has a bay window full of armorial glass. In the far court is a pretty garden with wrought iron railings. Around the courts are sets of chambers for the senior members (mostly attorneys) and students of the inn. The whole inn was demolished in the last century. Only Staple Inn (rebuilt after heavy war damage) retains its collegiate atmosphere today, though the ancient hall of Barnard's Inn has also survived.

The Law of the Land: The English Legal System

The King's Bench, Common Pleas and Exchequer survived as the three principal courts in law until their abolition in 1875. But their ways had set hard at least five centuries earlier, and became revered as 'due process' which could not be altered. An important part of this process was trial by jury. Only juries were allowed to try disputes of fact. Yet the jury was not the most perfect tribunal. Jurors might apply the law wrongly and they were likely to be corrupted or unduly influenced by unscrupulous litigants. The judges, on the other hand, being forbidden to investigate the actual facts, concentrated on the legal points raised by the laywers' Latin formulations on the plea rolls. Like umpires, they watched to see that no one won by a wrong move, whatever the absolute merits of a case. But the justice of a game is not necessarily perfect justice, and the price of formalism was sometimes hardship. These were among the reasons for the appearance of a special kind of royal justice, which developed in late medieval times from the king's residuary judicial prerogative of doing right where the regular system proved deficient.

The special royal justice was administered through the king's council in the Star Chamber and the Court of Chancery. In the latter court the Lord Chancellor sat without jury and decided each case according to the dictates of 'conscience' in the particular circumstances of the parties. By Tudor times the Chancery was developing its own jurisprudence, called 'equity', which supplemented the common law and mitigated its rigour. The chief invention of equity was the trust, which (in order to achieve a variety of ends) enabled a landowner to entrust the legal title in his land to others. The common law ignored such an arrangement and treated the trustees as the only owners, but in equity the trustees were bound in conscience to allow the beneficiary the rights of an owner and they could be compelled to do so by the Chancellor's decree. It is difficult now to imagine the English legal system functioning without the concept of the trust, and yet it is unknown to continental jurisprudence.

In and after the 16th century the common-law courts themselves remedied some of their procedural deficiencies, not by changing the rules of due process but by allowing lawyers some latitude in sneaking round them. The dodges included an abundance of 'fictions', such as that whereby most actions to recover land after about 1600 were brought by a non-existent person called John Doe against an equally fictitious defendant who had supposedly ejected him from the premises. Yet, although the common-law system had to sacrifice rationality to improve, the result was preferable in many ways to the situation in Chancery. By failing to adjust to changed circumstances, the Chancery became more and more bogged down in overwork and labyrinthine procedures. Dickens parodied the situation in *Bleak House*.

Between the 1830s and the 1870s the greater part of the old gothic legal edifice was dismantled and rebuilt, using where possible the old materials. John Doe was retired and other fictions swept away. Legal and equitable remedies were made available in the same courts. Procedure was made more sensible though not always more simple. The various courts and their officers were abolished and replaced by one High Court of Justice, with various divisions. (The Queen's Bench Division and the Chancery Division survive to the present. The Common Pleas and Exchequer Division were abolished in 1880, and the Probate, Divorce and Admiralty Division gave way in 1970 to the Family Division.) Above the High Court was set a new Court of Appeal, and these two courts formed the Supreme Court of Judicature. By a paradoxical afterthought,

another appeal was given from the Supreme Court to a still more supreme court, the House of Lords. Perhaps the most significant procedural change was that which enabled judges to try facts in civil cases. Since the First World War very few civil cases have been tried by jury, and this change has profoundly affected the character both of judgments (which now include detailed findings of fact) and of appellate decisions.

Criminal procedure has been in many respects the most durable part of the common-law system, both in England and in other countries which have inherited its traditions. Serious cases are still tried on 'indictment', as in medieval times, though the indictment (or accusation) now emanates from examining magistrates rather than a grand jury. The defendant still 'pleads the general issue' (not guilty), as in medieval times, thereby putting the prosecution to proof of its entire case. Trial on indictment is still by a jury of twelve lay people, though the system has recently been changed. Juries are now drawn from a wider class of citizens, the number of challenges without cause has been reduced, and in some situations majority verdicts can be accepted. The criminal law is still developed, as for centuries past, through consideration of the judges' directions to juries in particular cases, although Parliament has often stepped in to change the rules. At common law all felonies carried the death penalty, but by deft use of pardons, benefit of clergy and fictions the courts were able long ago to introduce a broader scale of penalties, including transportation and imprisonment. The distinction between felony and misdemeanour was abolished in 1967, by which time the death penalty itself had been abolished – except for treason and piracy.

The High Court of Chancery. This painting by Benjamin Ferrers shows the Court of Chancery sitting in Westminster Hall in the time of Lord Macclesfield (Lord Chancellor 1718–25). On the Lord Chancellor's left is Sir Joseph Jekyll, Master of the Rolls, and on his left a Master in Ordinary. On the table beneath them are the gilt mace and the embroidered purse containing the Great Seal, insignia which are still carried before the Lord Chancellor at Westminster. The lawyers with black patches on their wigs are serjeants at law. As late as 1720 there were few concessions to comfort. Counsel had to stand in crowded conditions, and even the Lord Chancellor had to rest his writing paper on his knee.

Criminal justice. Standing on the site of Newgate Prison, the Old Bailey has been the central criminal court of the London area since medieval times. The justices, headed by the Lord Mayor of London, sat by virtue of commissions of *oyer* and *terminer* and gaol delivery and had the same authority as the Justices of Assize had in the country at large. The assizes were usually held twice a year, in major towns throughout the country, to try serious criminal cases as well as civil actions. Less important criminal cases were tried at the quarter sessions of the peace. Assizes and quarter sessions were abolished in 1971 and their functions transferred to a new Crown Court. In the City of London the Crown Court still sits as the Central Criminal Court at the Old Bailey. The picture shows a trial at the Old Bailey in 1809.

Sir Edward Coke (1552–1634). In theory English judges do not make law, but merely declare what it is. From time to time, however, great judges (such as Lord Mansfield in the 18th century and Lord Denning in the 20th) exert considerable influence and point the law in new directions. Coke was dismissed from office in 1616 for resisting too strongly government by prerogative, but many of his decisions have lain at the foundation of English liberties and (more recently) of administrative law. Equally influential were his writings. His monumental *Institutes of the Laws of England* possessed an almost scriptural authority until the last century, and his 13 volumes of *Reports* summarized many of the legal changes of the 16th century. Between them, these books did more than any others to render obsolete the medieval learning of the year-books.

Her Majesty's Judges. Since time immemorial the legal year has begun soon after Michaelmas, and the first day has been marked by a procession of the judges to their courts in Westminster Hall. The courts moved to the Strand in 1882, but every year on the first day of the Michaelmas term the judges of the Supreme Court still meet at Westminster, for a service in the Abbey and a 'breakfast' given by the Lord Chancellor, before proceeding to the Royal Courts of Justice. This picture shows some of the High Court judges, in their full-dress robes, hoods and mantles of scarlet faced with white miniver, in procession with their clerks from Westminster Abbey to the House of Lords.

The Defence of the Realm: Before the Norman Conquest

Above: Maiden Castle, Dorset. The terraced ramparts of this iron-age earthwork hill-fort were built on the site of a Neolithic defence system. Maiden Castle was captured by the Romans under Vespasian in AD 43.

Right: Towards the end of the first millenium BC, fortified sites were spaced out across the landscape, each dominating a specific area.

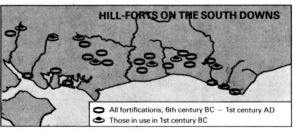

HILL-FORTS ON THE SOUTH DOWNS

○ All fortifications, 6th century BC — 1st century AD
● Those in use in 1st century BC

The traditional 'invasionist' view of early British history is one of fire and sword – a history of almost continuous fighting, in which only the early Roman period provides a brief respite. This of course is an exaggeration: signs of burning are very easy to detect when one excavates a site, and though quite often found do not appear nearly as regularly as the extreme 'fire-and-sword' theory demands. Contacts between peoples did not invariably mean warfare; a recent attempt to increase popular understanding of the Vikings for example, made much use of the slogan 'Traders, not raiders'. This, however, goes too far in the opposite direction. All the people of ancient Britain did not fight all the time, but most fought some of the time and some appear to have fought most of the time. Many impressive visible remains confirm this.

Whereas Neolithic and early Bronze Age monuments suggest a fairly peaceful society, those of the late Bronze Age and Iron Age show increasing preoccupation with the arts of war. The hill-forts of Wessex and the West Country are so large and numerous that the society which built them must surely have been 'baronial', similar to that of medieval England under one of its weaker kings. The late Iron Age in the south-east brought somewhat greater political unity, and with it even larger defensive works. These are technically known as *oppida*, from a remark by Julius Caesar: 'The Britons called it a town (*oppidum* in Latin) when they have fortified thickly wooded spots with a rampart and ditch'. The *oppidum* of *Camulodunum* (south of Colchester) was surrounded early in the 1st century AD by dykes enclosing altogether some 12 square miles (31 km²); its capture marked the climax of the Claudian invasion in AD 43.

Roman rule in its turn produced a new type of military work. In their advance across Britain, the Roman armies built numerous temporary camps (usually visible only from the air) and then forts with turf ramparts and buildings of timber. (One of these, the Lunt at Baginton near Coventry, has been partly reconstructed). As time went on, it became possible to abandon the forts in lowland Britain or to replace them by civil settlements; in Wales and the North, however, garrisons had to be retained, and their bases were gradually rebuilt in stone. Caerleon in Gwent, for example, began as an earth- and-timber fortress in about AD 75, but the stone buildings visible there today date from the 2nd century or later. Hadrian's Wall saw a similar change: its eastern part was of stone from the beginning, but its western part began as a turf wall and was rebuilt in stone later on. The more northerly Antonine Wall was of turf throughout its shortish life, as were most of the forts on it. Farther north still, beyond Roman direct rule, we find stone defensive works of other kinds – the towers known as brochs, in use from about the 2nd century BC to the 2nd AD, and the somewhat later stone forts with internal timber lacing, probably built by the Picts.

In the 3rd century new threats to Roman power caused new forts to be built, sometimes in regions previously regarded as safe, such as the 'Saxon Shore' of eastern and southern England (see page 103). The later 4th century saw further military constructions, with a new emphasis on defensive tactics; existing town walls had bastions added to them for catapults, forts were rebuilt, and new signal-stations and watch-towers were set up along the coasts, most notably that of Yorkshire. It was soon to become clear that the best defensive system in the world is useless without troops to man it.

Defence in the Dark Ages

The end of Roman rule and the beginning of the 'Dark Ages' brought a reversion to simpler methods of warfare. Several Iron Age hill-forts were re-occupied, among them Cadbury Castle in Somerset (traditionally but unprovably claimed as King Arthur's Camelot; it received new defences in the late 5th century, at about which time Arthur probably did exist and achieve something – though certainly not all the things afterwards credited to him). The earthwork known as Wansdyke, in Wiltshire and Somerset, may date from the same period or somewhat later. Better known is Offa's Dyke, built in the 780s to separate Offa's kingdom of Mercia from the Welsh (see page 45). And from the late 9th century onwards, wars between Saxon and Dane called for increasing use of fortified towns, some of Roman origin but others new.

Throughout ancient and medieval times, 'Defence of the Realm' usually meant defence on land. The Iron Age Britons presumably had ships that could be used for fighting (the people of Brittany certainly had, as Caesar mentions) but in the Roman invasions of Britain no such things as a 'British fleet' makes any appearance. The Romans, with their vastly greater resources, did have permanent fleets round Britain; but these, though apparently effective at first, failed to protect the coast as soon as the overseas threat became serious. Alfred the Great built warships (and thereby is sometimes claimed as 'Founder of the British Navy') but he too was unable to make them really effective. Seaborne attack was always likely to outrun seaborne defence. The 'sceptered isle' or 'Rule Britannia' approach to naval warfare, the idea that sea-power can stop an enemy from landing at all, is relatively recent; ancient ships on so long and exposed a coastline were never able to make it easy.

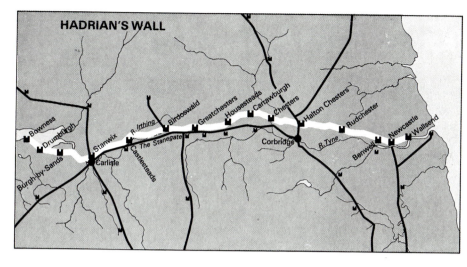

Above: Hadrian's Wall, built between AD 122 and 130 as a barrier against barbarians from the north.

Below: Porchester Castle, Hampshire, was a Saxon Shore fort built by the Romans at the end of the 3rd century AD.

Right: The Lunt, near Coventry – a reconstruction of a typical Roman camp.

The Defence of the Realm: Fortifications

England first became subject to fairly consistently unified political control – a realm – under the Romans. Their legions used fortified places, rural camps or walled townships, as part of the process of conquest and pacification. But there came a moment, as the legionaries tramped northwards, when an equation was reached between the logistics of expansion and the doggedness of resistance. A line had to be drawn – and was drawn – between AD 122 and 126, along the $73\frac{1}{2}$ miles (110 km) and the 16 back-up fortresses of Hadrian's Wall.

The frontier of stone – best studied through a tramp along it and a visit to the museum in Housesteads – was the first realm marker. The next came when control from Rome over the rest of north-west Europe faltered, and the Romans in Britain had to protect their coasts from fleets raiding across the North Sea. In the 3rd century, under a succession of Counts of the Saxon Shore, a string of fortresses was built in an arc stretching from Brancaster to Portchester. This last is the best preserved and, along with the still impressive remains at Pevensey, Richborough and Burgh Castle, show how massive was the investment in these walled and towered enclosures.

From Castrum to Castle

It was long after the break-up of the Roman realm that England was again occupied by foreigners who were also great builders of fortifications. From the motte-and-bailey defences of the decade immediately following 1066 to the later isolated keeps-within-private-enclosures and keeps-within-towns, the Norman and Angevin period saw the transition from *castrum* to castle, that is from fortifications built to protect whole settlements, whether of troops or civilians or both, to defensive works built primarily to protect an individual and his dependents: family, household troops and tenants. Paradoxically, it was Frenchmen who, by introducing the draw-bridge outside the front door,

Right: In the 3rd century the Romans built a string of coastal forts against the Saxon threat. Edward I's castle-building in Wales was designed to support his conquest of the area. Henry VIII's castles were built under threat of invasion.

Below: A ground plan of Porchester Castle, best preserved of the Roman forts (see also page 101).

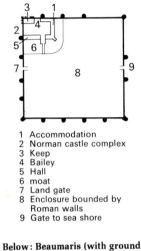

1 Accommodation
2 Norman castle complex
3 Keep
4 Bailey
5 Hall
6 moat
7 Land gate
8 Enclosure bounded by Roman walls
9 Gate to sea shore

Below: Beaumaris (with ground plan) expressed a new mood: no longer that simply of being a tough nut to crack but of constituting a danger to approach.

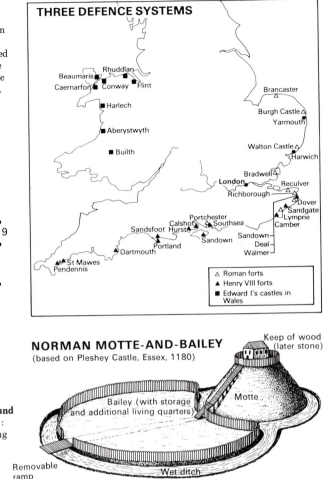

THREE DEFENCE SYSTEMS

- △ Roman forts
- ▲ Henry VIII forts
- ■ Edward I's castles in Wales

NORMAN MOTTE-AND-BAILEY
(based on Pleshey Castle, Essex, 1180)

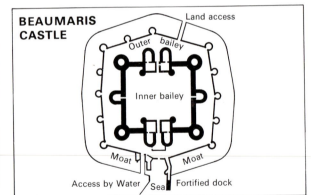

Keep of wood (later stone)

Bailey (with storage and additional living quarters)

Motte

Removable ramp

Wet ditch

BEAUMARIS CASTLE

Land access
Outer bailey
Inner bailey
Moat
Moat
Access by Water
Sea
Fortified dock

launched the cloying notion that an Englishman's home is his castle.

As with the early stages of Roman occupation the deployment of Norman castles was a product of conquest and pacification; the defence of the ruler and his lieutenants came before the defence of the realm. Indeed, the next occasion after the Saxon threat to the Romans when the imminence of an invasion led to the simultaneous planning of fortifications for national defence came as late as the reign of Henry VIII. In the meantime, the only major co-ordinated defensive system was the one designed from the 1270s to support Edward I's expansion of the realm into central and north Wales. This group of eight castles represents the apogee of 'picturesque' military engineering in Britain before the pounding of cannonballs enforced a squatter, less detailed and therefore less romantic elevation. Monarch of the group, and, as the latest to be built (from 1294) the one that incorporated the best of the new ideas more tentatively expressed in the others, was Beaumaris. Here, as at the almost equally well preserved Harlech, Caernarfon and Caerphilly, the keep, instead of being considered a defence of last resort, aggressively straddles the main entrance to the fortified enclosure. In the same spirit, in addition to the conventional round corner towers, two mid-wall towers shoulder themselves provocatively outwards. Thanks to its site, Beaumaris reflects its designer's instinct to achieve a perfect symmetry – thus the gate-keep is echoed by an equivalent strong-point on the opposite side. It also represents the most perfect example in England of a plan pioneered elsewhere (notably by the crusaders' engineers in the Near East) that aimed at doubling the task of besiegers by providing two separate, concentric rings of towered walls, the inner one high enough to provide a tier of missile–power suplementing that of the outer enceinte.

A New Mood

Beaumaris, in fact, expressed a new mood; no longer that simply of being a tough nut to crack but of constituting a danger to approach. And this was the mood perfectly suited to the new arc of fortifications cladding the Saxon shore that were erected on the orders of Henry VIII. In 1539 Protestant England was threatened by a major invasion from an alliance between the greatest Catholic rulers, Francis I of France and the Habsburg Emperor Charles V. A survey of the coasts led to the decision to build fortresses to guard landing beaches all the way from Harwich to Falmouth.

Again, symmetry, concentricity and tiers of aggressive fire-power were the guiding principles of design, though as the fire-power was now provided by heavy, recoiling guns, the architectural forms were dictated by the need for strong

Above right: Deal Castle, one of the many forts built along the south coast by Henry VIII as a precaution against French attack. Symmetry, concentricity and tiers of aggressive fire-power were the guiding principles of its design.

Right: One of Britain's latest contributions to the defence of the realm – the early warning radar installation at Fylingdales in West Yorkshire.

terraces and smoke-vented lower gun-chambers. The idea of planning inwards from a fortified perimeter has gone; Henry's forts cluster outwards from a central artillery tower. Living quarters are pared to the minimum. No protective space is offered to a fleeing tenantry. Now and henceforward the defence of the realm is entrusted not to walled camps or castles but to forts. And threat by threat the shapes of defences grew simpler, from the stolidly cylindrical Martello Towers of 1805–12 (103 of them studded along the familiar pressure point, the Saxon Shore) to the innumerable concrete gun emplacements of the two World Wars. Simpler, but not necessarily less beautiful: the traveller who moves from the Romans' Porchester to Edward's Beaumaris and on from Henry's Deal, Walmer or St Mawes to Britain's latest contribution to the defence of the realm, the early warning radar installation at Fylingdales in West Yorkshire, must surely agree that the last is the loveliest of them all.

The Defence of the Realm: Military Traditions _____

A tradition of the annual Passing Out Parade at the Royal Military Academy, Sandhurst: the Adjutant rides up the steps of the Old Building.

MILITARY MUSEUMS
The museums which recall the history of the British Army are too numerous to name: nearly every regiment has one. The most important are the Imperial War Museum at Lambeth, London; the National Army Museum in Chelsea; and the Scottish National Army Museum in Edinburgh Castle.

Military tradition is a pearl of great price. It is partly fact, and partly fiction. It has in it an element of Religion and an element of Mythology. At the same time it enshrines not only the ancient achievements of an army or regiment, but the good rules based on experience, which down the years have taught officers to look after the men, and the men to hit the targets they shoot at – and scores of other useful 'standing orders' besides.

The Standing Army dates its existence from the reign of Charles II, veteran of Edgehill (1642) and Worcester (1651), who wisely officered his regiments and his garrisons with Cavalier officers, who had fought for him and his father in the Civil Wars. A few of the less extreme Roundheads were retained out of deference to the former Parliamentarian, George Monck, who by careful selection of his officers had prepared his army so that he was able to bring about the Restoration.

But it would be absurd to date our army and our military tradition from so recent a date as 1660. The great victories of Crécy (1346), Poitiers (1356) and Agincourt (1415) are as much part of our tradition as Blenheim (1704) or Waterloo (1815) or El Alamein (1942). There are some units and regiments which can trace their lineage to Tudor times. These include the Bodyguard of Gentlemen Pensioners, who date back to Henry VIII; they fought at the battle of the Spurs (Guinegates, 16 August 1513), and at Edgehill. The Yeoman of the Guard and the Yeoman Warders of the Tower, have also existed since the 16th-century. They have long been chosen from senior N.C.os of exemplary character with many years of service. Another historic unit, which was reactivated in 1922, is the Company of Pikeman and Musketeers belonging to the Honourable Artillery Company. This unit, whose 'uniform' is that of Charles I's period, acts upon ceremonial occasions

as a Bodyguard for the Lord Mayor of London.

Military tradition is to some extent a question of drill, and discipline and dress. There are always those who find it irksome to take trouble about such things, but the truth is military success depends upon an unremitting attention to detail – to drill, turnout and strict discipline. These are the things which produce more effective soldiers: men who, if ordered out on a fighting patrol at a moment's notice, will have every item of their arms and equipment ready and in working order. This is the secret of all good units and especially, in the British Army, of the Household Cavalry, the Brigade of Guards and the King's Troop, Royal Horse Artillery.

There are good units in other armies, but there is really nothing to compare with the Brigade of Guards, which enshrine all that is best in British military tradition. Their expertise may be seen daily as they perform their public duties in the capital, and each year they celebrate the Queen's Birthday by performing the ancient ceremony of Trooping the Colour on the Horse Guards Parade.

And all the time, in the background N.C.os from the various regiments of Foot Guards, are preparing young officers for the Army at the Royal Military Academy, Sandhurst, and recruits for their own regiments at Pirbright.

Battle Honours
The ancient achievements of the regiments which make up the British Army are borne on their colours as battle honours. They include such famous names as Blenheim, Waterloo, Balaclava, Mons, Ypres, Dunkirk, 1940, El Alamein, Monte Cassino and Imphal. These names, embroidered in letters of gold, remind the soldiers of the present generation of the exploits of their predecessors.

Upon occasion other distinctions have been awarded such as the Sphinx, conferred by George III (6 July 1802) upon the units which had fought in Egypt under Sir Ralph Abercromby, 'as a lasting memorial of the glory acquired . . .' 'by their zeal, discipline and intrepidity in that arduous and important campaign'.

Honours and Awards
Just as the services of regiments are commemorated by battle honours and badges, the services of individuals are marked by medals awarded for gallantry in action, or for service in a particular campaign. Medals are also awarded for Long Service and Good Conduct and to mark events such as a Coronation or the Jubilee of a Sovereign. The awards for gallantry are somewhat sparingly awarded: the George Cross, the Distinguished Service Order, the Distinguished Conduct Medal, the Military Cross and on occasion the Military Medal. But the most famous of all British medals is the Victoria Cross.

The Victoria Cross, which was awarded for outstanding deeds of gallantry in the presence of the enemy, was instituted in 1856, but was made retrospective so as to cover the Crimean War of 1854. It was Queen Victoria's desire that the decoration 'should be highly prized and eagerly sought after'. Beyond question her wish has been respected. The garrison of Rorke's Drift, 104 strong, won nine V.cs in beating off the attack of 3500 Zulu warriors on their very indifferent fort (22/25 January 1879). The 1st Battalion of the Lancashire Fusiliers won 'six V.cs before breakfast' at Gallipoli (25 April 1915). Of the great Army which broke Hitler's vaunted Westwall in a single day (6 June 1944) only one soldier was awarded the V.c. He was C.S.M. Stanley Hollis of the 6th Battalion Green Howards, who appeared 'wherever fighting was heaviest'.

1.

2.

3.

4.

1. Trooping the Colour – an ancient ceremony that takes place each year on Horse Guards Parade, London to mark the Queen's official birthday.

2. A gun salute being fired in Hyde Park, London, by the King's Troop of the Royal Horse Artillery. Such salutes are fired to mark special anniversaries such as the Queen's Accession.

3. A bodyguard of the Company of Pikemen and Musketeers belonging to the Honourable Artillery Company escorting the coach of the Lord Mayor of London.

4. The annual parade of Chelsea army pensioners on Charley Day (29th May) celebrates the accession of Charles II, in whose reign the Royal Hospital was built. Its architect, Sir Christopher Wren, insisted that there should be no stained glass in the chapel, so that the old soldiers could see the sky. The six companies of In Pensioners consist of former NCOs and men over 65 years of age.

'A Wellington Boot, or the Head of the Army' – a caricature of the Duke of Wellington as Commander-in-Chief of the Army, published in 1827. A brilliant tactician, and victor of Waterloo, Wellington is regarded as one of Britain's greatest military commanders.

The Defence of the Realm: Battlefields of Britain

The battlefields of Britain are part of her historic heritage, but, sadly enough, a singularly ill-marked part. Romans, Celts, Saxons, Vikings and Normans fought each other with some skill and a great deal of ferocity, but where exactly they did so is, generally speaking, a very obscure subject indeed. The topographical details of their campaigns have vanished. Who can say with confidence where Julius Caesar or William the Conqueror crossed the Thames? Does the White Horse at Westbury mark some forgotten triumph of our Celtic ancestors? The great Neolithic fortress of Maiden Castle near Dorchester, is exceptional, for details of the storming of its eastern entrance by Vespasian's legion have been revealed by excavation. But it seems improbable that future generations of archaeologists will locate the field where Boudica's army was destroyed, or the site of Agricola's victory at Mons Graupius.

After the Conquest the records, while still far from satisfactory, at least reveal where the various battles took place. Nor do we have to depend entirely on written sources.

Traces of the fighting at Alton (1643), Colchester (1648) and Powick (1651), to name but a few examples, may still be seen. Occasionally, as at Lansdown, a monument was erected during the lifetime of the men who fought there. Some of the battlefields have a dramatic appearance far excelling anything that could be raised by the hand of man. Roundway Down where the Cavaliers drove Waller's cavalry down the slope that 'never horse went down nor up before' is a particularly horrifying example, with the Bloody Ditch at its foot.

From the military point of view the most important event in the history of the British Isles was not a military operation at all. It took place some 4000 years before our history began, when the seas broke through the English Channel, and set a most effective moat between Great Britain and Europe. Before that time England was open to invasion by any migrating horde that overran north-east France.

Thereafter it was still possible to make a seaborne attack

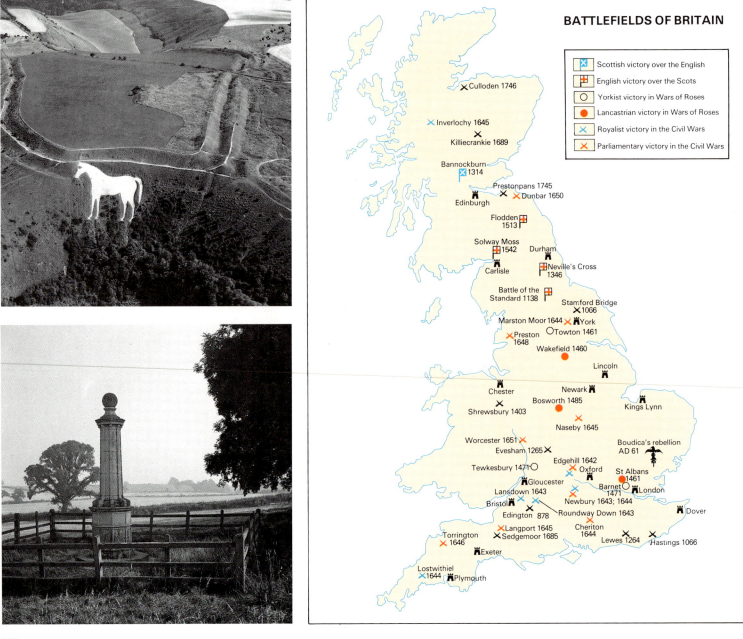

BATTLEFIELDS OF BRITAIN

⊠	Scottish victory over the English
⊞	English victory over the Scots
○	Yorkist victory in Wars of Roses
●	Lancastrian victory in Wars of Roses
✕	Royalist victory in the Civil Wars
✕	Parliamentary victory in the Civil Wars

Culloden 1746

Inverlochy 1645
Killiecrankie 1689

Bannockburn 1314

Prestonpans 1745
Dunbar 1650
Edinburgh

Flodden 1513

Solway Moss 1542
Durham
Carlisle
Neville's Cross 1346

Battle of the Standard 1138

Stamford Bridge 1066
Marston Moor 1644 York
Preston 1648 Towton 1461
Wakefield 1460
Lincoln

Chester
Newark
Bosworth 1485
Kings Lynn
Shrewsbury 1403
Naseby 1645

Worcester 1651
Boudica's rebellion AD 61
Evesham 1265
Edgehill 1642
St Albans 1461
Tewkesbury 1471
Oxford
Barnet 1471 London
Gloucester
Lansdown 1643
Newbury 1643; 1644
Bristol
Roundway Down 1643
Edington 878
Dover
Cheriton 1644
Langport 1645
Lewes 1264 Hastings 1066
Torrington 1646
Sedgemoor 1685
Exeter
Lostwithiel 1644
Plymouth

on these islands, but only after an administrative effort of which few were capable in the Dark or Middle Ages. Reading the ancient chronicles one is sometimes astonished by the fact that decades and even centuries go by unmarked by any great or decisive battle. And yet our ancestors were warlike people, never shy of putting their quarrels to the test of combat. This may perhaps be attributed to the fact that the warlords working by the light of their own practical experience, avoided when possible a pitched battle which could lose their only army at a blow, and destroy in an afternoon the fruits of a season's campaigning. Small wonder they preferred raiding or sieges, operations where the spoils of the victor were tangible prizes. Some of the fights which pass in our history books as battles were little more than big raids – Otterburn (or Chevy Chase, 1388), Chalgrove Field (1643) and Inverlochy (1645) are just some examples.

The location of many of our battlefields is explained by the special importance of London, populous and wealthy as well

of succeeding, when Charles I's with more than twice as many men had failed? London could muster and supply far more men – albeit raw soldiers – than any army of the olden days. She might be captured, but only if she allowed herself to be so.

Provincial capitals have their importance too. 'If York be lost,' Charles I wrote to Rupert, 'I shall esteem my crown little more.' Whereupon his rather literal-minded nephew proceeded to offer battle at Marston Moor – with disastrous results.

After Edgehill, King Charles took Oxford and made it his capital and headquarters. Thus it was determined that the main axis of both sides must be the lower Thames valley between Oxford and London, with the latter as the main Royalist objective. Parliamentarian strategy was a hand to mouth affair until the offensive of Cromwell's New Model Army, which destroyed the main Royalist forces at Naseby, Langport and Torrington. The fall of Oxford, not quite the last Royalist fortress to surrender, marked the end of the

as being a port, a fortress and a centre of communications. Rivers and mountains, marshes and forests, towns, ports and castles all had their influence on the strategic pattern of the campaigns of Simon de Montfort, of York and Lancaster; of Cavalier and Roundhead. But, however long the struggle, the winner in the end was always the one who held London. So it is not surprising that during the Wars of the Roses there were two battles at St Albans and another at Barnet both near the capital; or that the Cavaliers came near to putting their army at risk at Turnham Green. Prince Charles Edward was advancing on London, when his nerve failed at Derby. A rebellion on the defensive cannot succeed. But what serious chance had the Highland Army

Civil War.

The inhabitants of these islands, at least the generations alive in 1940, have seen a 'long-drawn battle in the skies', but the most recent Battle Honours won by the Army on British soil are 'Jersey 1781', and Fishguard (1799). Had it not been for the English Channel the map of Kent would certainly have been marked with symbols denoting the progress of Napoleon's *Grande Armée* and of Hitler's Panzer Divisions, to name but the most obvious of our would-be invaders. If England has seldom lain' at the proud foot of a conqueror', the reason has probably been geographical rather than military. There is something to be said for not having a Channel Tunnel!

The 'Death of Major Pierson' by the American historical painter John Singleton Copley. The painting depicts the climax of the battle of St Helier, Jersey, in 1781, when the British commander was killed at the moment of victory over the French. It was one of the last occasions when Battle Honours were won by the army on British soil.

The Defence of the Realm: The Royal Navy

A detail from a scene depicting the defeat of the Spanish Armada in 1588, in which the battle was mainly between the sleek English galleons and the Spanish 'floating fortresses'. As a result of the Spanish defeat a new and almost unknown navy made its entry onto the world stage.

Offa, king of Mercia, who died in the year 796, wrote in his testament that 'he who would be secure on land must be supreme at sea'. He was writing of Britain as an island, subject to periodic invasions by Saxons and Danes. His words are the first expression of what later grew into a realization that Britain's prosperity lies in her ability to control the seas around her coasts.

Exactly one hundred years later Alfred the Great built longships to attack the Danes as their fleets descended on England, but it is recorded that his ships were of little use, grounding in battle and later foundering in a storm.

There was then, and for the next 500 years, no continuing English navy. During wars the king would hire merchant ships, embark his fighting men, and disperse the ships when the war was over. Edward III fought the battle of Sluys against the French in 1340 with a fleet of cogs, the standard merchant ship of the day, and Henry V also took the cog as his model for his wars in France. His son sold the fleet as soon as he succeeded to the throne.

It is to the two succeeding Henrys that we look as the founders of the Navy as a permanent force. Henry VII built about eight warships and a naval dock at Portsmouth, to grow into the Royal dockyard we know today. Henry VIII continued his father's work, built new ships and dockyards, and in 1546 set up a permanent organization of administration and supply for the fleet.

It was with some of Henry VIII's ships, some new ones of her own built to a more seaworthy design, and some merchant ships armed for the purpose, that Queen Elizabeth had to face the first real threat to England since the days of the Danes and William the Conqueror. In 1588 the whole of Europe watched as Spain sent her Invincible Armada up the English Channel to embark a Spanish army at Calais and invade the small island that was beginning to challenge her supremacy at sea. It saw what was then the world's most powerful fleet harried up the Channel by Elizabeth's ships, forced from its anchorage off Calais in disarray, and driven north round Scotland to shipwreck and disaster. A new and almost unknown navy had made its entry onto the world stage.

There were English fighting seamen before the Armada, though mainly adventuring for private gain. Drake, Hawkins, Raleigh, Grenville, Frobisher and others were naval heroes in England before 1588 though the other nations of Europe looked upon them as pirates. Their marauding voyages were a foretaste of the pattern of English determination to rule the oceans.

But it was the defeat of the Spanish Armada and of Spanish sea power that really opened the door. The erstwhile privateers were absorbed into Elizabeth's navy and became its natural leaders. Within twelve years of that week-long battle England had formed her East India Company and broken into the Portuguese trade monoploy in India and the Far East, earning by sword and gun a share of the rich produce of this new market. Even earlier, England had planted her first, if unsuccessful, colonies in the Spanish monopoly of North America, an indication that there, too, she was prepared to maintain the challenge.

To those Tudor seamen who first put England's name on the maritime map of the world must be added later giants of the nation's sea story. Men such as Blake, Monck, Prince Rupert, and the gallant Myngs, who led the navy through the three bitter 17th-century wars against the Dutch and by their victories upheld the British claim of freedom of seaborne trade in European and foreign waters. Rooke and Russell, Benbow and Shovell ushered in the 18th century with the capture of Gibraltar and of new lands in the west, and blazed the trail for the great growth of empire

which followed a hundred years of wars against France and Spain. This was the century of admirals such as Anson, Hawke, Boscawen, Saunders, Rodney, Howe, Hood, Duncan, St Vincent and Nelson, and of battles such as Finisterre, Quiberon Bay, Lagos, Quebec, the Saints, the Glorious First of June, Camperdown, the Nile, Copenhagen and Trafalgar.

It was these two centuries of warfare, from the Armada to Trafalgar, which gained for Britain control of the world's oceans and the realization of her dedication to the freedom of the seas, that the oceans should be an open highway for the merchant ships of all nations. It was in defence of this freedom that the navies of Britain and her allies fought two great wars of the 20th century. It is a freedom that still exists, defended in times of challenge at heavy cost in lives and ships, but one that remains a foundation stone of the British naval heritage.

Perhaps Hilaire Belloc has best summed it up. 'The sea is the matrix of creation, and we have the memory of it in our blood.'

H.M.S. Victory. Ordered in 1758 she served for over 100 years and has now been restored to the same condition as when she was Lord Nelson's flagship at the battle of Trafalgar. Preserved in drydock in Portsmouth Dockyard, she stands as a permanent monument to the Royal Navy in its exercise of sea power.

Horatio, Viscount Nelson. The most famous of British admirals, his dedication and courage have been a shining example to naval officers and men since he lost his life in the moment of his most glorious victory.

The Royal Naval Hospital at Greenwich. Begun in the reign of William and Mary and completed in that of Queen Anne, it was designed by Sir Christopher Wren as a hospital and permanent home for British seamen wounded in battle. During the 19th century, with Britain largely at peace, the few men remaining at Greenwich were discharged with pensions and the building eventually converted into a naval college. Behind it lies the National Maritime Museum, a treasure house of the maritime history of Britain.

Chapter Five

The British Way of Life

The country house is perhaps Britain's greatest contribution to European civilization. Perhaps this is because it is in the country that the British are – or like to think that they are – most at home. The village, with its church, pub and pretty houses round the green; the hunting, the fishing and the cricket; the animals everywhere, especially dogs and horses – all this conjures up in the minds of many people an ideal image of Britain. We should also add to this picture the seaside, a passion for gardening and a love for old customs and traditions. But the vast majority of the population lives in towns and cities; and for these, despite the magnificent historic centres which many of them still possess, the British often have all too little respect. In the past 30 years, town planners and 'property developers' have accounted for as much loss of architectural heritage as did the bombs of the Second World War.

The Settlement of Britain

It was William Cowper who wrote in 1783 that 'God made the country and man made the town', a sentence that reads strangely to anyone who thinks about our landscape. It is true there is much about the English scene that is not human, for rocks and geological structure have gone into its making. But over these foundations a humanized veneer has been laid, first by the pre-Saxon inhabitants and then by later peoples. The settlements established by the invaders of Roman Britain were, very largely, the settlements of later times. Where the Englishman Babba made a 'stoc' or settlement in Wiltshire there stands Baverstock today, and where the Scandinavian Skeggi settled in Nottinghamshire there Skegby still stands. From these early centuries from say the 5th to the 10th, date a great number of terminations that give interest and variety to our place-names – e.g. the English *ham*, *ton* and *stede* and the Scandinavian *by*, *thwaite* and *toft*. With them must be counted those terminations that reveal how wood was being cleared over large stretches of countryside, names such as those which end in the English *hurst* or *ley*, or in the Scandinavian *scarth* (Aysgarth) or *skogr* (Litherskew).

By the time the Normans arrived in 1066, England was already an 'old country' in the sense that it was more or less settled and that it possessed a well-developed territorial organization. Twenty years after their coming the Normans instituted the inquiry that resulted in *Domesday Book* which shows a country divided into shires (or to use the Norman word, counties) that were to remain until the 20th century. The four northern counties were not surveyed. Over the rest of the country more than 13,000 settlements were named. Even this is not the total for many names covered more than one settlement. Whatever be the exact detail it is clear that the framework of the English countryside had been established. We cannot be sure to what extent

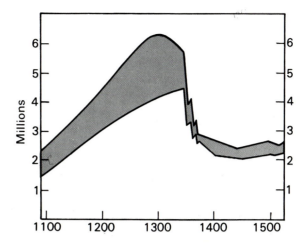

The Population of England between 1100 and 1525. Within an estimated range, this diagram shows the steady rise prior to the Black Death (1349) and the dramatic decline which followed. During the decline, however, settlements did not so much disappear as shrink in size.

the *Domesday* record of churches is complete, but whatever be the truth, stone-built parish churches were to become a feature of the countryside and to constitute a legacy to later generations. The population of *Domesday* England seems to have been between 1½ and 2 million. Such an estimate can only be uncertain, but a map of the distribution of *Domesday* population would probably not be far from the truth.

After 1066 reclamation continued for at least another two centuries, not by the creation of new settlements but by expansion around existing centres as nearby wood and waste were cleared. How great was the increase in population that accompanied this clearing is difficult to say. It may have doubled by 1300; some say even more than doubled to 4½ million. After about 1300, however, came recession which was greatly accelerated by the Black

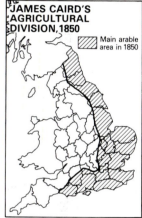

JAMES CAIRD'S AGRICULTURAL DIVISION, 1850

Main arable area in 1850

Enclosures in the 18th and 19th centuries were frequently accompanied by the conversion of arable land to grass, especially on the heavy clays of the Midlands. Thus arose the distinction between 'grazing counties' and 'corn counties' noted by James Caird.

Steam technology applied to agriculture in the 19th century. The illustration shows Howard's 'steam ploughing apparatus' using a stationary steam engine and windlass. Mechanization was eventually to lead to the uprooting of thousands of miles of hedgerows in recent years to provide prairie type fields. The enclosures of the 18th and 19th centuries in themselves transformed Britain's landscape as did earlier reclamations of heathland, the draining of marshes and the clearing of woodland in medieval times.

Death in 1349 when population declined to perhaps $2\frac{1}{2}$ million. Settlements did not so much disappear as shrink in size. Estimates of population in the 14th and 15th centuries are very uncertain. But one thing is clear. The recession of these years was once more succeeded in the 16th century by economic expansion.

Epics of the Countryside

The clearing of the wood may have been the great epic of the medieval countryside, but after 1600 came other epics. One was the draining of marshes such as the Fenland of eastern England. Another was the reclamation of heath-lands such as those in the light soils of north-west Norfolk and on the Wolds of Lincolnshire and Yorkshire. These changes were made possible by the adoption of new methods of agriculture and by new crops such as turnips and clover. Yet another transformation in the 18th and 19th centuries came from the making of landscape gardens which have been described as 'one of this country's major contributions to European art', and which still embellish great stretches of the countryside.

While these changes were in progress, the large open fields of the older agricultural areas were being enclosed so producing a chequer-board landscape of small fields divided by hedgerows. Enclosure was, moreover, frequently accompanied by the conversion of arable to grass, especially on the heavy clays of the Midlands. Thus arose the distinction between 'grazing counties' and the 'corn counties' noted by James Caird in 1851. His division must be modified by the addition of the potato and market-garden areas of the North-West especially on the reclaimed peat areas of south-west Lancashire. It is an interesting reflection that the main arable areas of 20th-century England are those that have been reclaimed since the Middle Ages.

Just as the impulse to improve was abroad in the countryside, so was the impulse to contrive and invent in the industrial areas. The age of steam had already begun when James Watt patented his engines in 1769 and 1781. The results were felt everwhere, but nowhere more so than upon the coalfields. As Arthur Young wrote in 1791, 'all the activity and industry of the kingdom is fast concentrating where there are coal pits'. The population of the country was clearly increasing. But to what extent? Speculation ended with the first census of 1801. Imperfect though this was, it left no doubt about the order of magnitude. It showed a total of 8.3 million for England and 0.6 million for Wales. Apart from London, the greatest increases were in Lancashire and Yorkshire, in Staffordshire and Warwick-shire, and in the North-East. By 1901 the total population had already quadrupled – from 8.9 to 32.5 million in England and Wales; and by 1971 the population had reached 48.6 million.

North and South

As a result of coal, iron and steam. Britain had become 'the workshop of the world', the country in which the Industrial Revolution had first exploded. A contrast was sometimes drawn between the industrial Midlands and the North, and on the other hand, the rural South with its many parks. But this must be qualified. In the North there are comfortable farming dales as well as open solitudes where National Parks were established after 1949. And in the South, successive censuses in the 20th century show greater increases of population than elsewhere. Britain's economic supremacy was over, leaving a rich legacy of industrial archaeology and a new challenge for the future.

Coal, iron and steam turned Britain into 'the workshop of the world'. Technological developments coincided with a rapid increase in population, providing ready supplies of cheap labour for the growing industrial centres, particularly in the Midlands and North. The picture shows an iron works in the early 19th century.

Cities and Towns

The towns and cities of Britain contain, despite successive waves of re-development, a visual record of history covering over 1500 years.

The word 'town' derives from *tun*, a native British word meaning homestead, but the concept of urbanization and civilization which the town or city implied, came from ancient Greece.

The earliest towns for which any visual evidence survives are those laid out by the Romans during the 400 years of their occupation. These Roman towns, often founded on defensive sites by the mouths of rivers, followed the form developed throughout the Roman Empire. Their streets were laid out on the grid plan which still persists in many of our towns today, just as many of the sites selected by the Romans have continued in occupation ever since. Chester, Chichester, Colchester, York, Gloucester, London, Lincoln, Carlisle and Canterbury were all important Roman towns. The first four still retain substantial remains of their city walls, all of Roman origin.

The Anglo-Saxons developed a pattern of urban life, accelerated by the need to defend themselves against Viking invaders, which continued relatively unchanged for another 1000 years until the Industrial Revolution. Many of our market towns and ports were founded during the Saxon period, for although the Romans built up a sophisticated system of supplies and communications, it broke down before the arrival of the Saxons. It took another 600 years for urban society to emerge, although the existence of Winchester and other great Saxon town palaces indicates a high level of sophistication at an early date. By 1086 the *Domesday Book* recorded 100 towns, ten per cent of the population were town dwellers, and every major river was controlled by a town near the coast and by a bridge which acted as a toll gate for traders and as a barrier to raiders.

The tenth and eleventh centuries saw a resurgence of town life not seen since the Romans. Most buildings, with the exception of churches, were of wood, but concrete mixers were in use in Northampton as early as the ninth century.

The early Christian Church established monastic sites during the Saxon period, many of which formed the nucleus of our cathedral cities. Of these Canterbury, York, Ripon, Durham and Lichfield were all founded before 800 by early Christian saints, St Augustine, St Wilfrid, St Cuthbert and St Chad respectively. The Normans, bringing from France the tradition of building in stone, rebuilt many of the 17 cathedrals already in existence, and most of the churches. (St Wilfrid's Saxon crypt at Ripon is a rare survival.) The Normans also fortified and strengthened our towns, and built the castles which are such a prominent feature to this day. In Wales the most important new towns built in the 13th century were established by Edward I during his campaigns to quell native opposition. These include the great fortresses of Caernarfon, Beaumaris, Conway and Harlech. During his reign Winchelsea and Hull were founded and Berwick on Tweed, captured from the Scots, given its first charter. This period marks the end of the first expansion of town life in Britain.

The Royal Scottish Burghs were initially founded by David I in the 12th century. At Edinburgh and Stirling existing settlements were granted royal status, while Inverness, Glasgow, St Andrews and Dingwall, among other, were founded soon after. The burghs consisted of guilds of craftsmen, later expanded into groups of merchant traders. Through trade with France and the Low Countries,

Conway Castle, one of several massive fortresses built throughout Wales by Edward I to defend his newly conquered territory. The town of Conway is surrounded by medieval walls. Thomas Telford's delicate ironwork bridge was built in 1826 and is still used by pedestrians.

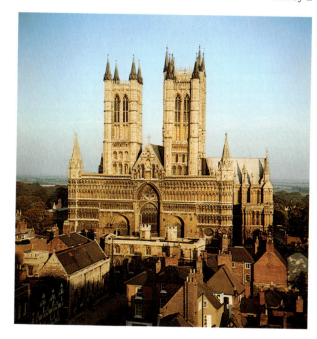

Lincoln Cathedral, arguably Britain's finest, stands at the heart of the city, surrounded by medieval buildings. Lincoln has been occupied since it was the site of a camp in Roman times.

Chester – the Rows, Bridge Street. The Rows, dating from the Middle Ages, are raised galleried streets reached from the road below by stairways. Chester was an important camp in Roman times and much of the original Roman enclosing wall survives.

Burford, a Cotswold town in Oxfordshire, dates back to Saxon times.

the burghs expanded rapidly during the 14th and 15th centuries. They promoted the founding of three universities before 1500, St Andrews, Glasgow and Aberdeen. But although Scottish trade increased during the 16th and 17th centuries, and included a busy wine trade with Bordeaux, the prosperity and control of the burghs declined.

Although the wooden houses, surrounded with walls of earth, have not survived, the lay-out of Edinburgh, Stirling and Elgin has. It consisted of a single street running the full length of the burgh, lined with narrow burgage plots of houses, with long gardens behind.

Many medieval towns were developed on the grid plan with a main street wide enough for a market. The houses were largely of wood and thatch, and although in Canterbury for example, it was laid down that two feet must be left between houses for 'eavesdrip', it was not until the disastrous fires, culminating in the Great Fire of London in 1666, that stringent controls were introduced, which tried to determine the width of the streets, and introduced the use of brick and stone as compulsory building materials. Although Sir Christopher Wren's re-planning of the City of London was never carried out and the medieval street plans persist to this day, his designs for houses, starting with 'houses of the greatest bigness', were adopted.

During the 16th and 17th centuries many of the great town houses were built, often by aristocrats on the sites of former medieval bishops' palaces, notably on the London riverside behind the Strand. To this period also belong some of the earliest examples of town planning, notably Covent Garden, developed by the Earl of Bedford, and by Charles I Whitehall and Greenwich to the designs of Inigo Jones.

After 1600 the cotton industry developed in Lancashire and Preston, where fustain was made from Mediterranean cotton; Liverpool and Chester grew, as the linen industry, using Irish flax, developed, and the invasion of Flemish immigrants in the South-East brought prosperity, with the manufacture of the 'new draperies', to Norwich, Colchester and London. The wool trade, which in the Middle Ages created the prosperous East Anglian towns with their magnificent churches, declined, but it flourished during the 17th century both in the Cotswolds, in Wiltshire, and in Devonshire, where the towns and ports were among the busiest in the country.

The 18th century saw the development of many of the great town estates by aristocratic landlords and by speculators, and the leisured classes cultivated the new spas and resorts of Bath (see page 150), Buxton, Tunbridge Wells, Bristol and Cheltenham. The great 18th-century New Town of Edinburgh arose beside its medieval neighbour, and John Nash followed up the formal 18th-century development of Bloomsbury with his classical terraces in Regent's Park and Regent Street.

At this period, the closes of many cathedrals were landscaped and cleared of medieval houses and tombstones, thus providing a setting unique in Europe, similar to the landscaped parks being created for country houses.

The 19th century gave birth to a social conscience, and with it came asylums, hospitals, prisons, baths, libraries, and all the appendages of the new welfare state. Rivers were embanked, railways and undergrounds constructed by roving teams of navvies. Cholera and pestilence created the need for cemeteries, civic pride the need for town halls and art galleries. Britain emerged as the leading industrial nation in the world, and the factories, warehouses, markets and offices were built which created the bones of our modern cities.

Evidence of these periods is visible in our towns and cities today, for those who know where to look. The chart on the opposite page, based on one compiled by the Council for British Archaeology gives some indication of the special features and characteristics to be found in each of the towns named. Nikolaus Pevsner's *Buildings of England* series provide the best travelling companions. They identify all the important individual buildings, and also contain descriptions of the towns and cities themselves, with suggested perambulations. The Council for British Archaeology estimates that 'of those historic towns which remain for study, the archaeological value of one fifth will most probably have been entirely destroyed in the next 20 years; and another two fifths will be developed in lesser ways. If nothing is done, most of these towns will be fundamentally changed without a record of their past being made.' The battles to save our towns and cities which have raged for the past 50 years and the organizations which have led them are referred to on page 200. The fact that any historical character has survived is largely due to them.

Left: The ancient fishing port of Whitby in Yorkshire, showing the sandstone ruins of Whitby Abbey, founded in 657 by St Hilda.

Above: The 18th-century New Town of Edinburgh which rose up beside its medieval neighbour.

The Shambles, York, a city which has successively been occupied by Romans, Danes and Normans. The city is still surrounded by medieval walls built on Roman foundations.

TOWNS WITH OUTSTANDING HISTORIC CENTRES

ENGLAND

Abingdon, Oxon
Barnard Castle, Durham
Beverley, Yorks
Bath, Avon
Blandford, Dorset
Bradford-on-Avon, Wilts
Bridgnorth, Shropshire
Burford, Oxon
Cambridge
Chipping Campden, Glos.
Cockermouth, Cumbria
Colchester, Essex
Hadleigh, Suffolk
Hereford
King's Lynn, Norfolk
Lavenham, Suffolk
Lewes, Sussex
Lincoln
Ludlow, Shropshire
Marlborough, Wilts
Newark on Trent, Notts.
Newcastle on Tyne
Norwich, Norfolk
Oxford
Pershore, Worcs.
Richmond, Yorks.
Rye, Sussex
Scarborough, Yorks.
Salisbury, Wilts
Sandwich, Kent
Stamford, Lincs
Tewkesbury, Glos
Thaxted, Essex
Totnes
Warwick
Wells, Somerset
Whitehaven, Cumbria
Wisbech, Cambs
Wymondham, Norfolk
York

WALES

Conway, Gwynedd
Monmouth, Gwent
Tenby, Dyfed

SCOTLAND

Aberdeen, Grampian
Cromarty, Highland
Culross, Fife
Edinburgh and Leith
Haddington, Lothian
Inverary, Strathclyde
Kelso, Borders
Stirling, Central

Key

Bridge
Waterfront
Towngate or wall
Castle site
Ecclesiastical building
Medieval –1714 ⎫
Georgian & Regency ⎬ building
Victorian ⎭

The 51 historic towns in a list of 324 which the Council for British Archaeology singled out as being so splendid and precious a part of Britain's heritage that the responsibility for them should be a national concern. The list takes into account not only the existence of buildings of historic and architectural importance but also of historic street plans – the skeleton of a town.

Villages

The village is an essential and much admired part of the rural heritage of England. To many people it is a symbol of 'roots' and stability, but we are only beginning to be able to assess the depth of these roots and to appreciate the complex and lively histories of most village layouts. The village as we now see it is less deeply rooted and far less stable than we might imagine. From pre-historic days through most of the Dark Ages, villages were the exception rather than the norm. They existed in all periods from the New Stone Age onwards, but in the ancient countrysides dispersed farmsteads, small hut clusters and hamlets were much more numerous. Most pre-historic village sites have been obliterated by later agricultural activities and can only be recognized in air photographs. Some ruined huts and associated streets or trackways survive in areas where stone rather than timber — wattle-and-daub was used and

which have been shunned by later ploughmen. Skara Brae on Orkney is by far the best New Stone Age village survival; Grimspound and Kestor (both on Dartmoor) are Bronze Age examples, while Chysauster in Cornwall is a relic of the Roman Iron Age.

Pre-historic villages were not only older than medieval examples, but different in vital respects. Never conceived of as truly permanent settlements, they were usually abandoned after a few decades of occupation. Often the villagers inexplicably migrated to a new site a few hundred yards away from their old homes.

An excellent reconstruction of part of a pagan Saxon village can be seen at West Stow in Suffolk. Another important early Saxon settlement site is at Mucking on the northern side of the Thames estuary.

The creation of permanent villages seems to have been part of a major reorganization and reappraisal of settlement and land-use which took place around the 8th- or 9th-century. The causes are not known, but the introduction of open-field cultivation, which created a more intensive use of arable land and so released some of the farmland as essential pasture, may have been partly responsible. The coming of Christianity and the construction of churches must also have played a part in the establishment of truly permanent villages. Though much has been made of the village green as an original component of the village plan, greens may not have been typical in late Saxon times; many are known to be later features inserted into the older village.

The popular perception of the village as that of an undisciplined and unplanned creation is also misleading, for many villages clearly preserve the outlines of medieval planning. A high proportion of northern villages, particularly those in the Vale of York are clearly planned creations based on regular rows of dwellings, each dwelling having a long plot of land or 'toft' attached, with the rows aligned along a

Far left: Some of the dwellings of the reconstructed early Saxon village at West Stow in Suffolk.

Left: Lower Slaughter, one of the least spoilt of the lovely stone-built villages in the Cotswolds.

Below left: The village of Newton, on Rawcliffe in Yorkshire, has a circular pond and a green as its nucleus.

Right: Finchingfield in Essex, often quoted as a 'typical' village (though its form is really quite complicated) was an important centre of the East Anglian textile industry during the Middle Ages.

Appleton-le-Moors in Yorkshire clearly preserves the outlines of early medieval village planning.

road or flanking a rectangular green set out on either side of the road. Many such villages were probably the work of Norman landlords following the 'Harrying of the North' of 1069–71 when older settlements were destroyed. Planned villages are not however confined to the North; often, as at Castle Rising in Norfolk and Castleton in Derbyshire, they are associated with the castles and markets of local lords.

Attempts have been made to group villages in a few simple categories: 'nucleated' or clustered villages, 'linear' villages where the dwellings are set out along a road or stream and 'green' villages, which have greens. The truth is much more intricate and complicated and therefore more interesting. Many villages are 'polyfocal'; that is to say they result from the merging of two or more different components. Other villages are quite recent features in the rural landscape, resulting from what has been called 'late nucleation'. Thus Birstwith in Yorkshire dates from only around 1800, a result of the organized industrialization of this part of Nidderdale. Then there are the several thousand lost, shrunken and shifted villages described on page 118.

Villages do not develop or persist without good reason. In less fertile parts of Britain and Ireland, where livestock was generally more important than arable farming, hamlets and farmsteads were more usual. Most of the villages which the Normans artifically created in Ireland have perished, while a high proportion of the villages in Scotland were built as planned settlements by landlords during the 18th- and 19th-century agricultural reorganizations. In England, villages survive only where new roles were discovered for them in the years following the Parliamentary Enclosures of 1750–1850 and the disastrous consequences of 19th- and 20th-century farm mechanization. So long as there are some opportunities for rural employment and commuters who prefer village life to the advantages and stresses of city life, the village will endure.

Lost and Shifted Villages

Dotted about Britain are thousands of 'lost' villages. Some are hidden beneath an overgrowth of nettles or woodlands. The site of others are marked by a ruined isolated church around which a village once clustered. In many cases the only reminder of a once thriving community is a faded pattern of green rectangles, the platforms on which houses once stood. Particularly as a result of air photography and the researches of the Medieval Research Group, new discoveries are continually being made. Local village studies are also demonstrating that hosts of living villages show signs of shrinkage, while a number are known to have completely shifted their sites. In areas such as Northamptonshire and Oxfordshire, which have been the subject of detailed survey, shrinkage, shifting and re-alignment almost appear to be the norm.

The cause of village deaths were various. Village desertion was normal in pre-historic times, but from the later Saxon period onwards villages were not normally abandoned without special cause. In the course of William the Conqueror's Harrying of the North of 1069–71 it is thought that about 850 out of 1900 Yorkshire villages were completely laid waste and another 300 partly destroyed. In the decades following, several Cistercian monasteries were established in the still partly deserted wastelands; and as monastic farms or granges were established on the abbey sites, peasant villages which

abandoned in places where the cold, heavy soils were waterlogged and slow to warm in the spring, or where the upland crops failed to ripen in the cool and cloudy summers. During the unusually violent coastal storms of the 14th century, some villages slithered into the sea as their cliff-top perches were eroded, while a clutch of settlements in the Humber estuary were completely inundated.

The 14th century had a worse horror in store, for in 1348 came the Black Death, killing at least a third of the population and recurring from time to time until the middle of the 17th century. Local folklore generally attributes any nearby lost village as a plague victim, but authenticated examples like Hale in Northamptonshire are not numerous. While a good number of villages may have been completely depopulated many, like Cublington in Buckinghamshire, were recolonized within a few years or decades of the disaster.

In the 15th and 16th centuries landlords discovered that livestock could be more profitable than collecting rents and services from peasants; the consequence was the removal of peasant settlements to create depopulated sheep runs — the commonest cause of village destruction during that period. These clearances were most severe in the Midlands and eastern counties: in Warwickshire, Oxfordshire and Northamptonshire chains of deserted parishes were created. Wormleighton in Warwickshire, devastated by the

intruded on their seclusion were removed. Cayton and Herleshow near Ripon in Yorkshire were among the dozen or more villages destroyed by the monks of Fountains Abbey.

Until about 1200, the medieval climate was equable and improving, encouraging peasant farmers in an over-populated countryside to establish new villages on poorer upland and clayland soils which had hitherto been shunned. After 1200, however, the climate underwent a prolonged deterioration. Scores of villages located in marginal lands, like Goltho on the Lincolnshire clay and Hound Tor on the uplands of Dartmoor, were gradually

Above left: Thaxted in Essex has atrophied since the decline of the town's important medieval cutlery industry, although the Cutlers' Guildhall is still impressive. The cutlery industry probably declined because of a shortage of trees on which it depended for fuel.

Above: The church tower – all that remains of the lost village of Godwick in Norfolk.

Spencer family, was one of the many hundreds of victims.

The final great onslaught on village England took place mainly in the 17th and 18th centuries in the course of the construction of great mansions surrounded by areas of deserted parkland. In some cases where 'emparking' took place as at Houghton in Norfolk, a new village was provided outside the park gate, but other villages like Hinderskelfe, which lies beneath the landscaped gardens and lake at Castle Howard in Yorkshire, were not replaced. Finally there are the recent departures, victims of local industrial decline like the deserted village of Porth-y-Nant in North Wales, of reservoir construction, like West End in Yorkshire, or of army training requirements, like Totington in Norfolk.

Shrunken Villages

Shrunken villages can often be identified by the neighbouring earthworks which mark the places of abandoned dwellings and streets. Sometimes shrinkage resulted from the same causes that we have described as producing village desertion: West Raynham in Norfolk was partly 'emparked' in the landscaping of land around Raynham Hall. Elsewhere the cause was the collapse of a traditional industry, the adverse effects of Parliamentary Enclosure on the smaller peasant farmers or the buying-up of the lesser farms in a locality by a few large landowners. Thaxted in Essex, today little more than a large village, was an important centre of the cutlery industry in the Middle Ages. Completely lost towns are far rarer than lost villages, but Caus in Shropshire, Torksey in Lincolnshire and Kincardine between Dundee and Aberdeen are examples.

The shifting of villages is often less easy to explain. The site of the original Castle Camps in Cambridgeshire is marked by the medieval village church which stands in the outer bailey of the local castle, but the present village is several hundred yards away. The cause for the move is unknown. Medieval Caxton in the same county seems to have been moved to a position astride the bustling Old North Road when the landlord obtained a charter to hold a market. Killinghall in Yorkshire reflects a later shift. The original village was sited on the edge of a large common in Forest of Knaresborough. At the end of the 18th-century the common was enclosed and two nearby roads were improved and turnpiked. Killinghall no longer had good reasons for being where it was and migrated a hundred yards or so to a new position at the convergence of the revitalized routeways. Thus, as new insights into village history accrue, we are able to recognize the fragility, complexity and also the vitality of the village which becomes much more interesting than the simple, stable place that we once thought we knew.

Ogle in Northumberland is a very shrunken village; from the air, the outlines of an elongated central green which was flanked by rows of dwellings set in rectangular closes are plainly apparent. The corduroy patterns of old ridge and furrow strip farming are also well displayed.

The Growth of London

London owes its origin to its strategic position on the Thames. In pre-historic times the Thames provided the principal means of access from Europe to the interior of southern England, but it was also a great barrier to northward penetration. An invader intending to conquer the whole country would therefore look for the lowest point where the river could be bridged or forded. After their arrival in AD 43 in the area of London the Romans found a sandbank leading across the marshy ground of the future Southwark on the south side of the river, matched on the north side by a low plateau. At that time the tide did not reach as far upstream as the site of London. This therefore was the ideal place for a permanent crossing, and around AD 50 the first London Bridge was built upon a site a short way east of the present bridge.

By this choice of site London became the focal point of the roads built by the Romans throughout Britain, and it has remained the hub of communications ever since, for the principal railways, motorways and air routes of more recent times all also radiate out of London. It soon superseded Colchester as the 'capital' of Britain and, with a population of perhaps up to 50,000, it also became an important port and commercial and financial centre. In the early 2nd century a large rectangular fort was built to the north-west of the city near Cripplegate. Around AD 200 the whole of the city, comprising (with the fort) an area of some 330 acres (133.5 ha) – by no means all of it fully built over – was enclosed by a great stone wall some nine feet (2.75m) thick and two miles (3.2km) long.

This wall marked the limits of London for over a thousand years. The protection which it provided probably ensured that after the Roman withdrawal in the 5th century the city was never wholly deserted during the Dark Ages; and so in the time of King Alfred (871–899) London was able to revive and become the greatest English city.

When Edward the Confessor (d. 1066) rebuilt Westminster Abbey and founded a royal palace nearby, London slowly began to divide into a city with two centres – Westminster, the seat of the sovereign, and later of Parliament, administration and courts of law, all later to be surrounded by the fashionable residential areas commonly called 'the West End'; and the City, the great financial and commercial citadel of the nation, later to be surrounded by workshops,

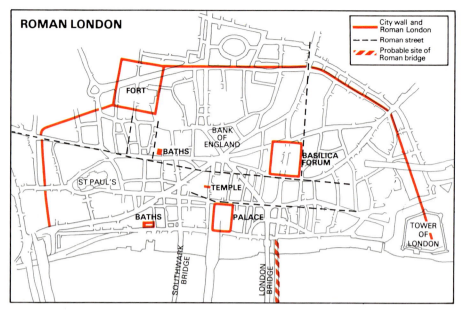

ROMAN LONDON

City wall and Roman London
Roman street
Probable site of Roman bridge

FORT
BANK OF ENGLAND
BATHS
BASILICA FORUM
ST PAUL'S
TEMPLE
BATHS
PALACE
TOWER OF LONDON
SOUTHWARK BRIDGE
LONDON BRIDGE

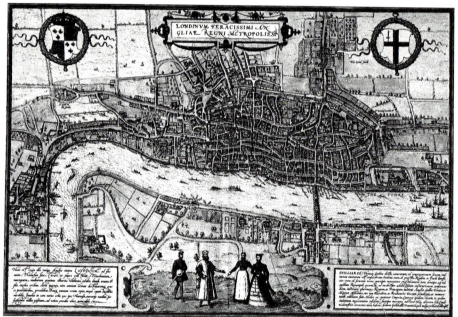

Top right: Roman London superimposed on a modern street plan.

Right: London as it was in the 1550s. The river was the city's main thoroughfare.

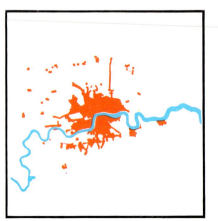

London in 1840, at the start of the railway age. The distance across the map is about 25 miles.

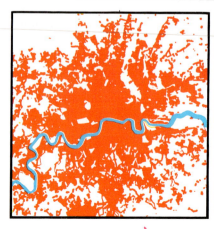

London in 1929, before the establishment of the Green Belt (far right) and the new towns beyond.

LONDON'S GREEN BELT, 1975

Stevenage
Welwyn Garden City
Harlow
Hatfield
Hemel Hempstead
Basildon
London
Bracknell
Crawley

The heart of London today. Outstanding landmarks are Buckingham Palace, the London home of the Sovereign; the Houses of Parliament, the seat of government; and Westminster Abbey, which many regard as the Church of England's 'ceremonial' centre. London's huge open spaces – parks, squares, and heaths – make it one of the greenest of the major capitals of the world.

warehouses and poorer suburbs of 'the East End' and by the wharves and docks of the Pool (or Port) of London. And under the powerful rule of William the Conqueror and his successors this bifurcated London had by the 13th century become, for the first time in the modern sense, the capital of the realm.

In the later Middle Ages some expansion outside the walls took place, particularly along the Strand and in Southwark. There was a setback when the Black Death killed some 25,000 Londoners in 1348–9. By 1500 the people of London probably numbered 75,000, out of a total population of two to three millions. This represented an increase of perhaps some 50 per cent since Roman times, but by 1600 London's population is thought to have more than doubled to 200,000. In 1666 nearly four-fifths of the City was destroyed in the Great Fire. Although rebuilding – in stone and brick – was virtually completed within five years, many homeless citizens had in the meantime established themselves in the suburbs, and by 1700 the total population of the capital amounted to 575,000. When the first census was taken in 1801 it stood at over 900,000, more than eleven times bigger than that of the second city, Liverpool, and some twelve times as great as it had been in 1500.

This gigantic growth was largely due to inward migration from the rest of the country, rather than to the natural increase of London's own inhabitants. In 1801 one in ten of all the people of England and Wales lived in the capital, and London had acquired a supremacy throughout the rest of the country which it has never lost.

Hundreds of streets and squares of terraced houses sprang up on all sides of London except south of the river, which until the opening of Westminster Bridge in 1750 remained inaccessible. Most of these houses were built by local men with locally made bricks under the leasehold system, which generally prevailed until the early 20th century; and until then there was never a shortage of building land.

By 1901 the population of Greater London amounted to over 6.5 million, or one fifth of all that of England and Wales. This vast 19th-century growth had been made possible by the development of buses, trams and railways (both on and below ground), by means of which London could spread far and wide, particularly southward. And also by 1900 London had ceased to depend for the maintenance of its inhabitants upon inward migration and became by its own natural increase a net 'exporter' of population.

In 1938 when, despite a decrease in the inner areas, the population of Greater London had reached 8.7 million, the Green Belt Act attempted to halt further outward spread by the creation of an inviolable rural girdle around the metropolis; and by 1964 nearly two thousand square miles (5180 km²) had been approved or proposed for inclusion in it. In 1947–8 eight new towns, all situated between 18 and 28 miles (29–45 km) from central London, were designated, and by 1968 their total population amounted to 450,000. By this time the population in almost all parts of Greater London had begun to fall, but in the London region as a whole (an area of about forty miles – 64 km – in radius from Charing Cross) it was still rising as inexorably as ever.

Gardens _____

Ever since the Romans taught them how, the British have gardened. And from the 18th century until today British gardens have been the most famous in the world. But what is particularly interesting about our garden tradition is that it is a truly popular one. While on the one hand we are past masters of the grand design as seen at Blenheim or Stowe, we have also evolved a strong tradition, nurtured in rectory and cottage gardens and dating back to the monasteries, of small individual gardens which not only provide useful plants for food, medicine and aesthetic delight but are a source of endless content to their owners. Of course the mild, wet weather is a help; but it can not entirely explain the Englishman's unique passion for decorating and nurturing his plot. And while this article deals largely with the grander examples of British garden heritage, you have only to drive through Kent in June to realize that the whole country is a garden.

In the 16th century British gardens looked to the Continent for inspiration and learned much from the Dutch and Italians in creating formal, departmentalized gardens. Topiary – trimming hedges into formal shapes – came from Italy and was enthusiastically adopted in gardens like Hampton Court. Low-cut hedges of box or herbs were used to create intricate knot gardens – a fashion still surviving in many herb gardens. Formal gardens on a larger scale began to appear, sometimes incorporating architectural features such as the splendid pleasure houses at Montacute, Somerset, built around 1590.

Sadly, many of the formal gardens of the 17th century like Wilton and Badminton have changed beyond recognition; we know them only from plans and illustrations. But some interesting ones remain such as the 'Dutch' or topiary garden at Levens Hall, Westmorland, designed in 1689 by a pupil of the great French gardener Le Notre, and glorious Compton Wynyates in Warwickshire. A good 17th-century garden would normally contain several hundreds of different plants and herbs, each in its allotted spot.

'Ideal Landscapes'

Such formal, limited gardens were swept aside by the landed gentry in the 18th century when the new freedom of thought and expression alive in the arts showed itself in a totally new approach to gardens. English gentlemen taking the Grand Tour of Europe, were much influenced by the paintings of Claude and Poussin depicting ideal landscapes with classical temples and statues, and decided that their gardens too, instead of being consciously artificial, must appear as nature at its most sublime. Out went restricting hedges; the simple invention of the ha ha enabled designer to create landscapes with park and garden apparently merged into one.

The first protagonist of this style was William Kent whose work can still be seen in its entirety at Rousham, Oxfordshire. Gone are formal flower-beds – in fact flowers altogether – and instead a lake, temples, ruins and statues dot the landscape in what he called 'landscape pictures' within the garden. Kent also worked for Lord Burlington at Chiswick, and also at Stowe where Lord Cobham boldly created a 500-acre park also employing John Vanbrugh and Charles Bridgeman. The head gardener at Stowe was Kent's most famous pupil Lancelot 'Capability' Brown.

Capability Brown's work was on an even larger scale. He did not flinch at moving hills or diverting streams to create his ideal and he became immensely popular. He worked at Chatsworth, Cliveden, Longleat and of course at Blenheim where he planted hundreds of acres of trees and laid out the well-known lake, spanned Vanbrugh's bridge,

Right: Montacute, Somerset. One of the two pavilions in the east forecourt of the Jacobean garden, which is among the most complete layouts of this date to survive. Montacute is now the property of the National Trust (see page 195).

which you see today on entering the grounds. Other famous gardens in this grand tradition created by Brown can be visited at Stourhead and at Wilton, both in Wiltshire, where in both cases their noble owners took a particular interest in them.

Such schemes, however, were limited to the immensely wealthy and the next generation saw a return to more contained styles subtly introduced by Humphry Repton, author of the influential *Observations on the Theory and Practice of Landscape Gardening*. He retained the wide sweeps, but resurrected flower-beds and terraces near the house. His changes coincided with renewed interest in individual flowers, trees and shrubs as plant-hunters returned from abroad with exotic but hardy shrubs and trees like camellias, rhododendron and laburnum to add colour and interest to gardens (page 124).

More modest gardens

Meanwhile more modest gardens sprang up around the smaller country houses and villas of the squirearchy and the new middle class. These gardens also reflected a growing interest in bedding plants raised in hot houses for mass planting in formal beds. Topiary returned to fashion and a formal lawn, previously cut laboriously with

Above: At Rousham, Oxfordshire, William Kent's landscape plan can still be seen in its entirety. Formal flower-beds have been replaced by a lake, temples, ruins and statues to form what Kent called 'landscape pictures'.

Humphry Repton (1752–1848) was also a talented painter; in order to show clients his proposed landscaping he prepared 'Red Books' with ingenious fold-over flaps to give his clients 'before' (above) and 'after' sketches of his ideas. He retained wide sweeps, but resurrected flower-beds and terraces near the house. His changes coincided with the renewed interest in individual flowers, trees and shrubs as plant-hunters returned from their travels abroad with exotic specimens.

With the invention of Budding's lawn-mower in 1830, a formal lawn, previously cut laboriously with scythes, was suddenly within the grasp of ordinary people.

Above: The Red Garden at Hidcote Manor, Gloucestershire. The gardens at Hidcote are laid out in a series of hedged compartments linked by a central vista, each compartment having a special characteristic. (National Trust)

Below: The White Garden at Sissinghurst, Kent, the creation of Victoria Sackville-West. (National Trust)

scythes, was suddenly within the grasp of ordinary gardeners with the invention of Budding's lawn-mower in 1830.

Capability Brown would have turned in his grave to see the bitty prettified styles adopted by the bourgeois enthusiasts. In fact much of the formal but eclectic tradition of Victorian gardening remains till this day. But the freer flower garden, complete with glorious herbaceous borders and wilder use of trees and shrubs was the invention of William Robinson, who used flowers naturalistically, massing daffodils in woods and orchards, and blending shrubberies within the landscape.

Robinson's style greatly influenced Gertrude Jekyll. She was a painter who turned to garden design. In partnership with the architect Sir Edwin Lutyens she created many rustic country homes and gardens between the 1890s and the early 1930s. Her own garden at Munstead Wood, Surrey, became famous as a model for the new kind of free but intimate gardening. She had enormous knowledge of plants and a considerable gift of putting that knowledge and enthusiasm across. Her books were immensely popular and are still widely read. It is the tradition of Miss Jekyll and William Robinson that we see varied but still carried on in such ravishing gardens as Sissinghurst Castle, the famous creation of Vita Sackville-West, and Hidcote Manor and which still exercises a lasting influence on gardeners today.

The Plant Hunters

The Temperate House at the
Royal Botanic Gardens, Kew,
built in 1848 to designs by
Decimus Burton, who also
designed the Palm House and
the fine wrought-iron gates at
the main entrance.

John Tradescant Senior – the
first important plant-hunter
who travelled through Europe
and Russia in search of plants,
in particular of bulbs, which
held high value.

As a small island race the British have always sought
adventures abroad, and in the search for unusual plants
British botanists have led the world. This great tradition,
which led to the founding and growth of Kew and other
exceptional botanical gardens as centres of research, goes
on to this day. It is these institutions, over the past century,
which have sponsored the majority of plant-hunting
expeditions to remote areas; but the original patrons were
private people, such as Lord Salisbury who sent John
Tradescant off to Europe and North Africa in the early 17th
century. Later, as the middle-class gardening public
burgeoned into a profitable market, there grew up a
number of independent nurseries, notably that of Veitch,
which spent enormous sums on plant hunting to increase
their stocks.

Serious botanical studies really began in England in the
17th century, with royalty taking a considerable interest.
John Tradescant was the first significant plant-hunter,
travelling throughout Europe and into Russia for plants –
and in particular for bulbs, which held high value. Such
was the value of tulips that by the mid-17th century they
had become a form of currency in Holland. Tradescant
became gardener to Charles I; his son, also named John,
made several journeys to North America, returning with
exciting plants which included red maples, lupins,
virginia creeper and the plant that is named after him,
tradescantia.

Men like Tradescant were working somewhat in the dark;
for as yet no scientific system of plant classification had
evolved. But in 1753 their problem was largely solved by
the great Swedish botanist Carl Linnaeus who published his
Species Plantorum which established a system of naming and
indexing plants which is used today. Linnaeus was famous
as a generous man who, from his position of Professor of
Botany at Uppsala, encouraged botany students and
collectors, particularly the American John Bartram who
gave to Europe the amazing magnolia grandiflora. When
Linnaeus died in 1778 his incredible library containing over
20,000 sheets of pressed plants, 2500 books, 3000 preserved
insects and 1500 shells was bought, together with his
copious correspondence, by a British collector and has
remained in Britain as an inexhaustible source for
botanists.

Banks – botanist and 'fixer'

The man who encouraged this purchase was the great
Sir Joseph Banks, Director of Kew. As well as being a great
botanist Banks was a great fixer. Having accompanied
Captain Cook on this three-year voyage round the world in
the *Endeavour*, he returned to become Director of Kew
Gardens – building it up, with the enthusiastic encouragement of his friends King George III and Queen Charlotte, as
an international botanical centre. By 1778 he was also
President of The Royal Society, and from these prestigious
positions he authorized plant-hunting expeditions led by
such intrepid men as Francis Masson, who brought back
Cape heaths and pelargoniums from South Africa and
plants from Madeira and the West Indies; David Nelson,
who sailed with Captain Bligh on the *Bounty*; and George
Caley, who sent plants from Australia and Jamaica.

British gardeners owe a debt to Banks as a founder in 1804 of the Royal Horticultural Society. It was the R.H.S. which sponsored David Douglas, the really great collector of the early 19th century. Douglas was a tenacious and apparently humourless Scot. During his short life – he was gored to death by a bull in Honolulu in 1834 at the age of 36 – he scoured the North American continent in dangerous and uncharted areas from California to Alaska to bring back more plants than any collector before him. He collected many conifers and is commemorated by his suitably sturdy Douglas Fir.

Collectors like Douglas always had to take the risk that their seeds and plants would dry or rot before they reached home. Later collectors benefited from the invention in the year of Douglas's death, of the Wardian case. In such an airtight glass case Nathaniel Ward discovered that plants could keep alive for great lengths of time. Thus the next generation of plant-hunters sent out by Sir William Hooker – Douglas's early patron in Glasgow and later Director of Kew from 1841–65 – could collect with confidence. Hooker greatly increased interest in Kew by opening it to the public. By 1865 there were 73,000 visitors annually.

Hooker's son, Sir Joseph, was a leading plant-hunter and later also a brilliant Director of Kew. His early expeditions were to South America where orchids, much prized by the Victorians, grew in abundance. Later it was the Himalayas that attracted him, and he collected camellias, rhododendrons and lilies, all charted in his beautifully illustrated *Himalayan Journals*.

While the Victorians adored exotics which they could grow under heat in their many conservatories – rich patrons like the Duke of Devonshire, as well as nurseries like Veitch, spent fortunes funding the search for these – there was a growing demand for hardy flowering plants. Many of these came from the cooler, more humid highlands of Japan and China. The great explorer in these countries was Robert Fortune, another Scot, who spent 19 years there after the Opium War treaties had opened many Chinese ports to westerners. His journeys were restricted to areas around the ports but he sent back such favourites as winter jasmine, weigelia, tree peonies and many species of azalea and rhododendron. He was also responsible for successfully introducing China tea to the East India Company and thus to India.

'The Edge of the World'

After the Boxer Rebellion of 1900–01 China was forced to open up her interior to exploration; at last the great collecting area known as the 'Edge of the World', bordering China, India, Burma and Tibet, could be fully explored. It was an Eden of hardy plants – fortunately, since by the time the collector E. H. Wilson arrived there in 1899 heat in Britain had become expensive and the demand had shifted firmly away from glasshouse plants to the wilder hardy plant gardening then being preached by William Robinson (page 123).

Wilson was sent to the East by the Veitch nursery, though later he collected for the Arnold Arboretum in Boston. He was the first collector systematically to use a camera. His first expedition was to find the davidia (handkerchief tree) named after the famous French botanist monk Arnold David. He returned with over 300 plant species including the davidia. It was Wilson who became world famous when, on sighting the glorious Regale lily in a mountain pass, he made his dangerous way towards it and was hit by an avalanche. He got the lily and for the rest of his life boasted a 'lily limp'.

Above: An illustration of *Rhododendron Thomsoni* from Sir Joseph Hooker's beautifully illustrated *Himalayan Journals*.

Far left: A photograph of the much-travelled naturalist and flower painter Marianne North (1830–90) at work.

Left: A Wardian case in which plants could keep alive for great lengths of time.

Customs and Folklore

Above: The Morris dancers of Thaxted in Essex hold a festival every June. Morris dancers are to be seen in many parts of England. Their dance probably dates back to pre-Christian ritual.

Above right: At Tissington and many other places in Derbyshire wells are dressed with elaborate pictures of flowers and leaves pressed on to clayboards.

In spite of the changes that have taken place since the middle of the 19th century, many of Britain's traditional customs are strongly alive and bound up in the social fabric of the country. As is to be expected, many of them can be traced to the deep-rooted beliefs and fears of our primitive forebears. We decorate our houses at Christmas time with evergreens – emblems of undying life – just as our pagan forebears did to ensure the fertility of the crops in the forthcoming year.

Bells have always played a large part in all Christmas customs. Church bells peal joyously to 'ring in Christmas' while handbell-ringers add their music to that of the carol singers. Thus in Dewsbury, Yorkshire, there is an unusual custom on Christmas Eve which is known as Ringing the Devil's Knell, or the Old Lad's Passing Bell, and dates from the early 14th century. The tenor bell of the parish church is tolled once for every year since Christ was born at Bethlehem. The ringing is timed to end exactly at midnight and so to usher in Christmas Day. The New Year, too, is welcomed in with the sound of bells, and of sirens and hooters, horns and anything else that will make a joyful noise.

In the North of England and in Scotland there are fire ceremonies, reminders of the age-old custom of lighting communal bonfires at the time of the Winter Solstice as a means of driving out evil and ensuring the future fertility of crops and animals. Particularly vigorous examples of this tradition are the 'Burning the Clavie' at Burghead, Morayshire, (on 11 January, the Old Style New Year's Eve) and the Fire Ceremony at Allendale, Northumberland.

Bonfires on Twelfth Night are not so frequent nowadays, nor is the custom of wassailing – though this can still occasionally be seen in the apple orchards of Devon and Cornwall, notably on Old Twelfth Night (17 January) at Carhampton and Roadwater in Somerset. Having selected one special tree to be wassailed, the owner of the apple trees and his men, armed with shot guns and a large pail of cider, go into the orchard. Cider is poured round the root of the tree, pieces of toast soaked in cider are placed in the fork,

and guns are shot through the branches while the on-lookers sing a traditional wassail song.

Hardboiled eggs with coloured and decorated shells are found on many breakfast tables at Easter. Called Pace Eggs in some parts of the country, these eggs are used in the Pace Egg play which is an Easter form of the Mumming Play. The boys of the Calder High School enact the play – the traditional story of life and death and resurrection – on Good Friday of each year. Egg rolling is another traditional Easter game: the coloured eggs are rolled down a slope until they are cracked and broken, when they are eaten by their owners. The Hare-Pie Scramble and Bottle-Kicking at Hallaton in Leicestershire on Easter Monday is another traditional custom kept up since medieval days. No one really knows the origin but no one would give up taking part in it.

The custom of Beating the Bounds reminds us of the days when maps were rare and parish boundaries were walked round and marked, and memorized by everyone. The Blessing of the Crops at Rogationtide is a service dating back to about the 18th century in this country, the prayers for good crops and harvest testifying to human dependence on nature. In many country districts these processions still take place regularly.

May the First was the first day of summer in the old Celtic calendar, so the month was welcomed in with much rejoicing and festivity. Winter was over, new life was already to be seen in the earth and a spirit of hope in the air. In Minehead and Padstow the Hobby Horses come out to 'Welcome the Summer', processing the streets all day long, and at Padstow enacting the age-long story of life, death and resurrection in the ritual dying and reviving of the Hobby Horse. The Furry Dance at Helston in Cornwall on 8 May is a relic of a pre-Christian ceremony of bringing in the summer. It is still danced with great vigour and gaiety and has lost little of its past history.

Garland Day at Abbotsbury in Dorset on Old May Day (13 May), with its procession of children carrying decorated garlands of flowers and greenery is all that

Far left: Up-Helly-aa – an old Norse fire festival – is celebrated at Lerwick, Shetland, on the last Tuesday of January to mark the end of the long winter nights. During the festival a model Viking ship is burned.

Left: Arbor Tree Day – a May festivity at Aston-on-Clun, Shropshire.

Below: At Padstow, Cornwall, Hobby Horses come out to welcome the summer, processing through the streets and enacting the story of life, death and resurrection in the ritual dying and reviving of the Hobby Horse.

remains of the centuries-old ceremony at the beginning of the fishing season, when wreaths and garlands decorated the fishing fleet as they put out to sea, and were then tossed into the sea. The fleet was blessed and the fishing season officially started.

Another ancient English tradition is a relic of the ancient pagan practice of well-worship. For centuries the wells and springs that bring life-giving water to man, his beasts and his crops have been revered and ceremonially decorated at certain times with flowers and votive offerings. At Tissington in Derbyshire the lovely pictures of flower petals and leaves pressed onto the clayboards are a comparatively modern development, having started in about 1818; but the dressing of the five wells, the processions and Service of Blessing is far older – a reminder to the villagers of either one of the two legends surrounding the origin of this custom. Was it an act of thanksgiving for the fact that in the Black Death in the 14th century no lives were lost there because the water from the springs was so pure, or was it because in 1615 when the rest of the country was devastated by drought Tissington springs never ran dry so that the village was able to supply water to other villages and hamlets? Whichever legend is true the act of thanksgiving is still shown today.

Few of the old Midsummer customs survive, but some bonfires are still lit on Midsummer Eve; summer fairs, rush-bearing and similar traditional festivities can still be seen in some districts.

The Horn Dance at Abbots Bromley in September is another example of the continuing traditions of centuries. The custom is mentioned in a book of 1686 but the very nature of the dance with its undertone of fertility rites, proves that it must be of non-Christian origin. A team of six men wearing reindeer horns, accompanied by a Fool, a man/woman character, a Hobby Horse, a Bowman and musicians parade the scattered parish, covering a distance of some 20 miles. Outside the farmhouses, cottages and other buildings they halt to dance their ritual dance. No one knows where the reindeer antlers come from or when – there have been no reindeer in England since the 12th century.

Most of the Hallowe'en customs are now incorporated in the fire festivals of 5 November, although some traditional games are still played on 31 October, together with divination rites played in a cheerful, half-believing way to read the future of one's love life.

There is no space to give more than a mention of such activities as the skipping on Scarborough sands at Shrovetide, Marbles Day on Good Friday, or Morris dancing at Whitsuntide, May Day and other summer celebrations; but these, and countless others, are still carried on enthusiastically in an ever-living continuation of our national heritage.

FOLKLORE

The folklore of a country is the living link between the beliefs and philosophy of the distant past and those of the present. The traditions and lore of the various invaders of Great Britain – all helped to build up the folkloristic foundation of our social life, from which spring many of our present beliefs and superstitions.

Our pagan forebears believed that everything in nature – trees, plants, rivers and wells, animals – possessed indwelling spirits with sacred and magical properties and should therefore be revered.

Some trees were considered lucky or unlucky. The oak was revered not only on account of its long life but also because it was thought to be a protector against fire and lightning. The rowan tree or mountain ash was another lucky tree, believed to be a sure protection against witchcraft and other evils. Loops made of its twigs were placed over house doors, or on railing spikes, or even carried in the pocket to keep one's home and person safe from such perils. A piece of rowan wood placed in a churn would prevent a witch from charming the butter, while a mast made of such wood would keep a ship safe from witchcraft.

The elder tree (sometimes called the 'witch tree') was considered very unlucky. Elder wood must not be burned. Nor should the tree be cut: there are many gardeners today who mutter 'please Old Lady may I cut off some of your branches?' before doing so.

Relics of tree-worship can be seen in many of our customs and superstitions. Can it be that we 'touch wood' lest that indwelling spirit might think we were boasting? Was it a protection against lightning that the bobbins at the end of blind cords were always in the shape of an acorn?

Many are the legends connected with springs and wells which keep alive the belief in the old water spirits. Although many of these wells were re-dedicated to Christian saints, some of the old beliefs surrounding our holy wells survive. Thus we believe in the healing power of the water from such wells, and we also drop coins into them to bring us luck.

Rivers were reported to claim a victim at some time or another. The Ribble had a spirit called Peg o' Nell which took a life every seven years, but could be placated by the drowning of an animal. Legend says that Peg o' Nell was a servant at Waddow Hall whose mistress drowned her by witchcraft. She haunted the district and was responsible for every drowning thereafter. The Trent is still said to take its toll each year when the spring tide known as the Aeger becomes dangerous. This is a memory of the Danish Jotun Aegir, for the upper reaches of the Trent run through the heart of the old Danelaw (the area of country once occupied by the Danes). These river legends are remembrances of the time when victims were ceremonially sacrificed to the river gods.

Stonehenge and the even older Rollright Stones in Oxfordshire created awe and fear among those who first saw them. Their size and the mystery of how such massive stones were transported and erected surely speak of magic. In fact all forms of standing stones, dolmens and barrows were treated with great respect. Little wonder that through the whole realm of nature there still runs the thread of fact and legend kept alive through the ages by partial memory, local tales attached to half-forgotten events, new heroes replacing old gods, and memories handed down.

This living link between the old and the new can be seen in our everyday life. Without thinking about sun- or moon-worship we salute the new moon, and we stir our puddings and sauces sun-wise. Many of our household recipies and remedies have come down to us from the 'white witch' or wise woman, although we would have no belief in her powers today.

Haunted Britain

Ghostly manifestation take many forms: some ghosts are actually seen; others simply make themselves felt. Some are terrifying, others quiet and gentle like the Radiant Boy occasionally seen at Corby Castle in Northumberland: a beautiful young boy with golden hair who appears quietly in a circle of bright light, stays a few minutes in the room smiling at the occupant and then glides away.

Some ghosts return as warnings of death and disaster, others return to right some wrong done in their lifetime. Some people see them, others do not.

There are spectral coaches and headless horses, packs of ghostly hounds and other animals, all of which have been seen by hundreds of people over the years. Inexplicable sounds that chill the blood, the sweet sound of bells or music from churches, all have stories connected with them.

Bisham Abbey in Berkshire remains much the same as it was in Tudor times when it passed into the Hoby Family. The story of the haunting there concerns Lady Elizabeth Hoby, wife of Sir Thomas Hoby, Ambassador to France in the reign of Elizabeth I. A great scholar, writer of Greek and Latin verse, Lady Hoby was also quick-tempered and easily exasperated by the unscholarly work of one of her sons, William, whose copybooks were untidy. William was often beaten by his mother and on one occasion when his books were worse than usual she beat him so hard that he died. Lady Hoby is still seen at Bisham Abbey, gliding out of a bedroom, washing her hands in a bowl which floats in front of her. An interesting fact about this apparition is that the ghost is seen 'in negative'.

Thorpe Hall in Lincolnshire is haunted by a woman who had never seen the house. When Sir John Bolle who owned the Hall took part in the expedition to Cadiz in 1596 he took charge of some Spanish prisoners. One of them, a wealthy woman, fell in love with him. She wanted to return to England with him. As he was married this was impossible, and the heartbroken woman retired to a convent. Among the presents she had given Sir John was a portrait of herself in a green dress, which was hung in Thorpe Hall. Her ghost is seen in the grounds at night; known locally as the Green Lady of Louth, she is seen wandering about the garden.

At Littlecote House, Wiltshire, a particularly gruesome murder took place in the 16th century. 'Wild' or 'Wicked' Will Darrell was suspected of murdering a new-born child by burning it to death, but was acquitted at his trial. The house is now haunted by Darrell himself, who is seen in the bedroom where the murder is reputed to have taken place. It is said that the floor of that room is under constant repair for the boards where Darrell walks about moulder away. The story of Darrell's death has a ghostly connection. It is said that when out riding an apparition of a baby in flames appeared in front of him, startling his horse so that he was thrown and broke his neck. The spot where this happened is known as Darrell's stile and is haunted by the man whose wicked spirit still pervades Littlecote.

When Theophilus Brome died in 1670 at Higher Chilton Farm in Somerset, he was buried in Chilton Cantelo Church. But he asked that his head be kept in the farmhouse. Several attempts were made to move the skull from the house but each was followed by such violent disturbances that it was always brought back. On the last attempt to bury it, in the 1860s, the sexton's spade broke into two and he vowed never again to attempt the job which proved to be so 'repugnant to the quiet of Brome's head'. The skull is now kept in a special cabinet in the house.

Of the many other skull-haunts the best known is probably that of the one at Burton Agnes Hall in Yorkshire. This beautiful house was built in the 17th century as the home of the three Griffith sisters. Anne, the youngest was

The Brown Lady descending the stairs at Raynham Hall, Norfolk. The Brown Lady has been seen by several famous people, including the writer Captain Marryat. It is thought that she may be the same ghost who haunts Houghton Hall – possibly Dorothy, the sister of Sir Robert Walpole.

intensely interested in the new house. Soon after the sisters had moved in, Anne was attacked by footpads and died a few days later. As she lay dying she made her sisters promise that when she was buried her head would be kept in the house she loved. The sisters presumably believing her to be delirious did not take her request seriously and buried her in the family vault. Not many days after the funeral, strange frightening noises were heard in the house: doors slamming, loud bangings and desperate cries. The disturbances reminded the sisters of the broken promise made to their dying sister; they had the grave opened and Anne's head removed into the house, whereupon the disturbances ceased. On the few occasions the skull was removed the noises and other manifestations returned so violently that the family decided to keep the skull in the house as promised.

It is an accepted theory that some violent and highly emotional events can leave their imprint on the surrounding atmosphere and appear as ghostly manifestations. This may be the reason why a group of men saw the Battle of Edgehill re-enacted in the sky a few months after the actual battle had taken place. Walking home between twelve and one at night on the Saturday before Christmas, 1642, these men heard the sound of drums and of soldiers coming near; then, to their terror, they saw in the sky the whole action of the battle taking place. After watching this phantom battle for about three hours they testified their experience before magistrates. The same vision was seen the following weekend by other witnesses, and officers sent by Charles I to investigate the matter also saw the battle and recognized some of the Royalists taking part whom they knew had been killed. On many other occasions – some in recent years – this ghostly Battle of Edgehill has been seen on 23 October, the anniversary of the actual battle.

This is not the only example of battle hauntings. An old house in St Albans was haunted by the sound of galloping horses and clashing weapons, and even when the house was eventually demolished and a row of shops built on the site, these noises continued to be heard. The original house was said to have stood on the battlefield of St Albans during the Wars of the Roses.

From these very few examples we can see how the ghost-lore, folklore and customs of Britain are woven into her national heritage.

Vernacular Buildings

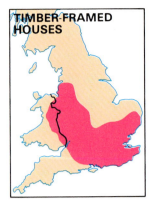

TIMBER-FRAMED HOUSES

Far right: Speke Hall, Merseyside, is a magnificent 16th-century half-timbered house. (National Trust)

WOOD

Before the second half of the 17th century the large majority of the inhabitants of the British Isles lived in timber-framed buildings. Until well into the Middle Ages these islands were abundantly wooded; it is known that in the 13th century there were over 60 forests in England alone, and at the accession of the Tudors England still had at least four million acres (116 m ha) of woodland, and Scotland was also extensively wooded. Often indeed the profusion of trees was an embarrassment; when the land was required for tilling they had to be felled, and often burnt.

There was therefore every incentive to make use of timber for building, even in regions where stone was abudant too. Wood was more easily obtained and much simpler to handle. England and the Scottish Lowlands were fortunate in being richly endowed with vast numbers of oaks, one of the best of all woods for building purposes. In the Scottish Highlands oaks were scarce and they had to rely chiefly on other trees such as Scots pines (excellent for roof-timbers), birches, alders and willows. When wooden flooring replaced the original beaten earth strewn with

Above: A 16th-century timber-framed wool merchant's house in Lavenham, Suffolk.

Above right: Weatherboarded cottages at Cranbrook, Kent.

rushes, elm was frequently employed in place of oak, and at all times the poorest people had to make do with inferior woods, which is why, except in south-eastern England, very few timber-framed houses survive that are earlier than 1500 and, farther north, earlier than 1600.

The very large majority of these houses were only partly timbered: that is to say, the skeleton was of wood and the spaces between the vertical beams, known as *studs*, were filled with some other material applied to a light wooden 'core': originally mud daubed on to wattles or sticks; later plaster spread over laths. Timber-framed houses that are wood-covered, are not so common here as in America, but there are some excellent specimens in Kent (Cranbrook for example).

The most primitive form of timber-framing is what is known as cruck construction. The framework consisted simply of pairs of tree-trunks, or sometimes a single tree sliced into two halves along its length, which, their ends having been scorched, were rammed into the ground at an angle, so that they met at the top: trees with a slight curve were therefore an advantage. Pairs of crucks were set at intervals of a few feet and linked together at the apex with a ridge-pole, and lower down by more slender beams known as purlins. On this framework lighter rafters were slung, to support a covering of straw thatch, brushwood or heather.

Later, vertical posts were added and the pitch of the roof reduced.

Cruck-frames were never employed in eastern or south-eastern England, but in the Midlands, the South-West (excluding Cornwall, which was not well supplied with timber), the Welsh border counties and most of Wales, northern England and most of Scotland cruck cottages were at one time very common. In Scotland crucks were generally known as *couples*. Survivors are comparatively few: today Herefordshire has easily the most, and otherwise most of them are to be found in the other counties of the West Midlands.

Nearly all Britain's timber-framed houses, however, have vertical walls – sometimes with the upper storeys overhanging, to make what are called *jetties* – and gabled roofs. There are a number of structural variations, but broadly speaking the better off the client was, the greater is the display of oak. Prosperous yeoman farmers in such counties as Kent, Sussex and Suffolk liked close-studded structures: that is to say, with plenty of robust oak uprights set fairly close together. In the less sophisticated and less well-to-do western counties the panels are usually broader and sometimes nearly or absolutely square; these offered opportunities for decorative panelling, often of the most exuberant kind, especially under Elizabeth I and James I.

Many thousands of timber-framed buildings survive, far more in fact than many people realize, for in the later 17th and 18th centuries the timber frame was often hidden under an overcoat of plaster or, mainly in the South-East, under a facing of brick, brick-tiles or hung tiles.

Distribution of these houses is, however, now very uneven. In northern England and in Scotland, partly perhaps for climatic reasons but also because they were less well built, survivors are few; nor are there many in the far south-western counties nor in most of Wales. To see good timber-framing we should visit all the five south-eastern counties, Essex and Suffolk, the South and West Midlands, Cheshire, South Lancashire and central Wales. Some of the surviving houses are surprisingly large, and can be extremely picturesque.

The best roofs are of limestone or sandstone slates, but most of the major houses are today roofed with tiles. Originally thatch was the almost universal material for the timber-framed house, on account of its availability and its lightness, and happily in some areas thatch is still by no means rare.

CLAY AND BRICK

Early builders in Britain had one other basic material besides wood, which was earth. All the Iron Age forts were earth-built, and, originally, most of the Norman castles too. Mud, which is just wet earth, was widely employed for building first huts and later cottages.

A fair number of these cottages still remain in Leicestershire and parts of the adjoining counties, also in central Buckinghamshire, where the unusually hard chalky clay was known as wichert. But the principal area for unbaked clay buildings is the South-West, where it is known as cob. In Devon alone many hundreds of cob cottages survive, and a few larger houses, such as Hayes Barton at East Budleigh, the house in which Sir Walter Raleigh was born. That is an indication of the surprising durability of this material, provided that the clay is right and the building carefully done. The process was laborious, as the mud was applied in layers; each layer was trodden down and then left to dry out before the next layer was applied. With its slightly undulating walls, curved angles and other signs of hand-moulding, a cob building, even under limewash or rendering, is often quite easy to recognize.

Only in East Anglia was the clay shaped before being lifted into position. This is the process known as clay lump, the English version of *adobe*. Clay lumps were like unfired bricks, but considerably larger. Farm buildings of this material were generally tarred, but cottages were usually rendered with lime plaster. The area in which they chiefly occur is north-west Suffolk and south-central Norfolk.

Clay fired to make bricks first appeared in Britain in Roman times. Their bricks were broad and thin, and more like tiles. They were extremely durable, and numerous examples survive, reused. But Britain had no completely brick building earlier than the 14th century, and only a very few which precede the Tudors. Moreover, all the early examples are on the eastern side of the country, from Sussex to Humberside. Probably because of the shortage of stone, apart from flint, in the eastern counties, and the relative scarcity of woodlands, over half the brick buildings erected before 1550 are in Norfolk, Suffolk and Essex.

Owing to the primitive conditions under which they were fired, these early bricks vary considerably in colour and shape, so need plenty of mortar. But 'homespun' though they may be, the brickwork of the Tudor period is often delightful, and chimney-stacks produced under Henry VIII can be spectacular. They too nearly all occur in the

Left: A cob cottage at South Milton, Devon.

Below: Spectacular Tudor brickwork chimney-stack at Lees Priory, Essex.

Hatfield House, Hertfordshire – a grand display of Jacobean brickwork.

Pantiles at Saxthorpe, Norfolk.

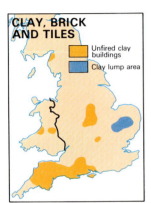

CLAY, BRICK AND TILES

Unfired clay buildings

Clay lump area

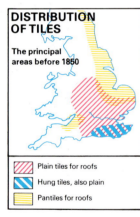

DISTRIBUTION OF TILES

The principal areas before 1850

Plain tiles for roofs

Hung tiles, also plain

Pantiles for roofs

Castle Combe, on the fringe of the Cotswolds.

South-East. Hampton Court Palace set a new standard in the employment of bricks on a large scale, and many of the big Elizabethan and Jacobean houses provide grand displays.

The greatest period of English brickwork was from the Restoration until the accession of George III exactly a century later. The craftsmanship in this period, especially in the South and East, the parts of the country which not only had the best clays for brick-making but which could best afford the refinements, has no equal anywhere in the world. Bricks were specially moulded before firing, rubbed to a smooth surface and to precise dimensions (what is called 'gauged'), and sometimes even carved, where elaborate decorative details were required.

Yet as late as this, brick was still quite the exception in Scotland and Wales, as also in Cumbria and Cornwall. Even today, in these parts of Britain, brick is not the natural building material, as it is over so much of England. This was not so much because of the absence of suitable clays – parts of the Scottish lowlands, for example, have excellent brick clays – as because of the abundance of building stone.

But when in the mid-19th century it became possible to manufacture bricks by machinery, no building material could rival them for cheapness. In the Victorian period vast industrial conurbations sprang up which were constructed almost entirely of brick. The tough engineering bricks known as 'Staffordshire blues' are not unpleasing, but many of the bricks made from the shales of the Coal Measures are harsh and ugly, and, alas, horribly durable.

Great improvements in the quality of bricks have been made in recent years and there is now a wider range of colours available than at any time in our history.

Tiles can make a most attractive contribution to the architectural landscape. Plain tiles were not only used for roofing, but in the South-East were also hung on battens to protect and enliven wall-surfaces: the rich terracottas of the hung tiles are often a great adornment to the villages of Sussex and Kent. Pantiles were first imported from the Netherlands towards the end of the 17th century. In the Georgian era they became the regular roofing material from Norfolk to Northumberland, and indeed on into eastern Scotland, expecially in the Lothians and in Fife. Outside the eastern counties they are rare except in Somerset where there are plenty, as Bridgwater also traded with Holland, and presently made its own. Many little towns and villages (Saxthorpe, Norfolk, for example) in these areas owe more to the rich colours and surface textures of their pantiles than to any other single factor.

STONE

Scotland and Wales are by no means devoid of interesting building stones, but perhaps no country in the world, in relation to its size, is so richly endowed in this respect as England. There is no marble. This would be a serious deficiency in the bright light of the Mediterranean, but in England it is not: imported marble never looks right. Otherwise there is hardly any desirable building stone which is not represented (see map on page 10).

For builders there is a fundamental distinction between the sedimentary rocks (mainly limestones and sandstones) on the one hand and the igneous (granite etc) and metamorphic (slate and marble) on the other. The impressive granite city of Aberdeen is largely a 19th-century creation; but until the mechanical advances of the 18th and 19th centuries granite and slate were very difficult to work, and this is where most of Wales and much of Scotland were at a disadvantage compared with England. In England these intractable rocks are confined to Cornwall, South Devon, the Lake District and a small area of Leicestershire. Scotland has some good sandstones, in Dumfriesshire, Fife, Angus, Morayshire and especially in Lothian, which yielded the durable Carboniferous Craigleith stone so much used in Edinburgh. But there is not much limestone, and none suitable for building.

England, on the other hand, has a wide variety of both limestones and sandstones, embracing some of truly exquisite quality. The most beautiful are the Jurassic limestones, the oolites and the lias, which, starting with an 'outlier' in the Isle of Purbeck, form the great ogee curve running from Portand Bill to the Cleveland hills. North of the Bristol Avon the limestone expands into a wide belt comprising the whole of the Cotswolds, where are to be found some of England's most seductive towns, villages and manor houses. Another specially fine limestone area is around Stamford. Along the Jurassic belt are situated many of the country's most prestigious quarries; not all, alas, are still working.

The Jurassic limestones vary in colour from white and light grey through pale honey shades to tawny yellow and rust brown. The older limestones tend to be whiter. Magnesian limestone is only important in Yorkshire. Aesthetically it is the equal of the finest oolite. Carboniferous or Mountain limestone, as it is often called, has given us some of our loveliest scenery, including the Yorkshire Dales, Dovedale and the Cheddar Gorge. As a building material it is rough and tough and cannot be ashlared but has been much employed in the northern counties, not least for miles of drystone walling.

At the other end of the geological time-scale are the Cretaceous limestones (chalk), which (except at Beer, in Devon) only occur to the south-east of the Jurassic limestone belt. They are usually too soft for building, but from the upper layers of the Chalk formation comes one of the strongest contributors to the pattern of English building: flint. This, being almost pure silica, is so hard as to be virtually indestructible, and was much used by builders in the South-East, but only for want of anything better; for it is in many respects a very unaccommodating material, and requires a great deal of mortar, which is always the vulnerable element in a flint building.

England also has sandstone in profusion: Cretaceous (Wealden and Greensand stones), Jurassic, Triassic and Permian (these two often termed New Red sandstones, although by no means always red), Carboniferous, Old Red and Devonian, to mention only the most important. Their range of colour is remarkable: from wine reds and plummy purples through red ochres, pinks and pinkish-browns to buffs, fawns, pale yellow, greens and greys, sometimes with a dusting of blue-grey lichen to add yet further interest. In a comparatively sunless climate this diversity of colour and tone is a great asset; but it has to be added that the sandstones do not reflect light as do many of the limestones. Some of the most attractive, such as the New Reds, the principal building stone of the West Midlands, also tend to weather indifferently.

The strongest sandstones come from the Carboniferous system: the Millstone Grits and the products of the Coal Measures. They tend to be dun-coloured and to collect dirt, but they have a property which was of great value in the industrial North in the 19th century: they stand up to atmospheric pollution better than any limestone, even Portland. Some of the best known quarries, such as Bramley Fall and Bolton Wood in Yorkshire and Dunhouse in Co. Durham, still flourish.

Both the limestones and sandstones have provided roofing slates in places where the stone is sufficiently fissile to lend itself to splitting. The best known limestone slates come from Stonesfield near Woodstock and from Collyweston near Stamford. They yield roofs that are a delight to behold. Sandstone slates are bigger and heavier – in the North they are known as flagstones of 'flags' – and not as gracious nor as subtle, but a sandstone roof can endow quite a modest building with a tremendous air of authority.

The gatehouse of St Osyth's Priory, Essex – a fine example of flushwork in which limestone is used in combination with flint.

Below: The east front of Houghton Hall, Norfolk – a fine example of Jurassic sandstone.

Bottom: Red sandstone: the corner of the Prior Slee Gateway in the Abbey grounds of Carlisle Cathedral, Cumbria.

The Historic House and Country House

English is a baffling language, because it manages to be loose and exact at the same time. So while the terms Historic House and Country House are often used as if they mean the same thing there is a significant difference between them. The Historic House is the broader for it ranges from buildings on the scale of palaces like Hatfield and Castle Howard to houses in towns and villages that range from the Jew's House in Lincoln, built in the late 12th century, and go on via Grevil's house at Chipping Camden, built about 1400 for a rich merchant, to 18th-century houses like Mompesson House in the Close at Salisbury, Peckover House at Wisbech, to William Morris's Red House at Bexley, and Amyas Connell's High and Over near Amersham, one of the first Modern Movement houses built in Britain, in 1931. It is a term that is purely to do with age – even some 20th-century houses are now officially accepted as historic buildings – and has no social or economic boundaries. The country house, on the other hand, is not just a historic house in the country, say a farm house or cottage, but is, or was, the focus of a landed estate. And it is for that reason that buildings that might seem to belong more properly to the castle tradition are regarded as country houses, in particular tower houses in Scotland and the defensible pele towers in the northern counties that often survive as a nucleus of later country houses, like Hutton-in-the-Forest in Cumbria, which comprises work of so many different periods as to be in itself a whole history of country house architecture.

It is the country house that some have seen as England's greatest contribution to the civilization of Europe, but that is because it has never been just a matter of architecture, or a setting for works of art, and the reason why it is

Left: Hutton-in-the-Forrest in Cumbria comprises work of so many different periods as to be in itself a whole history of country house architecture.

Penshurst in Kent, originally a simple manor house, became a great house expressing 600 years of history.

recognized as a unique British contribution to the European inheritance is because it is an institution that embraces not only architecture, collecting, planting and landscaping but grows out of attitudes to political and social life; landowning, agriculture and country pursuits, family inheritance and trusteeship. The country house is thus a complex place, fragile in that it is easily devalued through sales of contents, and yet adaptable and remarkably resilient; protected in the past through family settlements against wastrel heirs, now it is defended equally fiercely against the tax system; apparently obsolete, impractical and often increasingly uncomfortable, yet still able to dictate tough terms to the generation responsible for it. Perhaps most remarkable of all, country houses and the life they fostered have an increasing appeal to an ever widening public, inspiring not only the poetry of Drayton and the paintings of Turner, but also television serials like *To the Manor Born* and *Brideshead Revisited*.

It is this very complexity that makes a purely chronological and architectural approach so inadequate. Such an approach may provide a stylistic skeleton stretching from the barn-like manor house at Boothby Pagnell in Lincolnshire, built about 1200, to Meols Hall, largely designed by its owner in the 1950s and arguably the only recent country house approaching a complete work of art. But it is only a skeleton.

Meols is a classical house inspired by romantic ideas about architecture and family history, and thus reflects one of the chief characteristics of the country house: it looks to the present and the past at the same time. Country houses from at least the mid-15th century have often looked backwards, expressing family dignity and descent through towers and battlements, armorial bearings in carved stone, plaster and stained glass and collections of portraits. The castle continued to be an active theme long after it lost its defensive purpose, from Hurstmonceaux, Sussex and Tattershall, Lincolnshire, both begun about 1450, via the gatehouses at Oxburgh in Norfolk, Layer Marney in Essex and Coughton in Warwickshire to the Jacobean castles, Bolsover in Derbyshire, and Lulworth, Dorset, and the slightly later castles of Mar in Aberdeenshire.

Surely there is a link of nobility between their towers and the corner pavilions at Wilton House, Wiltshire, dating from the 1630s, the corner towers at Drumlanrig Castle built after the Restoration and the corner pavilions of Sir Robert Walpole's Houghton Hall begun in the 1720s; and it is no accident that the Dukes of Northumberland and Norfolk elaborated their castles at Alnwick and Arundel in the second half of the 19th century or that Lutyens should have explored castle themes at Lindisfarne and started from scratch at Castle Drogo in 1910.

Thus the country house is not unlike a double fugue: it consists of a continuously developing tune, doubled because of its two principal variations, the houses of the nobility and the houses of the gentry. In democratic times, when heraldry is a dead language to most people, the distinction between these two groups may not seem to be relevant; but houses like Burghley, Hatfield, Chatsworth and Holkham were the seats of great families with different intentions and purposes from Chastleton, Felbrigg or Dalemain.

Of medieval houses, the best surviving examples are all houses of country squires and of merchants who made good acquiring land and social status. Great Chalfield, Wiltshire, is in many ways the perfect example: it owes its character to Thomas Tropnell (d. 1480), who made the medieval form of the great hall and solar symmetrical by building gabled wings at either end of the hall each with an oriel, and balancing the hall bay window and the porch with lesser

gables. The sense of balance here is remarkable compared with the loose knit character of such a house as the 13th-century Stokesay Castle in Shropshire.

Some of these manor houses grew into great houses later, with the rising fortunes of their owners. So it was at Haddon Hall in Derbyshire, where between the 12th and 16th centuries the two courtyards became lined with buildings, with a great hall, private apartments, a chapel and with a long gallery. Penshurst in Kent has an even longer building history: the original manor with its great hall built by Sir John de Pulteney about 1341 later passed into the hands of a succession of noble owners including four dukes, acquiring a second hall with a curtain wall and eight towers. In the Elizabethan period the Sydneys gave it state apartments and their 19th-century descendants restored its fabric and extended it so that is became a great house expressing 600 years of history.

Drumlanrig Castle, Dum-friesshire, was built after the Restoration for the 1st Duke of Queensberry.

Below: Great Chalfield Manor, Wiltshire, in many ways a perfect example of a medieval manor house. (National Trust)

The Country House: The Classical Style

The English country house would not have developed as it did if Henry VIII had not dissolved the monasteries and redistributed most of their property among his supporters. Many of the landed estates in England include former ecclesiastical property, or at least possessed it in the past, and countless houses owe part of their character as well as their names to earlier religious houses on the same site. The courtyard plans of some great classical houses, Wilton, Woburn and Syon for example, hark back to long vanished cloisters, and at St Michael's Mount, Forde, Newstead, Lacock and Mottisfont the monastic origins of the secular building are clearly visible.

Forde and Lacock Abbeys are particularly interesting because they show the response of their respective owners to the architectural ideas of the Renaissance. At Forde in Dorset Thomas Chard(e), the last Abbot, had ambitious ideas; from what survives of his rebuilding we can see how he tempered the Perpendicular style with early Renaissance ornament. At Lacock in Wiltshire Sir William Sharington, who acquired the Abbey in 1540, built a polygonal tower topped by a balustrade in the Italian style and used other Renaissance motifs elsewhere. This interest in classicism reflects Sharington's position as a protégé of the Duke of Somerset, Edward VI's Protector, who had built one of the first English classical houses, Somerset House in London, and was responsible for a new understanding of the Renaissance style among his circle. These were a tough and unscrupulous group, largely opportunists who had done well out of the Dissolution and who were keen to be up-to-date architecturally and to be accepted as the new ruling class.

All these traits are apparent in the so-called prodigy houses of Elizabeth's reign, houses that reflect the prodigality and ambition of their owners. Particularly striking examples

Above: Kinross House, built between 1686 and 1693, is one of the finest examples of the work of Sir William Bruce. Sir William persuaded the Scottish lords to abandon their tower houses and their corbels for a more classical idiom.

Below: Longleat in Wiltshire – the most perfectly classical Renaissance country house in England.

A detail of stonework from Forde Abbey. Forde Abbey is particularly interesting in that it shows the very early response of its owners to the architectural ideas of the Renaissance.

are Longleat in Wiltshire and Burghley in Cambridgeshire, both built by associates of Somerset. Longleat is the distillation of some 20 years of thought and effort on the part of its owner Sir John Thynne, who built it after an earlier house, raised round the nunnery on the site, had been burned in 1567. It is the first great classical country house in England and has a highly individual character. Burghley, completed in 1587, is perhaps more characteristic of the age in its complex fusion of gothic forms with ideas derived from the foreign architectural books that Lord Burghley (William Cecil, Elizabeth's Lord High Treasurer) eagerly collected, and with material imported ready finished from the Continent. It is a vivid expression of the old and new worlds at the Queen's court, drawing upon the past to bolster up the present yet with the drive and confidence of a new society.

Internally, both Burghley and Longleat have been much altered. Fortunately Hardwick Hall in Derbyshire, another prodigy house built in the 1590s, retains intact not only its original interiors but also many of the furnishings and hangings that belonged to its builder, Elizabeth Countess of Shrewsbury. Hardwick is perhaps the earliest house in England where it is possible to get a sense of the processional quality of great houses. The extraordinary thrust of its elevations with their huge mullioned windows ('Hardwick Hall, more glass than wall') relate to the gradation of the rooms rising through the house: servants on the ground floor, the family living rooms above, and the great state apartments on the top, reached by a grand ceremonial staircase. The rich legacy of original tapestries, needlework, portraits and furniture surviving in these rooms reflects one of the unique aspects of the English country house: the existence of historic and documented contents which are not only magnificent in themselves but also provide valuable evidence for contemporary taste.

The men who built the Elizabethan prodigy houses had a sense of classicism, but not until Inigo Jones built the Banqueting House in Whitehall (see page 83) was the strict discipline of the Italian Renaissance style seen in England. His feeling for classical architecture was rarely expressed in country houses (though the pavilions at Stoke Park, Northants, are probably by him). At Wilton House, Wiltshire, however, where he advised on the design, this feeling can be seen in the relationship of the South front to the state rooms that lie behind, and in particular in the great Double Cube room lined with Van Dyck portraits. Wilton marks the end of the spring blossom of English classicism, when one can sense the frost of the Civil War beginning to nip. Inigo Jones's style was integrally linked to the Court: Charles I was beheaded outside the classical masterpiece built for him by Jones, whose particular genius was never recaptured, even by 18th-century Palladians.

Country-house building in the reign of Charles II was

The Long Gallery at Hardwick
Hall in Derbyshire. Hardwick
was built in the 1590s and is
perhaps the most spectacular
of all the great Elizabethan
'prodigy houses' of England.
(National Trust)

Below: The north drawing
room at Ham House, near
Richmond in Surrey. (National
Trust)

much less ambitious. Wren built hardly any country houses
(though was probably responsible for Winslow Hall, in
Buckinghamshire). Architects such as Robert Hooke, John
Webb and Hugh May did however evolve a marvellously
successful domestic style by tempering the severity of the
Italian Renaissance with the modesty of the Dutch to produce
houses in red brick and stone of rare felicity. Houses like
Groombridge Place, Kent, Ramsbury Manor, Wiltshire and
Belton House, Lincolnshire are in many ways the *beau
idéal* of the English country house. In Scotland Sir William
Bruce persuaded the Scottish lords to abandon their tower
houses with their corbels and crow-step gables for a more
classical idiom. Kinross House (1686–93) is his answer to
Ramsbury and Belton. What these houses lack in architectural show they make up for in the excellence of their
woodwork, often enriched with naturalistic carving of the
kind associated with Grinling Gibbons and with equally
brilliant plasterwork as at Sudbury Hall in Derbyshire.

The owners of these houses relied more and spent more
on interior furnishings than is generally realized. This
contemporary richness can be seen at Ham House, near
Richmond, where the modest scale and simple architectural
decoration contrasts with the marblized walls, veneered
furniture and elaborate upholstery, lavishly trimmed and
worked in combinations of contrasting textures and colours.
Though good pictures play a comparatively minor role in
the ensemble at Ham, the contemporary taste for works of
art can be seen at Burghley where part of the 5th Earl of
Exeter's collection remains, and at Lamport Hall,
Northamptonshire, where the small collection formed in
Italy in the 1670s by Sir Thomas Isham survives in the
house built by his father during the Commonwealth.

The Country House: The Grand Scale

The British are seldom good at grand architecture or formal planning, and by European standards the British royal palaces have always seemed unimpressive. Yet the ceremonial of the English court was one of the most elaborate in Europe, and had its effect in the planning of the great Baroque houses in the 1690s. At that time, in direct imitation of Charles II – who had himself been influenced by French ideas – the aristocracy began a furious burst of building and decorating. A surprising number of their Great Apartments survive, either within the shells of earlier buildings as at Burghley, or in the castles at Warwick and Powis, or in rebuildings and enlargements as at Chatsworth, Boughton and Petworth. The climax of these Great Apartments of four or even five rooms of increasing richness was the state bedroom with its towering bed hung with velvet, brocaded silk or needlework and finished with incredibly elaborate trimmings. None of these Great Apartments survives completely undisturbed but through what exists in these houses and the furniture at Knole, Penshurst and Ham, it is possible to get a vivid idea of how the work of joiners and house painters was enhanced by history painters on ceilings and walls and by carvers and gilders to provide a setting for tapestry weavers and upholsterers, who often sent in the largest bills of all.

To later generations these ceremonial arrangements seemed archaic, and in the 1840s the 6th Duke of Devonshire wrote of the state rooms at Chatsworth consuming 'in useless display the best habitable part of the house'. At Blenheim Vanbrugh had gone even further, designing two complete apartments flanking the Saloon as part of the national celebration of Marlborough's victories, but the state beds have now been removed and thus the Baroque processional quality has given way to the Edwardian luxury of a seemingly endless suite of drawing-rooms.

The Palladian reaction against the Baroque was partly a matter of style and taste, but it was also one of planning, in that it led to the spread of the villa as the ideal form for the small house – Lord Burlington's famous villa at Chiswick, in fact, was only an addition to an old house, designed to contain his works of art and not to be lived in – and to the modification of the great house plan as can be seen at

The tapestry room at Blair Castle, Perthshire. A surprising number of Great Apartments survives. The climax of such Apartments, of four or five rooms of increasing richness, was the State Bedroom.

Houghton and Holkham, and in several later houses designed by Robert Adam. At Houghton and Holkham as at Kedleston and Osterley, there are still impressive state beds, but in all four houses dining-rooms – an important innovation – are included as part of the state rooms and the state bed is counterbalanced by a greater emphasis on the display of works of art. At Holkham, for instance, the sense of architectural progression and the sequence of materials used for upholstery is related to the subject matter of the pictures, and classical sculpture plays a complementary role. Thus the house is not only a statement of family position but it is also a Pantheon of the Arts and Literature. For decades its owner Thomas Coke, Earl of Leicester, worked towards the achievement of a unity of architecture, decoration and furnishing, with pictures, drawings, books and manuscripts all playing their part, combining imports from abroad with a quite remarkable amount of furniture-making and upholstery done on the spot. And the house was only one part of his creation: it lies in a splendid park at the heart of a large estate that several generations of the family pieced together and improved. Holkham is not just a house: it is a world of its own and therein lies its real significance.

Painted Interiors

This feeling for order, balance and unity was taken a stage farther in the elaborately painted interiors designed by Robert Adam, particularly when he worked in collaboration with Thomas Chippendale the cabinet-maker and upholsterer, as at Nostell Priory and Harewood, both in Yorkshire. The Tapestry Drawing Room at Newby Hall, Yorkshire, is a brilliant example of his exceptional sense of control; for there, around a nucleus of French pier tables and pier glasses and a set of Gobelin tapestries with related chair coverings he designed a room complete down to the smallest detail, with an English carpet complementing the ceiling and even the gilt border for the tapestries matching the frames of the chairs. Largely under Adam's guidance interior design in England had a marvellous flowering in the last decades of the 18th century, with a succession of architects collaborating closely with furniture-makers, and upholsterers, carvers and gilders, decorative painters and house painters of exceptional skill in houses as far apart as Saltram in Devon, Attingham in Shropshire, and Inverary in Argyllshire.

The understanding, enthusiasm and means of the patron was crucial in that achievement, and it is no accident that the 18th century is a period rich in amateur architects and improvers, whose individuality gives it such character. Think not just of Lord Burlington, but of John Chute of the Vyne, Sir Roger Newdigate of Arbury, Sir Christopher Sykes of Sledmere and, perhaps most vivid of the Georgians, William Constable of Burton Constable, a Catholic who pursued the sciences as well as architecture, history and decorative art and died a rationalist, if not an atheist.

If it was the age of the amateur, it was also the age of women. It was they who introduced unsuspected notes of informality into the grandest houses and, describing it in their letters, it is they who bring it alive today. If one thinks of the 18th-century country house in terms of Vanbrugh and Kent, Adam, the Wyatts and Henry Holland, and their settings in terms of Bridgemann, Kent, Brown and Repton, and inhabited by the people painted by Huson and Kneller, Reynolds and Gainsborough, Ramsay and Raeburn, it is Mrs Delany, Mrs Lybbe Powis and the letter-writing daughters of the 2nd Duke of Richmond who give warmth to the gossip of Horace Walpole.

The drawing room at Chatsworth House, Derbyshire. Built by William Talman and Thomas Archer between 1687 and 1707 and a fine example of English Baroque architecture, Chatsworth comprises a block of lavishly decorated apartments arranged around a central courtyard. In the 1840s the 6th Duke of Devonshire considered that the state rooms 'consumed in useless display the best habitable part of the house'.

The Country House: The Romantic Revival and Modern Comforts

An early advertisement for a vacuum cleaner. Its message was for long ignored by owners of great houses.

Inverary Castle, Argyllshire, was built in the late 18th century in a Gothic/French château style.

If the Georgian builders of Palladian country houses thought that they were echoing Ancient Rome and the Renaissance Veneto in their parks, most of their successors looked back to an English, or a Scottish past. First came the Gothic Revival – not nearly as much the monopoly of Horace Warpole as he liked to make out, as can be seen at Arbury, such early castle-style houses as Inverary and abbey houses like Beckford's long-vanished Fonthill. To the 19th century, however, these buildings were neither 'serious' nor 'correct', and it is convenient to give that 18th-century phase of Gothic a 'k' to distinguish it from the more accusably medieval work of Pugin and his contemporaries. Tudor-style houses provided an attractive and often cheaper alternative, and so there developed in the 1820s and 1830s the first Old English style, as can be seen at Charlecote in Warwickshire. Alongside it grew up the first fashion for antique English furniture, much of which was made up, and for new pieces that were thought to be Elizabethan in style but owed more to the late 17th century. Partly under the influence of Sir Walter Scott and the Romantic idea of Scotland there was also a flowering of Scottish architecture: houses of every size from Balmoral to suburban villas sprouted features owing obvious debts to Glamis and the castles of Mar. The most successful country house architect of the time, William Burn, even introduced the Scottish Baronial style into England. However, for some of the richest patrons British styles were not exclusive or romantic enough, and for them the age of Louis XIV had an even stronger pull. Thus the Duke and Duchess of Rutland, who made Belvoir Castle, Leicestershire, externally the rival of Windsor, decorated much of the interior in the French manner, and that remained the favourite style of tycoons into the Edwardian period, when certain houses like Luton Hoo in Bedfordshire had the same luxurious character as Ritz hotels. The Italian Renaissance was yet another alternative, and at Alnwick Castle, Northumberland, in the mid-1850s the Duke of Northumberland swept away Adam's filigree, replacing it, within Salvin's new rugged exterior, with rooms that echo an Italian town palazzo. But Alnwick was an archaic concept of a great nobleman's house, and soon the emphasis switched to a revival of interest in the domestic architecture of the Wren period. 'Queen Anne' became the craze, and architects rediscovered the charm of unspoilt vernacular houses, so producing a second Old English Revival that was often paid for out of the profits of industry – though it affected to turn its back on it.

By then the period of the country house was drawing to a close, at least as far as new building was concerned: political changes and agricultural slump of the 1870s destroyed the confidence of the old families; instead there was an Indian summer of houses in the country – itself a romantic idea representing escape from the City, but seldom carrying with it the responsibilities of landowning.

This gave British domestic architecture a European reputation that it had never enjoyed before. Only now are we sufficiently far removed from it to be able to see its strengths; and Lutyens and, in Scotland, Lorimer are being restored to their pedestals.

The First World War was a watershed, and even Lutyens's country house practice never recovered from it. On the other hand there was already a growing appreciation of the qualities of old English country houses, and during the first 30 years of the century there were many poetic restorations of manor houses, like Great Chalfield, Lytes Cary and Westwood, which had such understanding lavished on their fabric, their interiors and their gardens that they were made into complete works of art. This led on to the re-discovery of Georgian country houses and the determination to preserve country houses intact, partly through the National Trust. Thus it is possible to see the romantic thread as continuing to be fruitful after 500 years.

Concepts of comfort are even more recent, and only became possible with technical advances to do with central heating, plumbing and lighting in the 19th century; examples are the Great Duke of Wellington's water closets at Stratfield Saye and the electric lighting at Cragside. But there was little thought of these being labour saving, and particularly under the influence of William Burn, the planning of the working side of country houses became much more elaborate than it had been in the 18th century. So when wages started to rise and servants found alternative occupations, the huge Victorian house was doomed.

One of the keys to the survival of houses of earlier periods has been the American influence between the wars that showed that comfort and convenience were quite possible to achieve. But just as it took a long time for the Renaissance to penetrate in the 16th and early 17th centuries, it was really only in the 1950s and 1960s that many country houses revolutionized; the last servants who needed other servants to wait on them retired, more bathrooms were contrived next to bedrooms, kitchens got closer to dining-rooms, even next door in some houses, and corridors ceased to be icy veins linking pools of warmth. These modernizations were as serious and significant as any matters of style, because they have enabled a significant number of owners to come to terms with their demanding inheritances and to give their houses a point in modern life.

Above right: Belvoir Castle, Leicestershire – externally the rival of Windsor, but designed by James Wyatt in 1801–13. Much of the interior is decorated in the French manner, a style which was soon to be repeated in other houses.

Left: A water closet at Stratfield Saye – an early concession to technical advances. Central heating, electric lighting and labour-saving gadgets only very slowly gained acceptance.

Right: The Great Hall at Charlecote, Warwickshire – a fine example of the Old English style.

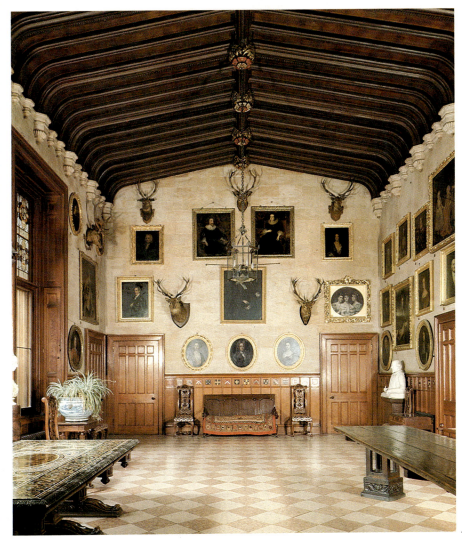

English Porcelain

English porcelain, which first began to appear in the 1740s, is an interesting mixture of Chinese, Japanese, German and French themes. The Chinese influence, evident in the vast output of blue and white wares, is to be seen on all the factories of the 18th century, at Chelsea, Bow, Longton Hall, Worcester, Derby, Lowestoft, Liverpool and Plymouth. The resultant products, however, often with shapes derived from silver are resolutely and unmistakably English.

The so-called 'Kakiemon' patterns, inspired by wares made in the Arita province of Japan, and found also on French and German porcelain, were produced at Chelsea, Bow and Worcester on a large scale from the early 1750s onwards.

The German influence of Meissen is clearly seen on the figures and wares of Chelsea, Bow, Longton Hall and Worcester. Often the figures were copied from Meissen originals by straight casts which resulted in a slight reduction in the size of the model. Thus the same models are to be found at Chelsea, Bow and Longton Hall. Though the basic shapes of the wares are frequently derived from German originals, the decoration was purely English in taste and inspiration. The classic example of this are the Chelsea botanical plates decorated with subjects taken from Ehret's illustrations to Philip Miller's *Figures of the Most Beautiful, Useful and Uncommon Plants*. After 1765 the influence of Sèvres was to have a marked effect on all these factories and at Derby bringing with it the introduction of solid ground colours and richly gilt cartouches enclosing panels of birds, flowers and figures.

In the early 1750s at Worcester the discovery of transfer printing on porcelain by Robert Hancock was a vital step towards the mass production of patterns. Though initially

Above: A pair of Chelsea
Botanical plates.

Right: A Caughley lobed oval
two-handled soup tureen stand.

Top: A Chelsea Kakiemon vase.

an exciting development, this was however to have a stultifying effect in the long term.

The late 18th century saw the extinction of most of the major factories. Only Derby and Worcester were to survive. The new generation, technically proficient and thus with few problems in production, was able to maintain a very high, if boring level of decoration in which the porcelain was entirely submerged in coloured decoration and gilding.

Much of the output of the 19th century continued on the lines and themes laid down in the previous century. Only at Worcester in the Hadley period, with its ivory toned and pierced porcelain in the Japanese taste, can any really positive development be observed.

Architecture Today

1880–1920 The Affluent years

At the end of the 19th century, with her huge Empire and enormous wealth, Britain was at the peak of her power. The remarkable eruption of building at this time was unprecedented, expressing the self-confidence of the new rich and powerful middle classes and, as Ruskin maintained, faithfully reflecting the social life of those it served. Its architects worked in every conceivable style – or mixture of styles – sometimes extravagant, pompous and exuberant, often showing great vitality and imagination and always with an air of value-for-money. This unparalleled display of wealth however did not go unchallenged. As long ago as 1841 the dedicated Gothic revivalist A.W.N. Pugin had written, 'the great test of architectural beauty is the fitness of the design for the purpose for which it is intended'. These stern words were to find response in those architects outside the mainstream who were desperate to break away from the indiscriminate artificiality of architectural practice.

A continuing belief in this philosophy of 'fitness for purpose' (never questioned by the great Victorian engineers) had persisted since Pugin through the work of such determined and original architects as William Butterfield and E.G. Street to Philip Webb and Norman Shaw. Inspired by strong socialist ideals, it was preached by Ruskin, demonstrated by William Morris and taught by W.R. Lethaby, and was the basis of the many Guilds formed at this time – the most important of which, the Art Workers' Guild, was the backbone of the Arts and Crafts Movement. This movement, which thrived between 1890 and 1910, attracted many of the liveliest and most imaginative architects of the time – such men as Lethaby himself and E.S. Prior. They believed in the revival of

EXAMPLES OF ARCHITECTS' WORK: 1880–1920

Historicists and Revivalists
Birmingham
The University   *Aston Webb*
Herefordshire
Church at Brockhampton   *William Richard Lethaby*
Lancaster
The Ashton Memorial   *John Belcher*
Liverpool
Anglican Cathedral   *Giles Gilbert Scott*
London
Admiralty Arch   *Aston Webb*
Battersea Power Station   *Giles Gilbert Scott*
Government Buildings, Parliament Square   *John M. Brydon*
Imperial Institute (tower)   *T. E. Collcutt*
Institute of Chartered Accountants   *John Belcher*
Kodak Building   *John James Burnett*
RAC Club   *Charles Mewes & Arthur J. Davis*
Ritz Hotel   *Charles Mewes & Arthur J. Davis*
St Cyprian's, Clarence Gate   *J. Ninian Comper*
Victoria and Albert Museum   *Aston Webb*
Oxford
Bodleian Library   *Giles Gilbert Scott*
Shenley
All Saints' Convent   *Leonard Stokes*
Wellingborough
St Mary's Church   *J. Ninian Comper*

Arts and Crafts Movement
Bridport
West Bay   *Edward Schroder Prior*
Bristol
Central Library   *Charles H. Holden*
Bournemouth
St Anne's Hospital   *Robert Weir Schultz*
Devon
Castle Drogo   *Edwin Lutyens*
Edinburgh
Hill House   *Charles Rennie Mackintosh*
St Peter's Church   *Robert S. Lorimer*
Glasgow
School of Art   *Charles Rennie Mackintosh*

Gloucestershire
Rodmarten Manor   *Ernest Barnsley*
Harrow
New Music School   *Edward Schroder Prior*
Kent
The Red House, Bexley Heath   *Philip Webb*
London
39 Cheyne Walk   *Charles Robert Ashbee*
25 Cadogan Gardens   *Arthur Heygate Mackmurdo*
Bedford Park, Chiswick   *Richard Norman Shaw*
Blackfriars House   *Francis William Troup*
Burlington Arcade   *Arthur Beresford Pite*
Christchurch, Brixton   *Arthur Beresford Pite*
Hampstead Garden Suburb   *Edwin Lutyens*
Heals   *Arnold Dunbar Smith & Cecil Brewer*
Horniman Museum   *Charles Harrison Townsend*
House for Mr Debenham   *Halsey Ricardo*
Mary Ward Settlement   *A. D. Smith & C. Brewer*
New Scotland Yard   *Richard Norman Shaw*
Rhodesia House   *Charles H. Holden*
Sanderson Wallpaper Factory, Chiswick   *C. F. A. Voysey*
Studio Cottage   *C. F. A. Voysey*
Whitechapel Art Gallery   *C. H. Townsend*
Manchester
Elm Street School   *J. Henry Seller/Edgar Wood*
Norfolk
Holm Place, Holt   *Edward Schroder Prior*
Northumberland
Cragside   *Richard Norman Shaw*
Oldham
Dronsfield Bros. Offices   *J. H. Seller/ E. Wood*
Roker, Sunderland
St Andrew's Church   *Edward Schroder Prior*
Sonning
The Deanery   *Edwin Lutyens*
Surrey
Tigbourne Court   *Edwin Lutyens*

The Glasgow School of Art
Library, designed by Charles Rennie Mackintosh, an original genius who developed *Art Nouveau* into a style very much his own.

Above: The Orchard at Chorley Wood, Hertfordshire, was built in 1899 by C. F. A. Voysey. It shows a return to local craftsmanship and skills.

Left: Castle Drogo, Devon, by Sir Edwin Lutyens, perhaps the greatest British architect of the 20th century.

Far left: The Horniman Museum in London, built in 1902 to designs by C. H. Townsend.

Westminster Cathedral, London, begun in 1895 by J. F. Bentley, was built in a vaguely Byzantine style.

Centre right: The dining room of the Ritz Hotel, London, designed by Charles Mewes and Arthur J. Davis.

Below: Cragside, Northumberland, built in 1870 by Norman Shaw, a firm believer in Pugin's dictum that 'the great test of architectural beauty is the fitness of the design for the purpose for which it is intended'.

Far right: Arnos Grove underground station, London – one of many stations designed by Charles Holden for London Transport. In their simple, functional and modest way Holden's stations have proved some of the most successful buildings of the period.

craftsmanship and integrity in the use of materials as passionately as they deplored structural or decorative dishonesty – such as the indiscriminate application of machine-made ornamentation on buildings. For 30 years these pioneers were responsible for some of the most significant and forward-looking architecture this country has ever produced. Although largely confined to domestic buildings, including the large model estates put up by the London County Council, its influence continues to be felt today.

On the Continent similar ideas were emerging, the most interesting of which was the Art Nouveau Movement. But it captured few supporters in Britain other than that original genius Charles Rennie Mackintosh, who made of it a style very much his own. In this period of conflicting attitudes and styles there was one man who seemed at ease with them all – Edwin Lutyens. A firm believer in the Arts and Crafts philosophy – though free of its socialist ideology – he stands out with his imagination, originality and wit as perhaps the greatest British architect of the 20th century.

1920–1940 International Styles

The gradual trend towards simpler architectural expression was accelerated by the economic effects of the First World War and the slow decline of national prosperity – culminating in the depression of the 1930s. The established architects such as Lutyens, Scott and Maufe continued to work in simpler versions of revivalism – stripped classic, simplified Gothic and Neo-Georgian. At the same time styles being developed in Holland and Scandinavia had great appeal for those architects searching for new forms of expression within traditional bounds. The strong simple brickwork characteristic of the Dutch and the elegant and friendly styles of Sweden and Denmark were adapted with some success to both public and private buildings here. But Art Deco and Art Moderne, so fashionable on the Continent and demonstrated in the 1925 Paris Exhibition, captivated only certain architects who, excited by its voguish originality, adapted it mainly for interior decoration and furniture.

By now frame construction using steel or reinforced concrete became common practice for most larger buildings – whether in or out of 'fancy dress'. London Transport's policy of extending its underground system to outlying areas of the capital required numbers of new stations; and to design these, its far-seeing and imaginative chairman Frank Pick commissioned the architect Charles Holden.

In their simple, functional and modest way Holden's stations have proved some of the most successful buildings of this period. Meanwhile, the seemingly uncontrolled spread of suburbia and the growing use of the private car stimulated a new and more urgent interest in planning. The early work of Raymond Unwin at Letchworth and later at Hampstead Garden Suburb was followed by the new Garden City at Welwyn – forerunners of the New Towns.

By now the younger architects were stimulated by ideas from the Continent – in particular those of Le Corbusier and the Bauhaus. Frustrated by the lack of opportunity to express themselves architecturally, they formed themselves into the pressure group MARS. This helped to promote their ideas but not until the arrival of many distinguished architect refugees from Nazi Germany, some of whom formed partnerships with their British counterparts, did the Modern Movement establish a footing – and then only a precarious one. Although unloved by the British public who found it didactic, over-solemn and lacking in cosy charm, it greatly inspired young members of the profession, as did the

outstanding Paris Exhibition of 1937. At first it was confined mainly to houses, but further opportunities soon began to open up in industrial, commercial and other fields. Among the most influential of these buildings were 'Highpoint' (a block of flats in Highgate, London), Bexhill Pavilion (a seaside entertainment centre), and the Boots Factory at Nottingham – each of which recognizably expressed in attitude, design and technology the principles of the Modern Movement. But perhaps the buildings which did most to win popular appeal for this new architecture were the animal houses at Whipsnade and the London Zoo, where the Penguin Pool in particular continues to be greatly loved and admired and beautifully illustrates the freedom gained by the use of reinforced concrete.

1940–1980 A Time of Confusion

War brought building virtually to a standstill. With peace came new problems – an acute shortage of materials and skilled labour. Not only had the nation to be rehoused but the industry itself had to be reconstituted. This encouraged the

Exuberant extravaganza. The interior of the New Victoria Cinema, London, designed by Walmesley Lewis.

Left: Bexhill Pavilion by Serge Chermayeff and Erich Mendelssohn. Refugees from the Nazi persecution of the Bauhaus (college of design) promoted a new architectural energy in their adopted countries.

Right: The Penguin Pool at London Zoo, by Bertold Lubetkin, helped win popular appeal for the Modern Movement and beautifully illustrates the freedom gained by the use of reinforced concrete.

Left: Peter Jones department store, London, designed by William Crabtree.

need to develop new methods and techniques to meet urgent needs, and much ingenuity went into the design of buildings assembled from factory-made components. Many versions of the 'pre-fab' house appeared in all parts of the country. Intended to last for no more than ten years, some proved so successful that they can still be found in use today.

The need for this kind of technology continued into the early 1950s; one of the most ingenious and successful

systems which became internationally famous, was devised by architects of the Hertfordshire County Council to meet their urgent school programme. Two further experimental efforts were made to tackle the continuing housing shortage – the use of system-built tower blocks, as elsewhere in Europe, which appeared to be quick to build and economical in land use, and the launching of a country-wide programme of New Towns, each self-contained and self-supporting with its own industry, schools and public buildings. These well-meant attempts at Utopia suffered many teething problems and received much critical abuse, but with time many of them have matured into pleasant towns which have proved acceptable to their inhabitants and aroused considerable interest abroad. The transformation to living in tower blocks, isolated from each other, has proved less successful: although these provided living units badly needed at the time, they have generally become so unpopular in Britain, largely for social reasons, that they are no longer built. Nevertheless when sympathetically

'High and Over' at Amersham, Buckinghamshire, was built by the firm of Connell, Ward and Lucas, who were strongly influenced by the Swiss architect Le Corbusier.

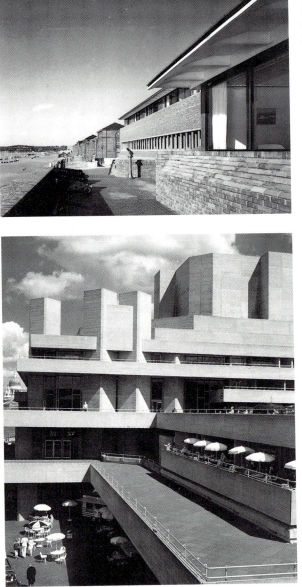

Right: Lloyd's Insurance building at Chatham, designed by Arup Associates.

Below: The Engineering Department at Leicester University, designed by James Stirling – a brilliant contribution to Britain's new university architecture.

Bottom: At St John's College, Cambridge, Powell and Moya solved with great sensitivity the delicate problem of inserting new buildings into old surroundings.

Above: Sir Denys Lasdun's National Theatre complex on the south bank, London, with St Paul's in the background.

Right: The Alton Estate, Roehampton in London, was built between 1956 and 1960 by the architects of the old London County Council. It is one of the more successful tower block developments which, in general, have become so unpopular in Britain, largely for social reasons.

planned in an agreeable environment, as by the London County Council at Roehampton and by Westminster City Council in Pimlico in the 1950s, they can be pleasant to live in as well as good to look at.

There was little private building at this time and many of the liveliest architects worked for Local Authorities and Government Departments which had now set up their own architectural offices to carry out the huge building programme required by the Welfare State. As a result architecture in the public sector reached a high standard – particularly in the London area. London's Royal Festival Hall formed an impressive and permanent feature of the 1951 Festival of Britain Exhibition on the South Bank – the first opportunity after the war for architects to see their designs built. Although in the event no revolutionary style emerged, many ideas were hatched which were to develop in later years. As the economy began to recover, so did the building industry: and architects were able slowly to return to their private practices. The rebuilding of Coventry Cathedral to a design won in competition by Basil Spence and the commencement of the enormous Barbican development in the City of London were both spectacular symbols of this resurgence.

During the 1960s, as the economy picked up and with the aid of Government incentives, an unprecedented building boom got under way which in the space of 15 years transformed most of our big city centres. Enormous funds were invested by property developers and investment companies, with the prime purpose of making a quick return. Buildings were rushed up with insufficient time to study the needs of the community, the effect on the environment or the needs of those who were to use them. New technologies, often imported from abroad and insufficiently tested, were employed as a means of cutting costs and saving time and were later to prove exceedingly expensive to maintain and repair. Planning authorities seemed unable for political and economic reasons to control even the worst excesses; and vast areas of our city centres which had escaped the bombs suffered the bulldozer in the interest of property tycoons, who preferred to employ architects more skilful at manipulating the system than in designing good buildings. But by the time the boom burst in the 70s and the property market had collapsed, some lessons had been learned. Not only had architects been forcibly made aware of the peoples' disenchantment and growing wish to have more say in the design of their surroundings, but there was an increased demand for more modest and

1940–1980

Beaulieu, Hants
Motor Museum   *Leonard Manasseh*
Brighton
Sussex University   *Basil Spence*
Cambridge
Caius College   *Leslie Martin*
Churchill College   *Richard Sheppard*
Clare College   *Ralph Erskine*
Cripps Building, St John's   *Powell & Moya*
Downing College   *Howell, Killick, Partridge & Amis*
Chatham
Lloyds Insurance   *Arup Associates*
Chichester
Theological College   *Ahrends Burton & Korelek*
Coventry
The Cathedral   *Basil Spence*
Durham (University)
Dunelm House   *Architects Co-Partnership*
Edinburgh
The Airport   *Robert Matthew & Partners*
Gatwick
The Airport   *Yorke Rosenberg & Mardell*
Halifax
Halifax Building Society   *Building Design Partnership*
Harlow New Town   *Frederick Gibberd & Partners*
Hunstanton
Hunstanton School   *Peter & Alison Smithson*
Ipswich
Wills Faber Building   *Foster Associates*
Leicester (University)
Engineering Dept.   *James Stirling*
London
Arts Centre, Christ's Hospital   *Howell, Killick, Partridge & Amis*
Barbican   *Chamberlain Powell & Son*
Bousfield School   *Chamberlain Powell & Son*
Chartered Accountants Hall   *Wm. Whitfield*
Colonnades, W.2.   *Farrell Grimshaw*
Flats in Pimlico   *Powell & Moya*
Horniman Primary School   *Michael Manser Associates*
Institute of Education & Law   *Denys Lasdun*

Oxford
Keble College, de Breyne & Hayward Building   *Ahrends Burton & Korelek*
St Anthony's College, Hall & Common Rooms   *Howell, Killick, Partridge & Amis*
St John's College, Sir Thomas White Bldg.   *Arup Assoc.*
St John's College   'The Beehives' *Architects Co-Partnership*
SPAN, The Paddox   *Eric Lyons*
Summertown House   *Howell, Killick, Partridge & Amis*
Portsmouth
Polytechnic Library   *Ahrends Burton & Korelek*
Sheffield
Crucible Theatre   *Renton Howard Wood*
Swindon
Reliance Control   *Foster Associates*
York
The University   *Robert Matthew & Partners*
Kensington Town Hall   *Basil Spence*
Lillington St. Flats, Pimlico   *Darbourne & Darke*
Lloyds Insurance   *Richard Rogers & Partners*
Royal College of Art   *H. T. Cadbury in association with Hugh Casson*
Royal College of Physicians   *Denys Lasdun*
Students' Residence, Imperial College   *Richard Sheppard*
Thamesmead Development   *GLC*
World's End Estate   *Eric Lyons*
Manchester
Exchange Theatre   *Levitt, Bernstein Associates*
NatWest Bank   *Casson Conder & Partners*
Milton Keynes, Bucks.
Shopping Centre   *Milton Keynes Development Corporation*
Newcastle
Byker Estate   *Ralph Erskine*
Norwich
Sainsbury Centre   *Foster Associates*

Above: Coventry Cathedral by Sir Basil Spence – an outstanding example of modern British ecclesiastical architecture.

Right: The Economist Building, London, designed by Peter and Alison Smithson.

Right: The Sainsbury Arts Centre, Norwich, designed by Foster Associates.

neighbourly architectural solutions coupled with a tremendous interest in old buildings and their conservation.

Plenty of lively architecture was, however, springing up, in industrial building and particularly in the new Universities. These set the design pace for the expansion of the existing and older Universities – not hitherto noted for enlightened or adventurous patronage – and resulted in many of most significant buildings of the post-war period. Perhaps the best of these can be seen at Oxford and Cambridge.

And what of the 1980s? We have seen how the continuing political swings between free-range market and the Welfare State have been reflected in the building patterns of the present century. The portents are gloomy. World depression and collapsing industries bring irresolution and uncertainty. Yet for architecture there are encouraging signs. Professionals have become more humble, the non-experts more discriminating. Old buildings are better respected and, when well preserved, are well looked after. New building technology will continue to fascinate and excite and there will be an increasing display of the 'tour de force' – sparkling, outrageous, confident. But along the middle road there is undoubtedly a rediscovery of that pleasure in simple forms, good materials and fine workmanship – the virtues which inspired the Arts and Crafts Movement a century ago and still have lessons for us today.

Below: Coutts's Bank in the Strand, London, designed by Sir Frederick Gibberd.

Below right: The Elephant House in London Zoo designed by Casson, Conder & Partners.

The British at Leisure: Games

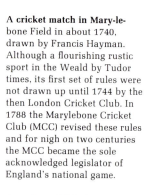

A cricket match in Mary-le-bone Field in about 1740, drawn by Francis Hayman. Although a flourishing rustic sport in the Weald by Tudor times, its first set of rules were not drawn up until 1744 by the then London Cricket Club. In 1788 the Marylebone Cricket Club (MCC) revised these rules and for nigh on two centuries the MCC became the sole acknowledged legislator of England's national game.

A rugby match between Lancashire and Yorkshire in 1895. Rugby Football first emerged as a game when, in 1823, a young Rugby schoolboy, William Webb Ellis, 'with a fine disregard of the rules of football as played in his time first took the ball in his arms and ran with it'. Since then the game has burgeoned overseas – notably in Australia, New Zealand, South Africa and France.

In Britain, as every schoolboy knows, nature and art have combined with especial creativity to 'invent' a remarkable range of games, both as a source of enjoyment and a kind of war surrogate, satisfying people's aggression not by vendettas or tribal conflicts but by ritual encounters played out in accordance with a code of rules and conventions accepted by both sides. Britain's later growth as a colonial power led to the export of both the sports and the values they reflected.

Cricket, a flourishing rustic sport in the Weald by Tudor times, may justly be called the first game to become national. There is no doubting the authenticity of the claim of John Derrick, Coroner of the County of Surrey, in 1598, to have played the game while a scholar in 'the free school of Guildeford', nor the splendid achievements of the Hambledon Cricket Club (1750–89) on Broadhalfpenny Down; nor the foundation, in 1787, with its headquarters at the present Lord's from 1814, of the Marylebone Cricket Club, which was to become for nigh-on two centuries cricket's sole acknowledged legislator; nor the games subsequent remarkable growth at home and overseas. How typically English that cricket's nomenclature should have been incorporated so effortlessly into the language, epitomized by the phrase, 'It isn't cricket' to connote unfair play or shady dealing.

Real, or Royal, Tennis, imported into Britain from France towards the end of the 14th century, is the only game with a continuous history as long as cricket's. The court at Hampton, the oldest of 17 surviving today, was built by Henry VIII, no mean player himself, and rebuilt by Charles II. The Victorian and Edwardian eras saw more courts built, including three at Cambridge to match an older one at Oxford. Royal support and the encouragement given to sports both by the major Public Schools, due largely to the influence of Dr Arnold, Headmaster of Rugby School (1828–42), and by the Universities of Oxford and Cambridge are recurring themes.

Rackets and Fives, two minority sports, also appear to have been well developed by the early 19th century, as the writings of William Hazlitt show, and a fillip was given to the former by the introduction of the Public Schools Championship in 1868, first at Prince's Club, London, and later at Queen's. The remarkable growth of both Lawn Tennis and Squash Rackets has been a 20th-century phenomenon, the outcome of changed financial, social and sporting patterns as well as of increased attention from the media.

Football, often of a violent kind, seems to have been played in England at least from the 12th century. Yet again, it was some of the major Public Schools and the Universities of Oxford and Cambridge which, from the 1820s, brought a more recognizable shape and system. The granting of half-days on Saturdays by the Factory Act of 1850 helped to encourage the interest of industrial workers also. Important landmarks were the formation of the Football Association in 1863, and the first F.A. Cup Final at Kennington Oval in 1872, before a crowd of 2000 – a far cry indeed from the 100,000 at Wembley today! Many clubs, like Aston Villa and Southampton, had their origins in schools; others, like Arsenal and Manchester United, in works teams. The one amateur side to hold its own, decisively, against professionals, was the Corinthians, founded by N.L. Jackson in 1883. Football has now become a world game and a vehicle for national prestige, helped by the Jules Rimet World Cup, started in 1930, and by the immense coverage given by the media. It was both a shock and a delight when, thanks to an irridescent display of footballing skills, England, the teachers, were defeated by Hungary, the pupils, at Wembley, in 1953 by 6 goals to 3.

A similar pattern emerges for Rugby Football, from the moment in 1823 when a 15-year-old Rugby schoolboy, William Webb Ellis, 'with a fine disregard of the rules of football as played in his time first took the ball in his arms and ran with it'. Oxford and Cambridge took up what Rugby School had started, and Guy's Hospital, the oldest surviving club, was founded in 1843, followed by the Rugby Football Union in 1871. The 1870s saw also an immense burgeoning of the game overseas, in Australia, New Zealand, and South Africa especially. Rugby League was to go its own way in 1895.

This article has found no room for athletics, which the English were probably the first to revive and redevelop in the 19th century; nor golf, which the Scots pioneered with single-minded devotion; nor badminton, nor hockey, nor rowing, nor a host of other competitive sports. Nor has it been able to elaborate the curses as well as the blessings of 20th-century sport: the growth of excessive nationalistic feeling, of commercial pressures, of aggressive, even violent, behaviour by both participants and spectators. Rather has its modest aim been to justify the assertion that games and sports, transmitted by our forbears and played for enjoyment as well as for the urge to win, have been, and still are, an indispensable and engaging ingredient of Britain's heritage.

Top: A scene from the Final Tie of the FA Challenge Cup Competition, Burnley v Tottenham Hotspurs at the Empire Stadium, Wembley on 5 May 1962.

Above: Virginia Wade – Wimbledon ladies' singles champion in 1977.

Above left: Sebastian Coe (wearing 717), Olympic Gold Medalist and holder of three world records.

The British at Leisure: Spa towns and the Seaside

The rush to the sea has characterized the British way of life for almost two centuries. But for many centuries before it was the lure of spa and spring water which attracted the seekers of pleasure and health. Roman spas (like Buxton and Bath) or medieval holy wells long remained important sites for 'taking the waters', for a variety of medicinal reasons. But it was in the 17th century that the custom – aided by contemporary medical opinion – developed into a major social habit. The spas of the 17th and 18th centuries became centres of secular leisure as ever more people found themselves able to afford the costly commercial delights of travel and entertainment at the spas. Sir Edmund Verney wrote of Bath in 1635, 'We pass our time awaye as merrily as paine will give us leave.' In response to the growing prosperity of the middle and upper classes, the spas proliferated in numbers and expanded their facilities. At Epsom, Bath, Tunbridge, Buxton, Harrogate and Scarborough – and many smaller ones – there developed sophisticated leisure facilities. The sick went in search of health, but the able-bodied went in search of pleasure – which they found in plenty in the summer round of balls, masques, concerts, dinners and assignations. To cater for these varied needs there grew up large urban settlements whose architectural masterpieces – for public and private pleasure – remain to this day as the unrivalled monuments to the tastes and fashions of the age.

The spas were first effectively challenged at the very apogee of their 18th-century popularity by a switch in medical opinion. Dr Richard Russell began to advocate the medicinal virtues of sea, as opposed to the spa, water for both bathing and drinking; and to test his theories lured patients to the Sussex coastal village of Brighthelmstone. Within a generation the newly named Brighton had become a latter-day Bath beside the seaside. In the North, Scarborough could provide both spa and sea water and was able to make a smooth transition from spa town to seaside resort, catering for the prosperous of the North. But initial development of the seaside resorts – duplicating the facilities, architecture and even social styles of the older spas – largely took place within easy reach of London – at Hastings, Folkestone, Southend, Margate, Ramsgate, Bognor, Lyme Regis, Brighton and Weymouth. Their fashionable appeal was often enhanced by royal and aristocratic visits but the crucial factor was their accessibility, by river or road. Architecturally and socially the new resorts consciously modelled themselves on the spas. Soon, however, there developed pronounced differences of social tone between them; the expansive early 19th-century middle class, keen to emulate their betters, flocked to the coast, often imposing on their favourite resorts what others regarded as a 'vulgar' social tone. Poorer people on the other hand were normally able to enjoy the delights of the seaside only if they lived close by.

The Transport Revolution

Like society at large, the resorts were transformed by the transport revolution. Steamships carried thousands of Londoners to resorts along the Thames. But it was the railways which put the coast within easy (and ever cheaper) reach of the new inland urban areas. Travel had traditionally been difficult and expensive but by mid-century a network of 7000 miles (11,000 km) of track provided a multitude of links to the coast (the farthest point from the coast in England is only 70 miles). From the 1840s onwards urban and industrial organizations – Sunday schools, churches, factories, temperance societies and of course the railway companies – began to organize excursion trains for a trip to the seaside. As soon as a railway link was opened, train-

'The Comforts of Bath' – a Rowlandson print of 1798 when the lure of spa and spring water still attracted the seekers of pleasure and health. To cater for the varied needs of the visitors to the spas there developed large urban settlements whose architectural masterpieces are unrivalled monuments to the tastes and fashions of the age.

FAMOUS SPA TOWNS

Bath
Buxton
Tunbridge Wells
Harrogate
Epsom
Droitwich
Cheltenham
Leamington
Llandrindod Wells
Malvern
Woodhall Spa

The Population of Major Seaside Resorts in 1851

Brighton	65,569
Blackpool	c.2000
Hastings	16,569
Ramsgate	11,838
Scarborough	12,915
Southport	4,765
Torquay	7,403
Weymouth	9,458
Whitby	10,899

loads of city-dwellers – often industrial workers – poured onto the coast, escaping the filth and routines of the cities and to enjoy the fresh air, the sights, and increasingly, the commercial delights of the resorts. In one week in May 1850, 73,000 people visited Brighton by train. The impact of such hordes on embryonic resorts, often catering for more refined souls, was dramatic. Writing of Blackpool in 1851 a Preston newspaper noted: 'Unless immediate steps are taken, Blackpool as a resort for the respectable visitors will be ruined'.

Where commercial interests began specifically to cater for working people (Blackpool) by offering cheaper, accessible pleasures, the social tone of the resort became plebeian. Elsewhere (Southport for instance) local landowners blocked the popular commercialization of the town and were able to preserve a more genteel social tone. Other resorts (Scarborough) managed to cater for various social tastes and classes.

Rapid Growth

The 19th-century seaside resorts grew more rapidly than any other type of town – including London and the expanding industrial cities. The 15 major watering places increased their population by 254 per cent between 1801 and 1851. The table shows the population of the major seaside resorts in 1851.

The seaside resorts were a permanent home for those people who sought a healthier escape from city life; the resorts offered fresh air to a society increasingly concerned with pulmonary illnesses. Some resorts failed to establish themselves or failed to capitalize on the growing vogue for seaside trips. In general however the resorts went from strength to strength, especially in the years 1870–1914, their attractions enhanced by the upsurge in national economic well-being. Despite the persistence of appalling urban poverty, ever more working people were able to save a little cash for an annual day (or longer) by the sea. In the process, customs of seaside trips and pleasures were bequeathed from one generation to another. And it was this force of social custom – and consumer power – which was tapped by those expansive commercial interests which invested so heavily in the leisure facilities of the seaside towns. The

Seaside resorts were transformed by cheap railway travel. By the 1840s, train-loads of city-dwellers – often industrial workers – streamed to the coast to enjoy the fresh air, paddling and such gaudier commercial delights as piers, theatres and music-halls. Today, despite competition from more exotic climes, 35 million people in Britain still travel to the seaside every summer.

A plunge from a bathing-machine – an early forerunner of the 'rude' postcard with its 'wish you were here' message for friends at home.

gaudier delights, of the pier, pleasure beaches, theatres, music halls and illuminations, were paralleled by more sedate offerings – of municipal gardens, parks, bandstands and promenades, for those of less robust tastes. In catering for these varied leisure interests of the British people, there developed the characteristic architectural and social institutions of the seaside resort.

Cultural Phenomenon

Despite the rapid process of modernization (and often destruction) since the 1950s, the resorts still possess many of the finest survivals of Victorian and Edwardian styles. Furthermore, although tastes have changed and the English coast faces competition from more exotic climes, a remarkable 35 million people travel to the seaside every British summer. The lure of the coast has become a cultural phenomenon, among all sorts and conditions of people, which has survived two centuries of remarkable social change.

The British at Leisure: Field Sports

Field sports have been practised in Britain for some 2500 years. During that time, however, some have expanded (fox-hunting, grouse-shooting and pheasant-shooting) while others have contracted (stag-hunting, partridge-shooting, salmon-fishing). This is in part due to changes in taste, economics and the technologies of both rearing and killing; but it mainly results from the modifications we have ourselves made to the environment. For example, the gradual clearing of the hardwood forests of southern England turned stag-hunting country into hare-and fox-hunting country. The huge population of wild partridges which gave most of rural England its principal fowling has been reduced almost everywhere to almost nothing by chemical sprays which kill its food. Pheasant-shooting has expanded into areas not naturally suitable by dint of coverts being planted and birds hand-reared, the motive being economic. Fox-hunting moved into countries far different from High Leicestershire, in response to the demand of sportsmen for more excitement than the old harriers gave; it was often made possible by the planting of gorse-covert (South Lincolnshire), the excavation of artificial earths for breeding (Essex) and the introduction of 'cat-footed' hounds better able to stand up to flints (Surrey). Sports are practised where conditions suit both quarry and chase, but often the conditions are in both senses artificial. This is itself a tradition which dates from the time of the Norman Conquest.

Like our ancestors, we pursue beasts, birds and fish.

A map of stag-hunting Britain in AD 1100 would comprise practically the entire British Isles. The beasts were hunted, shot, coursed, or a mixture of all three; on moorland they were driven. Farming has gradually expelled the extremely destructive Red deer to areas where they can do little damage: Exmoor, the Quantocks, the Scottish Highland. In the former deer are hunted, in the latter stalked and shot with rifles. These choices are made by geography: you cannot safely fire a high-powered rifle in agricultural Somerset, or ride up a perpendicular Grampian.

The modern fox-hunting map of England and Wales excludes only areas so industrialized as to be unhuntable (and includes some even of these, such as part of South

FOX AND DEER HUNTING COUNTRY

Foxhunting country

The Shires

Fellhounds

Stag and Buck

BRITAIN'S PRINCIPAL FISHING RIVERS

Principal salmon rivers

Principal dry fly rivers

Wet fly country

Yorkshire and South Wales). Fox-hunting as an organized sport dates from the Restoration; it covered England within a century and a half. The Scottish borders have always been hunted; elsewhere there are fox-hunting enclaves created historically by individual enthusiasts.

Hares were the staple chase of the countryside in the centuries between the disappearance of the forest and the arrival of the foxhound; say from 1550 to 1800. Hares are now hunted everywhere, by harriers, beagles or bassets, usually by arrangement with the local hunt. They are also coursed in competitive meetings, and often shot. On balance the sharing of a country between foxhounds and beagles benefits both sports, and entertains rich and poor, flamboyant and scruffy, brave and nervous.

For centuries the most important gamebird by far was the partridge. Now it is the pheasant. The change occurred between about 1830 and 1870; it was almost wholly artificial, and a consequence of taste, fashion and money. Good pheasant driving required hilly ground (natural), well-placed covert (either deliberately planted, or preserved for the purpose from axe and plough), and plentiful birds (few wild). It is no accident that the two periods of greatest growth in pheasant-shooting coincided with deep agricultural depression: 1815–40 and 1880–1900.

Grouse-shooting is restricted in location by the fact that grouse eat young heather and shelter in old, which effectively limits them to high moorland. It was further limited until the late 18th century by the impossibility of getting to Scottish moors; even when military roads were built after the Forty-five Jacobite uprising, few sportsmen used them until the 1820s. (The same is true of deer-stalking.) Grouse drives are the youngest major branch of shooting (grouse used to be shot over pointers, often from ponies) and to many people the most glorious.

Fishing

There used to be salmon in every considerable river in the British Isles. The Industrial Revolution expelled them from all except a very few in England and Wales. The geography of salmon is further determined by the fact that, after their adolescence in the sea, they return to spawn,

apparently invariably, to the river and even the pool where they were spawned.

Trout fishing now takes two completely different forms, determined by geography and geology. A stream-fed river, apt to spate, runs typically through rocky and peaty country, and is acid. A spring-fed river derives from rainwater absorbed by chalk and limestone; it hardly floods; it is alkaline. The two produce different flora, therefore different fauna, therefore different food for the trout, and so different ways of catching them. The former is wet-fly fishing, the latter dry. It is peculiar how very slow sportsmen were to appreciate the difference: on the alkaline Test in 1830 people were still fishing as though on the acid Tweed. Scientific dry-fly fishing – most delicate and donnish of all sports – was a late Victorian invention.

Above left: A hill stream. The water is too fast and too acid to admit the growth of much weed: the whole ecology of the river is different from that of a chalk stream. The trout are small, active and wild. They are caught with sunk flies drifted or dragged through the current: 'fancy patterns', seldom imitating specific natural forms. Wet-fly fishing is in no way an inferior sport to dry-fly fishing, but a completely different one, and at least five centuries older.

Left: Chalk stream. The Itchen above Winchester, flowing placidly through water meadows in fat farming country: one of the 'big three' of dry-fly fishing (with the Test and Kennet). The alkaline water is gin-clear and usually smooth. In it grows a jungle of weed which nurtures the grubs of flying aquatic insects. On these the trout feeds, and on exact imitations of these, for the last 100 years, he has been caught.

The British at Leisure: Racing

No one knows where or when people first set out to test one horse against another, so although there was horse-racing in Britain both before and during the Roman occupation this country has no claim to be the 'birthplace' of the sport. There is, on the other hand, no question that the thoroughbred, the highly specialized breed on which racing all over the world is now based, was an entirely British invention.

Amazingly, every single modern thoroughbred is descended, in direct male line, from one of the three Arab stallions imported into this country at the beginning of the 18th century. Known as the *Godolphin Arabian*, the *Byerley Turk* and the *Darley Arabian*, they were acquired in various ways, not all of them above reproach, from their original Middle Eastern owners and mated with British mares, of whose pedigrees, until then, no one had taken much notice. The 'selective' breeding which has been carried on ever since, based largely on race-course performance, has produced a creature much less durable than the original desert-bred Arab – but a great deal faster. Any modern thoroughbred, however humble, would easily beat the fastest Arab over any distance from 100 yards to five miles.

For most of the thoroughbred's short history, it was generally accepted that horses bred in England and Ireland tend to run faster than those bred elsewhere – and that breeders from other countries, America, for instance, must come back to the original source of 'quality' for regular transfusions to prevent their horses becoming coarse and slow. Even then there was the occasional exception – like Gladiateur who earned his proud title 'Avenger of Waterloo' by winning the Epsom Derby in 1855. But it was only after the war that the victory in our great races of horses trained in France and Italy (often, latterly, bred in America) became a painful commonplace.

Apart from the thoroughbred itself, the major contribution to modern racing made by the British Isles is National Hunt Racing, steeplechasing and hurdling – or simply 'jumping'. Here too, we and the Irish were the pioneers. It was in 1752 that two Irish hunting men called Blake and O'Calloghan challenged each other to race across country 4½ miles (still the distance of the Grand National) from Buttevant church to St Leger steeple. At that time the word 'steeplechasing' was self explanatory. Church steeples were simply the clearest, most visible landmarks and the winners were the man and horse who got fastest from A to B without benefit of flags, rails or grandstand. Messrs Blake and O'Calloghan would not see much in common between their carefree joyride and a modern steeplechase but it is jumping – steeplechasing over birch-fences 4 feet 6 inches high and hurdling over smaller gorse-laced sheep-hurdles – which gives British racing its unique variety. The first public steeplechase was held in 1830 at St Albans, in Hertfordshire. This steeplechase was run until 1839, which was the year of the first Grand National at Aintree, a race which has now become world famous. It was won by a horse called Lottery. One of the fences jumped in that first Grand National was a high fence and a ditch over which a certain Captain Becher came to grief, riding a horse called *Conrad*. This is the fence which is known as 'Becher's Brook' today.

With 60 separate courses and two race-meetings on nearly every weekday of the year, this country has more racing in proportion to its population than any other. Weather permitting, Good Friday and the three days over Christmas are the only weekdays when there is not a single scheduled meeting. Usually there are at least two – with four or five on Saturdays and as many as 14 on a Bank Holiday. Sixteen of the 60 courses are used solely for flat-

Top: The flat-racing season starts in March and ends in November. Its ruling body is the Jockey Club, set up in 1750 at Newmarket. In the five English races known as the 'Classics', horses run at level weights: 9 stone for colts and 8 stone 7 lb for fillies. The Classics, which are for three-year-olds are: the 2000 Guineas, the Derby and St Leger, open to colts and fillies; and the 1000 Guineas and the Oaks for fillies only.

Above: The Byerley Turk, one of the three founding sires of the English Thoroughbred.

racing, 25 solely for jumping and 19 are dual purpose, staging jumping in winter and flat in summer. Flat-racing, which starts in March and ends in November never has more than two months to itself. There are jumping meetings in August and the season lasts till the following June. Most of the year you can take your choice.

It needs a small army to keep this operation on the road. In 1981 about 6000 owners were paying in the region of £100 a week to have between nine and twelve thousand horses trained by 450 trainers and ridden by more than 600 professional jockeys. (These figures are of course, both

approximate and incomplete). There are also 600 amateur riders, 600 'Permit Holders' who can train their own or their family's horses – and nearly 5000 stablelads and lasses. It is estimated that around 70,000 people are employed in the betting industry – which now collects well over £200,000,000 for the government in betting tax.

The Controlling Bodies

British racing is controlled by two bodies. The Jockey Club is still, essentially, the self-electing social club which began to regulate racing in the 18th century. It has, however, moved with the times to such an extent that even its most bitter opponents find it hard to suggest a better way of enforcing discipline in a sport where millions of tax-free pounds are at stake every day. The second controlling body, the Betting Levy Board, is a statutory creation appointed by the Home Office and empowered to collect money from the betting industry for the benefit of racing as a whole.

Most of the Levy (now over £13 million) is distributed in prize money but although that is higher than ever before British owners and trainers still tend to look with envy across the Channel where the French enjoy a Tote Monopoly (no book-makers) which, since the war, has given their highly centralized racing a prosperity unique in Europe. But if centralization and no book-makers give prosperity, they also lead, the British race-goer might argue, to a certain lack of colour, atmosphere and variety. From the upmarket grandeur of Royal Ascot to the hurly-burly of a small jumping course like Newton Abbot on August Bank Holiday – that is the range which British racing spans and those who love it would not willingly accept much change.

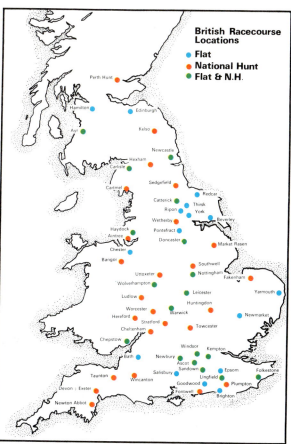

British Racecourse Locations
● Flat
● National Hunt
● Flat & N.H.

Perth Hunt
Hamilton
Edinburgh
Ayr
Kelso
Newcastle
Hexham
Carlisle
Sedgefield
Cartmel
Redcar
Catterick
Thirsk
Ripon
York
Wetherby
Beverley
Haydock
Pontefract
Aintree
Doncaster
Chester
Market Rasen
Bangor
Southwell
Uttoxeter
Nottingham
Fakenham
Wolverhampton
Leicester
Yarmouth
Ludlow
Huntingdon
Worcester
Warwick
Newmarket
Hereford
Stratford
Towcester
Cheltenham
Chepstow
Windsor
Kempton
Bath
Newbury
Ascot
Taunton
Salisbury
Sandown
Epsom
Folkestone
Wincanton
Goodwood
Lingfield
Plumpton
Devon & Exeter
Fontwell
Brighton
Newton Abbot

Steeplechasing is essentially British in origin, character and appeal. There are jumping meetings in August and the season lasts until the following June. The Grand National, run at Aintree during the Liverpool Spring meeting in March or April, is the most testing steeplechase of them all.

The British at Leisure: Equestrianism

The British Isles are acknowledged world-wide as being specially well suited to breeding horses. As a nation we have inherited a love and respect for the horse, based on our enthusiastic admiration of the many virtues which make it the most versatile, attractive of animals. Our climate is ideal with no extremes of temperature, and enough moisture to ensure the growth of rich nutritious grassland, especially in areas where the soil is based on limestone (as in parts of the West of England). Young horses thrive on our excellent pasture, growing strong, thick bone to withstand the hard work we often demand of them later. Although only a small area, Britain, remarkably, has produced nine truly indigenous 'Mountain and Moorland' breeds. Furthermore, each breed is distinctly different in both appearance and characteristics, but all have in common the ability to withstand hardship, being extremely tough as well as being sure-footed.

Below: Exmoor ponies in their natural surroundings. The Exmoor is believed to be the oldest pure indigenous breed, descended almost unchanged from its primitive ancestor, the Celtic Pony. The British Isles have nine native breeds of pony.

THE PRINCIPAL SHOWGROUNDS OF GREAT BRITAIN AND IRELAND

Badminton	National Three Day Event Championships
Burghley	Three Day Event
Cardiff	Wales and West Showground
Coventry	British Equestrian Centre
Dublin	Horse Show
Goodwood	Dressage
Hickstead	Show jumping
Newmarket	Hunter Show. Centre of British Thoroughbred breeding and racing
Peterborough	East of England Showground
Ardingley	South of England Showground
Wembley	Horse of the Year Show (October) International Show (July)
Windsor	Horse Show Three Day Event

BRITISH BREEDS OF PONY

The Shetland The strongest equine in relation to its size (10.2 hands). Once used as a pack-pony for carting sea-weed and as a pit pony. Now mainly a child's pony.
Colour: All colours.

The Highland Largest and strongest of the native breeds (12.2–14.2 hh). Quiet and ideal for slow hill work.
Colour: Black, brown, varying dun or grey (no white).

The Fell Smaller (13.2 hh) than the Dales pony. Once a pack pony, but excellent for riding and driving.
Colour: Black, brown, bay, occasionally grey or dun.

The Dales Larger than the Fell (14.2 hh) and more plentiful. May include Clydesdale blood. Used to carry lead and coal long distances. Docile, hardy and strong.
Colour: Usually black.

Welsh Mountain A most attractive native breed, and probably the best riding pony. Average height 12 hh. Used to cross with Thoroughbreds and other breeds, as it is intelligent, bold, sound and strong. Used to produce polo pony, hackney, hunter and of course the other Welsh breeds – the Welsh Cob and Welsh Pony.
Colour: All except piebald and skewbald.

The Exmoor Believed to be the oldest pure indigenous breed.

Average height 12.2 hh. Great hardiness and stamina, and popular with children.
Colour: Bay, brown or dun with black points. (No white.)

The Dartmoor A tough, small breed (12 hh). Used for riding and good jumpers.
Colour: Bay, black or brown. No white markings.

The New Forest Used to survive on poor pasture. Less distinctive in appearance than other breeds, having been 'improved' by alien blood. Average height 13.1 hh. Popular riding pony for all ages. Also suitable for driving.
Colour: Any, except piebald and skewbald.

The Connemara An ancient breed indigenous to Ireland. Renowned for strength and stamina. They make excellent jumpers. Shows traces of Arab and Spanish blood. Average height 14 hh.
Colour: Mostly grey, but can be bay or brown.

THE THOROUGHBRED

The 'English' Thoroughbred has been developed from native pony blood and the southern influence of the Barb, the Turk and the Arab. It is generally acknowledged as the most beautiful, practical and classical of breeds. It is most suitable for racing, being bred for speed and stamina, and is the ideal size (average 15.3 hh), with balanced proportions, strength and usually good temperament.

BRITISH HEAVY HORSES

The Clydesdale has size (17 hh), weight and activity, making it extremely useful, especially to farmers in the past. Usually bay or brown in colour, it has white on the face and legs.

The Shire This massive horse was once called the 'Great Horse of England'. Its strength has been used to draw enormous loads on farms or in towns. It is normally bay or brown, but it may have white feathers on the legs and feet. It can be as large as 18 hh.

The Suffolk Punch This heavily built horse (16 hh) is always chestnut. Unlike the Shire and Clydesdale it has clean limbs (no feathers). It is indigenous to Suffffolk and has a long life-span.

THE HACKNEY This versatile animal is usually driven in harness. The pony type (under 14.2 hh) has true pony characteristics, but the horse (up to 16 hh) has a longer history. It was bred for speed and stamina, but has become renowned as a trotter of brilliant, extravagant action.

THE CLEVELAND BAY – always bay with black points, is a long-established breed from Yorkshire which transmits its valuable characteristics to all its stock, whether pure or cross-bred. It possesses good conformation, strong legs, true action, and an excellent temperament.

A champion Welsh Mountain pony. Showing in-hand is as much of an art as showing under saddle. The horse is examined as a model of conformation, manners, performance and movement.

Below right: A Hackney Horse in harness, driven by Mrs Frank Haydon. The most distinctive characteristic of the Hackney is its action, which is both extravagant and spectacular.

Equestrian Sports

Showing a horse or pony satisfies the owner's or breeder's urge to display his stock in front of an expert judge. The animal must be judged either 'in hand' or ridden, and will be examined as a model of conformation, manners, performance and movement. Classes are held for every breed, height, type and age, with strong competition in every category. Shows are held throughout the year, but are most popular outdoors from May to September. The main attraction, particularly at indoor shows is the show jumping, which can often be exciting when speed becomes a factor: the winner is the horse and rider combination with the fewest jumping and speed penalties. Famous riders such as David Broome and Harvey Smith have made it a popular television sport.

Horse Trials or Eventing are less well known, being difficult to televise. The top competitors make few appearances, since Three-Day Events are very gruelling contests, and the horse must rest for at least a month after it. Most of the training is done at home, or at separate Dressage, Show Jumping or Cross Country competitions, to practise for each of the three phases. The horse and rider who can excel in all three aspects will be successful. It is the most demanding, but perhaps the most rewarding of the equestrian sports.

Polo does not require great horsemanship, but a combination of gamesmanship and horse control. The ponies must be fast and agile, and very fit to survive this high-pressure sport which requires galloping, stopping, turning and spinning. The rider must be skilled at hitting the ball from a full gallop, anticipating and teamwork.

Team racing is the newest sport in Britain, when four riders in a team cover about two miles of varied terrain, negotiating many different types of 'natural', hunting or cross country fences. The fastest team to complete the course intact, are the winners. The competition is an outlet for those who wish for exhilaration, but also enjoy the rewards of good horsemanship.

The British at Leisure: Food and Drink

also the predominant cereal, and in both places drop scones, oatcakes and pancakes are traditionally still cooked on the griddle.

The names of the hard cheeses, for which England is famous, are a roll-call of the rich dairy farming areas, Cheddar from the West Country, Cheshire, Double Gloucester, Caerphilly, Leicester, Derby, Lancashire, Wensleydale and Blue Stilton. Many are still made in local farm dairies. Hams too have a regional character and are cured in different ways in Yorkshire, Wiltshire, Cumberland and Suffolk (York ham was said to owe its flavour originally to being smoked with the oak chips left over from the building of the Minster). The meat pies of Cornwall, known as pasties, are totally different from the pork, veal, ham and egg pies associated with the Midlands, in particular Melton Mowbray. Pigeon pies and game pies are connected with sporting estates. Steak and kidney pies and puddings are universal, but faggots, made from pig's liver, are a speciality of Wales, and Black Pudding, made from pig's blood, is a northern one. Sausages too are subtly different in flavour depending on where they are made.

One outstanding characteristic of British food is the high quality of the ingredients and the corresponding simplicity of the way in which they are used. Fish is usually poached or fried, meat (the British have always been great meat-eaters) is roasted – originally on a spit over a fire – or boiled. Both are accompanied by traditional sauces (the accusation that 'the English have 60 different religious sects but only one sauce' is groundless). Parsley sauce accompanies cod, gooseberry sauce goes with mackerel, apple sauce with roast pork, bread sauce (found only in England and viewed with apprehension by foreigners) with chicken and game, Cumberland sauce with ham, caper, onion or mint sauce with lamb or mutton, horseradish sauce with beef. Fried fish is served with chips, roast beef with Yorkshire pudding. This dish, made of batter and cooked in dripping from the joint was originally served before the meat to blunt hungry appetites. For the same reason boiled beef was cooked with suet dumplings.

Fish is a prominent feature of British cuisine. Salmon and sole, lobsters and oysters are now usually reserved for special occasions, the days when salmon was so common that servants refused to eat it are gone. But trout, mackerel, herrings, fresh and smoked haddock, cod, plaice, shrimps, cockles, mussels and whelks are popular.

Poultry also figures in many recipes. Aylesbury duck with sage and onion stuffing, chicken pies and roast goose are all long established favourites. (Three hundred years ago flocks of geese were driven many miles to market, their feet first being 'shod' by making them walk through tar and sand.) A curious survivor is the northern boiled chicken dish known as Hindle Wakes – possibly meaning Hen de la Wake and formerly eaten in Wakes Week. Game too is much sought after, grouse and venison in Scotland, partridge and pheasant from the great estates, wild duck and snipe from the marshland demonstrate the English love of field sports. Jugged hare is a winter favourite on many country house menus.

The most common vegetable is the potato. Brought to England in 1585 by Sir Walter Raleigh, it is now so popular that it is eaten, in a variety of ways, at almost every meal. A runner-up used to be cabbage – it has been said that 'The English have three vegetables and two of them are cabbage'. The leek is traditionally connected with Wales (where it can be worn as a buttonhole on St David's day) as is laverbread (Bara Lawr) a smooth seaweed, sometimes called sea-spinach, which is cured and sold as a dark gelatinous puree for use in laver sauce or to be fried with oatmeal.

Fine fare from Scotland. The spread includes Tay salmon, grouse, roast sirloin of beef, haggis (with neeps and tatties), venison, Orkney and Dunlop cheeses, cock-a-leekie soup, shortbread and Dundee cake.

An English butcher's shop well stocked with traditional Christmas turkeys.

The best British food remains surprisingly regional. It is influenced by local agricultural conditions, themselves dependent on geography and climate. In Scotland, for instance, where oats grow better than wheat, local dishes use oatmeal rather than wheat flour. (Dr Johnson in his Dictionary was somewhat scathing in his definition of Oats as 'A grain which in England is generally given to horses, but in Scotland supports the people.) Scotland's national dishes, haggis and porridge, both use oats (the true Scot eats his porridge standing up flavoured only with a pinch of salt). In Wales, another Celtic country, oatmeal is

TRADITIONAL DRINKS

The traditional British drinks are beer, whisky, gin and cider. Beer, which might be regarded as the national drink, has a long history. Early Britons drank a fermented liquor made from barley, honey, or apples on festive occasions, and, by the time of the Roman invasion were tippling a kind of ale made from barley and wheat. From that time on beer has been the staple drink for adults of all classes. Different types include mild, bitter light pale, brown and Scotch. India pale is named from the type of ale first exported from Britain to India, Burton ale derives from the brewing centre at Burton on Trent where the water has its own peculiar properties and taste. Whisky is the national drink of Scotland; the word is an anglicization for the Gaelic 'usquebaugh', meaning water of life. Distilled from a mash of cereal grains with added malt, each brand was said to get its distinctive flavour from the different peat streams whose water was used. Gin, also distilled from grain, is flavoured with juniper berries, hence the word which is a shortening of the French word genièvre. London gin is world famous. Gin was one of the most popular working-class drinks in the 18th and 19th centuries when infamous 'gin shops' abounded. Cider and perry are made from fermented juice of special types of apples and pears respectively with a high acid content. Home made varieties are not very alcoholic but commercially made cider is fortified with brandy.

The Public House or Pub is one of the most typical British institutions, and in most places is a centre of social activity playing the role of the café or bar in European life.

A lunchtime drink at the local – still one of the most typical British institutions.

But perhaps Britain's special culinary offering to the world are its puddings, which balance the simplicity of the main dish. Some, like plum pudding, have beef suet as a base and are boiled or steamed, others, apple pie and treacle tart for instance, use pastry. Summer puddings and bread and butter pudding are made from stale bread; rhubarb and gooseberry fools are purees of fruit and cream. Trifle and syllabub date from medieval times, the mincemeat in mince pies comes from a recipe brought back from the Crusades. An enormous variety of cakes are also part of the British tradition, again often with a regional emphasis or connected with special occasions. Yorkshire Parkin is gingerbread eaten on 5th November to commemorate Guy Fawkes, Hot Cross Buns appear only on Good Friday, Devonshire and Cornish splits are buns filled with clotted cream, and there are Bath buns, Chelsea buns, Wiltshire lardy cakes, Eccles, Welsh and Dundee cakes and short-bread from Scotland.

Peculiar to Britain

Two meals are peculiar to Britain. The first is the English breakfast (Somerset Maugham rather waspishly advised the wise visitor to Britain to eat it all the time). This may include porridge, bacon, eggs, mushrooms, fried bread or potatoes, smoked haddock, grilled kipper or kedgeree (a legacy of the British Raj). The other is afternoon tea which first became popular with the upper and middle classes after the discovery of the Indian tea plant in Assam in the 1820s and is now an national institution. The classic tea consists of small sandwiches (the sandwich is also a British invention) bread, butter and jam, scones, sponge cakes, biscuits, and sometimes buttered crumpets. High tea, on the other hand, is the main meal in Scotland and the north of England. It is eaten at 6 o'clock and includes meat or fish as well as bread and cakes.

INN SIGNS

The pub, inn or ale-house has for centuries played an important part in English life. Together with the church, it is still the focus of local activity in most villages. So it is not surprising that many rural pubs are called after country pursuits and farm animals: *The Fox and Hounds, The Cock* and *The Cow* (in any colour you fancy). *The Lamb,* however, is more likely to be a reference to Christ and is an indication of the enormous influence of the Church on inn names. In the Middle Ages pilgrims formed perhaps the largest single group of travellers, and hostels or inns were built at abbeys to accommodate them. *The Mitre* has an obvious monastic connotation. The *Cross Keys* is the emblem of St Peter. Only remotely nautical, *The Anchor* is the religious sign of hope while *The Ship* may often be a reference to Noah's Ark. Travel, too, has left its mark on pub names. From the heyday of stagecoaches (the 1720s to the coming of the railways) we get staging inns with such names as *The Coach and Horses, Horse and Groom* or named after coaches that called there such as *The Bristol Flyer* or *The Quicksilver Mail*. The railways themselves have given names to pubs from *The Railway Arms* to the *Marlow Donkey*. But after the Church perhaps the most important influence on pub names has been royalty as the numerous *Crowns* and *King's Heads* testify. *The White Hart* was the symbol of Richard II and the innumerable *Royal Oaks* commemorate Charles II's escape from the parliamentarians by hiding in an oak tree. Inn signs also have sporting connections: *The Bull* and *The Bear* (bear- and bull-baiting) and the ubiquitous *Cricketers' Arms*. Great events and famous people are remembered in such names as *The Trafalgar* and the *Duke of York*, of 'ten thousand men' fame.

Chapter Six

Britain's Cultural and Religious Heritage

Christianity first came to Britain in Roman times. By the 8th century it had taken permanent root. Even in these secular days 75 per cent of the British say that they believe in God, and more attend Church on Sunday than attend football matches on Saturday. The Church has pervaded every aspect of British life. Britain's cathedrals still stand as the supreme achievement of her architecture, and her 12,000 medieval parish churches are unequalled by those of any other country. In secular architecture too, as in painting, music, the theatre, science and above all literature, British genius has enriched not only this country but the entire civilized world.

Religious Anatomy of Britain

Religion makes bad statistics. Figures are hard to compare and may not mean what they seem to mean. For example, Britain has the reputation of being an irreligious country with poor church-going habits. Yet 75 per cent of the British admit believing in God, and more people go to church on Sunday than attend football matches on Saturday. On the other hand, almost half of all believers think of God as being vaguer and more remote than the God of the churches.

The Church of England (mother of the worldwide Anglican Communion) is the official national church. The Queen is its Supreme Governor and 24 of its bishops sit by right in the House of Lords. No other church has that right. More than 27,000,000 Britons have been baptized by the Church of England. But only 8,700,000 have been confirmed, only 1,900,000 have put their names on the church electoral rolls, and only 1,700,000 take communion at Christmas and Easter. How many Anglicans are there?

The Roman Catholic Church has 1,300,000 regularly attending Sunday Mass, and so might claim to be England's most active single church. But the total Roman Catholic population is only 4,200,000. That figure includes Wales, where the Anglicans have an independent 'Church in Wales'. Both Anglicans and Catholics have separate branches in Scotland, but the official Church of Scotland is Presbyterian, governed by an Assembly without bishops.

Then there are the Free or Noncomformist churches – notably Methodists, Baptists and United Reformed (a merger of most of the former Congregationalists and English Presbyterians) – and a great variety of splinter-groups, independents and immigrant churches, down to the tiny Society of Friends (or Quakers) and the fast-growing Mormons.

Britain also has 95,000 Greek Orthodox, 400,000 Jews and even larger communities of Hindus and Muslims, as well as smaller ones of Sikhs and Rastafarians. There is no way of evaluating their impact from their gross numbers, but it might be argued that the Hindus, Muslims and Rastafarians have done more to change British society than any religious group since the time of the first Christian missionaries.

'Catholic and Reformed'

Christianity first came to Britain with the Roman armies, but was squeezed into Ireland by later barbarian invaders. It came back into the North as the Celtic Church but was soon replaced – after the arrival of St. Augustine in 597 – by the Church of Rome. Henry VIII and Elizabeth I 'nationalized' this Church and then adapted it to the Protestant Reformation: the Church of England still claims to be 'Catholic' (though not Roman) *and* Reformed. For some, it has never been reformed enough, hence the Nonconformist churches which grew up in the 17th and 18th centuries. John Wesley's Methodists were notably successful among the neglected working classes of the early Industrial Revolution. Roman Catholicism was driven underground for a time and Dissenters discriminated against, but by the mid-19th century religious toleration was the law. (The monarch, however, still must not be a Roman Catholic.)

As a kind of moral national health service, the Church of England has its branches everywhere: its buildings are the jewels of the national heritage. Working hand in glove with the political establishment, it influenced everything from education to law and order for at least four centuries. But with the rise of industry, it lost some of that influence to the Noncomformists who became strong within the Liberal and Labour parties. Nonconformism dominated the North of England, Wales and mining Cornwall, while Anglicanism fell back on rural areas, university and cathedral cities and the south-east of England, heartland of the ruling gentry and upper-middle class. Irish Catholics arrived in Merseyside and Clydeside and filtered down to other industrial areas, including London.

Today, boundaries (both geographical and spiritual) have become blurred and the churches are being driven slowly into each others' arms. The nation as a whole seems sceptical of them and finds television, the garden and the family car a better way of spending its Sundays. For the main Protestant churches, almost all the indices have been falling throughout the century. That the Catholics have fared better is largely due to immigration, and now even they are seeing a decline in attendance at Mass. In matters like divorce and contraception, Catholics are behaving more and more like the rest.

The churches believe they have now touched bottom, though people seem reluctant to take up full membership of a demonination. Where churches are booming, they are usually some form of Charismatic or else Bible-based Evangelicals.

HOLY PLACES

St Albans Named after the first British martyr, probably killed by Roman soldiers in about AD 209.

Armagh Fifth-century see of St Patrick. Now headquarters of both Roman Catholic and Anglican churches in All Ireland.

Canterbury Chosen by St Augustine in 597 as the headquarters of the Roman Church in the south of England. The martyrdom of St Thomas à Becket in 1170 made it England's leading place of pilgrimage. Its Archbishop is now Primate of All England and he also presides over the worldwide Anglican Communion.

St David's See of the semi-legendary patron saint of the Welsh. It is Britain's smallest Cathedral.

Edinburgh Headquarters of the Church of Scotland whose annual Assembly has a permanent building there.

Glastonbury Legendary association with Joseph of Arimathea, King Arthur and St Patrick. St Dunstan was Abbot about 940.

Iona Celtic Christianity was introduced here by St Columba in 563, and spread through Scotland and Northern England in rivalry with that of Rome.

Lindisfarne or Holy Island Headquarters of the Celtic saints Aidan and Cuthbert in the 7th century. Noted for its illuminated gospels, compiled by Bishop Eadfrith.

London St Paul's Cathedral, Westminster Abbey, Westminster Cathedral (R.C.) and numerous fine churches by Wren. Administrative headquarters of the Church of England.

Norwich The cell of Mother Julian, perhaps the most celebrated of the English 14th-century mystics.

Oxford England's most celebrated school of theology, rich with names such as Wycliffe, Cranmer, Wesley, Keble and Newman.

Salisbury Formerly Sarum, the birthplace of the English liturgy. Its cathedral is in the pure Early English style.

Scone Crowning-place of the kings of Scotland, of great significance to Scottish political and ecclesiastical independence.

Walsingham Medieval place of pilgrimage dedicated to Our Lady, recently revived.

Winchester Noted cathedral, the see of saints Swithin, Ethelwold and Alphege, also containing bones of the Saxon kings of Wessex.

York Headquarters of the northern Province of the Church of England, second only to Canterbury. Known to have had a bishop long before Augustine's colleague Paulinus arrived.

CHURCH NUMBERS

Church of England[1]	27,000,000
Roman Catholic[1]	4,200,000
Church of Scotland[2]	950,000
R.C. in Scotland[1]	820,000
Methodist[2]	487,000
Jewish[3]	410,000
Muslim[3]	400,000+
Baptist[2]	156,000
United Reformed[2]	150,000
Church in Wales[4]	133,000
Mormons[5]	112,000
Eastern Orthodox[5]	100,000
Salvation Army[6]	90,000
Welsh Presbyterian[2]	85,000
Scottish Episcopal[2]	71,000
Quakers[2]	18,000
Adventists[2]	14,000
Moravians[2]	2,800

1. Baptised. 2. Members.
3. By birth. 4. Communicants.
5. All ages. 6. Adherents.

Early Missionaries and Saints

Christianity was established in Roman Britain in the south among the town dwellers and villa owners. Mosaics or wall paintings bearing Christian symbols have been found in villas at Hinton St Mary and Lullingstone, and in the 4th century at least four major cities had bishops (York, London, Lincoln and perhaps Cirencester). However in the 5th century the south and east of the country was invaded and settled by pagan Germanic peoples. Churches and shrines were sacked and their possessions like the Water Newton treasure, were hidden or lost.

Survival of Christianity

In Wales, Devon and Cornwall, Cumbria, and later Ireland, Christianity survived and was maintained by the native rulers who supplied land for the establishment of monastic communities. In these non-urbanized regions bishops lived in monasteries, and the same centres fostered literacy, and the learning of the antique world. The 5th and 6th centuries produced many heroic churchmen; St Illtyd of Wales; St Patrick, who went from north-west Britain to evangelize Ireland; St Ninian, who worked from a base at Whithorn among the Britons and southern Picts; St Kentigern, who worked in Cumbria and southern Scotland, and St Sampson in Cornwall and Brittany. Although many sites are associated with their names, the details of their lives are shadowy and distorted by later legends. Only

Slabs such as these of the 5th century testify to the continuation of Latin traditions in the native churches. Among the Scots – in Ireland and in their colonies around Iona and Glasgow – graves, particularly in monastic communities, were marked by recumbent slabs incised with crosses and inscriptions which remind us of the pages of manuscripts. This type of grave-marker was adopted by the early Northumbrian converts of the Irish missions, as can be seen at Lindisfarne (right). Later very much larger slabs with raised crosses were adopted and these inspired Pictish copies in the 8th century.

BRITISH MUSEUM. HARLEY ROLL Y 6

The 7th-century English monk St Guthlac receiving the tonsure – the shaving of the crown of the head as a sign of a person's dedication to the religious life. The period from the mid-7th century to the mid-9th was one of rapid development in the English Church: the country was equipped with a full diocesan organization and religious communities proliferated. It was also an age of Anglo-Saxon missions to heathen Germanic peoples. Outstanding among the missionaries was the West Saxon Winfrid, commissioned in 719 by Pope Gregory II to preach to the 'unbelieving gentiles'. Taking the Roman name Boniface, he carried out the task with zeal, earning himself, by the time of his death in 754, the title 'the Apostle of Germany'.

Wooden preaching or memorial crosses were probably introduced by the Irish Church in the mid-7th century. But it was most likely the English who invented free-standing stone crosses. These were known from Glastonbury to Bewcastle in Cumbria or Aberlady in Scotland by the mid-8th century. The grandest of them, like Bewcastle (Left), reflect the influence of Mediterranean art in their plant-scrolls, animal and human naturalistic figures. This fashion spread to the Midland kingdoms in the late 8th century; The cross (above) is from Eyam. When the Vikings adopted Christianity they favoured a ring-headed cross of Irish/Scottish type and incorporated ornament and figure scenes from their native metalwork or textiles, such as the cross at Gosforth in Cumbria (above). More than 2500 fragments of pre-Conquest crosses survive in England today.

Columba – the Irish prince who founded Iona as a mission base for the Scots and later the northern English – is a well attested figure. He died in 597 – a year after Pope Gregory's missionary, St Augustine, was received in Kent by King Aethelberht (Ethelbert). From the time when land at Canterbury was granted by that king to Augustine, to the time when Edward the Confessor built Westminster Abbey in 1065, the English Church was deeply dependent on royal patronage and support.

Augustine's mission brought about a revival in the art of stone building – as churches built between 597 and 670 still testify at Canterbury, Lyminge, Rochester, or Reculver. In the North the island monastery at Lindisfarne, founded in 635 as an episcopal monastery after the model of Iona, was the focus from which many other centres developed. (It was later eclipsed by York, when that diocese became an archbishopric in 735.)

The early English Church developed under foreign missionaries but in the late 7th century English travellers abroad came into direct contact with Mediterranean culture and founded for themselves churches and monasteries modelled on what they saw. These were in stone, lavishly decorated with paintings and sculptures and well equipped with books. Such travellers were Wilfrid, founder of Ripon, Hexham, Oundle, and bishop of York, or Benedict Biscop, founder of Monkwearmouth and Jarrow, where Bede – the first historian of the English Church – spent his life.

Bede died in 735, and by that time Englishmen were widely dispersed on the Continent as missionaries to the still pagan Saxons or Frisians. They included the Northumbrian Willibrord, and two West Saxons, Boniface from Crediton and Lull (Lullus) from Malmesbury, both of whom became bishops of Mainz. Later an Englishman, Alcuin of York, established the court school of the greatest ruler of post-Roman Europe – Charlemagne. The fine metal work and illuminated manuscripts of the British Isles were much sought after, and profoundly affected continental art in the late 8th and early 9th centuries.

Post Viking Revival

Soon the raids, invasions and settlements of pagan Vikings from Scandinavia tore apart the old patterns of ecclesiastical contacts. The island monasteries around the British coast were no longer safe and in England new divisions emerged: the area north of the Thames and east of Watling street acknowledged Scandinavian rulers, while the rest remained subject to the kings of Wessex. Alfred, the first king to whom all the English owed allegiance, began to rebuild ecclesiastical life and learning, but it was left to his successors to win back the Viking-held territories and to restore their scattered churches. The far North never recovered its former glory, but under such kings as Athelstan and Edgar a new generation of southern churchmen flourished who raised Christian culture to new and more splendid heights. Pre-eminent among them was Dunstan, trained at Glastonbury, educated on the Continent, and for 28 years archbishop of Canterbury.

The Wessex royal family specially favoured Winchester Cathedral, which in the late 10th century became a centre for both ecclesiastical and cultural reform. Its greatest bishop, Aethelwold, reformed and revived the old religious communities, commissioning buildings and works of art over a wide area of southern England and the east Midlands. The last hundred years before the Norman Conquest was a period of great artistic energy in which many of the pre-Conquest churches which survive today were either built or refurbished.

CHURCHES AND ABBEYS

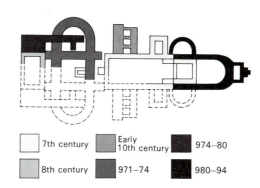

☐ 7th century	▨ Early 10th century	■ 974–80
▨ 8th century	▨ 971–74	■ 980–94

Plan of the excavations at the Old Minster at Winchester. Excavations have shown how the little 7th-century church built by King Ine of Wessex developed by the late 10th century into an impressive cathedral alongside the shrine of St Swithun.

Jarrow monastery. The model shows the excavated section of this Anglo-Saxon abbey.

Churches were founded on the estates of major landowners throughout this period. Escomb (left) probably dates from the early 8th century. Odda's Chapel of the Holy Trinity at Deerhurst is dated by an inscription of 1056 (below).

Ecclesiastical Buildings: Cathedrals

After many centuries of life and some very rough treatment, the cathedrals still stand as the supreme achievement of English architecture. The Scottish and Welsh cathedrals were always on a much smaller scale (St Andrew's, easily the largest of them, was about the same size as Chester); Elgin is today a beautiful ruin, but of St Andrew's only scanty remains survive. The best surviving cathedral in Scotland is Glasgow, the interior of which is, alas, cluttered with pews from end to end. In Wales St David's is without peer. The exterior is somewhat bleak, but internally this cathedral is a delight, and is by far the finest Welsh church.

The cathedral was the church in which the bishop, who was the principal man of the ecclesiastical province or diocese, had his *cathedra* or throne. (The word derives from Latin, and originally Greek.) It was therefore the mother-church of a considerable area, and, especially in the Middle Ages, a natural focus for legacies and endowments. There were only 17 English cathedrals when Henry VIII broke with Rome; he created six more sees, of which one, Westminster, was short-lived. Twenty new Anglican cathedrals have been created since 1836, so that there are now 42 in all. Of these, 12 are merely upgraded parish churches, while four (Truro, Liverpool, Guildford and Coventry) have been built since 1880. The venerable cathedral churches, all of medieval foundation (although London's St Paul's was completely rebuilt by Wren after the Great Fire of 1666) number 26.

Two features are special to the English cathedrals, to a far greater extent than elsewhere. One is the great divergencies of style within a single church. Because building – and sometimes rebuilding – continued over very long periods, being dependent upon the resources available, not a single one of the medieval cathedrals is in one consistent style. (Salisbury comes nearest to it.) As a rule this matters surprisingly little artistically, and may indeed be held to enhance the pleasure of a visit. It would matter, seriously, if later alterations or additions had been carried out in a different material, but until our own day this happily did not occur; builders had to make do with the nearest available stone. In this respect, certainly, some cathedrals were much more fortunate than others; those on or near the Jurassic limestone belt (see page 10), such as Salisbury, Wells, Peterborough and above all Lincoln, which had all the stone it required within a few hundred yards, were the luckiest. In contrast, those built of the all too friable New Red sandstones, Worcester, Lichfield, Chester and Carlisle, have had to undergo drastic refacing, and are seldom wholly without scaffolding.

The other specially distinctive characteristic of the English cathedrals is their great length in proportion to what, by French standards, is their decidedly modest internal height. This is due to the fact that no fewer then 11 of the 'vintage' 26 were also monastic. The bishop was also the titular abbot, and it was the monks who conducted the services. They occupied all the eastern portions, as well as the cloisters, so the nave had to be extended, and furnished with its own altar, to accommodate the laity. Specially impressive examples of long naves include Winchester, Norwich, Ely, Peterborough and St Albans.

Among so many splendid achievements it is not easy to make a choice, but externally the greatest glories of the English cathedrals are their towers and spires. In the Middle Ages many cathedrals had timber spires of prodigious audacity: two, those of Lincoln and Old St Paul's in London are believed to have exceeded 500 ft (152 m). But none of these survives. Of stone spires, Salisbury's is probably the most beautiful in the world, and soars to 404 ft (123 m), the loftiest of the Middle Ages. Other cathedrals with memorable spires include Norwich, Chichester and Coventry; Lichfield alone preserves three, 'the Ladies of the Vale'.

The finest single towers belong to the cathedrals of the Three Choirs Festival: Gloucester, Worcester and Hereford, to which should be added the noble tower of the recently completed Anglican cathedral of Liverpool. Several cathedrals have towers in groups of three, a glorious assemblage. Specially memorable are those which, all things considered, I would name as the four finest: Lincoln, Canterbury, Wells and Durham. Others include York, Ripon and Southwell. At Ely the central Octagon is an unique and thrilling conception.

Internally a special beauty of the English cathedrals is the elaboration of surface enrichment, rendered possible by the nature of the stone. This culminates in some of the world's loveliest vaults. In this respect Exeter and the Chapter House of Wells are the supreme examples of tierceron vaulting; later vaults of great beauty cover the naves of Winchester and Canterbury, the choir of Gloucester and the whole of the cathedral of Norwich. The choir of Oxford has an astonishing pendant vault; the retro-choir of Peterborough and the cloisters at Gloucester exuberant fan-vaulting.

The greatest misfortune that has befallen the British cathedrals has been the deliberate, fanatical destruction of their medieval stained glass. Today much can still be seen at York, and fewer but finer windows at Canterbury. At some cathedrals the Victorian glazing is a serious blemish.

VINTAGE CATHEDRALS

The 26 'vintage' cathedrals in England and one in Wales. The outstanding ones, which no cathedral lover should miss on any account, are in capital letters.

Bristol
CANTERBURY
Carlisle
Chester
Chichester
DURHAM
ELY
EXETER
GLOUCESTER
Hereford
Lichfield
LINCOLN
LONDON, ST PAUL'S
NORWICH
Oxford
PETERBOROUGH
Ripon
Rochester
St Albans
St David's
SALISBURY
Southwark
Southwell
WELLS
WINCHESTER
Worcester
YORK

The nave crossing at Ely Cathedral showing the magnificent octagonal 'lantern'. This lantern replaced the original tower which collapsed in 1322.

Above: Fan vaulting in the cloister of Gloucester Cathedral.

Above right: The nave of Exeter Cathedral.

Below: Bell Harry Tower at Canterbury, the grandest of the Cathedral's three towers.

Right: The three spires of Lichfield Cathedral, known as 'the ladies of the vale'.

Ecclesiastical Buildings: Abbeys and Priories

The role of the monasteries in Britain during the Middle Ages was of paramount importance, especially in the two centuries that followed the Norman Conquest. In a generally lawless society they were the principal practitioners of an ordered existence. For a long period they harboured the only men with any understanding of agriculture, as distinct from the chase. They regulated fairs and markets, maintained roads and bridges, dispensed hospitality in their guest-houses (which were in a large measure the hotels of the Middle Ages), provided the only libraries at a time when every book had to be hand-written and when few men outside their precincts could read, and encouraged music and the arts. As a result they attracted many gifts and legacies and sometimes became rich; this ultimately proved their undoing.

Their buildings were very extensive, comprising cloisters, chapter houses and generous domestic quarters which included refectories, libraries, dorters (dormitories) and lodgings for the abbot or prior, sometimes on a most imposing scale in the last century of their existence. But shortage of space precludes consideration of any but the most important buildings: the churches. The large majority

The vaulting in Sherborne Abbey, Dorset, originally a Benedictine foundation.

of these are Norman or early Gothic in origin, but some, like Tewkesbury, were later much embellished by generous benefactors. Here, early in the 14th century, the Despencers provided the eastern arm with a ring of chapels, some splendid stained glass and a superb vault, and a generation later the rest of the great church was also vaulted. Others, for various reasons, had later to be partly or wholly rebuilt; Melrose, for example, was a casualty of war during the reign of Richard II.

First came the Benedictines. Their abbeys were often located inside towns, and they shared their churches with the laity. In the early centuries of monasticism the towns greatly benefited from their presence, but later some of them became overbearing and oppressive, and bitter conflicts resulted. At Bury St Edmunds in 1327 and at Sherborne in 1437 the abbeys were plundered and set on fire, which was another cause of later rebuilding.

When the monasteries were dissolved by Henry VIII, the fact that many of the Benedictine churches occupied urban sites often saved them from destruction. Eleven were, or now became, cathedrals. Others were purchased from the Crown, to the eternal credit of the townspeople: these

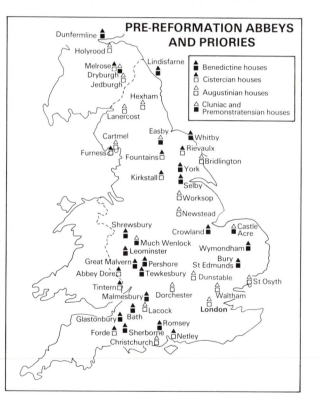

PRE-REFORMATION ABBEYS AND PRIORIES

- ▲ Benedictine houses
- △ Cistercian houses
- △ Augustinian houses
- △ Cluniac and Premonstratensian houses

included Tewkesbury, Sherborne, Selby, Malvern, Romsey and Bath, which are accordingly now among our very finest parish churches. More often, however, only part of the church managed to survive; at Pershore it was the choir, tower and south transept, but usually, as at Malmesbury, Leominster, Shrewsbury, Wymondham and Dunfermline (to mention only some of the best), it was the nave.

The Cluniacs, reformed Benedictines, were never very important in Britain, but two fine priories of the Order survive as ruins: Castle Acre and Much Wenlock. (At the latter the Prior's Lodge escaped, and has been inhabited continuously since the 1490s.) The Cluniacs were soon supplanted by Cistercians, who had a great success here as indeed all over Western Europe. This is surprising, for, unlike the other orders, they were unsociable; they built in

The ruins of the Cistercian Abbey at Rievaulx, North Yorkshire.

Below: The West front of the Cluniac priory church at Castle Acre, Norfolk.

remote country places, and never shared their churches with the laity. When they were not at their own devotions they were farmers, tilling the fields; every monastery had to be fully self-supporting. Their initial asceticism produced very austere buildings, devoid at first of any kind of decoration; happily for art, this austerity was later relaxed. But because at the Dissolution there was no alternative use for their churches, they are almost all in ruins; the only partial exception is Abbey Dore. The amateur of ruins, on the other hand, owes nearly all his greatest pleasures to the Cistercians, with their penchant for beautiful siting as an extra bonus. Fountains, Rievaulx, Kirkstall, Netley, Tintern, Furness and Melrose are only some of the most famous. Against this impressive list the Benedictines can only muster Glastonbury, Crowland, St Mary's York, Whitby and Lindisfarne as ruins of distinction.

The Augustinians
Another important group of abbeys and priories we owe to the Augustinians. They were not monks but regular canons, living like the monks in communities but less strictly. Though never as rich as the Benedictines, they built many beautiful churches; three that have managed to survive intact are the priories of Christchurch, Cartmel and Dorchester in Oxfordshire. In other cases only part of the church has survived, and usually the nave, as at Waltham, Dunstable, Worksop, Bridlington and Lanercost, among others. But at St Bartholomew, Smithfield, London, it was the choir that remained, and at Hexham it was the choir and transepts; a new nave was erected there in 1907–09. Of Augustinian churches surviving only as ruins, the two best known are in Scotland: Holyrood and Jedburgh.

The Premonstratensian canons founded few houses here. Like the Cistercians their preference was for remote places, often beautiful, so their churches too are mostly ruinous. The best are Easby and Dryburgh.

A few of the monasteries were converted at the Dissolution into country houses, usually with fairly drastic modifications. The most distinguished are Lacock, Newstead and St Osyth's, all Augustinian foundations, and Forde, which was Cistercian. They are but one more manifestation of the architectural inheritance which we owe to the monks and the canons.

Ecclesiastical Buildings: Parish Churches

In her parish churches England has an architectural achievement that is still, despite appalling destruction, unequalled by any other country. Moreover, the quality of craftsmanship in the smaller churches is often just as good as in the larger ones.

There are still in England rather over 9000 churches of medieval foundation: churches which have always been parochial, as distinct from monastic churches converted into parish churches at the Dissolution of the Monasteries. In 1066 there were already about 4500 churches in the country, but the majority at that time were only of wood. Nearly all the Saxon churches have perished, and it would be unreasonable to expect otherwise. On this subject both guide books and incumbents can be rather trying. For if our interest is in the churches as works of art, to be informed that a few stones at the base of one of the tower walls are 'undoubtedly Saxon' is, even if true, crashingly unimportant.

The Normans replaced nearly all the wooden churches with stone buildings, and erected many more, but the population in the 12th century was probably no more than

Below left: The nave of the exceptionally well-preserved little Norman church of Saint Mary and Saint David at Kilpeck, Herefordshire. Its sculptures are memorable.

Below: The church of St Mary and All Saints at Fotheringhay, Northamptonshire.

The large majority of the best parish churches belong to the Gothic period: i.e. from *c* 1180 to *c* 1540. Three phases are usually distinguished:

Three little names from school are we,
Graven upon the memory,
For every English Gothic church is bound to be
E.E., Dec. or Perp.

And oddly, enough, in the Victorian age this still holds good. The Early English is a style of sharply pointed architectural forms (arches, windows, vaults, gables) and of brisk, vital carving. The Decorated is less crisp but capable of glorious exuberance, especially in surface ornamentation and in window tracery. The Perpendicular is more worldly but at its best is the boldest of the three, the most stately and the most sumptuous.

If you read that a church is collegiate, it will almost always be worth visiting. Collegiate churches were served not just by one or two priests but by a group living together in what was termed a college. There were between 50 and

two million, so of course many of these churches were small and aisleless. Very few survive intact; eight hundred years is a very long time, and with continual increases of population it was almost inevitable that most of these early churches should have been enlarged and rebuilt. Moreover, materials decay. There has been a great deal more restoration of our Romanesque churches than writers of guide-books have sometimes been prepared to admit. Sometimes the restoration has been so drastic that, for all the asterisks, to the sensitive eye a great deal of the pleasure has been removed. An exceptionally well preserved little Norman church is Kilpeck in Herefordshire. Others, where the restoration has on the whole been well done, are Iffley in Oxfordshire and Barfreston in Kent.

THE CHURCH TOWERS OF SOMERSET

(The 20 finest. The 10 masterpieces are in capital letters.)

BATCOMBE	KINGSTON ST MARY
Bishops Lydeard	LEIGH-ON-MENDIP
Bruton	Mells
CHEWTON MENDIP	NORTH PETHERTON
EVERCREECH	Staple Fitzpaine
Glastonbury	Taunton
Hinton St George	Weare
HUISH EPISCOPI	WELLS, ST CUTHBERT
ILE ABBOTS	Weston Zoyland
ILMINSTER	Wrington

The church of St Mary, Batcombe, Somerset. The best of the Somerset towers are the most perfect parish church towers in England.

a monastery or a college, and served merely by a vicar, who was allowed only a share of the tithes. So we find churches like Woolpit (Suffolk), with a handsome nave rebuilt by the prosperous parishioners in the 15th century and a little 14th century chancel on which nothing was spent when the nave was rebuilt, because the vicar had not the money and the absentee rector just was not interested. With variations, this pattern recurs all too often.

Nevertheless there is a great deal to admire and much to enjoy. In an age when communications were difficult the great majority of people 'stayed put', and this favoured many local developments. Were I asked to make a tour of just one of these, I should choose the towers of Somerset. They all belong to the 15th or early 16th centuries and some are quite modest in scale, but bulk has nothing to do with good design. Built in a county well endowed with excellent stone, the best of the Somerset towers are visually an enchantment. Apart from the central tower of Wells Cathedral, from which some of them derive, Somerset has about 20 church towers of very fine quality and ten which might justly be described as masterpieces of tower design.

The handsome nave of the church of St Mary, Woolpit, Suffolk.

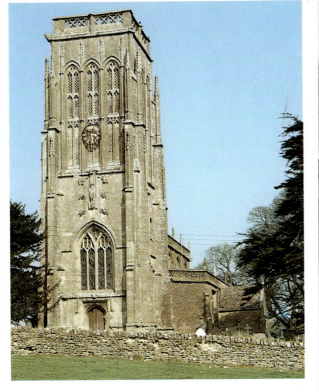

60 of these churches, three of which (Ripon, Manchester and Southwell) were elevated to cathedral rank in the 19th century. They were usually paid for by private benefactions, generally bequests, often linked with frequent prayers for the soul of the founder. Collegiate foundations usually have much finer choirs than other parish churches, and sets of stalls. Although Darlington, an imposing example, is E.E., nearly all these churches are Perp. Fotheringhay (Northants) and Denston (Suffolk), both full of light and air, are two examples of former collegiate churches much grander than were required by small villages.

Very often, however, it will be found in England that the chancel is unworthy of the nave. This was because, in the Middle Ages, the nave usually belonged to the parish whereas the chancel was the property of the rector. He might be almost anybody: often he would be a corporation,

Above: The church of the Holy Trinity at Long Melford, Suffolk.

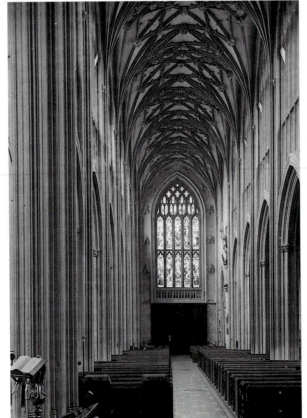

Right: St Mary Redcliffe, Bristol.

There is in truth not a large number of churches worth seeing in Scotland nor in Wales: the best in Wales, at Gresford (Clwyd), looks like a fine Cheshire church which has strayed across the border. But in England there must be at least 5000 deserving of a visit. Some of the town churches are truly magnificent. Two of them, St John the Evangelist, Beverley (always known as the Minster) and St Mary Redcliffe, Bristol, are as works of art superior to some of the cathedrals. But in general it must be said that village churches often give more pleasure than those located in towns, because, especially in counties where money was fortunately less plentiful in the 19th century, the village churches are the ones most likely to have escaped the pitch-pine pews, brass lecterns, prickly sculptured reredoses, magenta-hued memorial windows and Minton's encaustic tiles. The Victorians performed many heroic feats in rescuing decrepit churches from Georgian neglect, but unhappily they seldom knew where to call a halt.

Architecturally, the parish churches scarcely ever aped the cathedrals or other major buildings. They developed independently, which was only right and proper, for they had to serve quite different purposes. Their great period did not begin until after 1300, by which time English people were beginning to grow rather tired of the monks and wished to divert their financial support into other channels. The main factors contributing to the emergence of the English parish church in its full glory were (1) the growth of the spirit of independence and intolerance of foreign domination, particularly of seeing their hard-earned cash remitted to Rome; (2) the growth in the wealth and importance of the towns and of the various guilds; (3) wool. As has been well said, 'the Perpendicular churches were built on the backs of sheep'. Although the most opulent churches are not necessarily the best, some of these expensive buildings, like Long Melford and Southwold (Suffolk), Walpole St Peter (Norfolk) and Astbury (Cheshire), do rank very high indeed.

It might be supposed that the presence of good local stone would always have provided a temptation to build more imposingly: and there are, certainly, some very stately churches on or near the Jurassic limestone (Cirencester; Newark), the Magnesian limestone (Tickhill), and farther west, the sandstones: Old Red for Ludlow and New Red for Nantwich (see page 10). But how about East Anglia? This is an area very poorly provided with any stone except flint, yet the parish churches (and in Norfolk and Suffolk alone there are several hundred that should be seen) are among the noblest in the country. Their appeal, however, depends less on their fabric than on their furnishing. And this word is used to embrace the oak roofs, some of which were always at least as much ornamental as functional.

Were I asked to suggest a second tour of the parish churches of England, it would be to see some of the angel roofs of East Anglia. All the finest are of the hammer-beam kind: some are double hammer-beams. The structural justification of these bracket-like beams was to help the carpenters to bridge wider spans, but they also offered plenty of space for carvings of angels: not often complete

THE ANGEL ROOFS OF EAST ANGLIA

Single hammer-beam roofs
Badingham
Banningham
Cawston
Earl Stonham
North Creake
Trunch
Wymondham

Double hammer-beam roofs
Gissing
Grundisburgh
Knapton
March, St Wendreda
Swaffham
Tilney All Saints
Woolpit
Worlingworth

Composite roofs: hammer beams in conjunction with tie-beams or arched braces
Bury St Edmunds
Cotton
Fincham
Lakenheath
Mildenhall
Southwold
Upwell

Top right: The angel roof of St Wendreda at March, Cambridgeshire.

Right: The interior of the church of St Peter at Gayhurst in Buckinghamshire – one of the few Georgian parish churches which escaped rape by the Victorians.

figures, but heads and outstretched wings (and it must be said that the wings, an easy target for the shotguns of the puritanical iconoclasts, have mostly had to be renewed). Some of these roofs are positively a-flutter with angels. The double hammer-beam of St. Wendreda at March has 78 on the wing, and a lot more at rest on the cornices ('wall-plates'). March is in Cambridgeshire, but all the others are in Suffolk or Norfolk. The best are marvellous to behold. (There are other East Anglian churches with beautiful roofs which lack angels, often because misguided Puritan fanatics systematically decapitated them or had them sawn off.)

The East Anglian churches contain, in addition, some excellent screens and bench-ends. But these can also be enjoyed in hundreds of churches of Somerset, Devon and Cornwall. The best are a lovely sight, and a tour of these south-western churches would also prove very rewarding for those attracted to wood carving. In the far South-West the stone is granite or slate, so the fabrics, though sturdy, have little carved ornamentation.

Between 1540 and 1840 comparatively few churches were built in England except in London, where 87 were burnt in the Great Fire of 1666 and 51 rebuilt by Wren. These are specially notable for their steeples. Elsewhere there were usually plenty of churches; in some areas, in an age of luke-warm piety, too many. But among the relatively small number of Stuart and Georgian churches, mainly in the classical style, are some, like Gayhurst, Buckinghamshire, which are most delightful. Many, alas, were raped by the Victorians, who regarded the classical style as pagan. Victorian churches, nearly all Gothic, went up in their thousands, varying in quality from the noble to the outrageous.

Seats of Learning

Below: An Elizabethan
schoolroom, from a contemporary woodcut. Though Latin became less important for the professions in Tudor times, even the new grammar schools taught little other than the classics. This created an antipractical bias which still shapes educational values.

Below right: Thousands of
schools for children of the poor were founded in the 18th century. Surviving buildings can still be identified by the wooden or stone figures of children, like this bluecoat schoolboy, usually placed above the door.

Contrary to what most people believe, education in the past was not restricted to a few public schools, disreputable private academies like Dickens's Dotheboys Hall, and primitive dame schools in scattered villages. Teaching of some sort was much more widely available, and many hundreds of both primary and secondary schools today can claim descent from schools founded before 1800. Many go back much farther.

Some well-known schools have proudly kept features of their early foundations. But all have changed. Some remain the original school in name only, and a few have lost even that. Many have amalgamated with more recent schools, while others have divided into upper and lower, or boys' and girls' schools. Most have grown considerably, and in the case of the public schools in particular, most are far removed from the original charitable intentions of their founders.

Some schools, such as the King's School Canterbury, Ely, or Sherborne, still occupy monastic buildings. Others, particularly those founded in cramped town centres, have moved out to the suburbs. A few, such as Charterhouse or Cheam (one of the oldest preparatory schools, founded in 1646) have even changed county.

Appearances can be misleading. A substantial looking independent school, set in a magnificent historic mansion, with an august name and all the signs of having been there for hundreds of years, may actually be a modern reproduction. At the same time an undistinguished comprehensive in dreary new buildings may have roots in the 16th century.

Archaeologists have still to identify any of the schools that must have existed in the main towns during the Roman period, but it is a safe guess that these all disappeared between AD 450 and 600.

The revival of Christianity in the 7th century brought the return of some formal education, though it was almost wholly concerned with teaching future clergy to read and write Latin. In addition cathedrals set up choir schools to train choristers. St Peter's, York, and the King's school Canterbury, are survivors of this early period, and another dozen or so probably are as well.

A slightly clearer picture of British schools only starts to emerge in later medieval times. In England and Wales a succession of grammar schools was started either by churches directly or more commonly by charities, such as the chantries set up to pray for the dead. In 1384, for example, Katherine Lady Berkeley founded a chantry at Wotton-under-Edge, Gloucestershire, and a descendant of that school is now a mixed comprehensive. Other schools were associated with hospitals or almshouses, and a few, such as The Royal Grammar School, Worcester, which was in existence by 1290, relied for a while on civic support.

One of the first schools to be set up in its own right, and undoubtedly the most important foundation of the period, was Winchester College, started in 1382. It was to be the model of an even grander school, founded 60 years later by Henry VI – Eton – and was in many respects the first public school.

Below: The relaxed atmosphere
of a modern primary school contrasts with the stern discipline of the Tudor schoolroom above.

Right: The Fourth of June at
Eton in the 1930s. On this principal day of celebration speeches are made in the Upper School and there is a 'procession of boats' on the river.

In Scotland the oldest schools had been run by monasteries, though they were frequently sited in neighbouring towns, most of which had acquired a school by the 12th century. In 1496 Scotland made educational history by passing a law compelling the eldest sons of the rich to go to school. But this was never enforced.

Tudor Grammar Schools

The Tudor period, particularly the reign of Edward VI, is generally regarded as the time when most of the best known public and grammar schools came into being as a result of royal endowments. Scholars disagree about the numbers, but it is now clear that many of these 'new' schools were simply refoundations of older ones whose status and funding had been put in doubt by the Reformation.

Some, such as the King Edward schools at Bath and Birmingham were genuinely new. But the main growth in secondary schools in the following 200 years was as a result of benefactions by successful businessmen or city livery companies. These ranged from famous boarding schools like Rugby (started by a grocer in 1567) and Merchant Taylors', to Chard School, Somerset, (founded in 1671 and closed only in the 1970s). A handful achieved a national reputation at the outset but the majority stayed small local schools until the expansion of secondary education from the late 19th century onwards.

By the 18th century educational good works were increasingly aimed at the children of the poor, and hundreds of charity day schools were set up in towns and villages throughout England. They were normally run by one teacher, offered basic teaching in the three Rs (plus sewing for girls), and often had a purpose-built schoolhouse. A few of these buildings – almost all architectural gems – can be seen today, though they are usually now used for other purposes.

Reorganization and Expansion

In the 19th century primary education was reorganized and expanded, first as a system of so-called National Schools, and eventually as the local authority system of today. In the process many of the charity schools were absorbed, giving many present primary schools a much longer ancestry than is realized. For example, a free school at Sancton, Yorkshire, set up before 1609, was reorganized and rebuilt in the 19th century, and had 49 pupils on roll in 1977.

Scotland, which created a system of parochial education by law much earlier than England, can also claim a share of long established local schools. But Wales had rather fewer. In the 18th century many areas of Wales had to rely solely on itinerant teachers whose principal aim was religious instruction.

In the last 150 years Britain's schools have undergone their greatest changes as universal education from 5 to 16, public examinations, curriculum reform, and teacher training, have all been introduced. The abolition of the 11 plus was widely believed to herald the end of the ancient grammar schools, and a few became independent to preserve their character. But in fact many new comprehensives or sixth-form colleges, based on old grammar schools, are in some respects closer to their forbears. A much greater threat comes from the falling child population which in the next ten years will close dozens of both primary and secondary schools throughout the country. Small village schools, part of the country life for centuries, are specially vulnerable.

BRITAIN'S UNIVERSITIES

England
Aston (Birmingham)
Bath
Birmingham
Bradford
Bristol
Brunel (Uxbridge)
Cambridge
City (London)
Cranfield Institute (Beds.)
Durham
East Anglia (Norwich)
Essex (Colchester)
Exeter
Hull
Keele (Newcastle under Lyme)
Kent (Canterbury)
Lancaster
Leeds
Leicester
Liverpool
London
Loughborough
Manchester
Newcastle
Nottingham
Oxford
Reading
Royal College of Art
Salford
Sheffield
Southampton
Surrey (Guildford)
Sussex (Brighton)
U.M.I.S.T. (Manchester)
Warwick
York

Wales
Aberystwyth
Bangor
Cardiff
St David's, Lampeter
Swansea
U.W.I.S.T. (Cardiff)

Scotland
Aberdeen
Dundee
Edinburgh
Glasgow
Heriot-Watt (Edinburgh)
St Andrews
Stirling
Strathclyde (Glasgow)

University College at Buckingham ('The Independent University')
Open University (Milton Keynes)

UNIVERSITIES

Britain's university heritage is near enough intact. Unlike the thousands of schools which flourished briefly and disappeared without trace, the universities are much as they were founded. With the odd exception (Birmingham and Glasgow, for example) they occupy their original sites. Historic libraries and collections of treasures have not only survived, but have been added to constantly.

In view of the extraordinary influence – both good and bad – that Oxford and Cambridge have exerted for over six centuries, the history of the universities is inevitably largely the history of these two original foundations. But this ignores the four ancient Scottish universities, as well as a number of institutions which are part of the same tradition. For example, professional training – in law and medicine particularly – largely developed outside the universities, even though the earliest European universities made no distinction between academic and vocational education. A university education had the quite specific aim of preparing young men for a career in the Church (including teaching), the law and medicine.

Until the end of the 12th century, when Oxford University was slowly emerging from a loose collection of scholars and students in the city, this training had mainly taken place in cathedral 'schools'. As separate universities developed at Oxford and Cambridge, these schools concentrated on educating boys under 15, and so became schools in the modern sense. One or two, which survive today, are indirect descendants of the pre-university higher education.

Cambridge probably owes its origins to a mass walkout from Oxford by discontented scholars. But later migrations to Northampton, Salisbury and Stamford failed to establish universities.

At first the colleges were simply groups of scholars who lived and studied together. The oldest is probably University College, Oxford (1249), followed by Merton (1264) and Balliol (1263–68). Peterhouse (1284) is the earliest Cambridge college.

As individual colleges began to attract large endowments and put up their own buildings (of which Corpus Christi, Cambridge, is one of the most unaltered examples), they grew in power at the expense of the university as a whole. And as the Middle Ages progressed, the universities increasingly came to resemble the institutions of today. Oxbridge colleges started to admit undergraduates and do some of their own teaching. In Scotland universities were founded at St Andrews (1411), Glasgow (1450) and Aberdeen (1494); and law and medicine were taught wholly or partly outside the universities.

One or two monastic colleges were suppressed during the Reformation, but overall Oxford and Cambridge did well. New secular colleges were founded, while others received property confiscated from religious orders. By the Civil War they were enjoying a short-lasting boom, with at least 4000 students, an increasing number of whom were from rich or middle-class homes.

Though the universities had embraced the new humanism with its emphasis on the study of the secular science, literature and history of classical antiquity it was largely to London (home of the Royal Society) that students looked for science, mathematics and navigation teaching, and particularly to Gresham College. This college, founded in 1597, was the first serious challenge to Oxbridge, but it never developed into a university. The original foundation does survive however, in association with the modern City University.

The exclusion of Nonconformists from Oxbridge marked the start of a university decline in England that was to last

Oxford – 'a towery city and branchy between towers' – is as much part of the world's cultural heritage as it is that of Britain's.

nearly 200 years, and give rise to the dissenting academies. Small and short-lived though they were, they had a profound influence on the development of the modern university curriculum. In pioneering an education suitable for the new demands of the industrial revolution, they put a much needed emphasis on technical subjects. But there was a crucial gap between their decline at the end of the 18th century and the growth of the civic universities 80 years later.

Proposals for universities outside Oxbridge – at London or in the North – had cropped up on and off since the 16th century. It was not until well into the 19th century that the needs of an expanding economy made new foundations essential.

The first step was the unification of University College and King's College, London to form London University in 1836. Among its innovations was higher education for girls, which it began encouraging 12 years later at what became Bedford College.

Just as important was the introduction in 1858 of the external degree system (also adopted by Oxbridge). Not only did this give an impetus to the adult education movement, but it created a mechanism by which provincial technical and commercial colleges could eventually up-grade

themselves to full university status. Owens College, Manchester, was the first; followed by most main cities, which had acquired their own universities by the outbreak of the First World War in 1914. These included Leeds, Newcastle, Bristol, Sheffield, Birmingham, Nottingham, Reading as well as the University of Wales.

But in spite of its long ancestry Britain's university heritage is undoubtedly modern. Since the 1960s student members have risen dramatically. Brand new universities, such as York and Kent, have been set up. Former colleges of advanced technology have been up-graded to create universities like Aston and Loughborough. Existing universities have greatly expanded. New buildings – often spectacular – have gone up throughout the country.

There are now nearly 50 universities, 30 polytechnics, and many other colleges offering degree level courses. Throughout this growth Britain's higher education system has kept to its traditional mould. It remains highly selective, unlike the open access universities abroad. But for the next 15 years the number of 18-year-olds will plummet. For the first time since the 17th century the universities face the choice of contracting, or of substantially altering their character by admitting students without the present minimum entry qualifications.

The British Genius: Science and Medicine

Literature and science are the two fields of artistic and intellectual endeavour in which the British can be safely said to excel. And in each field Britain has produced an outstanding genius: William Shakespeare and Isaac Newton (1642–1727).

Perhaps Newton's most wonderful individual achievements – among many – were his laws of motion and the great law of gravitation published in the *Principia* in 1687. A Cambridge philosopher and mathematician, he was also a member of the Royal Society, one of the oldest scientific societies in the world and one which established London as a leading scientific centre. It has numbered among its members many of Britain's most distinguished men of science.

The Royal Society

The Society's origins date back to about 1645 when a group of *virtuosi* (men who loved to dabble in science) who had studied the teachings of Galileo began to meet in London. These gatherings led in 1660 to a learned society for the newly discovered 'scientific method'. In 1662 Charles II – never one to discourage enquiring minds – granted a royal charter to what now became known as the Royal Society for Improving Natural Knowledge. Half a century earlier, such a body would have conducted its proceedings in Latin; but at the Royal Society English was used from the first.

One of the Society's early members was Sir Robert Boyle (1627–91) – 'the father of modern chemistry' – who recognized the importance of publishing scientific discovery and observation. His law on the behaviour of gases began a long chain of discoveries culminating in the nuclear physics of the present century. A link in that chain is the ideas of John Dalton (1766–1844), a fellow of the Royal Society, who suggested that the behaviour of gases could be explained by envisaging all matter as indivisible 'atoms', the weights of which were characteristic of each element in nature. The chain also includes the discovery of William Thomson (later Lord Kelvin and president of the Royal Society) that all motion of particles constituting gases would cease at a temperature of minus 273°C.

Henry Cavendish (1731–1810), another fellow of the Royal Society, gave his name to one of Britain's great centres of scientific discovery, the Cavendish Laboratory in Cambridge; he was the first to measure the force of gravity and to weigh planet Earth. One of the Society's presidents, Sir Humphry Davy (1778–1829) used electricity to separate atoms and isolated several elements such as sodium and potassium. Michael Faraday (1791–1867), at one time Humphry Davy's assistant, is most famous for developing the first dynamo and discovering electromagnetic induction. He declined both a knighthood and the presidency of the Royal Society.

But perhaps the best remembered of Britain's scientists is known not for his physics or chemistry but for the theory of natural selection. The expedition of the naturalist Charles Darwin (1809–82) to the Galapagos Islands in the research ship *Beagle* has been described as the most important sea voyage in the history of science. Darwin's great work, *The Origin of Species*, published in 1859, won its latest legal battle for acceptance – as opposed to the biblical view of creation – as recently as 1982.

Contributions to Medicine

In medicine Britain has made a number of outstanding contributions, starting perhaps with William Harvey (1578–1657) who in 1628 published his account of the circulation of the blood. In preventive medicine the first

Isaac Newton – **an outstanding** genius among Britain's many distinguished scientists and thinkers.

The Library of the Royal Society, one of the oldest scientific societies in Europe.

175

Vaccination against the
scourge of smallpox was
one of the great British break-
throughs in preventive
medicine. At the end of the
18th century an English
country doctor named Edward
Jenner observed that dairy-
maids who had contracted the
mild disease cowpox became
immune against smallpox.
Jenner's discovery was not at
first generally acclaimed; this
cartoon of 1802 shows people
who had taken the cowpox
serum developing bovine
characteristics.

Max Perutz and Sir John
Kendrew at the Nobel Prize-
giving ceremony in 1962. Up to
1980 British scientists had won
61 of the prizes awarded in the
three categories of physics,
chemistry and medicine.

really great step forward was taken by Edward Jenner
(1749–1823) who in 1796 founded the science of
immunology through his work in the prevention of the
dreaded disease smallpox through vaccination. In 1847
Sir James Simpson, a Scottish obstetrician, demonstrated
the value of chloroform as an anaesthetic thus making
possible huge developments in surgery. Twenty years later
Joseph Lister (1827–1912) revealed that the risk of infection
to wounds could be greatly reduced by the use of carbolic
acid.

An astounding breakthrough in the chemical treatment
of diseases came when it was discovered that drugs derived
from living organisms could combat bacteria. The first of
these 'antibiotics' was accidentally discovered in 1928 by the
Scottish scientist Sir Alexander Fleming and was developed
as 'penicillin' by Sir Howard Florey and Ernst Chain at
Oxford in 1940.

Nobel Prizes

That Britain's scientific genius continues to flourish is
attested by an internationally recognized yardstick – the
annual Nobel Prizes for physics, chemistry and medicine,
first awarded in 1901. By 1982, British scientists had won
61 of these prizes, starting in 1902 with the medicine prize
for Sir Ronald Ross, for his explanation of the role of the
anopheles mosquito in the spread of malaria. Since then,
and particularly since the end of the Second World War,
Britain has regularly won laureates. In the 1960s and
1970s with the new science of molecular biology gradually
supplanting nuclear physics as the most exciting of
sciences British genius was well to the fore. This was
acknowledged by Nobel Prizes for Max Perutz, Sir John
Kendrew, Francis Crick and Maurice Wilkins, all in 1962, and
a second for Frederick Sanger in 1980 for his work on
nucleic acids. In 1982 Dr John R. Vane was awarded the nobel
prize for medicine for work on glandular hormones.

BRITISH NOBEL PRIZEWINNERS

Chemistry

1904	Sir William Ramsay	1953	Hans Krebs (German/British and joint)
1908	Ernest Rutherford	1960	Peter Medawar (joint)
1921	Frederick Soddy	1962	Francis Crick & Maurice Wilkins (joint)
1922	Francis Aston	1963	Alan Hodgkin & Andrew Huxley (joint)
1929	Arthur Harden	1970	Sir Bernard Katz (joint)
1937	Walter Haworth (Joint)	1972	Rodney Porter (joint)
1947	Sir Robert Robinson	1979	Godfrey Newbold Hounsfield (joint)
1952	Archer Martin & Richard Synge		
1956	Sir Cyril Hinshelwood (joint)	**Physics**	
1957	Sir Alexander Todd	1904	Lord Rayleigh
1958	Frederick Sanger	1906	Sir Joseph Thomson
1962	Max Perutz & John Kendrew	1915	Sir William H. Bragg & William L. Bragg
1964	Dorothy Crowfoot Hodgkin	1917	Charles Barkla
1967	Ronald Norrish & George Porter (joint)	1927	Charles T. R. Wilson (joint)
1969	Derek Barton (joint)	1928	Owen Richardson
1973	Geoffrey Wilkinson (joint)	1933	Paul Dirac (joint)
1978	Peter Mitchell	1935	James Chadwick
1980	Frederick Sanger	1937	George Thomson (joint)
Medicine		1947	Sir Edward Appleton
1902	Sir Ronald Ross	1948	Patrick M. S. Blackett
1922	Archibald Hill (joint)	1950	Cecil Frank Powell
1923	John Macleod (joint)	1951	Sir John Cockroft (joint)
1929	Frederick Hopkins (joint)	1954	Max Born (German/British and joint)
1932	Edgar Adrian & Sir Charles Sherrington	1971	Denis Gabor
1936	Sir Henry Dale (joint)	1973	Brian Josephson (joint)
1945	Sir Alexander Fleming, Sir Howard Florey & Ernst Chain	1974	Sir Martin Ryle & Antony Hewish
		1977	Sir Nevill Mott (joint)

The British Genius: Art

The best collections of British painting are to be found in London – at the National Gallery, the National Portrait Gallery and the Tate Gallery. There are also superb collections in certain country houses, notably the un-rivalled group of Turners at Petworth, and in the USA where interest has always been keen. On the European continent, by contrast, British art is less widely appreciated: not surprisingly perhaps, since only a few British painters – Reynolds, Gainsborough, Stubbs, Constable and above all Turner – can claim truly international standing. Whether the 20th century will be able to add to this list with names like Francis Bacon and David Hockney only time will tell.

Below: Prince Rupert
by William Dobson
(Lord Dartmouth's Collection)

Right: Clifford
by Nicholas Hilliard
(National Maritime Museum)

Below: The Marriage Contract
by William Hogarth
(The National Gallery, London)

Anne Hyde, Duchess of York
by Sir Peter Lely
(National Galleries of Scotland)

THE 16th CENTURY

NOBLE TRAPPINGS Henry VIII's patronage of Holbein introduced to England an artist of such formidable powers that it was inevitable that his style would be imitated; but Holbein's penetrating analysis of character was beyond the abilities of his followers. The portraiture of the period, which predominated over all other subjects in painting, tended to be the portrait of a dress: an evocation of wealth at a time when life was dictated by ceremony and when riches were worn as much on the person as they were reflected in household possessions. While such portraits of the family, of friends and of the nobility, would furnish the long galleries of Elizabethan houses, the mannerist refinement and sophisticated symbolism of the Elizabethan age are reflected most romantically in the miniatures of Nicholas Hilliard.

THE 17th CENTURY

CHARLES I A development towards a less schematic, more formal style preceded the accession of Charles I. With Mytens some blood began to course through the veins of sitters, with Cornelius Jonson their personalities began to reveal themselves. Both artists were to be affected by the example of Van Dyck, whose portraits became a mirror of the Caroline court. In the 17th century foreign artists (of whom Van Dyck was by far the greatest) still out-numbered those of native English birth, but in the 1640s the first distinguished native painter, William Dobson, initiated a style of portraiture to which Reynolds would be the true heir.

THE RESTORATION 'The Restoration brought back the arts but not taste' sniffed Horace Walpole; and if the florid opulence of the post-Restoration Sir Peter Lely is compared with the refinement of Van Dyck this statement is understandable. But while Lely with his large practice was the foremost portrait painter of the period, the miniaturist Samuel Cooper achieved a heroic quality not unlike Dobson. During these years the foundations of three other schools of painting, which were to become essentially British, were laid: marine (the Van de Veldes, father and son, both of whom settled in England); topography (the bird's-eye country house views of Siberechts and Knyff); and animals (Francis Barlow).

THE 18th CENTURY

BAROQUE TO CLASSICAL The baroque tradition, exemplified by the architecture of Vanbrugh and Hawksmoor, was reflected in painting by the decorative schemes of Sir James Thornhill and the portraiture of Kneller, whose sporadic brilliance illuminates every now and again a large output of stereotyped portraits. His style was adopted in Scotland by Medina and followed in England by Dahl. William Hogarth grew up when the baroque was about to be superseded by classicism, the style which characterizes the Augustan age. His training as an engraver – his strongly held social, political and aesthetic views were disseminated by his prints – is evident in his paintings, often overloaded with incident. But these paintings – conversation pieces, *genre* scenes and portraits – possess a beauty of handling allied with powers of observation, caustic or humorous, that places him above all rivals. His contemporary, Joseph Highmore, painted in a similar vein but without Hogarth's imaginative vigour.

Mr and Mrs Andrews
by Thomas Gainsborough
(National Gallery, London)

CLASSICAL COMPOSURE In the 18th century the classical tradition permeated every aspect of art. This tradition in painting was exemplified by Sir Joshua Reynolds, the most influential and esteemed British portrait painter of the age; when the Royal Academy was founded in 1769 it was inevitable that he should be elected its first President. But Reynolds never succeeded in his attempts to persuade collectors to patronize British artists in what was then regarded as the noblest form of painting: subject picture, historical, biblical or mythological. Success in this field, when it came, was achieved by the Americans West and Copley who, however, preferred history pictures of the heroic present to scenes of the past.

ROCOCO ELEGANCE European influences continued strong in 18th-century British painting, especially contemporary French portraiture and conversation pieces – repeated in the work of puppeteers like Arthur Devis who disposed stiff little figures in parks and bare interiors. Francis Hayman's larger groups and his scenes from romantic literature may have influenced Gainsborough – who was to become the most elegant and scintillating of the portrait painters of the century. His beginnings lay in his evocation of the Suffolk countryside in which he grew up; in his later years however, his landscapes like his portraits became increasingly artificial, sophisticated and romantic. The master of the conversation piece in the second half of the century was John Zoffany.

Sir William Chambers
by Sir Joshua Reynolds
(The Royal Academy, London)

LANDSCAPE AND SPORT In the 17th century landscape was thought of in terms of topography: the record of a site. The 18th-century collector preferred the idealized approach of Claude, Poussin and Salvator Rosa. In the middle of the century the topographical approach was given a new impetus by the visit of the Venetian painter Canaletto to England; and his style directly influenced the London views of Samuel Scott and indirectly the school of watercolourists of whom Paul Sandby was the leading figure (to be followed by the atmospheric drawings of Turner, Girtin and Cozens). The outstanding landscape painter was Richard Wilson. The few country house views of George Lambert may have been one source from which he drew; others were the paintings of the 17th-century Italian and Dutch landscape painters and his own memories of the blue distances of Italy – an amalgam from which an entirely integrated and felicitous style was to emerge. The formation of a school of animal and sporting painters was a British phenomenon not found elsewhere in Europe. On the whole the attainments of these artists were modest, but the sporting prints of John Wootton were – and are – deservedly popular and the school produced one classical genius in George Stubbs. His dissection and drawings of the rotting corpses of horses were the macabre genesis of some of the most beautiful animal pictures ever painted.

Above right: Five Mares
by George Stubbs
(Ascott House, Buckinghamshire)

The Air Pump
by Joseph Wright of Derby
(Tate Gallery, London)

ADDENDA For a time a rival to Reynolds existed in Allan Ramsay, of Scottish descent, a painter of understatement and sensitivity – something of an antithesis to George Romney, whose success a generation later was surpassed only by that of Gainsborough and Reynolds. His portraits – and those of the American Gilbert Stuart who spent 18 years in England – are characterized by an air of bravura: workmanlike, but unsubtle. John Hoppner was to carry a mixture of the styles of Reynolds and Romney into the 19th century. Reynolds' followers James Northcote, William Opie and Joseph Wright of Derby were among the many artists employed by Alderman Boydell when towards the end of the century he embarked on a project to form a gallery of paintings depicting scenes from Shakespeare. Wright, whose output comprised portraits, landscapes and subject pictures, was responsible for a few scientific candle-light scenes and dramatically lit views of early industrial England which are remarkable for their time.

THE 19th CENTURY

View from his Father's House
by John Constable
(Christchurch, Ipswich)

THE ROMANTIC REVOLUTION The history of art is partly a history of reaction. Among those who reacted most vehemently to the principles of Reynolds were the Swiss-born Fuseli with his morbid Gothic imaginings and – more important – William Blake who described his strange swirling paintings as 'visions of eternity'. The new style in portraiture was represented in London by Sir Thomas Lawrence and in Edinburgh by Sir Henry Raeburn. Only in landscape did a new truth to nature develop. The two great practitioners of the subject, J. M. W. Turner and John Constable, while trained in the classical tradition and observing minutely and with great sensitivity what was before their eyes, were nonetheless steeped in romantic feeling. Constable, who regarded himself as a natural painter, was able to integrate detail and atmospheric effect in a way that is almost hallucinatory. It was not until after 1830 that Turner increasingly studied the effects of light; in his late works, lambently bright and described by Hazlitt as 'tinted steam', it is the sky and not the earth that becomes the most substantial part of the picture.

The Village Holiday
by Sir David Wilkie
(Tate Gallery, London)

The Fighting Téméraire
by J. M. W. Turner
(National Gallery, London)

Claudio and Isabella
by William Holman Hunt
(Tate Gallery, London)

FROM 1850 ON The Pre-Raphaelite Brotherhood, formed in 1849 by Holman Hunt, Millais and Rossetti, was the major artistic and creative force of the century. Though the Brotherhood claimed to promote a new attitude towards realism, their paintings were no more realistic than was the notion that they resembled the artists who preceded Raphael. For inspiration they turned to Keats and other poets; stylistically they based themselves on the German painters known as the Nazarenes. Otherwise during the second half of the century an extreme insularity prevailed. Lord Leighton, as President of the Royal Academy, governed his neo-classic Academicians oblivious to developments in France. Reaction, to be found already in the vigour of Watts and the fastidiousness of Whistler, was strengthened at the end of the century with the New English Art Club, a rival exhibition centre to the Academy, which included Sickert, Sargent and Steer among its members. The consequent removal of insular barriers was to become the main feature of 20th-century art in Britain, with all its varied experimental advances – 'London impressionism', vorticism, abstract art – co-existing with the continuing traditionalism exemplified by such painters as Augustus John and Sir William Nicholson.

ANECDOTE AND ILLUSTRATION With a changing society after the Napoleonic Wars and the undermining of 18th-century humanist values a new type of patron was to emerge. For the first time paintings were produced speculatively and offered for sale. Turner and Constable were no longer the most admired artists of their day – still less Blake, who was regarded with derision. The palm was reserved for Sir David Wilkie, whose painstaking verisimilitude had its roots in the Dutch 17th-century tradition. A whole range of subjects hardly known to the 18th century had become fashionable. Illustration, no longer confined to the great authors or events of the past, could now depict contemporary scenes and stories: Gothic ruins by moonlight were romantic, poverty and near Eastern markets picturesque. The so-called 'grand manner' of painting, hitherto the most highly acclaimed form of art, was replaced, with William Etty the single exception, by anecdote and illustration. In sporting art Ben Marshall was followed by Edward Ward, who as an animal painter echoed the vision of Constable and was in turn superseded by the anthropomorphism of Sir Edwin Landseer.

The British Genius: The Theatre

The unequalled greatness of Shakespeare has distorted the history of the British theatre. Because he was also our greatest poet he has made us see theatre as a branch of literature; because his miraculous range and depth has not only survived the 350 years since his death but has been increased by persistent study and performance, he has almost made subsequent playwrights unnecessary. All the emotions, all the human types and phases of life, all the public and private dilemmas are there. 'He was not of an age, but for all time,' wrote his friend and rival Ben Jonson. With Shakespeare's 36 plays on the shelf and first-rate actors to interpret them freshly, the stage need never be out of touch with the reality of its time. The true history of the British theatre, however, is the history of its actors and its actor-managers, with intermittent help from the writers.

The Elizabethan theatre derived from the players employed by Elizabeth's grandfather, Henry VII, and they in turn from the professional and amateur groups (wandering players and university scholars) who performed farces and 'moral interludes' in the Middle Ages. The first British playwright we know by name is John Heywood, who had a comedy produced at court in 1520, but the anonymous texts of four complete cycles of medieval Miracle plays are still extant, as is that of the most popular 'moral interlude', *Everyman*.

The first public playhouse – called simply the Theatre – was built in 1576 by the great actor-manager James Burbage, father of one of Shakespeare's leading actors, and by the time Shakespeare's first plays were being performed in the 1590s there were several companies of actors, under the patronage of various noblemen as well as the Queen herself. The unique quality of Elizabethan theatre was its unprecedented and never since rivalled scope and variety – its unabashed mixture of poetry and prose, farce, comedy, history and tragedy, realism and fantasy in defiance of academic rules. It appealed equally to the 'groundlings' and 'wits', it called for players and writers who knew both the market place and the court.

The Jacobean theatre, first with the dark Italian tragedies of Tourneur and Webster, then with elaborate 'masques' in which scenery and music grew more important than text and performance, gradually withdrew into the court. In the Civil War the Puritans, who had always been vociferous and dangerous enemies and remain so to this day, at last got the theatres closed; when they re-opened after the Restoration they were mainly an upper-class diversion, concerned with heiresses and fortunes, love and adultery, metropolitan wit and rural witlessness. In Dryden's hands tragedy turned into a literary more than a theatrical form, though Thomas Otway contrived to write the last great English theatrical tragedy, *Venice Preserv'd*, whose subject was a revolution and its betrayal. It was an age of comedy, crowned by Congreve's *Love for Love* and *The Way of the World* which explored the relationship of men and women as deeply as Shakespeare had done. But Shakespeare's range was not available to any writer of such purely domestic pieces, however psychologically exact. After Congreve the playwrights grew softer and more ingratiating. The best of them in his *genre* – Goldsmith, and Sheridan in the 18th century, Boucicault, Wilde and Pinero in the 19th century,

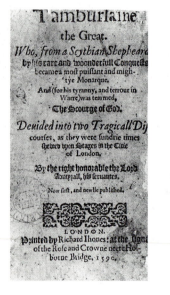

Tamburlaine the Great was produced by the Admiral's Men in 1587. Christopher Marlowe's magnificent iambics and his overweening Renaissance characters prepared the way for Shakespeare's histories and tragedies.

David Garrick and Mrs Cibber in an 18th-century revival of the last great English tragedy, Otway's **Venice Preserv'd**, first produced in 1682. But Colley Cibber, Mrs Cibber's father-in-law was largely responsible for the rise of sentimental comedy, which at the outset of the 18th century ended the Golden Age of English drama.

Coward and Rattigan in the 20th century – wrote light social comedies for the respectable classes.

The powers and scope of the performers, however, did not decline. The great adult male and boy actors of Shakespeare's day, when women did not appear on the stage, were followed by male and female stars – such as Betterton and Mrs Bracegirdle – in the Restoration period. The actor-manager David Garrick was the greatest theatrical figure of the 18th century: reviving Shakespeare, he set the pattern of British theatre up to our own day. 'The drama is an aesthetic phenomenon,' wrote James Agate, the drama critic, in 1926, 'the theatre is an economic proposition'. Fearing to be left with the bare aesthetic phenomenon, managements have tended to seek safety in the drama of the past.

kind of new Elizabethan range and variety has so far failed to find more than a token audience. There is a new generation of playwrights, many of whom are certainly not inferior to the lesser Elizabethans; but although they enjoy, thanks to the cinema and television, opportunities and audiences undreamed of by their predecessors they lack a sense of their real importance to the society and the world they live in. It seems unlikely, given the competition of books, newspapers, sport etc., that there can ever be another Golden Age of playwriting in Britain, but the Golden Age of performance has lasted some 500 years and we are still in it.

'The name Ellen Terry,' said Bernard Shaw, 'rang like a chime through the second half of the 19th century.' John Singer Sargent painted her playing Lady Macbeth during her 20-year reign as Sir Henry Irving's leading lady at the Lyceum.

Ellen Terry's great-nephew, Sir John Gielgud, in the famous 1943 production of *Love for Love*: Congreve revived in the age of Noel Coward.

Below: A dash of 'absurdism' puts a little sparkle back into the old domestic comedy. Jonathan Price and Warren Mitchell in *The Caretaker* by Harold Pinter.

Shifting the Balance

Until the end of the 19th century plays – whether revivals, melodramas, farces or light comedies – were treated almost entirely as vehicles for the leading performers, but in the 20th century brave attempts have been made to shift the balance back towards the 'aesthetic phenomenon' or at least towards a theatre which dealt with the serious issues of the day and was not simply light entertainment. Miss A.E.F. Horniman's Manchester Repertory Theatre found new local plays as well as players. Harley Granville-Barker's Incorporated Stage Society produced Shaw and Galsworthy as well as Barker's own plays. George Devine's Royal Court Theatre groomed a stable of socially conscious and 'absurdist' playwrights in the 1950s and 60s. But although Shaw, a great self-publicist, gained a spurious reputation for his shallow and wordy paradoxes, these writers were all minor figures, still treading the narrow pound of domestic comedy even if in reaction to its respectability.

The two leading contemporary companies – the National Theatre and the Royal Shakespeare Company – rely principally on classic revivals; the commercial theatre of London's West End and the provincial repertory theatres are dominated by star performers; and the alternative or 'fringe' theatre which sometimes looks as if it may achieve a

The British Genius: Literature

'Chaucer at the court of King Edward III' by Ford Madox Brown (painted in 1851 with the poet, Dante Gabriel Rossetti, modelling for Chaucer). The canvas was originally meant to include virtually every other major writer in the language so as to show Chaucer's seed flowering down four and a half centuries.

Sir Walter Raleigh (1552–1618), one of Queen Elizabeth's favourites, wrote the *History of the World* and, like so many of his contemporaries at court, could turn his hand to poetry as readily as to scholarship, exploring, war or government.

Sir Philip Sidney (1554–86), poet, courtier, diplomat and soldier, was idolized on all four counts by the English people at the time, but himself rated poetry above all other pursuits: 'Nature never set forth the earth in so rich tapestry as divers poets have done – neither with pleasant rivers, fruitful trees, sweet-smelling flowers, nor whatsoever else may make the too much loved earth more lovely. Her world is brazen, the poets only deliver a golden.'

English literature, like Milton's landscape in *Paradise Lost*, is a large prospect, made up of shaggy hills, lawns and level downs, palmy hillock and hairy wilderness, flowery plots, 'umbrageous Grots and Caves/Of cool recess'; and, like any other landscape worked by man, it is in a state of constant flux. With each fresh generation, new tracts are cleared, old workings covered up or over grown, landmarks come and go. At their head stands Chaucer, friendliest and most accessible of ancient monuments, still recognizably the predecessor of our own contemporary practitioners whether for psychological acuteness or minute observation, the casual conversational tone, humour, irony, and tragic penetration that make him in some ways the first novelist as well as one of the finest poets in the language.

Chaucer worked from Latin models for an illiterate, aristoractic audience in a medieval English that had barely been used as yet for literary purposes. Two hundred years later Shakespeare belonged to what is already very much our modern world, mirrored in his plays by an imagination so copious, rich and fertile that like the subterranean river in Milton's Eden, it has shaped the contours of the literary landscape ever since. But Shakespeare himself meant posterity to remember him less for the plays than for his 154 sonnets, perhaps the most brilliant and perplexing achievement of an age whose glory was its lyric poetry. Few readers today are likely to find time for the stiff and cumbrous spendours of Elizabethan or Jacobean prose. But the poets, secular and religious, from Spenser and Sidney to Cowley and Marvell, Herrick and Davenant still have the delicacy and pristine freshness of the gay enamelled flowers that deck their verses in profusion.

Fiercer, darker and more complex strains in the 17th century shape the work of the metaphysical poets and that strange divine, John Donne who, having dazzled and dominated his contemporaries, remained for the next two hundred years and more a forgotten oddity until dug up, by T.S. Eliot and others, as a new and powerful influence in the 20th century. Nothing illustrates the unpredictable vitality of our literature more vividly than Donne's fluctuating reputation. Beside him Milton towers like a granite crag, remote and lofty, scaleable only with difficulty even in his lifetime. Always a source of more pride than pleasure, *Paradise Lost* marks the highest point in the long struggle to make English not only as mellifluous, supple and expressive as Latin but also as stupendous and sublime.

The Augustan Age that followed, from Dryden to Pope and Swift, seemed at the time and since to have come out on a plateau, sunny and well tended, more or less securely fenced against the unclaimed waste beyond. Even at their

Left: Thomas Hobbes (1588–1679), author of *Leviathan*, was with Locke, Hume and Berkeley among the earliest and most influential of British philosophers, possessor also of a splendidly pithy, vigorous and trenchant prose style.

'The chief glory of every people arises from its authors' wrote Dr Johnson (1709–84) who – pundit, poet, biographer, lexicographer and one of the best talkers in the language – did more than most to celebrate English authors and their work.

Samuel Pepys (1633–1701), wrote his *Diary* in a code known only to himself, and can scarcely have anticipated that posterity would honour him not as a pioneering civil servant but as master of a racy, capricious, conversational, even gossipy art form peculiarly congenial to the English, then as now.

Left: One of the masterpieces of English romanticism, *Weymouth Bay*, painted on his honeymoon in 1816 by John Constable who summed up his feelings at the time with a passage from Byron's *Childe Harold*:

There is a pleasure in the
   pathless woods,
There is a rapture on the lonely
   shore,
There is society where none
   intrudes,
By the deep sea, and music in
   its roar . . .'

gentlest and most prosaic, the poets of this and the next generation – Gray, Cowper, Crabbe and the ebullient Robert Burns – were only too well aware that urbanity is a precarious defence against a world of misery and chaos. But this was beyond all else the age of print, of increased circulation in clubs and coffee shops, of a new and growing middle class readership which required more flexible, less ornate and constricting forms: prose romances, verse epistles, skits and satires, collections of letters and gossip in periodicals like the *Spectator*, above all the novel itself which, after vigorous efforts on the part of writers like Bunyan and Defoe, burst suddenly into full flower in the middle of the 18th century with Richardson, Fielding and Smollett. In some ways the prospect of expansion seemed limitless, in others the horizon was deliberately restricted: Dr Johnson, who left both Chaucer and Donne off his list of poets worth recording, reckoned that Pope had already taken poetry as far as it could ever hope to go ('To attempt any further improvement of versification will be dangerous').

But the point at which things seem for once to be fairly well under control is (as Milton's gardeners also found) the natural moment for violent upheaval; and less than a quarter of a century after Johnson's encomium, Pope's name was mud with Romantic critics. Hostilities were first tentatively declared in Wordsworth's famous preface to his and Coleridge's *Lyrical Ballads* in 1800. Forces long dormant erupted in a surge of energy that seemed, according to which way you looked at it, demonic or divine: inspiration and enthusiasm were to take over from artifice and thought, nature would oust the dead hand of tradition and the poet himself take on godlike powers of creation, prophecy and leadership.

    A rock with torrents roaring, with the clouds
     Familiar, and a favourite of the stars
was the metaphor Wordsworth used for his own soul.

Romanticism, the only major literary movement ever initiated by the English, spread rapidly to the Continent carried by exiles like Byron and Shelley whose lives were perhaps more influential than their art. It is hard to exaggerate the effect of liberation and renewal. Poets like Wordsworth and Keats not only changed the actual countryside, so that to this day we see it through their eyes; they left us with a radically altered view of poetry itself as an emanation of man's inner, spiritual and moral landscape.

But the most far-reaching revolutions are the most effectively tamed and domesticated by time. Popular adulation in the latter part of the 19th century succeeded

Jane Austen (1775–1817) – drawn by her sister Cassandra'. Jane Austen was one of the first and greatest practitioners of one of the few art forms in which women have been from the start men's acknowledged equals.

The Gin Shop, one of George Cruikshank's illustrations to *Sketches by Boz*, the book with which the 24-year-old Dickens first electrified the reading public in 1836: 'The gin-shops in and near Drury Lane, Holborn, St Giles's, Covent Garden and Clare Market, are the handsomest in London. There is more filth and squalid misery near these great thoroughfares than in any part of this mighty city.'

'**Robert Browning taking tea** with the Browning Society'. A cartoon by Max Beerbohm showing the ludicrous lengths to which Victorian literary snobbery regularly went in adulation of perhaps the nearest contemporary equivalent to pop stars. (Browning himself declined to accept responsibility for the 'strenuous twaddle' talked about his work by fans like these.)

on the one hand, in reducing the cult of the hero to manageable proportions in the persons of literary oracles like Carlyle, Ruskin and Macaulay while, on the other, appropriating the more innocuous, optimistic and nature-loving elements of romanticism to shore up rather than split society apart. Poets like Tennyson and Swinburne made up in richly glittering imagery and verse patterns for any want of intellectual rigour. But there is a sad shrinkage of a long and honourable poetic tradition embodied in Matthew Arnold's crushing dictum – first adumbrated by Coleridge in the 1790s and echoed until at least the 1930s by wan latterday romantics like A.E. Housman – that Dryden and Pope 'are not classics of our poetry, they are classics of our prose!

Arnold looked forward rather than back, to Hopkins, Hardy, Yeats and Eliot, to the austere beauties of a century that has set less store by rhetoric than by the intense difficulty of telling anything so complex as truth. But whole areas that once belonged to poetry – satirical, polemical, epistolary and didactic verse, for instance, and for that matter the erotic song – had been enthusiastically given up, and have since proved tricky to reclaim, in spite of

enthusiastic attempts at salvage by the political poets of the 1930s, or the university wits and popular performing poets of our own day.

The Novel

Where poetry lost ground, the novel gained it, expanding throughout the 19th century into an almost infinitely capacious and accommodating medium. 'Three or four Families in a Country Village is the very thing to work on,' wrote Jane Austen who, painting with the finest possible brush on what she herself called a 'little bit (two Inches wide) of Ivory', achieved a depth and strength seldom equalled by even her most ambitious successors. 'The big bow-wow strain I can do myself like any now going; but the exquisite touch which renders ordinary common-place things and characters interesting . . . is denied to me,' wrote Scott, marvelling at Jane Austen's economy. She ranks high in the long line of novelists, descending from Richardson via the Brontës and George Eliot to Hardy and Henry James, who have found a comparatively narrow domestic compass in no way set boundaries to their

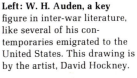

Left: **W. H. Auden, a key** figure in inter-war literature, like several of his contemporaries emigrated to the United States. This drawing is by the artist, David Hockney.

Above: Henry James (painted for his 70th birthday in 1913 by his fellow American, J. S. Sargent), one of the several literary colonists who have from time to time enriched and vitalized the English novel, in which he found possibilities that no one else had seen before.

Right: T. S. Eliot was, with W. B. Yeats, one of the twin poles of the modern movement in poetry, though works like *The Waste Land* – which once seemed the last word in barbaric dislocation and cynical disillusionment – have come more and more to look like classics in a long and high tradition of gravity, harmony, lucidity and beauty.

The satirist George Orwell (1903–50), author of *Animal Farm* and *Nineteen Eighty-Four*.

exploration of the human heart in its subtlest and most intricate recesses.

At the opposite extreme stands Dickens, working with bold strokes and lurid colours on anything from crowded city slums to scenes of wild and sombre desolation, exaggerated burlesque to bleak social comment, all jammed down higgledy-piggledy in the light of a powerfully freakish imagination. This is a line going back at least to Fielding, Sterne and Defoe – racy, impressionistic, indiscriminate; and the English novel owes its unrivalled luxuriance and scope partly perhaps to the endless possibilities for interaction, opposition and mutual replenishment between these two broad streams with their innumerable tributaries. Reaction to the Victorian superabundance meant a marked lightening of tone among Edwardian novelists, followed by a period of confusion and regrouping in the experiments of James Joyce, Virginia Woolf and D.H. Lawrence. Alternate spurts of vivacity and languor in the domestic novel ever since have been overtaken by what looks like a recent doubling back to the comical, 18th-century picaresque manner; and the tradition has been constantly enriched by importers and outsiders from Conrad and his

contemporary disciple V.S. Naipaul, or pioneers like Kipling who plundered the spoils of empire, itself a fruitful source of something like a modern version of Scott's brand of historical romance.

The golden age of the novel has also been the heyday of biography, always an English speciality from Aubrey's *Brief Lives* in the 17th century and Boswell's *Life of Johnson* in the 18th – works that raise gossip to an art form – to the more formal pleasures of the official, Victorian double-decker. No other country has produced anything comparable to our own monumental *Dictionary of National Biography*, yet another illustrious offspring of Virginia Woolf's father Leslie Stephen. The 20th century began with Lytton Strachey's *Eminent Victorians* – biography used as Milton's Eve used billhooks to 'Lop overgrown, or prune, or prop, or bind' – and, in an age inclined to rate documentary at least as high as fiction, biography has flourished like the bay tree ever since. It is a taste natural enough in a people as individualistic as the English, humane, inquisitive, rhapsodical, pragmatic, and as ill disposed to regular discipline in literature as in that other peculiarly English art of landscape gardening.

The British Genius: Music

The history of British music is, as with most things, somewhat chequered. Between periods of glorious creativity there have been long, barren years of inactivity. Frequently some years behind the Continent, the British have, by and large, produced music that is steadfastly idiosyncratic.

Sadly, very little music before 1400 has survived, but we do have a considerable quantity of 15th-century manuscripts and it is from these that we can get an idea of the music of the earliest known important British composers, such as John Dunstable (c. 1384–1453) who is considered to be the first 'great' English musician. In those days – and indeed until the mid-18th century – formal music was fostered by the Church and the court (with its attendant aristocracy). Outside these two institutions trained musicians were almost non-existent and the ordinary man's experience of music was restricted to the popular, improvised or folk tradition – a tradition of unwritten music.

The most important characteristic of music before 1500 is that it existed almost exclusively in a vocal form; when the limited instruments of the period *were* available they usually played a subsidiary role, providing support for the singers by doubling the vocal lines.

With John Taverner (c. 1495–1543), Thomas Tallis (c. 1505–85) and William Byrd (1543–1623) came the great flowering of Tudor music – unsurpassed by contemporary continental works, except perhaps those of Palestrina in Italy and Victoria in Spain. Even in music of this period, a peculiarly cool English quality is detectable, which sets it apart from Mediterranean polyphony.

From the Tudor era was to evolve the rich age of the madrigalists, such as Thomas Morley (1557–1602), John Wilbye (1574–1638) and Orlando Gibbons (1583–1625). Rooted in the works of the Elizabethan lyrical poets, the English madrigal was quite distinct from similar compositions by European counterparts; the pure madrigals of William Byrd or Thomas Tomkins (1573–1656) are worlds apart from the passionate writing of such composers as Monteverdi or Willaert.

By the mid-16th century, purely instrumental music was beginning to assert itself and the madrigal composers were turning their attention to what we would now call chamber music. They wrote mainly for lute or virginals, and small consorts of viols and recorders. Towards the end of the century, however, the singer was once again to become the dominant force in English music. One man in particular, the lutenist John Dowland (1563–1626), devoted the greater part of his output to the lute song which was in the 16th century what lieder and ballads were to become in the 19th – an exceptionally intimate and concentrated form of domestic music.

The central figure of the Baroque period was Henry Purcell (1659–95) who in spite of his very short life, managed to produce an extraordinarily large quantity of music for the Church, the theatre and the consort. His genius is tellingly evident in his incomparable settings of the English language, his almost bizarre sense of harmony and his exuberant feel for rhythmic vitality. He wrote the first English opera, *Dido and Aeneas*, almost by accident. Though incidental music for the theatre was common in 17th-century England, a completely staged music drama, uniting elements of the cantata or ode, play and masque had not been attempted; yet Purcell somehow thought it a suitable concept to be mounted not by a theatre company as such but by the pupils of a girls' school in Chelsea. If Purcell was the first British composer of opera, he was also virtually the last of any international significance until the present century, when Britten's *Peter Grimes* achieved world acclaim. (The sparkling products of the partnership

between W.S. Gilbert and Sir Arthur Sullivan are more properly described as operettas.)

The most important musician in England during the first half of the 18th century was not an Englishman, but a German, George Frederick Handel (1685–1759), who settled in London in his late twenties. In adopting Handel, the musical establishment was allying itself not so much to the stylistic conventions of Germany as to those of Italy, where Handel worked between 1706 and 1710. He managed to fulfil the almost insatiable demand for biblical oratorios as well as writing Italianate operas, *concerti grossi* and chamber music. His main English contemporaries were Thomas Arne and William Boyce.

Following in Handel's footsteps – from Germany via Italy – was the youngest son of J.S. Bach, Johann Christian (1735–82) who arrived in London at the age of 27 in 1762. He was joined by one of his father's pupils, Karl Friedrich Abel (1723–87) and together formed a mainstay of musical life in London, composing and organizing many of the capital's concerts, including regular subscription seasons at the Spring Garden and the Hanover Square Rooms. But by the late 18th century, music in England had begun a decline, fashions changed and the patronage of the aristocracy and the Church was not forthcoming.

Although music making naturally continued throughout the 19th century, when numerous concert-giving bodies, festivals and choral societies were born, England went through an undeniably thin period in composition. There were competent musicians and even competent composers, but no creative giants like Beethoven or Liszt.

Only by the end of the 19th century did English composers begin to re-establish their importance. Edward Elgar (1857–1934) in particular was to become something of a national institution; while he gained international respect for *The Dream of Gerontius*, the two symphonies and the two concertos, he won affection at home with the *Enigma Variations*, the Serenade, the Introduction and Allegro, and, of course, the *Pomp and Circumstance* marches. Frederick Delius (1862–1934) on the other hand somewhat distanced himself from the musical public by totally abandoning classical traditions and writing music inspired by nature. The music of Ralph Vaughan Williams (1872–1958) and Gustav Holst (1874–1934) veered away from the romanticism of Elgar and moved towards a kind of neo-classicism, inspired to some extent by their interest in and revival of folksong and Tudor music.

The past hundred years has thus seen a remarkable resurgence of composition in Britain equal to that anywhere else. The list of established composers is extensive: at the forefront of the pre-war generation are William Walton (1902–), Lennox Berkeley (1903–) Michael Tippett (1905–) and Benjamin Britten (1913–76).

In the world of popular music Britain has produced a truly original voice in the shape of the Beatles with John Lennon (1940–80) and Paul McCartney (1943–) producing songs as universally loved as those of the Americans Cole Porter and Irving Berlin.

In the same way as composition was fostered by the Church and court in the 17th century, the great patrons of the 20th have undoubtedly been the BBC and the many festivals that have sprung up throughout the country. Vital to the continuation of new music are the Arts Council and more recently, commercial sponsors.

Spearheaded by composers like Peter Maxwell Davies (1934–) new generations of British composers are beginning to secure reputations both at home and abroad which gives hope that not only should we be grateful for the past but look forward with eagerness to the future.

1.

2.

1. Orlando Gibbons (1583–1625) belonged to the golden age of the English madrigal.

2. George Frederick Handel (1685–1759), German-born but stylistically Italian, satisfied the demand for biblical oratorios.

3. Arthur Sullivan (1842–1900) wrote sparkling, easy-going operettas, with libretti by W. S. Gilbert.

4. Frederick Delius (1862–1934). His Romantic/Impressionist style of music won acceptance largely through Sir Thomas Beecham's sensitive interpretations.

5. Edward Elgar (1857–1934) is thought of as the most 'English' of composers.

6. Ralph Vaughan Williams (1872–1958) was much influenced by English Tudor music, both sacred and secular.

7. Gustav Holst (1874–1934) – neo-classical in style but inspired by national folk music.

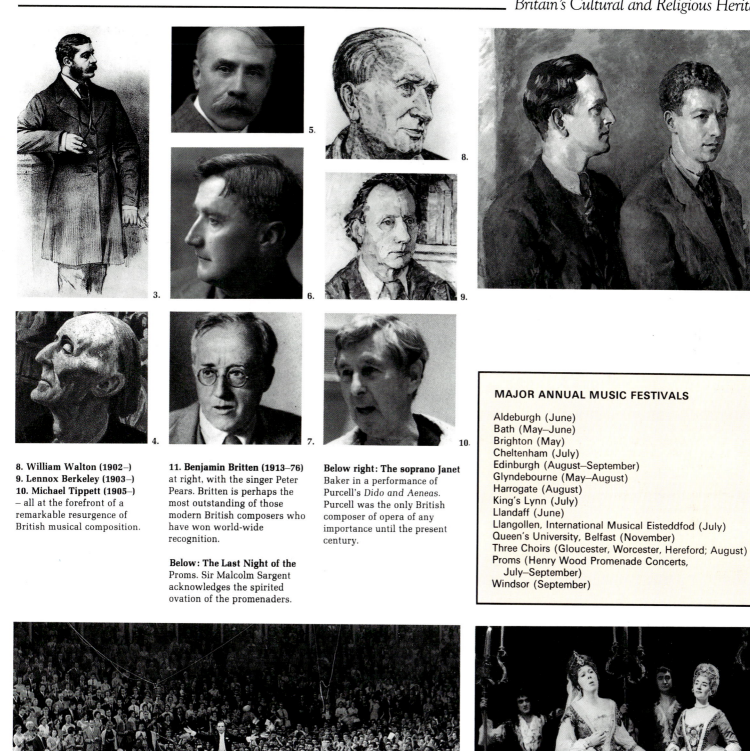

8. William Walton (1902–)
9. Lennox Berkeley (1903–)
10. Michael Tippett (1905–)
– all at the forefront of a
remarkable resurgence of
British musical composition.

11. Benjamin Britten (1913–76)
at right, with the singer Peter
Pears. Britten is perhaps the
most outstanding of those
modern British composers who
have won world-wide
recognition.

Below: The Last Night of the
Proms. Sir Malcolm Sargent
acknowledges the spirited
ovation of the promenaders.

Below right: The soprano Janet
Baker in a performance of
Purcell's *Dido and Aeneas*.
Purcell was the only British
composer of opera of any
importance until the present
century.

MAJOR ANNUAL MUSIC FESTIVALS

Aldeburgh (June)
Bath (May–June)
Brighton (May)
Cheltenham (July)
Edinburgh (August–September)
Glyndebourne (May–August)
Harrogate (August)
King's Lynn (July)
Llandaff (June)
Llangollen, International Musical Eisteddfod (July)
Queen's University, Belfast (November)
Three Choirs (Gloucester, Worcester, Hereford; August)
Proms (Henry Wood Promenade Concerts,
   July–September)
Windsor (September)

The British Genius: Architects

The great master-masons of the Middle Ages, like Henry Yevele at Canterbury and William Wynford at Winchester, brought to the international Gothic style an individuality that instantly marks out the English cathedral from its French and German counterparts. But it was the Reformation, setting Britain apart from the rest of Europe politically and culturally, that gave rise to a new class of professional architect in the modern sense of the word, concerned almost wholly with secular buildings. Elizabethan and Jacobean 'prodigy houses', like Hardwick and Wollaton designed by Robert Smythson, or Hatfield and Blickling by Robert Lyminge, may depend on Italian and Flemish pattern-books for their decoration; but their soaring proportions, and huge windows like walls of glass, seem developed instead from the triumphs of the English Perpendicular style.

The purer classicism of the Italian Renaissance and Palladio's theories of harmonic proportion were first introduced to this country by Inigo Jones, court architect to Charles I, whose Banqueting House at Whitehall and Queen's House at Greenwich were revolutionary for their period. Due to the upheavals of the Civil War, however, they had less influence on the gentlemen-architects of the Restoration, figures like Hugh May and Sir Roger Pratt, who developed the idea of the 'double-pile' house. Eltham Lodge and Coleshill (now alas destroyed), their best-known works, are indebted rather to the sober Dutch and French classicism of the 1650s.

The man who must be regarded as the greatest of all English architects, Christopher Wren, began life as a scientist, and combined brilliant technical and engineering skills with equally remarkable artistic gifts. Wren's great opportunity came with the Fire of London in 1666; over the next 20 years he built more than 50 City churches, with the crowning achievement of St Paul's Cathedral, only completed in 1710. But Wren was equally active in the secular field, and it would be hard to find nobler public buildings than his hospitals at Greenwich and Chelsea, his Library at Trinity College, Cambridge, and his additions to Hampton Court for William and Mary. His assistants at Hampton Court, William Talman and Nicholas Hawksmoor, joined by the unlikely figure of the soldier and playwright, Sir John Vanbrugh, developed the Baroque style in the country house field; but the drama and movement of Vanbrugh's palaces at Blenheim and Castle Howard look back also to the fantasy of the Elizabethan prodigy houses. Among other proponents of the short-lived English Baroque, Thomas Archer and James Gibbs brought a more consciously Italianate flavour to the style with details borrowed from Bernini and Borromini.

The Classical Ideal

The Hanoverian Succession coincided with a revolution in taste, which again set Britain on a quite different course from the rest of Europe. Lord Burlington's protegés, Colen Campbell and William Kent, turned the clock back a century and revived Inigo Jones' reverence for the buildings and writings of Palladio. Chiswick on a small scale, and Wanstead and Houghton on a much larger one, set the pattern of the Palladian villa plan which was to dominate country-house building for the next 50 years. The search for the classical ideal continued to obsess architects for the rest of the century; but archaeological discoveries in Italy in the 1750s, and a new interest in Greece stimulated by James Stuart and Nicholas Revett's *Antiquities of Athens*, led to the purer and more scholarly neo-classical style that is associated above all with the work of Robert Adam and his chief rival, James Wyatt. Strict as were the rules he

Above: Hardwick Hall, Derbyshire, built by Robert Smythson for Bess of Hardwick, Countess of Shrewsbury, between 1590 and 1596.

Right: St Paul's Cathedral — the Great Model made in 1673 and representing Wren's original conception.

Below: Blenheim Palace, Oxon, designed by Sir John Vanbrugh for the 1st Duke of Marlborough and completed in 1716.

advocated, Adam brought an unrivalled imagination and delicacy of touch to the interiors of Syon and Osterley, Harewood and Kedleston – to name only a few of the great houses where he was employed. More fastidious but less prolific than Adam, Sir William Chambers practised in the same period in a style closer to French neo-classicism, a theme developed by the younger Henry Holland's chaste Louis XVI interiors.

With the dawn of the 19th century came a parting of the ways – between the high seriousness of the Greek Revival, which achieved its most individual expression in the work of Sir John Soane, and the eclecticism of John Nash, designer of the Prince Regent's Brighton Pavilion. Even the return of the Gothic style advocated by Pugin in the 1830s and 1840s could not paper over the cracks, and much the same division can be seen among the architects of the High Victorian period. On the one side lay the ecclesiologists such as Street, Bodley and, to a lesser extent, Gilbert Scott; and on the other the eclectics, from Barry and Salvin to William Burges, the creator of Cardiff Castle and Castell Coch. The powerful influence of John Ruskin and William Morris meanwhile urged a return to the basics of building practice, and with the Arts and Crafts Movement (a reaction against some of the worst aspects of the Industrial Revolution), architects like Norman Shaw and Philip Webb late in the century pioneered a simpler 'Queen Anne' style. In a sense the career of Sir Edwin Lutyens, coinciding with the Indian summer of the English country house, can be seen as tying together all these threads. Brought up in the Arts and Crafts tradition, he could build in almost any style, yet stamp each commission with his own unmistakable identity. From the mock-medieval Castle Drogo to the neo-Palladian Gledstone, from the vernacular of Folly Farm to the simple majesty of the Cenotaph, his work is as English in character as the music of Elgar.

The Anteroom at Syon House, Middlesex, one of Robert Adam's finest interiors of the 1760s.

Cardiff Castle, built by the 3rd Marquess of Bute between 1868 and 1885, to designs by William Burges.

Below left: The Palladian villa at Chiswick, designed by Lord Burlington and built c. 1723–29.

Below: Folly Farm, Sulhampstead, Berkshire, one of Sir Edwin Lutyens' best-known essays in the vernacular style.

English Silver

England may justifiably be regarded as the leading producer of silver throughout the ages. The rigid assaying laws, and the high quality of the metal used provided a clear and reliable structure in which the craft could thrive. Although the making of fine silver had flourished from the reign of Elizabeth, and splendid pieces engraved with Chinoiseries were among the finest creations of the reign of Charles II, it was a political event across the Channel that radically changed the face of British silver. When Louis XIV, in 1685, revoked the Edict of Nantes, thus exposing the Huguenots to persecution, a wave of skilled silversmiths crossed the Channel to continue their craft in the Protestant British Isles. This ushered in a remarkable age of silver making which was to last for 150 years.

The early Huguenot goldsmiths such as Harache, Platel and Willaume combined robust forms made with generous use of the metal with brilliant and inventive engraving. The plate supplied to the courtiers of William, Mary and Queen Anne was a solid and confident assertion of the values of the new century. The second quarter of the 18th century was dominated by one of the greatest exponents of the silversmith's art, Paul de Lamerie (1688–1751), whose output spanned the transition from the Baroque to the Rococo. He was, however, but the best among hundreds of very gifted craftsmen working all over the country throughout the century. The styles of silver adhered closely to developments in the field of furniture. Chinese Chippendale is reflected in Chinoiserie silver, and the architecture and designs of Robert Adam find their counterpart in the silver of Fogelberg and Gilbert, John Schofield and the Bateman family.

The Regency, with the lavish tastes of the Prince of Wales and his circle, produced the atmosphere conducive to another great burst of creative activity. Here silver gilt was all the rage and clients such as Lord Lascelles and Lord Lonsdale were splendidly equipped with the output of Paul Storr and the partnership of Benjamin Smith and Digby Scott.

Until the arrival of the Arts and Crafts movement, the Victorian era saw few major developments or great names. The era was epitomized perhaps by massive candelabra and figure compositions.

Unlike the majority of European states, where much silver has been lost in wars, or melted to finance them, English silver has survived intact since the Restoration of Charles II.

Chapter Seven

Guardians of Britain's Heritage

What of the future? Can what remains of Britain's diverse and beautiful countryside survive the insatiable demands of industry, modern farming and urbanization? What hope is there for the rarer species of wild life and plant life when the habitats on which they depend are increasingly threatened? Nowhere in Britain is too remote that it is not imperilled by 'progress' – an oil spill in the Shetlands could inflict incalculable damage. Progress and re-development have already wantonly defaced Britain's towns and villages. Hundreds of churches and historic buildings are slowly decaying through neglect. Will they be lost for ever? The answer to these and many similar questions is encouraging. Up and down the country is a surprising number of organizations, all varied in their individual objectives, which are united in their determination to preserve all that is best in Britain – from a rare species of butterfly or a village pond to a redundant church or ancient barn. Such organizations, together with an amazing variety of museums and collections, are helping to preserve Britain's heritage for posterity.

Museums and Treasure Houses

Museums are a nation's memory, and the better the museum the better its memory. British history contains more than a modest ration of looting, theft and forced sales abroad – these things are an unfortunate concomitant of all empires – and our museums and great houses contain correspondingly large collections of works of art, curiosities and ethnological material of all kinds brought back from Africa, India, China, the Pacific and other parts of the world in which British commercial interests had been strong during the 18th and 19th centuries and in which the British Army and Navy had been able to exercise a powerful influence.

Whether the Benin bronzes, Chinese porcelain and Egyptian and Classical antiquities acquired in this way can fairly and decently be considered part of the British heritage is a matter of opinion, although they do beyond doubt belong to the stock of our treasure houses. One could perhaps express the problem in another way, by saying that there would seem to be much stronger reasons for keeping a painting by Stubbs, Constable or Lowry, a vase by Wedgwood or Doulton, or a table or set of chairs by Chippendale or Sheraton in this country than for preventing the sale and export of a Rembrandt or Donatello or a French Empire sofa. A Stubbs is part of our heritage in a way that a Rembrandt is not.

From this point of view, there is no essential difference between a museum and a house. Both serve to remind us of the way in which our ancestors, both powerful and humble, lived and worked, of the style and the values of their existence.

With nearly 1700 museums and almost the same number of house open to the public to choose from, any selection is bound to be somewhat arbitrary, but certain of them do, even so, appear to provide complete answers to the question, 'Where would one advise a person with no knowledge of Britain or its history at all, to go, in order to discover not only the basic facts but the flavour and the balance of our heritage?'

The dividing lines between one kind of museum and another are and should be vague – neither history nor human activities can be put into neat and tidy compartments – and for this reason it seems more sensible to think of museums and museum collections as illustrating periods in our history, rather than different kinds of activity. Within these time divisions, there are the museums which tell the story of the labouring poor and those which perform the same task for the well-to-do. There are the museums of craftsmanship and practical ingenuity, the museums which document the traditions and tastes of a single family, the museums of artistic creativity. There are the national shrines, the house-museums of distinguished people, the archaeological site-museums and, a matter of much importance in a country with such splendid horticultural traditions, our great gardens, which are as fully entitled to be regarded as museums as anything with four walls and a roof and, as living historical monuments to the highest degree of care, attention and conservation (see page 122).

Rich, poor and technical

From the 17th century onwards, the pattern of English civilization becomes more complex, and museums reflect the change. Exploration and the creation of an empire brought enormous additions to the national wealth and a corresponding increase in luxuries and domestic comfort. The upper and middle classes acquired personal possessions – pictures, furniture, jewellery, horses, carriages, clothes – on an unprecedented scale, and it is these possessions,

The Alfred Jewel is kept in the Ashmolean Museum, Oxford. It is widely thought that Alfred the Great, who died in 899, owned the jewel for it bears the Anglo-Saxon inscription 'Alfred made me'. It is gold, decorated with *cloisonné* enamel. It was found near the Island of Athelney, Somerset, in 1693. The jewel may have been a pointer for following the lines of a manuscript.

BRITAIN BEFORE THE NORMAN CONQUEST

Fine pre-historic exhibits can be found at the National Museum of Wales, Cardiff; the Museum of the Wiltshire Archaeological & Natural History Society, Devizes and the Museum of Antiquities, The University, Newcastle-upon-Tyne. Finds from the Bronze Age hill-fort at Maiden Castle are on show at the Dorset County Museum, Dorchester and exhibits from the lake village settlement at Mere, near Glastonbury can be seen at the Somerset County Museum, Taunton.

Britain is rich in museums concerned with the Roman period. Among the most interesting are the Verulamium Museum, St Albans, Herts; the Roman Fort museums at Caerleon, Gwent and Caernarfon; and those at the villa sites at Bignor, West Sussex and at Chedworth (Yanworth, Cheltenham, Glos.) where there are remarkable mosaic pavements. Also highly recommended are the Roman Palace Museum, Fishbourne, Chichester, West Sussex (the largest Romano-British residence so far to have been discovered in Britain) and the Roman Baths, Bath where the museum is arranged in the baths complex and presents a wide range of local material dating from the Roman period.

A great mass of interesting material relating to the Anglo-Saxons and the Vikings has survived and is well distributed throughout museums and the southern and eastern parts of Britain. Apart from the immense riches of the British Museum, there are particularly good collections at Winchester City Museum; God's House Tower Museum, Town Quay, Southampton, Hants; Castle Museum, Norwich; The Yorkshire Museum, York, and the Manx Museum, Douglas, I.O.M. At Durham Cathedral Museum one can see a fine series of Anglo-Saxon carved stones, the relics of St Cuthbert and a display of plate, books, seals, scrolls and robes.

The murder of Thomas à Becket, Archbishop of Canterbury, in his own cathedral in 1170. This illustration is from a manuscript by Matthew Paris, the 13th-century historian of medieval England.

NORMAN AND MEDIEVAL BRITAIN

In Britain, the Normans are best represented by their churches and their castles, which introduced to this country styles and techniques already developed on the Continent. Their contribution to art was almost entirely through the religious movements which they fostered and their only significant achievements were in the military field, from which a not very impressive legacy is preserved in museums. Recommended are the following: Dunster Castle, Somerset (National Trust), built by William de Mohun soon after the Norman Conquest, sold to Lady Elizabeth Luttrell in 1376 and in the possession of the family until 1976; Bodiam Castle, East Sussex (National Trust), built in 1385 and very little changed since; Berkeley Castle, Gloucestershire, lived in by the Berkeley family for more than 800 years;

together with the buildings which accommodated them, which form the bulk of the stock of most of our museums today.

Until the middle of the 18th century, Britain was still largely rural. Most of its people lived in villages and small towns and maintained themselves by working in agriculture or in craft workshops which catered essentially for the local technologies based on power-driven machinery. The old economy, rooted in agriculture, slowly declined, as money and people moved into the manufacturing areas and out of the countryside. Great fortunes were made and spent, large numbers of the working classes lived in dreadful poverty and squalor, and a favoured élite lived at a standard which would have been unimaginable 200 years earlier.

All this is illustrated in our museums, where the problem has been increasingly to find room for all the material which has been offered to them. Between 20 and 30 new museums are created each year, and still the

pressure grows. The legacy of the more recent past is the most vulnerable, mainly because few people recognize the historical importance of what was made and done ten or fifty years ago, while objects dating from earlier periods are likely to be considered old enough to be interesting and therefore worth collecting.

One might, therefore, usefully divide museums which tell us about life and work during the past 300 years or so into three broad groups – the museums of the rich, the museums of the poor or relatively poor, and the museums of changing technology.

The 17th century, one might, add, was a period of great destruction and vandalism. The religious fervour of the Cromwellians annihilated or damaged a high proportion of the religious art which had managed to survive the iconoclasts during the reign of Henry VIII, so that unfortunately we cannot see today what we could have seen in the early 1640s.

Cotehele, near Calstock, Cornwall (National Trust), the home of the Edgecumbes from 1354 to 1947, with the furniture, tapestries, and armour accumulated by the family during 400 years.

The finest and most adventurous architectural work of medieval Britain went into its churches, cathedrals and monasteries. The Cathedral Exhibition in the crypt of Canterbury Cathedral explains how the medieval builders carried out their work, the materials and tools they used, and the way in which the construction of the cathedral was planned. The Exhibition of Monastic Life in one of the surviving buildings of the great Cistercian Abbey at Beaulieu Abbey, Hampshire, illustrates the daily life of a Cistercian monk and sets out the political and social context in which Beaulieu operated. Visitors can follow the story of the Abbey from the late 13th century, when more than 4,000 acres were under cultivation, to the years just before the Dissolution, when the community contained fewer than 30 monks.

Of the many museums which illustrate the crafts, agriculture, seafaring and trading of medieval Britain, the following are outstanding: Wool House Maritime Museum, Southampton; The Lynn Museum, King's Lynn; Winchester City Museum; and the Museum of London, The Barbican, London.

THE TUDORS

Perhaps the best way of understanding the immense strength, drive and creativity of Tudor Britain is to study the faces of some of its most successful and influential people. The most convenient method of doing this is to visit the Gallery of Tudor and Jacobean Portraits at Montacute House, Somerset which reveals the tough, ruthless, unsmiling characteristics of the First Elizabethans.

The new wealth of the period and the anxiety to parade it is well illustrated by the great houses which the successful Elizabethans built for themselves: Montacute (begun in 1588); Longleat (1566–8, but very Victorianized inside); Hardwick Hall (1591–97: see pages 137, 188) and many others.

These were the homes of important people. More modest and therefore more typical buildings, showing the development of English domestic architecture from the 14th to 18th centuries, can be seen at Lacock in Wiltshire where the whole village, which owed its existence to the prosperity of the local wool industry, is now in the care of the National Trust. The construction of barns, houses, and other buildings dating from the late

The staircase at Hatfield House, Hertfordshire, the home of the Cecil family. The original building, completed in 1497, was the palace of the bishops of Ely. It was seized at the Dissolution and the present house built from 1608–12 by Robert Cecil, 1st Earl of Salisbury, and Queen Elizabeth's Secretary of State. Though Jacobean, it retains the usual E-plan of Elizabethan houses.

The Soane Museum, Lincoln's
Inn Fields, London, was
founded in 1812 by Sir John
Soane and contains collections
for 'the promotion of the study
of Architecture and the Allied
Arts'. These include the
sarcophagus of the Pharaoh
Seti I and Hogarth's series of
paintings of the The Rake's
Progress.

medieval and Tudor times can be studied at the Avoncroft
Museum of Building, Bromsgrove, Worcs. and the Weald and
Downland Museum, Singleton, Chichester. At both these
museums the story of English vernacular building is carried
forward to the early 19th century.

PICTURES AND FURNITURE
Museums are well enough in their way as places in which to
store and show off furniture and portraits, and one must be
grateful to the National Gallery, the Scottish National Portrait
Gallery, the Victoria and Albert Museum and to the great number
of provincial museums for the public duty they perform in safe-
guarding treasures which would otherwise have disappeared
abroad long ago. But these things mean most in the surroundings
for which they were originally intended and, in many cases,
designed. These are just a few of the places where furniture and
furnishings are to be seen at their best:
Stourhead, Wilts. Furniture by Thos. Chippendale, the Younger.
Woburn Abbey, Beds. 18th-century English furniture.
Pencarrow House, Bodmin. 18th-century English furniture.
Firle Place, Lewes. 18th-century furniture and porcelain.
Wightwick Manor, Wolverhampton. William Morris wallpapers
and furnishings.
Leighton Hall, Carnforth, Lancs. 18th–19th century furniture by
Gillow of Lancaster.

THE TASTES AND HABITS OF THE RICH
One thinks first of the houses, because, without houses, there
would have been nowhere to put the huge quantities of furniture
and works of art which rich people acquired as Britain became
steadily more prosperous and more powerful. There was great
competition to acquire the services of the most celebrated and
successful architects and interior designers — Inigo Jones, Sir
Christopher Wren, Robert Adam, James Wyatt, Sir Edwin
Lutyens and others — and most of the houses they built or
transformed are still standing; many indeed still occupied, often
by the same family which commissioned them in the first place.
The following are some outstanding examples of the work of
such architects and interior designers.
Inigo Jones   The Queen's House, Greenwich. Begun in 1616.
Sir Christopher Wren   Marlborough House, London. Early 18th
    century.
Sir John Vanbrugh   Castle Howard, near York, 1699. Blenheim
    Palace, Woodstock, Oxon. 1705–16.
Colen Campbell   Stourhead, Stourton, Nr Mere, Wilts. 1718–24.
William Adam   Haddo House, Nr Methlick, Scotland 1732.
    Floors Castle, Kelso, Scotland 1721.
Robert Adam   Kenwood, Hampstead Lane, London 1764.
    Syon House, Brentford, Middlesex.
Henry Holland   Althorp, Northampton 1790. Berrington Hall,
    Leominster (N.T.) 1778–81.
James Wyatt   Heaton Hall, Prestwich, Greater Manchester
    1722. Plas Newydd, Isle of Anglesey (N.T.) 1793. Doddington
    House, Chipping Sodbury, Glos. 18th century.
Philip Webb   Standen, East Grinstead, (N.T.) 1894.
Sir Edwin Lutyens   Castle Drogo, Devon (N.T.) 1910.

MUSEUMS OF THE POOR
Our heritage covers a much wider field than the fine decorative arts, and it is in the collection and conservation of the more
mundane and workaday objects of the past that many museums
make their contribution. Farming and rural life, industrial and
technical history, ships and navigation, transport — these are the
aspects of the past which depend on museums for keeping the
memory of the people alive.
North Cornwall Museum, Camelford. Display of household
equipment.
Somerset Rural Life Museum, Glastonbury. Farmhouse kitchen.
Beamish, Stanley, Co. Durham. Interior of miner's cottage.
Kingston-upon-Hull, Local fishing and whaling industries.
Ironbridge Gorge Museum, Shropshire. Abraham Darby's
furnace.

The National Trust

The National Trust, despite its name, is a private charity, with membership open to everyone. It was founded in 1895, in the drawing room of the Duke of Westminster's Grosvenor House, by three people – Octavia Hill, the social reformer, Sir Robert Hunter and Canon Hardwicke Rawnsley. The founders had the vision to see that Britain's heritage of natural and man-made beauty required organized protection if it were to survive. Their aim was to establish a responsible body 'to act as a Corporation for the holding of lands of natural beauty and sites and houses of historic interest to be preserved intact for the nation's use and enjoyment'.

Until its foundation there had been no association with the legal power to hold both land and buildings for the nation. This power was further expanded in the National Trust Act of 1907 when the right was first conferred to declare property inalienable. This right is the cornerstone of the Trust's success, as property so designated cannot be sold, given away, or in any way 'alienated'. It follows that inalienable buildings or land cannot be compulsorily acquired by government departments, local authorities, or any other agency without the express will of Parliament. It is this right therefore that confers ownership in perpetuity and enables the Trust to protect against all comers the heritage it holds for the nation.

Above right: Langdale, Cumbria. Langdale Fell with its mountain backcloth of the Langdale Pikes, Bowfell and Crinkle Crags is one of the most majestic scenes in Britain – and mercifully preserved for posterity by the National Trust.

Right: This map is purely selective, marking some of the more important National Trust properties. Apart from the Neptune coastline National Trust open spaces are not included.

In 1896 the National Trust acquired Dinas Oleu, 4½ acres (1.82 ha) of cliff land overlooking the Barmouth Estuary. Octavia Hill who was the Trust's conscience and driving force, noted 'we have our first property, will we ever get another?' She did not have long to wait, for in the same year the Trust bought for £10 – a virtual gift – the clergy house at Alfriston, Sussex, typical of the small, mainly medieval buildings that it was to acquire during its early years.

From modest beginnings has sprung an organization which is now the largest private landowner in Britain, owning almost half a million acres (over 200,000 ha) of its most beautiful country, protecting by ownership over 400 miles (643 km) of unspoiled coastline and opening to the public over 200 houses and gardens – the largest and most successful conservation society in the world.

Many of Britain's major sites, monuments and country houses are in its care, and when you realize that the White Cliffs of Dover, the Needles, Helvellyn, Box Hill, Avebury, Knole, Petworth House, Sissinghurst gardens, Telford's suspension bridge at Conway, the Giant's Causeway, are but a random sprinkling of the places that it protects, some idea can be gained of the importance of the National Trust in conservation.

After conservation, the Trust's second duty is to make available its properties for the 'nation's use and enjoyment'. Over six million people now visit these properties each year. The standards of preservation and presentation that they see are probably second to none, while the whole of the Trust's holding of coast and country is open free to all, subject only to the needs of agriculture and observance of the Country Code. Visitors to the Trust's houses can also enjoy programmes of concerts, often organized during the

SOME OUTSTANDING NATIONAL TRUST PROPERTIES

☐ Houses and other buildings
○ Gardens
— Neptune Coastline

London
Carlyle's House
Fenton House
Ham House
Osterley Park

Below: Craigievar Castle, Grampian is an outstanding example of the Scottish Baronial style – a tall tower house, plain below, but crowned with turrets, corbels and cupolas. The house was completed in 1626.

Right: Selworthy, Somerset – a beautiful village within the Trust's large holdings on Exmoor.

winter months when the houses are otherwise closed. In the summer there are out-of-door theatrical productions, pageants, water festivals, fêtes champêtres and serenades.

Scotland has its own National Trust, founded in 1931. The membership is now over 110,000, a higher proportion of the population than its sister organization achieves in England, Wales and Northern Ireland. Crathes, Craigievar, Culzean and Haddo Palaces are among its great houses, while Brodick and Inverewe are gardens of superlative quality; but perhaps its finest possessions are the great tracts of wild country such as Torridon, Glencoe and Ben Lawers, or its remote islands, Fair Isle, St Kilda and – most numinous of all – Iona, the holy island and burial place of the kings of Scotland.

Enterprise Neptune

Enterprise Neptune, the National Trust's campaign to save the coast, has been described as the 'outstanding act of conservation of the 20th century'.

A Trust survey, made in 1964, showed that some 980 miles (1577 km) of coast was of outstanding natural beauty and worthy of permanent preservation by the Trust. In March 1965 Enterprise Neptune, initiated and run by the Trust, was launched by HRH the Duke of Edinburgh.

Neptune was an immediate success and is now an established and continuing part of the Trust's work. More than £4 million has been raised and the Trust now protects more than 420 miles (676 km) of outstandingly beautiful coastline. The ownership of almost half the 'heritage' coast of England, Wales and Northern Ireland by the National Trust is of incomparable benefit to all lovers of unspoiled coastal scenery, and enables us and visitors to walk and bathe in wild, beautiful places, that are becoming rare in other European countries.

The Trust has been particularly successful in acquiring coastlands in Devon and Cornwall, South Wales and Norfolk. It is now beginning to achieve a significant holding in North Yorkshire. In Northern Ireland the Giant's Causeway, the Antrim coastal footpath and the Murlough nature reserve come under its protection.

The National Trust for Places of Historic Interest or Natural Beauty
42 Queen Anne's Gate, London SW1 H9AS
01 222 9251

National Trust for Scotland
5 Charlotte Square, Edinburgh EH2 4DU
031 225 2184

Both Trusts welcome new members, who are admitted free to all properties that the public pays to visit.

The Needles Headland at the westernmost extremity of the Isle of Wight is a Site of Special Scientific Interest – a sanctuary for sea-birds.

Below left: Penrhyn Castle, Gwynedd, was built in the 19th century by Thomas Hopper in a neo-Norman style. The castle houses a huge collection of dolls and, in curious contrast, a museum of industrial railways.

Below: The gardens at Blickling Hall, Norfolk, are largely Georgian in layout, with wooded walks, an orangery, topiary and numerous rare trees.

National Parks

Britain's countryside is fast vanishing; and the face of the countryside that remains continues to undergo profound and ravaging changes. As a result, in many places an environment is being created that is fundamentally hostile to wild life. Every year thousands of hectares of open land are built over to satisfy the greedy requirements of urban man: new roads (12,000 hectares alone of motorways), new houses, factories and airports, have buried huge tracts of rural Britain. Quarries, gravel pits and pylons deface the scenery. New farming methods have grubbed out hedgerows, cleared woodlands, drained wetlands – all to the detriment of wild life. By AD 2000 it is reckoned that 14 new towns the size of Birmingham will be needed to accommodate a 14 million increase in Britain's population.

But the story is not entirely a bleak one of wither, decay and destruction. Some 15 per cent of England and Wales

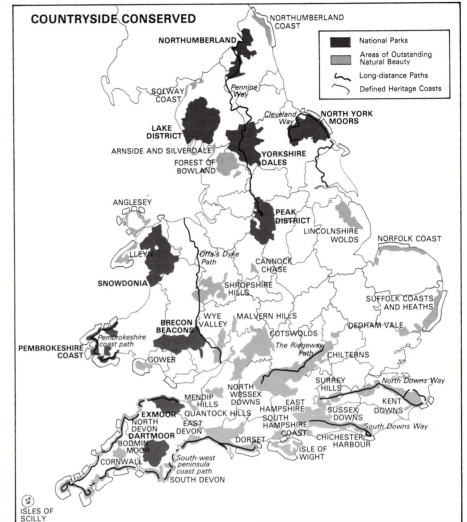

COUNTRYSIDE CONSERVED

Legend:
- National Parks
- Areas of Outstanding Natural Beauty
- Long-distance Paths
- Defined Heritage Coasts

NATIONAL PARKS
The ten areas of wild and splendid scenery in England and Wales which have been designated as National Parks.

	area in sq.km. (sq. miles)	date of designation
The Brecon Beacons	1344 (519)	17. 4.1957
Dartmoor	945 (365)	30.10.1951
Exmoor	686 (265)	19.10.1954
Lake District	2243 (866)	9. 5.1951

This is England's biggest park with England's highest mountain (Scafell Pike 987m/3210 ft) and largest lake (Windermere 17km./10½ miles long).

	area in sq.km. (sq. miles)	date of designation
Northumberland	1035 (398)	6. 4.1956
North York. Moors	1431 (553)	28.11.1952
Peak District	1400 (542)	17. 4.1951
Pembrokeshire Coast	583 (225)	29. 2.1952
Snowdonia	2188 (845)	18.10.1951
Yorkshire Dales	1761 (680)	12.10.1954

is protected by designation either as a National Park or an Area of Outstanding Natural Beauty (AONB). The campaign to establish them was long and hard fought.

As recently as 1949 the National Parks and Access to the Countryside Act went on the statute book. The Act set up the National Parks Commission for England and Wales (but not Scotland) with powers to designate National Parks and Areas of Outstanding Natural Beauty, to propose Long Distance Paths and to provide information. This was the culmination of much pressure and many reports (including that of the 1942 Scott Committee on Land Utilization in Rural Areas which specifically called for the establishment of National Parks). But the new legislation fell short of what the campaigners had sought. Instead of placing the parks under the protection of a powerful national executive body it left them to be administered by committees or boards of local county councils. The twin requirements that dominated these committees were: firstly to preserve, and where possible to enhance the splendour of the scene, and secondly to make it available to the people.

Despite legislation, the Parks and AsONB have not totally been able to withstand violation by industrial and technological intrusion. For instance, it was found that the 'national interest' justified potash mining and the establishment of Fylingdales Ballistic Missile Early Warning Station on the North York Moors, an atomic power station in Snowdonia and oil installations on the Pembrokeshire

coast. The only consolation left to those who struggled from the start to pass on intact to future generations the beauty inherited at the date of the designations is the reflection that 'things' would have been far worse today had they not so struggled.

Nature Conservancy Council
In some ways the 1949 Act has done more to protect wild life habitats than it has done to preserve scenery. The Act squarely placed the main responsibility for the conservation of 'nature' on central government. It established the Nature Conservancy Council by Royal Charter. This charter requires the provision of 'scientific advice on the conservation and control of the natural fauna and flora of Great Britain; to establish nature reserves; and to develop the scientific services related thereto'.

The 10,450 acres (4230 ha) of Beinn Eighe in Rosshire, established in 1951, was the first of a series of National Nature Reserves. By 1954 Scolt Head in Norfolk, Yarner Wood on Dartmoor and 10,000 acres (4050 ha) of Moorhouse in Westmorland had followed. By 1958 some 70 Reserves, totalling 133,081 acres (53,850 ha), had just in time saved remnants of some ancient habitats- chalk downland, lowland moss, fen and carr. At the end of 1981 the purchase of 638 acres (258 ha) of chalk downland on Salisbury Plain, with 40 different plants to the square metre; of 492 acres (199 ha) of reedbed, open water,

The map shows England and Wales only, for in Scotland there are neither National Parks nor Areas of Outstanding Beauty. The reason for this is that at the time the classifications were made it was considered that over half of Scotland would have to be included. Nevertheless, Scotland does have four Forest Parks which are owned by the Forestry Commission. They are Glen More (south of Inverness), Argyll, Queen Elizabeth (in the Trossachs), and Glen Trool. A part of the Border Forest Park is in Scotland.

woodland, sand dunes and cliffs at Stackpole in Pembrokeshire; and another 297 acres (120 ha) of Ribble marshes to add to the original 5392 (2182 ha) indicate how effectively the Nature Conservancy spent its tiny income.

The NCC controls some 3,900 Sites of Special Scientific Interest (SSSI). Such areas are notified by the NCC to local planning and water authorities, the Forestry Commission and other bodies as having special scientific interest, either biological, geological or physiographical. No change of use may be accepted without prior consultation with the NCC. The SSSI sites cover $5\frac{1}{2}$ per cent of Britain's land surface. Of these some 3000 are biological; these include the best examples of undisturbed habitat types within which ever rarer communities of plants and/or animals may be saved for posterity. Some are just big enough to save, say, the last example of a particular orchid.

In addition, the NCC by the Wildlife and Countryside Act (1981) has been enabled to establish National Marine Nature Reserves and to endorse those already supervised by voluntary bodies off Wembury, Purbeck, St Abb's Head, Lundy and Skomer. These were needed largely to ward off predation by skindivers.

Conservation by voluntary bodies

Despite the Acts of Parliament, the beauty of the landscape and the scientific importance of reserves are still largely and effectively protected by private owners.

A network of voluntary county naturalists' trusts now covers the whole of Britain. Their work is co-ordinated by the Royal Society for Nature Conservation. Since 1960 they have accumulated some 1200 reserves, totalling over 100,000 acres (40,500 ha).

Meanwhile the 340,000 members of the Royal Society for the Protection of Birds (founded in 1891) have built up a series of 83 reserves. At first the RSPB set out to provide safety for birds, but it long ago learnt that it is the total habitat that is important with its complicated biological relationships.

The National Trust

By 1977 the National Trust (founded in 1895) was the owner of 342 of all the Nature Conservancy Council's designated reserves, totalling 203,000 acres (82,150 ha). The Trust is the largest private owner of nature reserves in Britain. In addition it owns more than a further 200,000 acres (81,000 ha) of beautiful countryside in which scientific interest is not nationally important. The Trust also has over 200 gardens of historic or artistic importance. On top of all this the National Trust prompted its Enterprise Neptune in 1965 which, by 1981 had raised enough money to buy 230 miles (370 km) of the most beautiful coastline to add to the 185 miles (298 km) owned before Neptune was launched.

Despite all these facts and figures it should not be forgotten that only about 15 per cent of England and Wales (and much less of Scotland) is protected by any kind of designation to conserve. However feeble many of the defences may be, they are better than the near-nothing that fails to prevent inroads into the beauty of the rest of rural Britain.

The Green Bridge of Wales – one of the Pembrokeshire Coast National Park's most famous geological features. It is a natural arch formed in the carboniferous limestone which outcrops in the Castlemartin Peninsula of Pembrokeshire.

Heritage Organizations

Far right: The Pennine Way at Malham's Cove, one of several long-distance paths managed and maintained by the Countryside Commission (see map on page 198). The Pennine Way goes through some of the most remote areas of Britain. It starts at Edale in the Peak District National Park and passes through the Yorkshire Dales and Northumberland National Parks before crossing the Scottish border to end at Kirk Yetholm.

The Pineapple, Dunmore, Airth, Stirlingshire. This eccentric two-storey summer house dating from 1761 is leased to the Landmark Trust by the National Trust for Scotland. It is built of the very finest masonry, with every leaf separately drained to prevent damage by frost. The Landmark Trust rescues small and unusual buildings in distress and then gives them life and a future by letting them as holiday homes.

200

The crusade to save our environment has always depended upon the inspiration of a few individuals, supported by a rearguard action of scholarship. These two elements have, over 400 years, created the pressure groups and the documentation upon which the legislation, which gave their initiative some permanence, was based.

Society of Antiquaries

The Dissolution of the Monasteries between 1536 and 1539 added £1.5 million to the Royal Exchequer, but the deliberate programme of pillage and destruction unparalleled in our history also created an interest in medieval buildings as historic monuments, and was partly instrumental in bringing the Society of Antiquaries into being.

'From about 1585 a number of persons, in and about London, eminent for learning, had regular meetings for the improvement and illustration of the history and antiquity of England.'

The survey of Stonehenge, commissioned by James I (VI) from Inigo Jones in 1620, shows that official interest in ancient monuments was awakening. It was not, however, until 1720 that the Society received its charter, and 1721 before it took an active interest in preservation, when Waltham Cross was protected 'from injury by carriage' by the 'setting up of two oak posts', at the cost to the Society of ten shillings. It still stands, heavily restored, in the same position today, still menaced by traffic as it was in 1721.

During the late 18th and early 19th centuries the Society became increasingly involved in the fight to stem the tide of restoration then sweeping over the cathedrals and churches of Britain, the principal practitioners of which were James Wyatt, known in his lifetime as 'the destroyer', and Sir George Gilbert Scott.

Encouraged by the brilliant draughtsmanship of John Carter, and later, by the invective of John Ruskin, both eminent Fellows, the Society halted, in 1801, Wyatt's systematic transformation of Durham Cathedral, and prevented the demolition of the Galilee Chapel, and the 14th-century reredos. They also fought unsuccessfully, after the Napoleonic Wars, against the proposed destruction of the screen at York, the north-west tower at Canterbury, and the Lady Chapel at Southwark. They campaigned against the destruction of several Roman sites, including part of the amphitheatre at Verulamium, and against the damage being done to pre-historic sites by ploughing methods. In 1850 they opposed the restoration of the Royal tombs in Westminster Abbey, and in 1869 they prepared for the government a list of historic tombs and monuments worthy of preservation. In 1871 they supported Sir John Lubbock's proposals to introduce the first Ancient Monuments Bill, which finally became law in 1882. While the first Ancient Monuments act offered protection to 68 sites, mostly pre-historic, among them Avebury and Stonehenge, it marked the entry of the government into the field, and from this grew the immensely elaborate structure of Historic Buildings and Ancient Monuments Acts with which our environment is protected today.

Council for British Archaeology

The Society of Antiquaries gave birth in 1780 to a similar body in Scotland, and also in 1944 to the Council for British Archaeology, with the responsibility for recording and excavating sites. The C.B.A. has played a vital role in the protection of our historic towns and cities during the past 30 years, firstly by the presentation of its report and analysis of their archaeological importance (see page 115), and secondly by the setting up of an Urban Research Committee. This has prepared a study of historic towns affected by modern development in England and Wales and Scotland entitled 'The Erosion of History'.

The Society for the Protection of Ancient Buildings, founded by William Morris in 1877, to prevent the restoration of Tewkesbury Abbey, fought successively against the restoration of St Albans, Peterborough, Rochester and Canterbury Cathedrals, and Westminster Abbey. It opposed with the help of Thomas Carlyle the systematic destruction of Wren's churches in the City of London, alterations to the Tower of London, and even extended its efforts to prevent the demolition of the Ponte Vecchio in Florence, and the restoration of St Mark's in Venice. The Society gave practical advice on 'conservative repair', and on the ethics of preserving buildings as historical evidence, and continues to do so today. The Society helped to found the Georgian Group and the Victorian Society.

Georgian and Victorian Societies

The Georgian Society was founded in 1937 as a result of the destruction of Rennie's Waterloo Bridge and of the Adelphi by the Adam brothers. At that time both Bath and Cheltenham were in decline, Chiswick House and Marble Hill House were derelict, Abingdon Street threatened, and the systematic destruction of important examples of 18th-century town planning in Bloomsbury, London, was proceeding unopposed. After the Second World War the Group fought successfully to protect John Nash's Regent's Park Terraces and Carlton House Terrace, both in London, and regarded at that time by the authorities as unworthy of preservation owing to the poor quality of Nash's building.

The Victorian Society was founded in 1958 in order to fight for the recognition of 19th-century buildings and industrial monuments as valid in their own right. Led by Sir Nikolaus Pevsner they failed to save Euston Station, but successfully prevented British Rail from demolishing Paddington, St Pancras, King's Cross and Liverpool Street stations, as well as saving many important stations, bridges and industrial monuments all over Britain. They saved most of Parliament Square and much of Whitehall from destruction during the 1960s, and led battles to protect many of Britain's monumental 19th-century town centres.

The Scottish Georgian Society carries out similar work to these two organizations in Scotland.

Association for Industrial Archaeology

The interest aroused in Britain's great industrial past, and the systematic destruction of much of the technology which made Britain the world's leading industrial nation in the 19th century, gave birth to the Association for Industrial Archaeology. Based at Ironbridge, itself the cradle of the industrial revolution, the Association led by Neil Cossons, stimulates interest in industrial monuments and campaigns to save important surviving examples, although most of the original evidence has alas already been lost, and the involvement of the government came too late.

The Inland Waterways Association campaigns for the restoration and use of our canals, once such a vital link in our transport system, but which now, alas, are increasingly neglected.

Saving country houses and town centres

As long ago as 1950 the catastrophic destruction of the great country houses, brought about largely by high taxation and declining incomes, was presented, in the Gowers Report, as a tragedy comparable in scale and importance with the Dissolution of the Monasteries 400 years earlier. This led to the establishment of the Historic Buildings Council to provide grants for beleaguered owners, and later to the Historic Houses Association to fight for their rights.

In 1957 Lord Duncan-Sandys, recognizing the disastrous effect of the post-war clean sweep redevelopments on our historic towns and cities, founded the Civic Trust. This, in establishing over 1250 local civic societies, has successfully encouraged a return of civic pride and a desire for a more civilized environment than that created by the post-Corbusian planners of the 1960s. As well as fighting against larger roads and heavier lorries, the Trust was instrumental in bringing about by-passes for many of our more vulnerable towns and cities. It has also, with its Civic Trust awards, played a leading role in stimulating good modern design, within the fabric of historic settings.

In the mid-1960s, recognizing the limitations of the National Trust, and the need to save by ownership smaller buildings threatened with redundancy and destruction, Mr John Smith M.P. founded the Landmark Trust. The Trust has acquired an amazingly varied collection of buildings, ranging from medieval priories and castles, to 19th-century water towers and Martello Towers which, when restored, are rented to the public for holidays. The Trust has saved over 200 buildings, and the list continues to grow.

Redundant churches

While the struggle to save some remnants of Britain's secular buildings raged, a similar tragedy was ravaging our churches. Although appeals for cathedral repairs, combined with increasing revenue from visitors, have succeeded in keeping our cathedrals open and standing, the same cannot be said for churches. Despite the efforts of the Historic Churches Preservation Trust, the Council for Places of Worship, and the Friends of Friendless Churches, the number continues to rise, and in East Anglia alone, has reached catastrophic proportions.

The Redundant Churches Fund restores and maintains the 170 churches in its care, none of them in regular use, but all of outstanding importance, and the Historic Buildings Council helps to keep a small proportion of the churches in use in reasonable repair.

For the rest, which represent the summit of our medieval achievement, the future is bleak indeed. Nothing short of a religious revival coupled with a major revival of interest from the visiting public, can save them. The gradual erosion of our ecclesiastical fabric today is less dramatic than the Dissolution of the Monasteries, but just as far reaching, and may finally result in an even greater level of destruction.

Protection of the Countryside

The protection of the countryside of Britain was initiated as with buildings and sites, by a few visionaries with no funds or recognition. Sir Robert Hunter, later a founder of the National Trust, saved, through the Commons Preservations Society, many London commons, and Epping Forest from despoilation and development. Similarly Octavia Hill, also a founder member of the National Trust, campaigned for Hampstead Heath, the North Downs, and 'King Arthur's Castle' at Tintagel.

Canon Rawnsley, the third of these great visionaries, led the battle to save the Lake District from exploitation by railway companies and developers. They all fought for the rights of the public to use footpaths and bridleways, and

The nave of St Andrew's, Winterborne Tomson, Dorset – one of the many churches of architectural and historic merit cared for by the Redundant Churches Fund.

regularly walked them to keep them open. They would rejoice in the popularity of our long-distance walks today. While much of the responsibility for the countryside has now been taken over by the government, the initiative of the early pioneers is still reflected in the work of the Ramblers Association, the Council for the Preservation of Rural England, the Royal Society for the Protection of Birds, the Naturalists' Trusts and many more.

Octavia Hill's vision for the protection of the coasts of Britain has been magnificently implemented by the National Trust in Enterprise Neptune, and that of John Dower in the foundation of the National Parks. Between them they hold safely much of the finest landscape in Britain. In no other country have volunteers managed to save so much.

Acknowledgements

The editors wish to thank Kingfisher Books Ltd, London, for permission to reproduce their wild life illustrations on the pages listed here: 22 (fish); 24 (amphibians and reptiles); 25 (insects); 26–27 (butterflies); 30–32 (mammals).

The editors also thank the following photographers, agencies, galleries, museums and other establishments for their help in supplying photographs for this book.

Pages 10–11 Dr R. Muir. 12–13 Cambridge University Collection. 14 E. T. Archive. 16 Charles Sinker. 17 *top right* Michael Chinery *centre left* Heather Angel *bottom left & right* Charles Sinker. 18 Charles Sinker. 19 *top* Michael Chinery *centre right* Dr C. E. Jeffree *centre left & bottom* Charles Sinker. 20 Charles Sinker. 21 Tricia Moxey. 23 Fotomas Index. 25 Michael Chinery. 26–27 F. Baillie/NHPA. 28 Heather Angel. 29 *top left & right* Heather Angel *bottom* National Museum of Wales. 30 James Hancock/Nature Photographers. 31 Lacz Lemoine/NHPA. 32 Stephen Dalton/NHPA. 33 National Coal Board. 34 Shell (UK) Ltd. 36 Fotomas. 37 *top* British Museum *bottom* British Tourist Authority. 38 Research Laboratory for Archaeology, Oxford University. 39 Cambridge University Collection. 40 *top* Michael Holford *bottom* Peter Clayton. 41 *top* Scottish Tourist Board *bottom* Peter Clayton. 42 Andy Williams/The National Trust. 45 *right* Janet & Colin Bord *left* British Museum. 46–47 *left* Werner Forman Archives. 47 *right* Mansell. 48 *left* Aerofilms *right* Ronald Sheridan *bottom* Public Record Office. 50–51 Stanley Elles, University of Leeds. 50 *centre left* Oxford University Press. 54, 55 & 56 Dr R. Muir. 57 Cambridge University Collection. 58 Mervyn Blatch. 59 *top & centre* British Tourist Authority *bottom* Ercol Furniture, High Wycombe. 60 Science Museum, London. 61 Walker Art Gallery, Liverpool. 62 British Leyland. 63 IBM. 64 Yorkshire & Humberside Tourist Board. 65 *top* Fotomas *bottom* Aerofilms. 66 *top* England Scene *bottom* Derek Pratt. 67 Hulton Picture Library. 68 Mansell. 69 *top left & right* Ironbridge Gorge Museum *bottom* Hulton Picture Library. 70 *top* Aerofilms *bottom* Derek Widdicombe. 71 *top* Aerofilms *bottom* Hulton Picture Library. 75 British Tourist Authority. 76 *top* Scottish Tourist Board *bottom left* Bodleian Library, Oxford. 77 *left* British Tourist Authority *right* Picturepoint Ltd. 79 Michael Holford. 80 By Gracious permission Her Majesty The Queen, Windsor Castle. 81 *top left* National Portrait Gallery, London *right* J. Allan Cash. 82 Fotomas. 83 By Gracious permission Her Majesty The Queen, Department of the Environment. 84 National Portrait Gallery, London. 85 *top* By Gracious permission Her Majesty The Queen, Department of the Environment *bottom* Michael Holford. 87 *top* S. Nuttall *bottom left & centre* Mansell *right* John Topham. 89 Fotomas. 90 *top* Zefa *centre left & bottom* Fotomas. 91 *top & bottom left* Fotomas *bottom right* John Topham. 92 Islington Libraries. 94 & 95 *centre* E. T. Archive/Hon. Society of Middle Temple. 95 *bottom* Public Record Office. 96 Dr John Baker. 97 *left* Dr John Baker. 97 *right* Guildhall Library, London. 98 National Portrait Gallery, London. 99 *top left* Courtauld Institute/Holkham Hall *top right* Fotomas *bottom* John Topham. 100 Cambridge University Collection. 101 *top* Peter Clayton *bottom* F. H. C. Birch/Sonia Halliday Photos. 102 Janet & Colin Bord. 103 *top* Aerofilms *bottom* Yorkshire & Humberside Tourist Board. 104 *top* Royal Military Academy, Sandhurst. 105 British Tourist Authority. 106 *top* Aerofilms *bottom* Janet & Colin Bord. 107 Tate Gallery, London. 108 & 109 *top* National Maritime Museum, Greenwich. 109 *centre* National Portrait Gallery, London *bottom* J. Allan Cash. 111–112 Fotomas. 113 *top* Janet & Colin Bord *bottom left* F. H. C. Birch/Sonia Halliday Photos *bottom right* J. Allan Cash. 114 *top* English Scene *bottom* Derek Widdicombe. 115 *top* Aerofilms *bottom* Halcyon Photos. 116 & 117 *top* Dr R. Muir. 117 *bottom* Cambridge University Collection. 118 Dr R. Muir. 119 Cambridge University Collection. 120 G.L.C. Map Collection. 121 Aerofilms. 122 *top* The National Trust *bottom* Rousham House, Oxon. 123 *top left & centre left* RIBA Drawings Collection *top right* Doris Nicholson/The National Trust *centre* Science Museum, London *bottom* John Bethell/The National Trust. 124 *top* Richard Bryant. 124 *bottom* & 125 *top & bottom right* Crown copyright, by permission of the Controller HMSO & Director of the Royal Botanical Gardens, Kew. 125 *bottom left* Fotomas. 126 *top left* British Tourist Authority *right* Robert Estall. 127 *top left* Scottish Tourist Board *top right & bottom* Janet & Colin Bord. 129 Fortean Picture Library. 130 *top* The National Trust *centre left* Michael Holford *centre right* Derek G. Widdicombe. 131 *top* S & O Mathews *bottom* Hatfield House. 132 *top & bottom* Derek G. Widdicombe. 133 *top* Michael Holford *centre* Mervyn Blatch *bottom* Derek G. Widdicombe. 134 *top* Country Life *bottom* Aerofilms. 135 *top* Country Life *bottom* John Bethell/The National Trust. 136 Country Life. 137 *top* Tony Davison/The National Trust *bottom* John Bethell/The National Trust. 138–139 Country Life. 140 *top* Hulton Picture Library *bottom* The National Trust for Scotland. 141 *top & bottom left* Country Life *bottom right* The National Trust. 142 Christies, London. 143 *Centre left* Mackintosh Library. Glasgow *centre* G. Beech/Architectural Press *right* British Tourist Authority *bottom left* Will Green *centre bottom* Aerofilms. 144 *left* J. Allan Cash *centre* The Ritz *right* London Transport. 145 *top right* Hulton Picture Library *centre right* Richard Bryant *centre left* Architectural Press *bottom left* J. Allan Cash *bottom right* Richard Bryant. 146 *top & centre left* Martin Charles/Architectural Press *centre* J. Allan Cash *bottom left* Henri Snoek/Architectural Press *bottom right* Richard Bryant. 147 *top left* British Tourist Authority *top right* Wm J. Toomey/Architectural Press *centre right* J. Allan Cash *bottom right* F. Gibberd/Architectural Press *bottom right* De Burgh Galwey/Architectural Press. 148 *top* Fotomas *bottom* E. T. Archive. 149 Colorsport. 150 Mansell. 151 Dr J. Walvin. 152 *top* Mary Evans Picture Library *bottom* Jim Meads. 153 *top* G. L. Carlisle *bottom* Dermot Wilson. 154 Ed Byrne. 155 *top* Ed Byrne *centre* Fores Gallery. 156 *top* Fred Spencer *centre* Sally Anne Thompson. 157 Kit Houghton. 158 *top* Scottish Tourist Board *bottom* M. Newitt Butchers, Thame, Oxon. 159 J. Allan Cash. 162 T. Middlemass. 163 *top* Rosemary Cramp *centre* T. Middlemass *bottom* Janet & Colin Bord. 164 Edwin Smith. 165 *top left & right* Michael Holford *bottom left* J. Allan Cash *bottom right* Derek G. Widdicombe. 166 Edwin Smith. 167 *top* British Tourist Authority *bottom* Mervyn Blatch. 168 *left & right* British Tourist Authority. 169 *left* Mervyn Blatch *right* O. G. Jarman. 170 *top* Michael Holford *bottom* British Tourist Authority. 171 *top* Michael Holford *bottom* Edwin Smith. 172 *top left* Hulton Picture Library *top right* Martin Trelawny/The National Trust *bottom left* J. Allan Cash *bottom right* Keystone Press Agency. 174 *left* British Tourist Authority *top right* Hulton Picture Library *centre* J. Allan Cash. 175 *top* Science Museum, London *bottom* The Royal Society. 176 *top* Mary Evans *centre* Keystone. 177 *top* National Maritime Museum, Greenwich *centre left* By permission of Lord Dartmouth *centre right* National Gallery of Scotland, Edinburgh *bottom* National Gallery, London. 178 *top left* National Gallery, London *top right* The Royal Academy *centre* Ascott House *bottom* Tate Gallery. 179 *top* Ipswich Museum Committee *centre left* National Gallery, London *centre right & bottom* Tate Gallery, London. 180 *left* Bodleian Library, Oxford *right* National Theatre, Maugham collection. 181 *left* Tate Gallery, London *right* Cecil Beaton/Courtesy Sotheby's *bottom* Catherine Ashmore. 182 *left* National Gallery, London *centre top & bottom* National Portrait Gallery, London. 183 *top left* Gift of Ed. B. Greene, The Cleveland Museum of Art, U.S.A. *top right* National Portrait Gallery, London *centre left* National Portrait Gallery, London *centre right* National Gallery, London. 184 *left* National Gallery, London *right* Ashmolean Museum, Oxford *centre* Mansell. 185 *top left* National Portrait Gallery, London *top right* David Hockney/Petersburg Press *centre left* National Portrait Gallery, London *centre left* National Portrait Gallery, London *centre right* BBC. 186 Fotomas. 187 (3) Mansell (4) National Portrait Gallery, London (5, 6, 7 & 10) Mansell (8) National Portrait Gallery, London (9) Keystone *top right* National Portrait Gallery, London *bottom left* BBC *bottom right* Zöe Dominic. 188 *top* John Bethell/The National Trust *centre & bottom* Ronald Sheridan. 189 *top* Syon House *centre* City of Cardiff *bottom left* Richard Bryant *bottom right* Dan O'Neill. 190 Christie's. 192 *left* British Museum *right* Mansell. 193 British Tourist Authority. 194 Richard Bryant. 195 Mike Williams. 196 *left* B. Norman/Ronald Sheridan Library *right* Andrew Priddy/The National Trust. 197 *top* Brian Bradbury/The National Trust *bottom left & right* The National Trust, 199 Cyngor Sir Dyfed (Dyfed County Council). 200 *left* John Wilkie, Edinburgh *right* Mike Williams. 201 Redundant Churches.

Index